MULTINATIONAL CORPORATIONS AND FOREIGN DIRECT INVESTMENT

MULTINATIONAL CORPORATIONS AND FOREIGN DIRECT INVESTMENT

Avoiding Simplicity, Embracing Complexity

STEPHEN D. COHEN

OXFORD
UNIVERSITY PRESS

2007

OXFORD
UNIVERSITY PRESS

Oxford University Press, Inc., publishes works that further
Oxford University's objective of excellence
in research, scholarship, and education.

Oxford   New York
Auckland   Cape Town   Dar es Salaam   Hong Kong   Karachi
Kuala Lumpur   Madrid   Melbourne   Mexico City   Nairobi
New Delhi   Shanghai   Taipei   Toronto

With offices in
Argentina   Austria   Brazil   Chile   Czech Republic   France   Greece
Guatemala   Hungary   Italy   Japan   Poland   Portugal   Singapore
South Korea   Switzerland   Thailand   Turkey   Ukraine   Vietnam

Published by Oxford University Press, Inc.
198 Madison Avenue, New York, New York 10016

www.oup.com

Oxford is a registered trademark of Oxford University Press

Library of Congress Cataloging-in-Publication Data
Cohen, Stephen D.
Multinational corporations and foreign direct investment: avoiding simplicity,
embracing complexity / Stephen D. Cohen.
   p. cm.
Includes index.
ISBN-13 978-0-19-517935-4; 978-0-19-517936-1 (pbk.)
ISBN 0-19-517935-8; 0-19-517936-6 (pbk.)
1. International business enterprises—Finance.   2. Investments, Foreign.   I. Title.
HG4027.5.C64 2006
332.67'314—dc22   2006010605

9   8   7   6   5   4   3   2   1
Printed in the United States of America
on acid-free paper

Acknowledgments

Given what for me was a formidable challenge to say the least, it is no pro forma courtesy to thank a number of people whose assistance was invaluable in researching and editing this book. First off, I extend a deeply felt appreciation for the contributions of Daniel de Torres and Craig Matasick, who performed magnificently during their two-year stints as my graduate assistants. The exact same feelings are extended to Erin Teeling and Christopher B. Doolin Jr.; their tenures as my graduate assistants were shorter, but their contributions were of the same high quality. It is fact, not just courtesy, to say that without their collective research and editing talents, my work schedule would have been much longer, more painful, and less productive, not to mention the end product being less accurate and more verbose.

The text of several chapters has benefited from the expertise of professional colleagues and personal acquaintances. I thank them very much for the time and effort they spent in offering me many valuable suggestions on the chapter or chapters they read. In alphabetical order, they are Michelle Egan, Roger Golden, Louis W. Goodman, Tammi Gutner, and Stephen Kobrin.

Given the content and approach of this study, the standard disclaimer needs to be emphasized: None of the acknowledged persons is responsible for factual errors, subjective interpretations, or conclusions. These should be attributed solely to the author.

Finally, I thank my wife, Linda, and children, Sondra and Marc, for their patience while I spent a lot of time working on this project.

Contents

Abbreviations   ix

Introduction   3

Part I   Fundamentals

1   A Better Approach to Understanding Foreign
Direct Investment and Multinational Corporations   11

2   Defining the Subject: Subtleties and Ambiguities   27

3   From Obscurity to International Economic Powerhouse:
The Evolution of Multinational Corporations   41

4   Heterogeneity: The Many Kinds of Foreign Direct
Investment and Multinational Corporations and
Their Disparate Effects   62

5   Perceptions and Economic Ideologies   93

Part II   The Strategy of Multinationals

6   Why Companies Invest Overseas   117

7   Where Multinational Corporations Invest and
Don't Invest and Why   148

Part III   Impact on the International Order

8   Effects of Foreign Direct Investment on Less Developed
Countries: Vagaries, Variables, Negatives, and Positives   179

9   Why and How Multinational Corporations Have
Altered International Trade   205

10   Multinational Corporations versus the Nation-State:
Has Sovereignty Been Outsourced?   233

11   The International Regulation of Multinational Corporations:
Why There Is No Multilateral Foreign Direct
Investment Regime   252

Part **IV** Three Bottom Lines

12 The Case for Foreign Direct Investment and
Multinational Corporations   283

13 The Case against Foreign Direct Investment and
Multinational Corporations   308

14 An Agnostic Conclusion: "It Depends"   332

Part **V** Recommendations

15 An Agenda for Future Action   355

Index   365

Abbreviations

AFL-CIO	American Federation of Labor and Congress of Industrial Organizations
BIT	Bilateral Investment Treaty
EPZ	Export-Processing Zone
EU	European Union
FDI	Foreign Direct Investment
FIRA	Foreign Investment Review Agency (Canada)
GATT	General Agreement on Tariffs and Trade
GDP	Gross Domestic Product
IMF	International Monetary Fund
IT	Information Technology
LDC	Less Developed Country
M&As	Mergers and Acquisitions
MAI	Multilateral Agreement on Investment
MNC	Multinational Corporation
NAFTA	North American Free Trade Agreement
NGO	Nongovernmental Organization
OECD	Organization for Economic Cooperation and Development
OPEC	Organization of Petroleum Exporting Countries
R&D	Research and Development
TNI	Transnationality Index
TRIMS	Trade-Related Investment Measures
UN	United Nations
UNCTAD	The United Nations Conference on Trade and Development
WTO	World Trade Organization

MULTINATIONAL CORPORATIONS AND FOREIGN DIRECT INVESTMENT

INTRODUCTION

W hy another book on multinational corporations? The answer begins shortly after the new millennium, when an involuntary end came to what had been my nimble effort spanning three decades to avoid teaching the course on multinational corporations (MNCs) offered by American University's School of International Service. The simple truth is that although I have long been an avid student of international economic relations, I was not enamored with the scholarly and policy literature on foreign direct investment. Most of what I read sooner or later became either a strident all-out defense or condemnation of MNCs. To my personal way of thinking, this was an oversimplified and ultimately not very compelling intellectual exercise—one in which the two opposing sides were unable to find any common ground even after much discourse. Seeing no resolution of their disagreement in sight, they began yelling at each other.

My preparations for teaching our MNC course forced me to confront the issues in a much more detailed and systematic manner than ever before. As I read extensively and looked for good class readings, two thoughts began to dominate my approach to the subject. First, the advocates and critics of MNCs continued to talk past one another mainly because they shared a faulty frame of reference and an inadequate appreciation of how much an observer's ideology and perceptions had come to define the reality of MNCs and foreign direct investment (FDI). Second, the literature suffered from an important gap that needed filling. Scattered throughout were many insightful comments on the subject as a whole and many good studies and essays on narrowly focused aspects of the FDI and MNC phenomena (e.g., their impact on less developed countries). What was missing was a nonjudgmental study of FDI and MNCs in full economic and political context, one that treated them as heterogeneous and still evolving subjects that did not lend themselves to the usual black-or-white evaluation. Too many authors were writing with an attitude, one that either advocated or opposed these phenomena. I found no analytical pieces proclaiming that the authors were neutral concerning the net virtues and vices of FDI and MNCs because of their diversity and the gaps in our knowledge about them. Nor did I find many authors urging a case-by-case approach in lieu of generalization. In short, an opportunity existed to contribute to closing what I perceived as a major void in our understanding of an important subject.

Unlike most people, I agree partially with much of what I have read and heard on both sides of the argument. Also unlike most people, I do not identify with either the pro or con schools of thought on these subjects. My feeling is that both sides have made valid points on parts of the subject while maintaining a blind spot as to the big picture. No one seemed to be expounding the seemingly obvious thesis that a dispassionate inquiry would see that the phenomena of FDI and MNCs were far too complex and heterogeneous to warrant all-inclusive labels being applied to their nature, behavior, and effects. It seemed that I was the only one answering "it depends" to most questions about these phenomena and endlessly railing against generalization. My credo became "never say never" and "never say always" about them. Eventually, I came to believe that being outside of not one but two mainstreams of thought was something to build on, not try to overcome. Given my many years of scholarly inquiry into the economics and politics as well as the domestic and international aspects of international economic policy, I felt I possessed good credentials for having something new to say about a subject for which I claimed no long, deep expertise. Once convinced this self-evaluation was not mostly hubris, I began outlining and researching this book. In designing an innovative approach that can make a meaningful contribution to advancing knowledge of FDI and MNCs, I have played the roles of believer, skeptic, and synthesizer. The big fascination for me was not pretending to have mastered the subject and come up with a multitude of breakthrough answers but in understanding how and why these phenomena could be viewed—incorrectly—in one of two diametrically different lights for so long with virtually no movement toward consensus.

A study whose premise rests heavily on the importance of perceptions should be sensitive to the possibility that some people will anticipate a work that replicates their view of how to assess the subject or is devoted mainly to the specific subtopics in which they are most interested. It is wholly appropriate, therefore, to present a succinct statement of what this book is *not* about and what it does not try to do. It is not about telling readers what to think about multinational companies, but it does suggest *how* to think about them. This is not a political science book about the governance of corporations, appropriate regulation of them by government, or the "proper" distribution of income and economic power. Nor is it a business administration text about the management, product mix, and marketing techniques of MNCs. And it is not an economics treatise examining the theory of the firm or the implications of oligopoly in the marketplace. No attempt has been made to do what I think is the impossible: producing a single integrating economic theory that accurately and consistently explains why FDI exists in such large volume or a single comprehensive conclusion explaining the behavior and measuring the effects of MNCs as a collective entity. In many cases, efforts to understand the issues being examined are better served with an inquiry as to why inconclusiveness prevails rather than a presentation that purports to have transformed limited soft data into hard facts. Although not a sentiment shared by many academics, I feel no personal need or desire to reach a firm conclusion on the much debated question as to whether these international business phenomena are, on balance, good or bad. As this study argues, that is not the right question, anyhow.

The process of producing an accurate interpretation of the FDI/MNC phenomena is different from assembling a jigsaw puzzle. The latter has a finite number of smooth-edged pieces designed to produce a perfectly assembled end product with a fixed image. The step-by-step process to connecting them is a physical reality that can be precisely reproduced an infinite number of times. Unlike jigsaw puzzle pieces, the ever-changing numbers and shapes of pieces that form the collective personae of FDI and MNCs do not necessarily fit neatly together to produce a demonstrable, enduring reality. Even if they could all be neatly connected at a given time, some of the pieces periodically need to be moved about, reconfigured, or discarded, and some new ones need to be added to accurately depict an ever-changing, multifaceted abstraction. Final assembly of the foreign investment puzzle is further complicated by the need to keep a few pieces blank in recognition of the significant gaps in our knowledge of the subject.

My main objective is to raise the level of understanding that we should have about the nature and diversity of these international business phenomena and about the range of effects they have had on domestic economies and the international economic order. Hopefully, the arguments developed will contribute something to narrowing the long-standing, unresolved public policy debate conducted between those ardently in favor of MNCs and those bitterly opposed to them. A recent book on this subject said that "most theoretical frameworks are still based on the simplifying assumption of homogeneous agents, and theories encompassing heterogeneity are still in their infancy."[1] A major goal of this volume is to nurture the heterogeneity concept at least as far as young adulthood. The fifteen chapters that follow will not and cannot provide a definitive explanation of these issues. No matter how responsive a chord this book hits, it is still just one step in a very long journey to a fuller, more accurate understanding. The need for continuing research and additional data in this field remains unequivocal.

Structure of the Book

Different levels of analysis are used throughout this study because it examines its subject in both a vertical and horizontal manner. Depending on the specific topic at hand, the focal point may be the international economic order, MNCs as a whole, categories of FDI and MNCs (e.g., extractive, manufacturing, or service sector), categories of countries (home and host; rich and poor), or case studies involving specific countries or companies.

The first of the book's five parts lays out a series of fundamental concepts to set the stage for the analytical and thesis-advancing chapters that follow. Chapter 1 explains how the approach and perspective of this study are different and why they can enhance the current level of understanding of FDI and MNCs. The second chapter deals with the deceptively tricky subject of definitions and terminology. The third chapter is on one level a straightforward chronological summary of the history of multinational companies; on another level, it speaks to the usually understated external forces that have played a large role in shaping these enterprises. A separate section examines their contemporary economic importance. Chapter 4 moves to a second stage of fundamentals by developing a critically important theme: The largely ignored diversity of FDI and MNCs undermines the validity of most of the generalizations that have long been the main elements of their public image. The fifth chapter looks at the broad economic ideologies that shape differences of opinion on these phenomena and perpetuate two mutually exclusive, partially valid arguments over the relative merits of multinationals.

The two chapters of part II look at two core strategies of MNCs. The first analyzes the very important issue of *why* companies establish subsidiaries in countries outside their home market, when in fact this activity is seldom mandatory or easy. This chapter reviews the main academic theories purporting to explain management's rationale for doing this and then outlines the expanding list of real world practical reasons encouraging the proliferation of direct investment overseas. Chapter 7 examines the main variables determining where companies choose to invest and not invest abroad. In doing so, it identifies the economic and political conditions in countries that tend to attract or repel foreign companies looking to invest overseas.

Part III looks at four key links between the international political and economic order and the FDI/MNC phenomena. Chapter 8 looks at the multiple ways that their effects on economic growth in less developed countries can be gauged. Chapters 9 through 11 analyze the impact of FDI on the international trading system, examine three interpretations of the allegation that MNCs have nullified the sovereignty of nation-states, and explain why the nature of these phenomena has precluded establishment of a multilateral framework to impose norms and rules on them.

The thesis that FDI and MNCs can be judged in at least three ways is laid out in part IV. Chapters 12 and 13 are similar in style and diametrically opposite in content. The first makes the case in favor of the argument that the FDI/MNC phenomena are on balance beneficial, while chapter 13 argues that on balance they are harmful. Both views are presented debate-style, without qualification or endorsement by the author; the purpose is not to advocate one side or the other but to faithfully re-create the main arguments advanced by both sides in the debate. A synthesis of the two arguments, emphasizing the appropriateness of making positive or negative evaluations only on a case-by-case basis taking individual circumstances into account, is the subject of chapter 14.

Finally, chapter 15 offers recommendations that are intended to be useful and feasible measures to reduce the downside and increase the upside of FDI and the companies that engage in it.

Note

1. Giorgio Barba-Navaretti and Anthony J. Venables, *Multinational Firms in the World Economy* (Princeton, NJ: Princeton University Press, 2004), p. 281.

PART I

Fundamentals

1

A BETTER APPROACH TO UNDERSTANDING FOREIGN DIRECT INVESTMENT AND MULTINATIONAL CORPORATIONS

In an old tale, six blind men have come into contact with an elephant for the first time. They are curious to know what it is like. The first blind man touches its side and says an elephant is like a hard wall. The second puts his hand on the trunk and disagrees, saying an elephant resembles a giant snake. The third blind man touches its tail and compares the animal to a fuzzy piece of rope. The fourth feels the legs and says the elephant is like four tree trunks. The fifth touches the ear and describes it as a soft carpet. The last blind man touches the tusk and proclaims an elephant to be sharp like a spear. Confused that they all had come to radically different conclusions, they seek a wise man to ask which one of them has it right. He tells them that they all are right. The reason, he explains, is that "Each of you has 'seen' only one part of the elephant. To ascertain the truth, you must see the whole animal."

Speaking metaphorically, this book is about a better way to analyze the nature and impact of things that are having an increasingly important effect on our lives—things that receive much attention but are not easy to comprehend. More to the point, it is about using largely ignored analytical techniques to assess the nature and impact of the process of foreign direct investment (FDI) and the business entities known as multinational corporations (MNCs). It is intended to add to our far from comprehensive knowledge of what they are and how they really affect the domestic and international economic and political orders. This is a deceptively difficult task for several reasons. Far more layers and variants of these international business phenomena exist than are commonly recognized. They are constantly assuming new shapes and permutations. Perceptions frequently substitute for facts in defining reality.

Subsequent chapters will show that consensus has been unable to extend much beyond agreement that FDI is growing in importance and that MNCs are growing in number, and like untethered elephants, they cannot be ignored. The clash of ideas centers on the questions of nature and effect. Do MNCs excessively exploit the majority to benefit the relatively few owners of capital and harm the environment? Or are they mainly a vehicle for enhancing the standard of living of workers and consumers while doing relatively little social and environmental harm? Returning to metaphor, should the multinationals be allowed to roam relatively freely in search of profit or be constrained by the chains of vigorously enforced governmental regulations aimed at ensuring they operate in what is defined as the public good? "Touching" one part of them produces not only the image of excessive concentrations of power in the hands of management and wealth in the pocketbooks of shareholders but a precipitous decline in the power of labor as well—all of which perpetuate social inequities. Touching another part of the FDI/MNC phenomenon produces the image of unprecedented efficiency, good jobs, and competitive prices for a constant array of new goods and services—all of which make people's lives better. Touching other parts reveals the possibility of neutral effects and the presence of unknown factors suggesting conclusions should be tentative.

"Foreign direct investment" and "multinational corporation" are composite phrases describing two separate but related phenomena. Both exist in many different forms, as will be spelled out in chapter 4. The number of valid generalizations that can be made about the approximately 70,000 companies that meet the definition of *multinational* dramatically declines when they are viewed in anything but the broadest terms.[1] Plentiful exceptions exist to almost any specific rule about them. Patterns discerned in studies of all FDI in a single country or FDI by a single industrial sector in many countries may or may not be legitimately extrapolated to broader conclusions; it depends on specific circumstances.

Unambiguous black-or-white positions and generalizations tend to be the outgrowth of inquiries based on too few data and too much preconceived bias. Given its emphasis on objectivity and its tilt toward ambiguity, this study does not (consciously) take sides. It is neither an endorsement of the criticisms by detractors of FDI and MNCs nor an endorsement of the praise offered by their supporters. To play advocate for a single point of view would contradict and undermine the core thesis that depending on circumstances, these phenomena can be very beneficial, very harmful, neutral, or uncertain in their impact.

Needed: A More Accurate and Productive Method of Evaluating FDI and MNCs

The most frequently asked question about FDI and MNCs (as defined in the next chapter) is whether on balance they are a positive or negative thing for the international community—and by extension whether governments should or should not tightly regulate them. A two-tiered cottage industry exists to provide evaluations of both. One floor cranks out proof that their collective contributions to economic growth and efficiency comfortably outweigh the effects of their self-aggrandizing oligopoly power and harm to society. The second floor generates proof that the situation is in fact the other way around. The popularity of the good-versus-bad question notwithstanding, this is not the most intellectually productive avenue of inquiry into this subject. To be blunt, this is the wrong way to frame the question. It typically leads to a very unrewarding least common denominator approach. The whole is composed of so many dissimilar and constantly evolving parts that generalizations about good and bad are superficial at best and inaccurate at worst. Placing a list of pros and cons on either side of a scale and then rendering a sweeping endorsement or condemnation of all FDI and MNCs is an oversimplified and all-around unsatisfactory exercise.

A far more fruitful line of inquiry and the integrating thesis of this study is the inevitability of *heterogeneity* in FDI and MNCs and accordingly, the imperative of *disaggregation*. Nuance is too pervasive to permit many valid generalizations. This leads to the hardly earth-shattering but surprisingly infrequently offered conclusion that FDI in the form of foreign-owned or controlled subsidiaries is sometimes a positive thing on balance, sometimes a bad thing on balance, sometimes neutral or irrelevant on balance, and sometimes has an indeterminate effect. This conclusion results in the phrase "it depends" being the mantra of the approach taken in this study. Massive numbers of foreign subsidiaries operating in hundreds of different national and regional environments generate a sliding scale of economic effects that ranges from highly deleterious to highly beneficial. Facts and circumstances are seldom if ever identical and need to be considered on a case by case basis according to circumstances.

A disconcertingly large percentage of policy advocates and researchers of all ideological persuasions has failed to explicitly recognize the seemingly obvious: Different kinds of businesses produce different kinds of corporate activity and diverse results. Stated another way, the result of different input is different output. The nature, objectives, and effects of specific kinds of foreign subsidiaries are not applicable to others. This guideline applies within countries, within business sectors, and on a global basis. Even the notion that all multinationals are big companies is a false generalization. No two MNCs are organized exactly alike, share the same production profile, have the same business culture, and produce identical effects on host and home countries. Some are genuinely socially enlightened, perhaps because they are based in countries that literally legislate the requirement that corporations serve the interests of the larger community of stakeholders (see chapter 2). Some are socially amoral with no discernible concerns beyond serving the interests of their executives and shareholders. Few MNCs find themselves in such a static business environment that their current management strategy is the same as it was twenty to thirty years ago. Furthermore, very few (if any) foreign subsidiaries, even of the same company, are identical in their output and impact on the local economy.

The concepts of heterogeneity and disaggregation are essential elements in providing a relatively objective and balanced explanation of the infinite number of combinations within and among three main variables: the nature and the effects of tens of thousands of individual foreign subsidiaries plus the conditions in countries where they are located. MNCs and FDI have genetic codes that, virus-like, are able to mutate in response to new external threats and opportunities. Hundreds of variables create a complex, seldom (if ever) duplicated confluence of factors that shape the characteristics and actions of each of the world's estimated 700,000 individual foreign subsidiaries, the end product of FDI and the operating arm of MNCs.[2] These foreign-owned factories, service facilities, and natural resource extractive projects operate in dozens of different business sectors in more than 200 countries and territories, each of which has its own distinctive political, regulatory, and commercial milieu. Foreign subsidiaries are created for different reasons (see chapters 4 and 6) and pursue their goals differently. Among the diverse tasks they can be assigned are production of services, components, or finished goods; wholesale distribution; retail sales; and research and development. Different tasks and different locations mean that few, if any, subsidiaries have identical needs for labor skills and identical schedules of pay and benefits for workers.

Every overseas subsidiary faces a one-of-a-kind mix of pressures from customers, headquarters, host governments, workers, and civil society. Each subsidiary responds to its total environment in a unique way. Some provide lasting benefits for the country in which they are operating, others exploit it and then leave. Some countries hosting incoming FDI are powerful, highly developed, and longtime practitioners of capitalism. Other host countries are just a few years removed from bloody civil wars or communist economies where the concepts of markets and private enterprise were alien. Companies founded in what are popularly dubbed less-developed countries (LDCs) are now regularly becoming multinationals with subsidiaries in industrial countries, thus reversing the historical North to South direction of FDI (see chapters 4 and 8).

Disaggregation also is an essential diagnostic tool to identify and measure the different levels of *quality* by which an individual foreign subsidiary can be assessed. As discussed in chapters 4, 12, and 13, certain kinds of FDI have a high statistical probability of providing a favorable impact on the country in which they are located, whereas other kinds have exhibited a high propensity for unfavorable, costly results. As argued throughout this book, the compatibility of MNCs with the welfare of the countries in which they operate and those in which they are headquartered is mainly determined by specific circumstances. A universally applied label of benevolence or malevolence is at best misleading, at worst inaccurate. So, too, is an operating assumption that all necessary data needed for evaluating FDI and MNCs are available and accurate. If one accepts the hypotheses of the dominance of heterogeneity and the need for disaggregation, no compelling economic or political logic exists to demand that an all-inclusive guilty or innocent verdict be issued regarding the cumulative net desirability of all foreign-owned or -controlled subsidiaries in all countries. Most of the important questions, such as "Do MNCs promote economic growth and employment?" "Do MNCs seek unconstrained market power?" "Does FDI promote exports and upgrade local labor skills?" and "Do MNCs threaten local companies and culture?" have only one thing in common. The appropriate answer to all of them begins the same way: "sometimes." Whether these questions should be answered in the affirmative or negative depends on the nature of an individual subsidiary, the specific pattern of economic and social effects by a foreign subsidiary on its local surroundings, and the economic-political conditions prevailing in the host country. The answer to the question of whether governmental policy should emphasize market forces or government regulation is: *It depends* on one's values.

The diversity of MNCs creates the opportunity for subjective research to find at least one or two examples of just about any kind of corporate behavior, from the most abhorrent to the most beneficial. The appropriate research question is and always has been whether the presence of one or two case studies is adequate to confirm existence of a larger truth as opposed to merely demonstrating isolated anomalies. The answer is that it depends on the circumstances. Even multiple case studies can strain credibility if the corporate behavior patterns cited no longer are in effect. It is all too easy to start from a preconceived notion and find at least some scattered examples for affirmation of a specific point of view. Accuracy is more likely to be forthcoming from a research strategy that starts with a blank ideological slate and no agenda, conducts a broad and deep examination of the many forms and behaviors of MNCs, and then reaches conclusions integrating both the charms, warts, and intangibles of heterogeneous phenomena.

Another guideline for a more accurate and productive line of inquiry is to appreciate that MNCs respond in large part to the larger business environment in which they operate; they are not exclusively proactive movers and "shapers." Yes, they are the proximate *cause* of major changes in the way that business is conducted throughout the world. But they are better described as the middlemen of change because they themselves are largely the *effect* of even larger phenomena. The two most important are technological changes that restructured the international economic order and the post–World War II relaxation of official barriers to international trade and capital movements. Multinational companies are mainly the offspring of the bigger, more powerful forces that rendered obsolete the concept of national markets, meaning that producers of sophisticated manufacturing and services products no longer can remain competitive if they produce and sell only in their country of origin (see chapter 6). A more specific cause-and-effect conundrum is whether incoming FDI is a cause of accelerated economic development or whether a country's success in achieving high rates of economic growth and development attract foreign companies/cause inward FDI (see chapters 8 and 14).

International business issues should be viewed in context, not as stand-alones. MNCs long ago became a natural extension of corporate activity. The conflicting attitudes toward the costs and benefits of private enterprise are similar whether considering them on a global scale or in terms of a single country. Issues involving multinationals are derivatives of larger divisive issues, just geographically wider in scope and introducing the political/psychological variable of foreigners being involved. The optimal division of wealth between owners of capital and workers; the growing concentration of market power in fewer, increasingly large companies; business's influence on government policy makers; and environmental damage are as much national as they are worldwide concerns. The pros and cons of a handful of large nationwide retail chains driving out locally owned stores by charging low prices and skimping on employee benefits (the Wal-Mart syndrome) have many similarities with the mixed message of a large, aggressive MNC amassing increasing market share on a country-by-country basis through low prices and excellent customer service.

One of the very few generalizations that accurately characterize FDI and MNCs is that their benefits have been exaggerated by advocates and their harm has been exaggerated by critics. The massive proliferation of foreign-controlled subsidiaries cannot accurately be characterized in the aggregate as a zero–sum game as its harsher critics argue, nor can it accurately be labeled a positive-sum game as its most enthusiastic advocates do (see chapters 12 and 13). Both sides of the public debate have tended to oversimplify and share the same methodological deficiencies.

Shortcomings of Traditional Diagnosis

The approach to the study of FDI and MNCs advocated here is tantamount to arguing the need to take the tale of the blind men to the next level. To see the whole elephant in front of you is a necessary but not sufficient means to achieve an adequate understanding of the full range of characteristics and behavior of an entity that exists in multiple forms. When the men in the story heard the one-sentence explanation as to why each had a different experience when touching the animal, their curiosity was satisfied—but prematurely so. They still were far removed from becoming fully informed about the subject of their inquiry. This is the overlooked fallacy of the story. The men did not achieve full enlightenment about elephants simply because a sighted person told them that all descriptions of their individual tactile experiences had been correct, albeit limited in scope. They learned only that there is utility in aggregating data to resolve apparent contradictions. Errors of omission are still possible if some important parts of the elephant were not touched by the six sets of hands and therefore could not be entered into the equation. Seeing only a few aspects of FDI and MNCs similarly provides only partial, potentially misleading understanding.

The limited inquiry conducted by the blind men in the tale provides a second valuable lesson for students of the FDI/MNC phenomena: The specific object being observed may or may not be representative of the entire range of the object's forms and variants. Examining only one form of the object under scrutiny can result in inadequate data sampling that leads to inaccurate extrapolations rather than a genuine mastery of the subject. If sightless people seeking to learn about elephants touch only a three-month-old animal, their assessment of the physical dimensions of the species will be faulty. However, it would be the same situation if twenty people with perfect eyesight attempted to learn about elephants by looking only at a relative newborn.

In addition to the need to account for age as a variable, a full understanding here requires knowledge that the elephant family is composed of different species. Asian and African elephants are not physically identical. Hence, both need to be touched, if not visually examined, to assemble critical data on the different forms of these animals. In some cases, information gathering done solely by touch would be wholly inadequate. A rare strain of white elephant actually does exist, but its most distinctive feature would elude the touch of 100 highly educated blind people.[3] Similarly, the heterogeneous nature and impact of FDI and MNCs cannot be fully understood by touching only one, two, or three of the many forms that they take.

The larger lesson of this classic tale goes beyond the virtue of information seekers combining several perspectives to provide broader insights. It is a lesson about the need to recognize the limits of partial knowledge and the need to pursue further lines of inquiry to attain larger truths. The story never suggested that after the blind men learned why each of their tactile experiences was different from the others, they realized the possibility that they were still missing key pieces of data, that is, they were still ignorant of certain physical attributes of the elephant. Another lesson that is transferable to study of FDI and MNCs is that all six assessments by the blind men were equally valid because each correctly portrayed partial reality. None negated the accuracy or usefulness of competing descriptions.[4] No one assessment could claim to have described the most important trait of the animal, that is, none could claim to be the definitive explanation of what they had touched. Additional fact finding and data analysis would be necessary to produce such an explanation. At times, it is appropriate that pursuits of a definitive study of elephants and a definitive understanding of the world of FDI and MNCs incorporate a Hegelian dialectic to seek synthesis between the valid points of numerous theses and antitheses.

A major shortcoming of most prior studies and discussions of FDI and MNCs is their failure to emphasize that neither is cut from a single mold. They defy all-inclusive labels and need to be understood as generic terms encompassing a variety of formats. They are heterogeneous. A few studies have made this critical point, but regrettably only briefly, without emphasis, and no follow-up. In an incisive observation made too quickly and with no fanfare, David Fieldhouse wrote, "Each corporation and each country is a special case. Individual examples can neither prove nor disprove general propositions."[5] Buried in the middle of a paragraph on page 450 of a well-known 1978 book on the subject, the authors quickly noted in passing that one of their "principal findings is that foreign direct investment is an extremely heterogeneous phenomenon."[6] The need to emphasize diversity goes beyond academic methodology; it has an important implication for public policy as well. To the extent that systemic heterogeneity is recognized, national laws and international agreements can be designed to deal with specific contingencies and address specific infractions rather than regulate on a broadly indiscriminate basis. As the authors of the just cited book said, generalizations, including theirs, about the effects of FDI "must be treated with extreme care, as must calls for sweeping policy approaches."[7]

Although the issues surrounding FDI and MNCs are numerous, difficult, and not conducive to easy answers, they ultimately are about the two most complex policy issues in political economy. The latter can be stated succinctly and clearly: (1) what is the optimal trade-off for society between fairness and efficiency in the economic order, and (2) where in economic policy is the optimal dividing point between government regulation and free markets on both a national and global basis? The wording of these two mega-questions never changes, but countless responses over the years have failed to provide answers simultaneously satisfactory to the opposite ends of the political spectrum. All of the chapters that follow directly or indirectly touch on these questions. They are not intended to provide definitive answers one way or the other but to analyze the two sides of the argument in a way that helps point the way for a mutually acceptable common ground between two clashing perspectives.

Thousands of articles, books, and reports, together with uncountable speeches and debates, collectively provide a vast body of information on the many facets of our subject. Large quantities, at least in this case, are not synonymous with complete, accurate, and up-to-date data. Though this is a personal opinion, the combined written and oral efforts of practitioners, advocates, and researchers do share at least one demonstrable failing: They have been unable to change a measurable number of preexisting attitudes—pro, con, and noncommittal—regarding FDI and MNCs. Scant progress has been made toward reaching consensus on what kind of public policies should be applied to them. Closure has been blocked in part because so many opinion makers, scholars, and casual observers on both ends of the political spectrum either embrace international business as a whole with open arms or attack it with a clenched fist. The standard rhetoric of the opposing sides exudes the erroneous belief that the generic terms FDI and MNCs are compatible with a one-size-fits-all set of government regulations, lenient or restrictive as the case may be. In fact, these terms are holding companies for infinite variations of economic and business situations.

That relatively few people have switched from being favorably disposed to opposed and vice versa seems to be a function of the continued paucity of uncontestable universal truths, real and perceived. New arguments have not come along that were convincing enough as to be capable of changing people's perceptions. This is part of the explanation for a forty-year-old public debate about the virtues and implications of FDI and MNCs that is better known for its intractable, occasionally strident inconclusiveness than for its intellectual acuity. Given their present and future importance to a growing percentage of the world's population, this is an unsatisfactory state of affairs. FDI is an important variable in determining economic growth, employment, incomes, and international trade flows. By dominating global production of many key capital and consumer goods, MNCs have become the most important nonstate actors in the international political order, so much so that legitimate but not necessarily accurate concerns have been raised about their ability to diminish the sovereignty of nation-states (see chapter 10).

Another basic shortcoming of many of the words written and spoken on this subject is failure to explicitly recognize how important *perceptions*, *value judgments*, *ideology*, and sometimes *self-interest* are in shaping discussions by both advocates and critics. When "attitude" fills a vacuum caused by a shortage of incontrovertible data, a contest between diametrically different positions is likely to provoke and perpetuate disagreement and crowd out objectivity. People tend to view the FDI/MNC phenomena through differently configured lenses that have been individually molded by the unique mix of values and experiences that shapes our thinking. Greek philosopher Epictetus said some 2,000 years ago, "Men are disturbed not by things, but by the view which they take of them."

Assessing what one sees when considering FDI and MNCs is somewhat akin to taking a Rorschach test made up of concepts instead of ink drawings. Evaluations of FDI and MNCs are prime examples of perceptions defining "truth." (Full disclosure: The text of this book is largely a manifestation, sometimes subconsciously, of the author's values and preferred methods of processing information.)

When the need to make choices takes place in the absence of proven fact and in the presence of perceptions, a political process is at work. Blanket condemnation and praise of MNCs and FDI stem from divergent personal philosophies and ideological beliefs (see chapter 5) that are subjective in nature. They cannot definitively be proved or disproved by controlled laboratory experiments that, as might be possible in the natural sciences, produce exactly the same result after hundreds or even thousands of replications. Only a few things about these phenomena can be deemed factual or be precisely quantifiable, such as corporate sales, profits, and assets and the most popular country destinations of overseas subsidiaries. The exact amount of annual worldwide FDI flows and the total value of cumulative FDI outstanding are unknown due to data collection shortcomings and different definitions in national statistics (see chapter 14).

Subjectivity, the stuff of politics, is also deeply rooted in our subject matter because of the totally hypothetical nature of the "what if" scenario. Definitive assessments of the gains or losses that would have accrued to a host country from nonexistent FDI that *might* have been established, or of the net effects of *not* introducing foreign subsidiaries that were in fact established are not possible. Counterfactuals by definition are hypothetical statements and pure guesswork. Irrefutable impact assessments could be achieved only by the science fiction device of freezing time, turning back the clock, then either creating new foreign subsidiaries that were not established or eliminating those that were, and finally restarting time. The results of the new chain of events could then be definitively compared to the original version of history.

Reduced to its essence, different perspectives in this case equate to a referendum on big capitalism. Persons with very liberal or very conservative political views are likely to process information in such a way that they perceive domestic and international business operations mainly with skepticism or enthusiasm, respectively. It is yet another case of honorable people looking at the same abstract phenomena and seeing two mutually exclusive albeit completely legitimate versions. Both sides remain dogmatic and dug in for the long haul even though neither can offer irrefutable proof that its position is the most accurate and equates to first-best public policy strategy.

In the introductory lecture of my course on MNCs, the potential ambiguity of perceptions is illustrated by showing students optical illusions in which two images are entwined in an especially clever manner. When one looks at the classic

FIGURE 1.1.

illusion in figure 1.1, the initial perception most likely will be the profile of an old woman; a second look eventually will reveal the profile of a young woman. It's all a matter of perspective, not unlike viewing MNCs and FDI.

Scholarly Inquiry Needs to Keep Up with a Rapidly Changing Business World

Finally, studies of FDI and MNCs should avoid a common error of commission in the debate: failure to explicitly assert that these are not static phenomena. Their dynamic properties have been clearly demonstrated historically in two opposite ways. The first is the multinationals' nonstop ability to adapt to and then exploit changing economic and market conditions. The second face of dynamism is big companies' tendencies to restructure, fail outright, or be bought out by bigger, more successful companies. To revert to cliché, the only constant has been change. The new economics of high-technology production and the advent of the information and telecommunications revolution have helped fuel an accelerated flow of new products and new forms of international business operations since the 1980s. The continuing pace of change also reflects the overlapping rise in the need for a successful multicountry business strategy and the decrease in the difficulty of establishing foreign subsidiaries. The bottom line is that relentless change in international business operations has reduced much of what has been written about them to an interesting but somewhat outdated snapshot of a particular point in time (a fate awaiting at least parts of this book) rather than an accurate reflection of present-day conditions.

The start of a new millennium is a propitious time to suggest that more persons and organizations on both sides of the pro/con argument need to recognize the wide gap between conventional wisdom and changing real-world conditions. MNCs have changed at a far faster rate than is commonly recognized. Several of the contending arguments' most cherished, longest used images and allegations date back to the early 1970s and before. Continuing to repeat them without modification has become more a reflex action than an intellectually sound analytical exercise. Several long-running allusions now qualify for antique status and are badly in need of updating—if the objective is to construct timely and accurate characterizations. The forecast of an operatic drama featuring apocalyptic struggles between gargantuan, avaricious, unaccountable, monopoly-seeking, amoral-exploit-the-workers commercial baronies and altruistic protectors of the people but overmatched government officials has not quite materialized. Neither have the promises that MNCs could work wonders in reducing poverty and economic backwardness and that a new age of enlightened corporate executive embraced the practice of responsible corporate behavior.

The accumulated literature seldom highlights the extent to which the continuing evolution of FDI and MNCs impedes formulation of a permanently accurate analysis or critique of how they behave, what their objectives are, or what effects they have. A good example of this syndrome is *Global Reach—The Power of the Multinational Corporations*, a book Richard J. Barnet and Ronald E. Müller, published in 1974. It became a major source of grist for the mills of an entire generation of skeptics and critics who saw a dangerous if not disruptive and harmful trend in the making. When examining this much-quoted book three decades later, one finds a largely accurate description of the unprecedented scale and scope of MNCs, the implications of which had not previously been articulated in such a detailed manner.

Some of its arguments, however, invite an update or a disagreement. In response to the statement that "Driven by the ideology of infinite growth, a religion rooted in the existential terrors of oligopolistic competition, global corporations act as if they must grow or die,"[8] one should begin by noting that big corporations are anything but immortal. *Any* company faced with aggressive, smart, and persistent competitors will eventually confront financial death if it is too incompetent or self-assured to innovate, cut costs, and serve customers in a way that allows it to protect and increase its profits. It is common for those who criticize large corporations and markets to downplay the degree to which changing conditions in the latter can render summary judgment on the former. Permanence is not a fringe benefit that comes with a company growing in size and profitability; "here today and gone tomorrow" is the more prevalent syndrome. One-third of the corporate giants listed in the *Fortune* 500 in 1980 were not there in 1990 because of decline, acquisition, or bankruptcy; another 40 percent of the 1980 class was gone by 1995.[9] The constant change in the composition of the Dow Jones Industrial Average is additional testament to the ebbs and flows of business success. Sometimes the cause is management mistakes, for example, they ignore what Andrew Grove called inflection points—full-scale transformational changes in a business sector that can provide a responsive company with an opportunity to "rise to new heights" or signal the demise of a nonresponsive one.[10] At other times, hot-selling products fall by the wayside, victims of new technology or fickle consumers.

When the authors of *Global Reach* offered a list of firms in support of their argument that a global company is by definition an oligopoly,[11] they unintentionally demonstrated the fallacy of overlooking the fact that only a select few companies remain dominant in their product line for extended periods of time. The list began with IBM, who in the 1970s was the prototypical mighty MNC. No one could have guessed then that a few years later it would have to rush to reinvent itself after it suffered a nearly fatal disregard during the 1980s for the shift away from its one-time core product, mainframe computers. More recently, as part of its transition to becoming a business services company, IBM sold its personal computer division to, improbably, a Chinese company.

Ford and General Motors, two other companies cited in the *Global Reach* list of market-dominating oligopolists, remain huge global corporations, but they have become symbols of American manufacturing giants in distress. A steady erosion in their domestic market share, high fixed costs (especially for workers' health benefits and retiree pensions) relative to their foreign competition, slim-to-nonexistent profit margins, and lack of confidence in management's ability to turn the situation around resulted in credit ratings agencies downgrading their debt (i.e., bonds) to "junk" status in 2005. No outside financial analyst could rule out the possibility of either or both of these one-time corporate icons needing to seek protection under U.S. bankruptcy law. Other companies listed as examples of big oligopolists included the seemingly omnipotent international oil companies known as the seven sisters. They would later have to adjust to nationalizations of their oil concessions and respond to the rising costs of oil exploration by engaging in a spate of mergers, which reduced their number to four. Of the four remaining firms on the list, National Biscuit was acquired by a cigarette company, and Du Pont, Dow Chemical, and Bayer no longer command the status of market-dominating, rapidly expanding kings of the universe.

Barnet and Müller's claim that "The global corporation is the first institution in human history dedicated to centralized planning on a world scale" is an oversimplification. It can be countered with the observation that many MNCs prefer decentralized, that is, subsidiary-by-subsidiary decision making by executives of various nationalities who are closer to and more knowledgeable about local market conditions and changing tastes of customers throughout the world. Successfully standardized "world products" have proven to be the exception rather than the rule. Elsewhere, the authors raised a two-part question as to whether the rise of "world managers" would lead to "a new golden age or a new form of imperial domination," and whether MNCs represent "mankind's best hope for producing and distributing the riches of the earth" or "an international class war of huge proportions, and, ultimately ecological suicide?"[12] Offering only these diametrically opposite, black-and-white choices incorrectly ignored what unsurprisingly, subsequently occurred: a large gray area of mixed, sometimes ambiguous results that falls between the extremes.

There was and is no good reason for the world not to be vigilant against allowing excessive power to accrue to MNCs. Still, a better assessment of the major changes then under way in the international order and the role of multinational firms in these changes can be found in a 1968 book by renowned management guru Peter Drucker:

> Genuinely new technologies are upon us. They are almost certain to create new major industries and brand-new major businesses and to render obsolete at the same time existing major industries and big businesses.... We face an Age of Discontinuity in world economy and technology.... The one thing that is certain so far is that it will be a period of change—in technology and in economic policy, in industry structures and in economic theory, in the knowledge needed to govern and to manage, ... While we have been busy finishing the great nineteenth-century economic edifice, the foundations have shifted under our feet, ... Imperceptibly there has emerged a world economy in which common information generates the same economic appetites, aspirations, and demands—cutting across national boundaries and languages and largely disregarding political ideologies as well. The world has become, in other words, *one market*, one global shopping center. (emphasis in original)[13]

The Paradigm to Be Examined

An opening exists for an even-handed, "no attitude" analysis that connects more dots than its predecessors and illustrates more clearly how irregularly shaped pieces relate to the larger picture. In seeking new clarity and more accuracy, this study is distinctive from the mainstream by virtue of emphasizing diversity and presenting a menu of answers, not definitive conclusions. Instead of searching for a uniform, predictable set of behavior patterns, it stresses the nature and implications of heterogeneity in the subjects being analyzed. Hence, the emphasis placed on the use of disaggregation and the avoidance of generalization. No attempt is made to pursue the arguably unattainable quest to formulate unified theories about the nature and net welfare effects on countries of FDI and MNCs. The "anti" theory presented in this study is that there is no provable, all-encompassing hypothesis capable of synthesizing the aggregate character, relative merits, and overall impact of FDI and MNCs. The already large and still growing numbers of foreign-controlled subsidiaries share too few specific, nonobvious characteristics to justify stereotypes.

This new methodology is actually a throwback to one of the first academic books written specifically on FDI and MNCs. In the introduction to his 1969 work, Charles Kindleberger advised his readers, "We shall encounter a variety of attempts to prescribe general precepts, and I will find it possible as a rule to suggest circumstances in which they are not appropriate."[14] This is also my intention. Some readers of this book will dismiss such an approach as a cop-out lacking in intellectual vigor and appreciation of theory. Their numbers will be reduced to the extent that subsequent chapters are convincing in their arguments as to why it is the best and most accurate assessment, or at worst, the least imperfect.

In sum, the integrating theme of the chapters that follow is that our cumulative knowledge about FDI and MNCs is still inadequate and the heterogeneity of corporations and countries is too great to permit generalized conclusions that can be defended as accurate and enduring. The subjects being observed are too dissimilar, fluid, and ambiguous to permit more than a handful of "correct" analytic answers and "optimal" government policies to regulate FDI and MNCs at any given time. In the past, most of the judgments made about international corporate behavior have had to be revised and expanded as MNCs continuously adapted to relentless forces of change. Extrapolations have amassed more of a record of medium-term obsolescence than sustained accuracy. The forces of change will continue to manifest themselves, and the results cannot be predicted with any more certainty than upcoming patterns in a turning kaleidoscope.

Notes

1. Data source: United Nations Conference on Trade and Development (UNCTAD), *World Investment Report 2005*, p. 13, available online at http://www.unctad.org; accessed November 2005.
2. Ibid.
3. In theory, the potential for pachyderm heterogeneity goes further. Drunks reportedly have seen pink elephants, though no scientific evidence exists to confirm their exis-

tence. Furthermore, ever since 1941, the movie classic *Dumbo* has implanted the image in the imaginations of successive generations that given sufficiently large ears, an elephant could fly. After the blind men, the second most famous fictional collective to contemplate the characteristics of an elephant was a group of talking crows in *Dumbo*. They, too, fell short in their elephant IQ when they initially dismissed Dumbo's chances of taking flight.

4. George J. Marshall, "Hegel and the Elephant," available online at http://www.bu .edu/wcp/Papers/Inte/InteMars.htm; accessed October 2004.

5. David Fieldhouse, "'A New Imperial System'? The Role of the Multinational Corporations Reconsidered," in Jeffry A. Frieden and David A. Lake, eds., *International Political Economy*, 4th ed. (Boston: Bedford/St. Martin's, 2000), p. 176.

6. C. Fred Bergsten, Thomas Horst, and Theodore H. Moran, *American Multinationals and American National Interests* (Washington, DC: Brookings Institution, 1978), p. 450.

7. Ibid.

8. Richard J. Barnet and Ronald Müller, *Global Reach—The Power of the Multinational Corporations* (New York: Simon and Schuster, 1974), p. 364.

9. "The World's View of Multinationals," *The Economist*, January 29, 2000, p. 21.

10. Andrew S. Grove, *Only the Paranoid Survive* (New York: Currency Doubleday, 1996), pp. 3–4.

11. Barnet and Müller, *Global Reach*, p. 34.

12. Ibid., pp. 14, 25.

13. Peter F. Drucker, *The Age of Discontinuity* (New York: Harper and Row, 1968), pp. ix, 10, x; emphasis in original.

14. Charles P. Kindleberger, *American Business Abroad* (New Haven, CT: Yale University Press, 1969), p. 36.

2

DEFINING THE SUBJECT
Subtleties and Ambiguities

In what might be called a retro innovation, the substantive assessment of the nature and impact of foreign direct investment (FDI) and multinational corporations (MNCs) begins in a relatively unusual manner. It pauses to explain in detail precisely what these terms mean because their definitions are neither self-evident nor common knowledge. The absence of consensus about their overall nature and effects begins at a very rudimentary level: What are the defining characteristics of these complex, diverse, and abstract entities?

Before defining FDI and MNCs, this chapter takes two steps back to advance the simple, but somewhat unconventional argument that there are two important issues that are even more basic than definitions of our subject matter. The first section examines the conflicting perceptions and definitions of that which preceded and later gave birth to FDI and MNCs: the domestic corporation. The next section assesses the very basic question of whether *multinational corporation* is the most appropriate term for that which is to be defined. Finally, the chapter's third section presents a broad range of definitions covering this study's subject matter. This would seem like the logical starting point, but definitions of FDI and MNCs are best presented after a generic description of the corporation and a look at the conceptual difficulties associated with determining the most accurate term for what is to be defined.

What Is a Corporation? What Is Its Mission?

Insights into the nature, functions, responsibilities, and impact of MNCs begin with insights into the same four aspects of that which spawned them: the *domestic corporation.* A corporation is the most important private sector institution for creating wealth and allocating resources on a country-by-country basis. MNCs serve this role in the global economy. As a consequence, domestic corporate issues extrapolated to the international business arena shed light on the underlying themes of most major MNC/FDI-related issues. In some cases, domestic and international corporate questions are the two sides of the same coin.

The domestic-international parallels begin with the difficulties inherent in constructing a consensus definition of either type of corporation and in setting criteria for measuring their net impact, either good or bad. Given the eclectic approach of this book, the appropriate starting point is to quote the observation by two business analysts that definitions of the corporation "reflect the perspective (and the biases) of the people writing the definitions."[1] The near impossibility of devising a single concise, universally accepted definition of the modern corporation reflects the important roles of perceptions and value judgments, as well as the nature of the beast. Another obstacle is the multiple dimensions inherent in the corporate phenomenon: legal status, purpose, internal governance, external responsibilities to society (if any), and so on. Is there an order of priority among these subthemes? Do all have to be considered or just some? If the objective is to make a one-sided case for the corporation's net virtues or net drawbacks, a succinct, deliberately worded, unnuanced definition would suffice. Given this book's broader perspective and commitment to an objective study emphasizing heterogeneity, legitimate differences in perceptions are inevitable, and the need for disaggregation, multiple definitions and descriptions of the corporation are necessary.

In the most literal, basic terms, a corporation is a business entity that has met certain legal requirements and has had its incorporation papers approved by designated national and/or local government authorities in the country where the new corporation resides. From a narrow legal perspective, at least under U.S. law, a corporation is no more than a web of contracts and other legal documents that tie together various parties to a specific company. In broader legal terms, a corporation (as distinct from a sole proprietorship or a partnership) is a freestanding entity separate from its owners and is a de facto citizen. It possesses separate legal rights, liabilities, and responsibilities; these include the ability to buy and sell assets, enter into contracts, issue debt, and sue or be sued in the judicial system. Three other important characteristics of corporations are that they

1. Have an unlimited life that allows them to continue even though owners and managers come and go.
2. Allow easy transferability of ownership interests by shares of stock that can be transferred from one owner to another quickly and easily.
3. Have limited liability. Owners' losses are limited to the funds they invested in the corporation, that is, owners cannot be assessed to cover corporate deficits or obligations.[2]

Beyond these legalistic characteristics, definitions often demonstrate value judgments, if not outright biases. Critics of free markets and those with doubts about capitalism would sympathize with the caustic definition of a corporation as "an ingenious device for obtaining individual profit without individual responsibility."[3] Disdain for corporations can be taken to the next level by branding them as ruthless seekers of self-aggrandizement with a genetically embedded, irrepressible desire to seek enough market power to fix prices for its goods at levels that guarantee maximum profits for the long term. This goal is derided as an effort to provide limitless riches to a relatively small capitalist class, with little or no concern about possible negative costs to society as a whole or the relative lack of benefits accruing to workers whose toil produces the goods and services being sold. The implication of this characterization is that governments must systematically monitor, tax, and regulate companies to limit their alleged natural inclinations to exploit the majority and abuse their power in a perpetual, single-minded drive to maximize profits.

Most critics of corporations would go one step further and express concern about the diminishing likelihood of proper government regulation when the financial power and reach of corporations continue to grow beyond what these critics perceive as already being at disturbingly large sizes. They would define corporations in terms of their supposed ability to convert economic power into the ability to co-opt government officials' interpretation of the public good. They presumably could do this through massive increases in donations to politicians and political parties and by means of threats to move the company and its jobs to a different jurisdiction.

Most people embracing a right-of-center political ideology would offer a very different core definition: A corporation is a business entity designed to make profits by pleasing customers. By doing so, it justifies the confidence placed in it by its owners. Profits enhance the wealth of shareholders through rising stock prices and higher dividends. The idealized version of perfectly functioning markets affirms that the quest to create wealth for shareholders is a positive-sum game because to achieve it, companies must serve the public interest. The unrelenting need to maximize efficiency—for which corporations are superbly designed—in producing goods or providing services presumably translates into rising living standards for the public at large. Companies do this by optimizing output (usually through high volume), increasing the ability of people to consume by keeping prices low (in economic terms, the result is increased real incomes), and by widening consumers' choices. The pro-corporation line of reasoning explains that superior management is acquired and retained by competitive salaries and bonuses linked to increased corporate profitability and rising stock prices, neither of which can be generated for long by overpriced or underperforming goods and services.

To depict private corporations as efficiency-driven, positive-sum game institutions is to argue that a successful company does what no government agency can do. Relentless competition and unforgiving market forces afford the private sector no alternative to utilization of resources in the most efficient manner, constant innovation, quick adjustment to changing tastes and needs of consumers, and taking risks to keep one step ahead of competitors. New technology creates new business opportunities and pushes obsolete businesses into oblivion. Corporate growth translates into additional jobs. Unlike the typical government agency, a commercial company must be able to meet its customers' present and future needs to perpetuate itself. Only government agencies can enjoy permanence and increased budgets through statutory authority.

Another useful insight into the nature of the corporation is to examine the evolution of its structure as logical responses to constantly changing external stimuli. Until the second half of the nineteenth century, most manufacturers were relatively small, unincorporated sole proprietorships or partnerships serving geographically limited markets. An unprecedented progression of innovations in transportation, communications, and power generation that began in the second half of the 1800s encouraged the move to ever larger factories to utilize economies of scale (see chapter 6) through larger volumes of production and sales—a trend that continues today. Individual owners needed increasing amounts of capital to keep growing, and many found incorporation and selling shares in the company (above and beyond borrowing) to be a cost-effective means of doing so. As production techniques became more complex, corporations continued growing in terms of size and the number of owners. Gradually, many companies became so large that they began replacing their founders with professional managers hired from outside or promoted from within. The continued growth in the number of shareholders meant an increasing disconnect between ownership and control of corporations.

By the mid-twentieth century, the larger, more successful manufacturing corporations extended their capabilities beyond the production line to include marketing, distribution, research and development, and international divisions.[4] A significant organizational innovation became commonplace after World War II, first in the United States and soon elsewhere, establishing subsidiaries in numerous foreign countries; in other words, growing numbers of firms were transforming themselves into MNCs.

A definitive definition of the corporation must go beyond what thus far has largely been a U.S.-centric point of view. Deeply held beliefs throughout much of Europe and Asia go beyond the legal, economic, and organizational definitions to include assigning it an organic role as a societal institution. This concept puts less emphasis on corporate profits and stock prices and more emphasis on the need to fulfill what are deemed essential obligations to the broad public interest.

Country-by-country differences in assigning priorities to serving the interests of society relative to shareholders largely derive from differences in deeply rooted cultural values. Acceptance of the proposition that corporate operating guidelines can differ from country to country adds credence to the school of thought that the world is populated by transnational companies with distinctive national qualities and priorities that do not universally fall into the category of like-minded stateless MNCs. As globalization proceeds and business interaction among countries intensifies, it is logical to wonder whether their differing systems for regulating corporations, based as they are on strong cultural preferences, present opportunities for convergence, cooperation, or conflict[5]—or all three. (The questions of how and to what extent MNCs should be regulated are addressed in chapter 11.)

The issue of corporate obligations and goals is frequently framed as a question of primacy between two contending interest groups. For whom should a corporation *primarily* be run? On one side are the *shareholders* who bought stock in a company for the purpose of receiving a return on investment and who ultimately own it. On the other side are the *stakeholders,* a broader, more inclusive group that is composed of all persons or entities that are affected by the activities, successes, and failures of a corporation. This "public commons" is composed of the community at large (including the environment), employees, customers, other companies doing business with the corporation, national and local governments, lenders (banks, bondholders, etc.), along with shareholders. Which set of interests should be served first and foremost is a decision that tends to flow from one's place on the political left-to-right spectrum (see chapter 5).

The Anglo-Saxon model (so named because it has mainly been used in the United States and the United Kingdom) favors a market-oriented economic ideology. It therefore tilts in favor of giving priority—not exclusivity—to the interests of shareholders. *The Economist* opined that a corporation placing social responsibility ahead of profits is "philanthropy at other people's expense." Managers are entrusted with the care of assets belonging to the company's shareholding owners; if executives want to support good causes out of their own pockets, that would be admirable. Besides, asked the article, "is it really for managers and NGOs to decide social-policy priorities . . . ? In a democracy, that is a job for voters and elected politicians."[6] By encouraging maximum corporate freedom and efficiency short of violations of laws and regulations, the private sector has been instrumental for many decades in generating steady increases in standards of living. Hence this viewpoint argues that government should encourage and support the dynamism of business, not stifle efficiency and innovation with red tape.

The majority of Western European and developing countries plus Japan have a different set of values. They believe that the primary purpose of economic activity is to serve and protect the population as a whole, not an economic elite. They embrace a government-dominated model to pursue a "just" society that serves the vast majority. Pursuit of full employment, worker benefits, and a comprehensive social safety net at some cost to corporate profits and after-tax income of the owners of capital is deemed fully justified.

The efficiency maximization and societal enhancement models of the corporation are not mutually exclusive. Although it would be naive to suggest that they will eventually meet in the middle and merge into a single theory of economic structure, both versions of corporate missions and responsibilities have seen the need to adopt some principles of the other. Many persons who still define the ultimate justification of the corporation in terms of its unmatched ability to generate physical output, efficiency, and wealth would probably accept Peter Drucker's definition that the "modern corporation is a political institution; its purpose is the creation of legitimate power in the industrial sphere."[7] They likely would have more reservations about more "progressive" assertions, like "The corporation cannot—and should not survive if it does not take responsibility for the welfare of all of its constituents and for the well-being of the larger society within which it operates."[8]

Committed advocates of stakeholder rights think that the legitimacy of the contemporary corporation—its social charter—"depends on its ability to meet the expectations of an increasingly numerous and diverse array of constituents."[9] Much to the dismay of these activists, some companies and policymakers in Western Europe and Japan at the start of the millennium were reluctantly conceding that swelling global competitive pressures necessitated at least a small step in adopting the unsentimental brand of U.S. capitalism that allows forced layoffs and a frozen benefit scale for workers, accepts most corporate bankruptcies, and seems content to accept a secular decline in the power and size of unions. In its most polarized form, the shareholder-stakeholder debate extrapolated to the global stage has long been a major contributing factor to the backlash against globalization (see chapter 5).

The larger reality is that the corporation is still a work in progress. Its organizational structure and mission continue to evolve and diversify, for better or worse. No matter how someone defines it at any given time, the terms used inevitably will need to be modified and expanded—on more than one occasion— if obsolescence is to be avoided.

Until the late 1990s, *governance* had been an arcane aspect of the corporate process largely ignored by the public. It became a hot policy topic that swelled in importance as news headlines trumpeted the latest in what seemed to be an endless series of corporate financial scandals engineered by senior executives, mostly in the United States but also in Europe, Japan, and elsewhere. Corporate governance as discussed here is a term roughly synonymous with oversight of management.

(Lacking a precise meaning, it can also be used to refer to the structure of internal, day-to-day corporate decision making and procedures for resource allocation). The better the oversight by a select group of informed, independent outsiders that outranks senior operational executives, the less likely that the latter will commit such crimes as "cooking the books" to inflate earnings, siphoning funds from the company, engaging in insider stock trades, making patently false statements about the company's financial health, and so on. Good corporate governance also hastens the exit of executives guilty of such noncriminal acts as recklessness, repeated poor business decisions, unethical acts, and so on.

Externally, corporate oversight is administered by government agencies such as the U.S. Securities and Exchange Commission, the Internal Revenue Service, and by private entities such as the two major national stock exchanges. Internally, corporate governance is centered in the board of directors, a body mandated by government statute in many countries. In the United States, it is charged with establishing and adjusting the levels of salary and benefits earned by senior managers and, when necessary, with firing them. Boards also approve broad changes in corporate strategy, examine and certify company financial statements, and (at least in the United States) ensure that the interests of shareholders are reasonably protected. In Germany, a different philosophy about corporate priorities and responsibilities led to a governance practice known as codetermination. Medium and large corporations are required by law to have a supervisory board (roughly analogous to the board of directors of U.S. corporations) that is equally divided between members chosen by employees and members representing shareholders.

Depending on one's perspectives, a good board could be defined as a toothless group that stays out of the way of senior managers. The latter in theory are full-time executives with distinguished credentials who are the best informed on current market conditions and the intricacies of the company's operations. A "see no evil, hear no evil, and speak no evil" board of directors that eschews second-guessing management begins with having the chief executive officer (CEO) double as chairperson of the board, as opposed to having an independent member of the board of directors hold the position. The all-important second step is recruiting a majority of directors who will not rock management's boat. These kinds of directors include personal friends and relatives of the chairman/president, employees of the company, executives of outside businesses that want to retain their contracts to sell goods or services to the company, and persons too busy or untrained to pore over corporate documents.

A genuine "checks and balances" board operates very differently and corresponds to the opposite definition of desirable oversight. It is one composed mainly or totally of independent, knowledgeable directors and a chairperson with no conflicts of interest. They conscientiously keep close tabs on what management is doing and saying. The board is prepared to bare its sharp teeth and has the inclination and competence to vigorously hold management responsible for running the corporation efficiently and honestly in the home country and, in cases of MNCs, in host countries abroad. This is the kind of board of directors that the U.S. government has mandated for U.S.-based companies. The most tangible response of the U.S. Congress to the early twenty-first century parade of corporate scandals was the Sarbanes-Oxley Act of 2002. Designed to reduce conflicts of interest at the highest corporate echelons, the legislation mandated several requirements to ensure a minimum level of independence for boards of directors, prohibited accounting firms from performing a number of (usually lucrative) consulting functions for the companies they audit, and so on. It is an open question as to whether these and additional safeguards can ever entirely prevent unscrupulous executives from bending the rules or attempting the perfect white-collar crime.

What's in a Name? Are MNCs Really "Multinational"?

A second step needed before defining the subject matter of this book is trying to resolve the seemingly pro forma task of determining what to call the internationally oriented business entities that will be defined and later analyzed. No universal consensus on the most basic terminology exists. The term *multinational corporation* is employed throughout this book because it is the most commonly used, and it satisfactorily (though perhaps imperfectly) conveys the nature of this kind of business enterprise. A number of scholars and analysts use the equally suitable term *enterprise* in lieu of *corporation*. Arguably, the choice here is mostly a matter of semantics. In theory, a business with foreign subsidiaries might not be incorporated in the headquarters country; even fewer could be government-owned enterprises, often referred to as parastatals. However, these rare exceptions are so greatly overshadowed in size and importance by traditional corporations that there seems to be no compelling intellectual reason to opt for *enterprise* on the basis that it has a more all-encompassing connotation.

A far more significant question is whether to use *multinational* or *transnational* as the adjective before *corporation*. The choice of words in this case involves more than semantics. These two modifiers symbolize a conceptual disagreement about how, at their core, MNCs are organized and managed and how they establish priorities. On one side is the belief that MNCs are a new kind of stateless entity with no allegiance to any particular country or business style. Such companies allegedly represent an economic and political revolution in the form of a radically new business paradigm, one unusually disdainful of government authority and dismissive of what they see as obsolete old-order constraints, such as national loyalties and borders. MNCs are sometimes depicted as new age global players that have methodically shed a single national identity in favor of the multiple identities needed to conquer multiple national markets. Their goal is a new level of cosmopolitanism in the quest to successfully compete in dozens of far-flung countries having diverse cultures. Japanese business consultant Kenichi Ohmae once exhorted executives to accept that neither an MNC's country of origin nor the location of its headquarters matters. "The products for which you are responsible and the company you serve have become denationalized," he wrote.[10]

To those who subscribe to this viewpoint, *multinational* connotes a blending of various national traits. The end product is a novel form of enterprise that operates in as many different ways as countries in which it maintains subsidiaries and major sales operations. Decisions on where to produce what goods presumably are based on worldwide searches by globally oriented technocrats guided solely by the credo of seeking maximum efficiency with minimum costs.

The opposing theory holds that MNCs are in fact transnationals, because ultimately they are nothing more than big national companies with operating subsidiaries in at least one other country, not a mixture of multiple nationalities. The statistically average MNC employs about two-thirds of its workforce and produces more than two-thirds of its output in the home country, typically a large industrialized economy.[11] Some scholars reject the notion that a new breed of denationalized corporation has emerged, one having an entirely new modus operandi shaped by a truly globalized mindset. This school of thought holds that even the most geographically dispersed companies do not and cannot totally divorce themselves from the national heritage that shaped their growth, corporate culture, and operating rules. A globally active corporation can "go native" on the surface, but not systemically. For example, a Japanese company operating in any country is likely to bring with it its native predilection for long-term growth and market share over immediate profits. As already noted, governance requirements under German corporate law preclude companies from dismissing the interests of their employees in the race to maximize shareholder value.

In *The Myth of the Global Corporation,* one of the most widely cited books espousing what, with only a slight exaggeration, might be dubbed as the uni-national overseas corporation thesis, the authors argue that "the most strategically significant operations of MNCs continue to vary systematically along national lines." "Distinctive national histories have left legacies that continue to affect the behavior" of even the largest MNCs. History and national culture allegedly "continue to shape both the internal structures of MNCs and the core strategies articulated through them." The authors further assert that MNCs should not be depicted as engines of globalization because they "are not converging toward global behavioral norms" devoid of their respective national origins. "The global corporation, adrift from its national political moorings and roaming an increasingly borderless world market, is a myth."[12] Another scholar argues that the typical MNC does not "leave" country A for country B; she feels that it is not an either/or situation. The management, governance, and organizational structure of a corporation overlap the political boundaries of home and host countries.[13] The global nature of multinationals also has been questioned on grounds that many have a very high percentage of their sales in their home country and a limited number of foreign markets.

In some cases, the relatively recently coined term *multidomestic* company may be the appropriate appellation. This would be applicable to MNCs that emphasize global decentralization and maintain small headquarters operations. Some or all of their overseas subsidiaries are given above-average autonomy and a relatively free hand to act as much as possible as a locally owned company in host countries. The managerial ranks at these stand-alone subsidiaries usually are staffed mainly or even totally with local nationals. Another relatively new term, *global corporation*, may catch on if only because it has a nice ring to it. Finally, two seldom used terms suggest a more value-free, all-inclusive label: *multination business* and *transnational production*.

Definitions of FDI and MNC

Foreign direct investment and *multinational corporation* are two inextricably intertwined concepts but not perfect synonyms. They are subtly different facets of the phenomenon of international business operations, but are often jointly referred to in the chapters that follow.

FDI is a *financial process* associated with companies operating and controlling income-generating facilities in at least one country outside their country of origin. Governments adopt and administer FDI policy. An MNC is a *tangible entity* that in some way will impact a *home* country, which is where its main headquarters is located, and one or more *host* countries, the recipient(s) of incoming FDI. Although a company might designate a tax-haven country as its official place of incorporation, in practical terms the headquarters or home country is where the offices of the top echelon of management are located. In most cases, this is also the country where the corporation began and where the largest percentage of its shareholders resides.

The terms FDI and MNC share the problem of inexact definitions. In considering the definitions that follow, one should be mindful that they are not immutable. They have been altered over the years and are likely to undergo further modifications in the future. Moreover, a few countries use definitions that differ from the one most commonly used.

FDI is a term used in at least four ways. First, it is the corporate activity that confers the status of multinational on certain firms. It is what MNCs *do* to become MNCs. Second, FDI is a financial activity. It normally consists of an international capital flow from the home country to the host country for the purpose of acquiring partial or full ownership of a tangible business entity, such as a factory, extractive facility, or wholesale distribution system. As a branch of international finance, FDI has implications for the balance of payments of both home and host countries. Third, *FDI* is the generic term used to designate the economic policies toward MNCs and international investment flows maintained by governments and international organizations. Finally, *FDI* is the generic term used by official statistical agencies to measure in monetary terms the annual incoming and outgoing *flow* and the cumulative value, that is, the *stock* of inward direct investments, on a country-by-country basis.

Two important technical qualifications are necessary. First, an FDI transaction does not literally need to involve an international capital flow to conform to these definitions. MNCs occasionally opt to finance the building, acquisition, or expansion of an overseas subsidiary by raising the needed funds in the host country's capital markets through bank borrowing or issuance of stocks and bonds. When expanding an existing operation, a corporation might tap the subsidiary's retained earnings (profits) as opposed to transferring capital from the home country. Second, FDI can take place without an MNC being involved; for example, a group of independent investors in one country could acquire a 10 percent or more (see following discussion) equity stake in a company incorporated in a foreign country. An always accurate but unwieldy definition of FDI would be: "significant" ownership in an income-producing entity in at least one country other than the one in which the controlling company or group is domiciled.

Certain specific criteria differentiate FDI from other international capital flows, even other kinds of international investment.[14] *Portfolio investment* is frequently and erroneously confused with FDI. The former occurs when an individual or financial institution (a mutual fund in most cases) buys a relatively small number of shares in a company located in another country because of the expectation that those shares will appreciate in value and can be sold at a profit sometime in the future. The investor in this case has no influence over management decisions and no long-term commitment to the company, just the visceral hope that he or she eventually will profit from rising share prices and dividends.

FDI is further defined on a qualitative and quantitative basis. Qualitatively, it is about ownership and control. FDI is done by companies with the intent of having sufficient ownership to ensure a partial or total say on a lasting basis in the management of a corporate entity located in a foreign country. In other words, a company based in the home country has at the least a meaningful long-term voice in shaping output, production, and marketing strategies; constructing corporate budgets; selecting senior managers; dealing with labor relations; and approving new product development in a company incorporated and doing business in the host country. FDI is about long-term, perhaps permanent relationships that could have a significant financial impact—good or bad—on the foreign company making the investment. It involves relatively large transfers of capital that cannot easily be reversed (whereas stocks and bonds can usually be sold in seconds). When establishing a foreign manufacturing subsidiary, a corporation commits more than a relatively large amount of capital—it also commits its prestige.

For manufacturing subsidiaries in particular, the foreign company will inject into the host country's economy a package of resources that typically include advanced, possibly state-of-the-art management skills and production techniques, technology, and marketing savvy. Increased jobs and exports are often associated with FDI. None of these qualities apply to the purchase, say, of 100 shares of Toyota Motor Corporation stock by an American citizen. This would be foreign portfolio investment.

Quantitatively, the nearly universally accepted definition of FDI is ownership of at least 10 percent of the common (voting) stock of a business enterprise operating in a country other than the one in which the investing company is headquartered. Having an active voice in an enterprise's management does not require 100 or even 51 percent ownership of the foreign entity's voting shares. In most countries, 10 percent ownership is considered sufficient for a foreign company to have entrée to at least some control over management decisions; in addition, it usually ensures selection of at least one member of the board of directors or its equivalent. According to the stylebook of the International Monetary Fund (IMF) and the Organization for Economic Cooperation and Development (OECD), a foreign *subsidiary* is an incorporated enterprise with a foreign investor having more than 50 percent equity ownership; the parent of a foreign subsidiary would normally have the right to appoint a majority of the members of its board of directors. The IMF/OECD stylebook uses the term foreign *associate* for an enterprise with a foreign investor having 10 to 50 percent ownership. Because the vast majority of FDI undertaken by large MNCs involves majority to full ownership by a single parent company, the term *subsidiary* will be used throughout this book for simplicity's sake. (For consistency's sake, the synonymous term of foreign *affiliate*, preferred by some government agencies, will not be used.)

A foreign subsidiary can be an entirely new entity or be formed through a merger with or acquisition of an existing company. FDI may also take the form of a joint venture with another company; in this case, a new, jointly owned corporate identity is created. A foreign branch involves ownership of an unincorporated business entity by a company headquartered abroad.

A few countries utilize other formulas to designate FDI, thereby preventing a uniform global statistics gathering standard. Some of these countries establish a higher minimum level of stock ownership, usually 25 percent, to define FDI. A very few make exceptions to the 10 percent rule in certifying FDI. If the investing company meets or exceeds that threshold but apparently will not have an effective managerial voice in the foreign firm, the transaction will not be classified as FDI. On the other hand, if the foreign investor appears to have secured a meaningful management role in the firm with less than 10 percent ownership, these countries will include the transaction in their FDI statistics.[15] Limitations on the cumulative data are further imposed by the difficulties facing even the best government statistical agencies in recording *all* FDI flows in a given year and in assigning accurate monetary values to those flows that are recorded. Some less developed countries do not have an established capability to accurately and fully compile such statistics.

MNCs, in contrast to FDI, are a kind of living organism because they are actively engaged overseas in producing goods and services and may be disseminating technology, managerial skills, and capital. The nearly universally accepted definition of a multinational corporation is one that owns outright, controls, or has direct managerial influence in income-generating, *value-added* facilities in at least two countries. Prior to the 1990s, the definition referred to a simpler, more concrete term: *production* facilities. However, relatively rapid rates of growth in FDI by service sector companies such as banks, engineering firms, accountants, and advertising agencies necessitated terminology that went beyond portrayals of factories, oil wells, and mines.

The relative precision of the definition of an MNC does not prevent conceptual problems. A company doing business on a global scale is not necessarily an MNC. Neither exports nor the presence of salespeople or wholesale distribution centers to distribute imports in a foreign country meet the definition of managerial control of an incorporated subsidiary in at least one foreign country.

A very wide range of companies are designated as MNCs. The broad spectrum ranges from small enterprises whose overseas subsidiary might consist of one small factory with statistically insignificant output and a handful of employees in just one other country, to huge corporations owning factories in thirty-plus countries that garner large market shares in host countries. A small number of purists want to deal with this incongruity by imposing additional statistical requirements before labeling a company an MNC. One suggested criterion is to require foreign subsidiaries to collectively contribute some minimum percentage of a company's annual total sales and/or profits. Another proposal is to require that a company have value-added facilities in more than two countries, perhaps four or more, before being classified as a multinational.

Notes

1. Robert A. G. Monks and Nell Minow, *Corporate Governance* (Malden, MA: Blackwell, 2004), p. 8.

2. For details on the legal nature of the corporation, see Eugene Brigham and Michael C. Ehrhardt, *Financial Management: Theory and Practice*, 11th ed. (Mason, OH: Thomson/South-Western, 2005), chap. 1.

3. Ambrose Bierce, *The Enlarged Devil's Dictionary* (Garden City, NY: Doubleday, 1967), p. 48.

4. Roger W. Ferguson Jr., "Lessons from Past Productivity Booms," press release of the Board of Governors of the Federal Reserve System, January 4, 2004, pp. 12–14.

5. Jeswald W. Salacuse, "European Corporations and American Style? Governance, Culture and Convergence," draft of paper presented April 2002; available online at http://www.ksg.harvard.edu/cbg/Conferences/us-eu_relations/salacuse_corporate_culture.pdf; accessed October 2004.

6. "Two-Faced Capitalism," *The Economist,* January 22, 2004, p. 53.

7. As quoted in Laurence J. Peter, *Peter's Quotations—Ideas for Our Time* (New York: William Morrow, 1977) p. 85.

8. James Post, Lee Preston, and Sybille Sachs, *Redefining the Corporation—Stakeholder Management and Organizational Wealth* (Stanford, CA: Stanford University Press, 2002), pp. 16–17.

9. Ibid., p. 9.

10. Kenichi Ohmae, *The Borderless World: Power and Strategy in the Interlinked Economy* (New York: Free Press, 1990), p. 94.

11. "The World's View of Multinationals," *The Economist,* January 29, 2000, p. 21.

12. Paul Doremus, William Keller, Louis Pauly, and Simon Reich, *The Myth of the Global Corporation* (Princeton, NJ: Princeton University Press, 1998), pp. 9, 1.

13. Mira Wilkins, "Comparative Hosts," *Business History,* January 1994, p. 24.

14. As noted by the UNCTAD Secretariat, " 'Investment' does not have a generally accepted meaning." UNCTAD, *World Investment Report 2003*, p. 100, available online at http://www.unctad.org. A generalized definition of *investment* is the purchase of financial or tangible assets with a view to obtaining a relatively high financial return.

15. International Monetary Fund, *Foreign Direct Investment Statistics—How Countries Measure FDI 2001*, October 2003, p. 23.

3

FROM OBSCURITY
TO INTERNATIONAL
ECONOMIC POWERHOUSE

The Evolution of Multinational Corporations

Multinational corporations (MNCs) did not suddenly appear on the scene or emerge as part of a calculated design by a group of avaricious captains of industry lusting after more sales and less competition. In fact, the nature, size, power, and number of the current generation of MNCs are at least as much the outgrowths of larger events that were *not* of business executives' own making. The timetable and twists and turns of foreign direct investment's (FDI) long evolutionary process were determined to a significant extent by external forces. Entrepreneurs and corporate managers did not set out to create the soaring costs of producing new generations of high technology goods that made an international presence necessary for companies in this sector. They did not create investor pressures for steady increases in sales and profits. Nor did they create the governmental policies that produced the business-friendly international order that allowed modern-day MNCs to flourish. The manufacturing and to a lesser extent services sectors acted at least as much defensively to external forces as they acted opportunistically to make a lot of money selling goods and services that a lot of people wanted to buy. Some have been pleased with the overall results of the pursuit of profit on a global basis by private enterprise; others have been bitterly critical.

This chapter examines the historical record in an effort to explain how the various kinds of MNCs evolved into their current corporate structures. Stereotypes and neatly wrapped conclusions are not consistent with the long, winding, and at times bumpy road that preceded the emergence of modern MNCs. The first section provides an overview of the infancy and intermediate stages of international business operations that spanned 350 years. This is followed by a closer look at the mix of factors causing the relatively recent onset of the modern era of mature and seemingly ubiquitous MNCs. The third and final section examines the reasoning and statistical data behind the assertions that (1) FDI and MNCs have reached the top echelon of issues in international economic relations, and (2) their economic impact is now sufficiently powerful to make them politically significant on a global scale.

The Initial and Intermediate Stages of MNC Development

The path that would eventually lead to the modern MNC followed a circuitous route, displaying no consistent pattern in either content or timing. Periods of rapid growth in multinational operations were interrupted by years of stagnation or even decline. In different periods, corporations made different choices between alternative modes of operating abroad and among alternative forms of internal organization.[1] The long gestation process for the full blossoming of the MNC was due to the need to wait for the arrival of a long succession of technological discoveries and nurturing economic conditions and public policy changes. History suggests that the larger political, technological, and economic environments mainly influenced the nature and timetable of the evolution of international business, not vice versa. According to one of the preeminent scholars in the field, John H. Dunning, the history of the development of the multinational corporation is

> The story of a series of political and social events that have affected the ownership, organization and location of international production.... The growth of international production in modern history essentially reflects the way in which changes in the structure and organization of the world's resources and capabilities impinge on the cross-border production and transaction strategies of companies. While historically the role of the [MNC] has been both a pro-active and re-active one ... the discovery of new territories, increases in population, advances in the stock of knowledge of production and organizational techniques, and the response of governments to these changes have been the prime movers.
>
> Enterprises have responded to these developments by realigning the extent, form and geography of their value-added activities. ... In many ways the growth of international production is a microcosm of changing commercial relationships, as they evolved from the personal trading of individuals ... through ... the industrial ... revolution ... to the computer ... revolution.[2]

Most economic historians trace the origins of the MNC back to the seventeenth century. The age of exploration was followed by colonization and large-scale expansions of trade and human migration outside of the European Continent, trends that gave birth to the first multicountry business enterprises. The British East India Company and the Dutch East India Company, established as trading companies in the beginning of the seventeenth century, are generally considered to be the first version of the MNC as we know it today.[3] The Western Hemisphere version of this genre was the Hudson's Bay Company, recipient of a monopoly charter bestowed by the British Crown to operate a fur trade monopoly and establish settlements in the Hudson Bay region of North America. None of these three enterprises bear much resemblance to the contemporary model because they were formally established by ruling monarchs for the purpose of enhancing the wealth and power of the home country. The first generation of MNCs also differed by undertaking overseas operations as soon as they were chartered, not after compiling a successful business record in the home country.

With long-distance communication primitive, the two East India companies received little direct supervision from their home countries. Having been granted monopoly power and broad authority to develop trade with the Far East as they saw fit, they often transacted business by brute force more than by commercial wiles. They were given authority to acquire territory if they deemed it necessary, maintain their own army and warships, and issue their own currency. At the peak of their power, these companies acted more like colonial governments than commercial enterprises. The British East India Company eventually became the de facto ruler of most of the Indian subcontinent, and its presence extended to Hong Kong, Burma, and Singapore. The Dutch counterpart controlled regions in Indonesia and built fortified posts in other locations to protect its Asian trade routes. For a time, these companies enjoyed enormous profits from exporting goods such as spices, cotton, silks, tea, and coffee to Western Europe and by engaging in intra-Asian trade. Their propensity for overreach and new competition eventually contributed to their demise.

Transition to the contemporary version of the MNC hit full stride in the second half of the nineteenth century, the catalyst being an extended series of interrelated events hitting critical mass. The Industrial Revolution had reached its peak, and in its wake widespread changes appeared in the economic landscape. Large-scale factories began to replace individually owned small businesses. The sprouting of manufacturing companies forced the liberalization of British corporate law, an approach adopted by other countries. Corporations no longer needed to secure a royal charter to begin operation. Subsequent changes allowed them to legally function as an "artificial person" that could issue tradable shares to investors who would have limited financial liability, that is, they could lose only the money they had invested. As manufacturing spread from Great Britain to other countries, so, too, did demand for new sources of energy and raw materials and for varieties of food that the industrializing countries lacked physically or could not produce efficiently. The increased opportunity for profits stimulated foreign investments in the primary sector.

An important indirect effect of the Industrial Revolution on the growth of international business was its significant enhancement of technological capacity and human skills in the production process. Once created, these two assets

> often became the proprietary rights of the owners. . . . They were also potentially mobile across space, opening up the possibility that firms might utilize the human and physical assets they generated . . . in one country to produce goods and services in another.
>
> Taken together, these events heralded a watershed in the history of international business. The age of merchant capitalism which had dominated international commerce for the previous two centuries was now replaced by an era of industrial capitalism. . . . Although the [MNC], as we know it today, did not emerge until later in the 19th century, firms from Europe and North America began to invest in foreign plantations, mines, factories, banking, sales and distribution facilities in large numbers.[4]

As a consequence of the ratcheting up of technological progress and increased worker skills in the late 1800s, wrote Dunning, "both the global structure of value-added activities and the modalities in which goods and services are exchanged across national borders have helped push back the industrial and territorial boundaries of firms, and have refashioned the competitive advantages of countries."[5]

The intermediate stage of FDI, which runs roughly from the 1850s through the 1950s, was created and sustained far more by exogenous events and trends than calculated corporate planning. The most important changes in the global commons were major technological advances in transportation and communications that allowed people, goods, and information to move long distances more quickly, cheaply, and reliably than ever before. The nineteenth-century inventions of the steam engine and the telegraph, the laying of undersea cables, the spread of railroads, and the opening of the Suez Canal geometrically enhanced the ability of corporations to operate and supervise distant operations. A second stimulant was the gradual escalation of tariffs in the second half of the nineteenth century in the United States and most European countries other than Britain. A classic reason for establishing an overseas subsidiary is the need to jump import barriers imposed by the government of a lucrative foreign market (see chapter 6).

FDI was simultaneously facilitated by accommodating governmental policies that placed no significant restrictions on international capital movements. Host countries were universally amenable to what was still a limited stream of incoming MNCs, although in some cases openness was a function of a country's being a colony with no indigenous government to voice objections.

The exact amount of FDI on the eve of World War I is not known. Governments measured only total foreign investment. No need was felt at that time to make a distinction between the direct and portfolio investments made by their citizens in other countries because both were viewed as being parts of the larger process of seeking a greater return on capital. A crude estimate of FDI at that time is somewhere in the $14.5 to $18.2 billion range. Ownership of overseas subsidiaries in 1914 was heavily concentrated in just five countries. An admittedly rough estimate puts Great Britain's share at 45 percent, the United States and Germany 14 percent each, France 11 percent, the Netherlands 5 percent, and the rest of the world accounting for the remaining 11 percent. "Given that a considerable amount of the service sector investments was concerned with financing, insuring, transporting and otherwise making possible international trade in raw materials and foodstuffs, it can be estimated that at least three-quarters of world FDI [in 1914] was concerned with the exploitation of natural resources."[6] In addition to such high-profile companies that would become notorious for the power they wielded in host countries (Standard Oil and the United Fruit Company, for example), a growing number of manufacturing companies sought a secure supply of critical raw materials by buying, among other things, rubber, tobacco, and palm oil plantations; mines; and cattle ranches in developing countries. Dunning estimated that more than 60 percent of FDI (by value) in 1914 was located in developing countries; an important component of this amount was U.S. investment in mining operations in Latin America.[7]

The second half of the nineteenth century was notable for the initial appearance of multinational manufacturing companies. Unlike their counterparts in the primary sector, these companies shared the pattern of contemporary MNCs: starting out selling goods in their home country, becoming successful exporters, and then becoming "first movers" in establishing overseas subsidiaries to enhance sales in key foreign markets. In 1855, Siemens built a factory in Russia to manufacture equipment for a nationwide telegraph network after receiving a contract from the Russian government. Twelve years later, the Singer sewing machine company opened a factory in Scotland that is considered to be the first sustained overseas American manufacturing subsidiary.[8] In some ways it can be considered as the original prototype of the contemporary manufacturing MNC; Singer's Scottish factory was built in an effort to maximize direct sales to foreign customers by taking a step beyond exports and not relying on European licensees.

By the turn of the century, Singer probably became the first truly global manufacturer by virtue of also having established factories in Canada, Austria, Germany, and Russia.

Ford Motor Company opened an automobile assembly plant in Britain in 1908; five years later it had become that country's largest carmaker.[9] In buying the Opel automobile company in 1929, General Motors can be given credit for what may be the first recorded cross-border acquisition of consequence. Kodak opened a factory near London in 1891 to produce film and cameras after its export efforts in Europe had become so successful that combined international and domestic demand exceeded the capacity of its headquarters in Rochester, New York.[10] Early in the twentieth century, Lever Brothers expanded beyond its British base by establishing soap-making factories in three European countries, the United States, Canada, and Australia.[11] A vanguard of manufacturing companies from France, Switzerland, Germany (mainly chemical companies), Sweden, and Japan also began establishing production facilities outside their borders.

As the twentieth century began, the estimated values of foreign trade and foreign investment (portfolio and direct) as a percentage of world output were at historic highs. The unprecedented scale of international economic integration, however, was temporary. Turbulent events in world history intervened to deflate what potentially was FDI's coming of age; by most calculations, it was not until the early 1990s that MNCs returned to the same relative importance to global gross domestic product (GDP). Two world wars and years of recovery from their devastation knocked the upward trajectory of commercial economic activity well off course for many years. A similar effect was experienced between the wars as the Great Depression shrank economic growth by double-digit percentages in many countries, and triggered a worldwide adoption of "beggar thy neighbor" policies. Import barriers and capital controls were implemented in a futile effort to protect jobs at home and export unemployment. The deteriorating international economic and political atmosphere encouraged manufacturing and raw materials companies in sectors with a relatively small number of producers to shift strategies from expanding production facilities in foreign countries to collusion with competitors to control markets. International cartels spread in the 1930s; their principal attraction was giving participating companies the benefit of being able to influence prices and output on a global basis without incurring the growing risks of investing overseas.[12] The Soviets' nationalization of foreign-owned enterprises following the Russian Revolution and later the formal collapse of the gold standard in the early 1930s were two additional factors dampening enthusiasm for new FDI ventures between 1917 and 1939.

In the years after World War I, MNCs in the secondary sector began to more closely resemble the traits later exhibited by their contemporary counterparts.

The biggest difference was that prior to the 1970s, overseas subsidiaries of big manufacturers were too few in number to be seen as a threat to the economies of either home or host countries. Nor were they portrayed as forerunners of an economic revolution. In retrospect, we know that in some ways that is exactly what they were. Although their numbers and profits were not noticeably rising, a handful of multinational manufacturing companies operating in a limited number of countries were, by the 1930s, regularly introducing new products at attractive prices, changing consumer tastes, and winning a growing market share in host countries.

In contrast to minimal growth in FDI activity by the manufacturing sector during the interwar period, resource-seeking investment increased in Latin America and Canada (mainly by American companies) and in Asia, the Middle East, and Africa (mainly by companies based in one of the European colonial powers). Companies engaged in extractive activities still accounted for a clear majority of the value of total world FDI on the eve of World War II. This situation was transitory, like so many others involving international business. The steep increases after the war in MNCs operating in the secondary and tertiary sectors would relegate the primary sector to a minority share of the world's stock of FDI in the third stage of MNC development.

MNCs at Full Maturity and Full Force

The start of the 1960s saw the full effects of a "perfect storm" of synergistic forces that triggered a period of unprecedented increases in the amount of FDI and in the numbers and new forms of MNCs. A new chapter in the history of FDI materialized by virtue of the relatively sharp increases in the value of foreign subsidiaries output, the sharp increases in the number of subsidiaries, and the surge in the value of their output as a percentage of domestic economic output, that is, world GDP. As seen in figure 3.1, the value (stock) of cumulative inward FDI hit take-off in the 1960s, and relatively high growth rates continued in the early years of the new century. The estimated 7,000 MNCs in 1970 more than quadrupled to about 30,000 in 1990, and then more than doubled to approximately 77,000 in 2005.[13] These trend lines move steadily and sharply upward only when viewed over a long time horizon. Annual increases in new FDI flows have demonstrated short-term volatility because of large, sudden shifts in corporate foreign investment commitments or reactions to global economic crises, such as the two great oil price shocks of the 1970s and early 1980s.

Unfortunately, data are not available to provide detailed, year-by-year insights on the first two decades of the newest era in the history of FDI and MNCs; there was little recognition of the utility in documenting their coming of age. The most

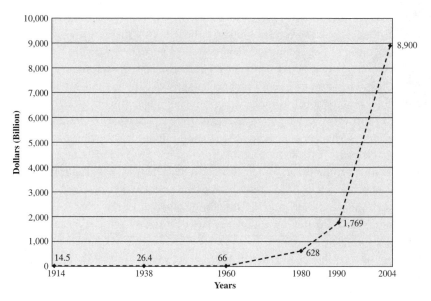

FIGURE 3.1. Estimated global inward stock of FDI. *Sources:* UNCTAD for 1980 and beyond, various academic estimates for pre-1980 data.

comprehensive compiler of global FDI data, the United Nations Conference on Trade and Development (UNCTAD), publishes a database going back only to 1982. Nevertheless, using this as a starting point still produces a dramatic quantitative portrait. The dollar value of global FDI outflows recorded by this UN agency increased about ninefold, from $27 billion in 1982 to $239 billion in 1990; outflows of $730 billion in 2004 were triple the 1990 level. UNCTAD data show sales of foreign subsidiaries surging from an estimated $2.8 trillion in 1982 to $18.7 trillion in 2004. Total recorded assets of these subsidiaries grew seventeenfold between these years from $2.1 to $36 trillion.[14]

The blossoming of the modern MNC post-1960 was brought about by multiple forces.[15] In addition to synthesizing the more important aspects of conventional wisdom, the analysis that follows contains some important causal factors that have received little or no attention.

The international economic climate in the post–World War II era was infinitely better and more nurturing than the two decades of economic turmoil following World War I. The tragic historical record of the 1930s provided a very clear guideline of what not to do, and the costly economic mistakes were not repeated. A core element of the ensuing Pax Americana was a remarkably successful set of policies designed to help rebuild and restore the shattered economies of allies and former enemies alike. The U.S. government provided generous foreign aid to Western Europe and Japan, kept the American market open to their exports, and maintained a high tolerance for the discriminatory import barriers erected by these countries. For their part, the Europeans and Japanese implemented growth-friendly domestic economic policies that complemented the American efforts. Despite the beginning of the Cold War, the industrialized countries of the U.S.-led bloc enjoyed an unprecedented long-term run of noninflationary growth during the 1950s and 1960s, a period later dubbed the golden age of the international economy. With increased prosperity came increases in corporate sales, profits, exports, and concerns about how to protect growing foreign markets.

The largest single source of new FDI flows in the 1960s and 1970s was American manufacturing companies opening factories in Western Europe.[16] They began arriving en masse in response to the creation in 1958 of the European Union (originally called the European Economic Community). The movement to regional economic integration in Western Europe presented foreign companies with a classic good news/bad news situation. On the one hand, the move to internal free trade held great promise for above-average economic growth rates in member countries. On the other hand, the largest regional U.S. export market was at risk: It was about to be surrounded by a common external tariff that would put exports from nonmembers at a potentially serious price disadvantage. One phase of a two-pronged U.S. response to this potential financial hit was to negotiate deep reciprocal tariff reductions beginning with the Kennedy Round of trade negotiations. The second was a private sector initiative: history's largest surge of FDI designed to leapfrog newly introduced trade barriers. A foreign-owned factory had the same status as a European firm: It could produce in any EU country and freely ship its output to all other member countries.

Many U.S. MNCs in important sectors like computers, electronics, motor vehicles, pharmaceuticals, and machinery established commercially successful—in terms of rising market shares and profits—subsidiaries in the countries of the so-called Common Market. The proliferation of American companies on the Continent was so great that it inspired a best-selling book still discussed today. *The American Challenge*, originally published in French by Jean-Jacques Servan-Schreiber in 1967, galvanized European and world thinking with the warning that if existing trends were not reversed, the third greatest world economic power after the United States and the Soviet Union would soon be, not Europe, but American-owned industry in Europe. Depending on the value judgments of the individual commentator, the book's message is variously depicted as a positive call for closer European cooperation and increased emulation of American business methods to prevent a serious loss of economic sovereignty, or an agitated warning of an American scheme to dominate the world economy.

Not all regions experienced major inflows of FDI. The three and one half decades after 1945 were wilderness years for direct investment in the less developed countries (LDCs). To say that most of them viewed MNCs with great suspicion is an understatement. Many looked back at bad experiences with arrogant foreign-owned extractive companies. As newly independent countries, they looked forward to exercising full sovereignty and making a clean break with their colonial past. Furthermore, widespread preference for extensive and intensive government involvement in the economy led most LDCs to turn their backs on free market economic principles and a foreign-owned corporate presence.

The growing belief that a market-based international economy would only preserve and widen the North–South income gap culminated in a collective LDC demand through much of the 1970s that a new international economic order be created. The system they wanted would have used multilateral intervention by governments to ensure a sustained increase in the flow of financial resources from rich to poor countries that was well above what the market mechanism was providing. Among the specific demands to this end was recognition of the right of LDCs to expropriate foreign companies (which is accepted in international law) *and* the unilateral right to decide if they should pay compensation to the company whose property had been seized and if so, to unilaterally define what was appropriate compensation (which is *not* accepted in international law). The effects of an overtly hostile atmosphere can be seen in the amount of recorded FDI flows into LDCs in 1970 being virtually zero.[17] The other major reason for the geographical shift of FDI flows from South to North was the surge in direct investment in the manufacturing sector. For the first time, the cumulative book value of that sector exceeded that of the relatively stagnant FDI in the primary sector. The gap has grown ever since.

The slow but steady increase in global FDI flows during the 1970s and 1980s partly reflected the resumption of overseas direct investments by Western European nations and Japan, a by-product of their full recovery from the physical devastation of World War II. The time when U.S. companies accounted for 80 percent or more of new FDI came to an end by 1970 as the result, like most MNC-related trends, of a changing international economic landscape. The amount of FDI flowing from the United States did not decline in absolute terms; instead, the number of companies headquartered in other countries opening overseas subsidiaries swelled. The first wave came mainly from Great Britain, France, the Netherlands, and West Germany, countries whose companies historically had been active foreign investors.

The next wave consisted of construction of overseas subsidiaries by dozens of Japanese manufacturers that within the span of the 1980s propelled their country from statistical insignificance to the number two position on the list of MNC home countries. Corporate Japan was forced to abandon its postwar reluctance to rely on foreign assembly line workers, deemed to be less dedicated and disciplined than their Japanese counterparts, because of a confluence of events imposed on Japan's corporate chieftains not of their own making. The most important events were a rising protectionist sentiment in many of Japan's trading partners (especially in the United States) kindled by resentment toward its chronic trade surpluses, rising domestic salaries that had reached the upper echelon of world wages, and a seemingly endless appreciation of the yen.

The 1990s witnessed record growth in the flows and stock (historical value) of FDI across a wide geographic front. The collapse of communism and increased reluctance of banks to lend to LDCs following the Latin American debt crisis of the 1980s further encouraged countries in Latin America and the Caribbean, Asia, and to a lesser extent, Africa to embrace market-oriented domestic economic policies and to shift from indifference to proactive policies to attract MNCs. Similar measures were adopted by Central European countries in transition from planned to market-based economies. These decisions were made easier by growing empirical proof that a significant statistical correlation existed between relatively extensive government ownership of the means of production and involvement in the economy and below-average increases in a country's economic growth and productivity. Developing and transition countries contributed to an upward blip in global FDI in two ways: first, by becoming more open and appealing to foreign companies, and second, by privatizing scores of state-owned industrial companies and public utilities, many of which were bought by foreign companies operating in similar sectors.

Later in the 1990s, the volume of FDI hit all time highs in large part due to a temporary upsurge in mergers and acquisitions (M&As) between companies headquartered in different countries. Most of this spate of international business marriages was attributable in dollar terms to a spike in European acquisitions of U.S. companies. FDI in the form of M&As soared from an annual average of about $10 billion in the 1987–94 period to an average of about $65 billion in the years 1998 through 2003.[18] As the century drew to a close, yet another new source of outgoing FDI emerged, this time from the growing number of elite companies based in the relatively advanced developing countries (a.k.a. emerging markets) that increasingly felt the need to move to the next level and establish a multinational presence. The final years of the century also were the time that FDI in China grew from negligible in the early 1980s to moderate in the early 1990s to some $50 billion annually; in 2003, it temporarily surpassed the United States as the world's number one recipient of FDI inflows in dollar terms.

A new series of space- and time-shrinking technological advances in transportation and communication has further simplified and reduced the costs of managing manufacturing and services subsidiaries scattered around the world.

Larger ships, cargo containers, cheap and fast travel by passenger and freight aircraft, fax and telex machines, satellite communications, powerful computers that rapidly talk to one another, and last but far from least, the Internet collectively brought about what is often called the death of distance. Easy collaboration among white-collar workers and between production lines thousands of miles apart became common. In sum, national borders and physical distance have been marginalized as considerations when corporations calculate the most cost-efficient places to produce their products or offer their services.

Inadequate emphasis has been placed on the economics of high-tech production in pressing companies to pursue global production as part of a strategy to maximize sales. Computer, semiconductor, pharmaceutical, automobile, and machinery companies typify the extraordinarily high fixed costs (research and development, factory machinery, and training highly skilled workers) that accrue to high-tech companies before the first sale of a new product is made. Failure to achieve economies of scale for these companies brings with it near certainty that competitors who do so—usually through FDI—will have lower unit costs and higher profits (see chapter 6).

The intricacy of high technology production largely explains the development of yet another new form of FDI. Vertical integration occurs where subsidiaries in various countries produce the many specialized components that are assembled into sophisticated goods like electronics and automobiles. In these cases, no one factory can efficiently make all the complex parts needed, the result being that rising transactions among specialized subsidiaries of the same company is a major cause of the dramatic increase in intrafirm trade since the early 1980s.

The information and communications technology revolution has further spurred FDI by unleashing a revolution of rising expectations that arguably has raised competition to a new level. Never before has the public expected producers of computers and consumer electronic devices (e.g., cell phones, personal digital assistants, digital cameras, and high-definition TVs) to constantly enhance the performance of these products while simultaneously lowering their prices or at least keeping them steady. To the extent that bigness equates with cost competitiveness, multicountry production and sales by fewer and larger MNCs will be the order of the day in emerging technologies. UNCTAD's 2002 investment report explained the new business pressures in these terms: "Heightened competition compels firms to explore new ways of increasing their efficiency, including by extending their international reach to new markets . . . and by shifting certain production activities to reduce costs. It also results in international production taking new forms."[19] In sum, defensive reactions to economic realities are part of the reason why virtually every major manufacturer of capital-intensive commercial goods is or will be an MNC.

A big boost to the growth of FDI in recent years has come from the services sector. More services companies are investing overseas because in recent years there have been steady increases in the number of these companies and in the kinds of services they provide, especially in informatics and telecommunications. In addition, a growing number of accounting, law, and advertising firms followed their clients overseas. Although high-tech is the fastest growing segment of FDI by services companies, traditional sectors—finance, wholesale trade and distribution facilities, transport, hotels, utilities, and construction—still account for most of the value of overseas investment in the tertiary sector.

The move to a more liberal international economic order is yet another cause of the proliferation of MNCs. A steady dismantling of controls on international capital movements reduced the obstacles to corporate expansion overseas. This factor is related to the argument that political factors also played a role in creating and sustaining the proliferation of FDI. Noted political economist Robert Gilpin has been the chief advocate of the view that MNCs were able to become powerful actors in international relations only because hegemonic powers, first Great Britain and then the United States, felt it was in their political and economic interest that their corporations flourished on foreign soil. "While economic factors are obviously important for the emergence and success of MNCs, they could not exist without a favorable international political environment created by a dominant power whose economic and security interests favor an open and liberal international economy."[20] In addition, leadership exerted by the United States beginning in the 1950s has been the single greatest force promoting successive rounds of multilateral trade negotiations that progressively lowered trade barriers. Freer trade was another postwar trend facilitating the conduct of multinational business operations.

The Importance of FDI/MNCs

When economic issues are considered to be very important, they cross an invisible line and attract the attention and concern of senior government leaders. In a word, they become politicized. The process of FDI and its agents of implementation, MNCs, began moving into the advanced stages of politicization in the 1970s. This was the time when it was becoming widely understood how extensively the multinationals were dominating critical systems of the international economy: production, technology, finance, trade, and energy and raw materials. The power and financial stakes involved in the spread of big international enterprises are so high that the executive and legislative branches of many countries find themselves directly involved in FDI-related issues. In addition to frequently seeking to attract incoming MNCs, politicians are caught in the middle of conflicting demands about policies and regulations from two powerful and committed political forces—one condemning and the other defending MNCs. Opinions sharply diverge on their costs relative to benefits, but unanimous consensus exists concerning their importance.

If perceptions define reality, then the FDI/MNCs phenomena have introduced extraordinary, perhaps revolutionary changes to the international order. The prevailing belief that these phenomena have had an extraordinary impact in the way goods and services are produced and income distributed is illustrated by the following arguments:

- MNCs are "huge organizations with considerable control over economic resources; they are not just business firms, but the most complex and most highly developed organizations in world capitalism, operating in the most important branches and the most highly concentrated sectors of the economy. . . . [We] should regard MNCs not only as *a* new feature of the world economy, but as *the* emerging new organizational form of that system in recent decades. (emphasis in the original)"[21]
- The increasing importance of MNCs has profoundly altered the structure and functioning of the global economy. These giant firms and their global strategies have become major determinants of trade flows and of the location of industries and other economic activities . . . These firms . . . have become major players not only in international economic but in international political affairs as well. . . . [They have created] 'a qualitatively different set of linkages' among advanced economies."[22]
- The preeminence of MNCs "in world output, trade, investment and technology transfer is unprecedented."[23]

In statistical terms, the importance of MNCs to the international economy begins with the fact that for more than twenty years, FDI has regularly grown faster than world GDP (output) and other macroeconomic measures of activity. The result is that international production is becoming an arithmetically more significant component of world economic activity.[24] Between 1982 and 2004, the value added (also referred to as gross product) of foreign subsidiaries worldwide increased sixfold, whereas world GDP only tripled (as explained in box 3.1, it is incorrect to compare GDP and *sales* by MNCs). The value added total in 1982 as a percentage of world GDP was a little bit above 5 percent; by 2004, it had doubled to slightly above 10 percent.[25]

The result of inward FDI becoming an increasingly larger percentage of virtually all middle-income and advanced national economies is to make it a more important variable of how well or poorly a country's workers and businesses fare.

BOX 3.1 How *Not* to Demonstrate the Importance of MNCs

One of the oldest statistical series used to dramatize the size and, by implication, power of MNCs is to compare their sales with the GDPs of countries. "Of the 100 largest economies in the world, 51 are corporations; only 49 are countries."*

The attention-grabbing technique of claiming corporations are as big as large countries is *not* used in this study because it is a seriously flawed puree of statistical apples and oranges. GDP is calculated on the basis of value added by the private sector. Otherwise, double counting would seriously exaggerate the value of a country's total output of goods and services. Double counting is inherent in corporate sales numbers. By way of example, suppose that Worldwide Widget Corp. assembles its product from two sets of components supplied by two contractors; each set costs Worldwide $50 million a year. After adding assembly costs, overhead, profit, and so on, the company's final sales come to $125 million. That means the net addition to the country's overall economic output is only the $25 million added to the value produced by the two contractors; only value added is counted as the widget company's contribution to national GDP, not $125 million. The $100 million in sales made by the contractors also includes double counting if they used subcontractors.

The proper way to measure the size of MNCs against country GDP is to try to calculate and then compare value added by corporations, not their final sales. Two researchers, De Grauwe and Camerman, estimated (based on a sample of high-ranking companies in the *Fortune* 500) that the average worldwide value added by manufacturing and services MNCs in 2000 was 25 and 35 percent, respectively.** By these criteria, only two of the fifty "biggest economies" in the world were MNCs; Wal-Mart ranked forty-fourth and ExxonMobil forty-eighth. However, thirty-five of the second fifty biggest economies were judged to be MNCs. This methodology puts the MNC-GDP comparison into the proper perspective. On the one hand, the data in this study show that very few MNCs rank with the biggest national economies; the U.S. economy in 2000 was 200 times bigger than the largest MNC ranked by value added, and Belgium was 5 times bigger. When measured in comparable terms, even the largest MNCs do not rival the larger economies in size. On the other hand, the data clearly indicate that the largest MNCs, again by value added, are as big as or bigger than the GDPs of most medium to small countries. Using slightly different data, an UNCTAD analysis (*World Investment Report, 2002*) produced similar results.

* Sarah Anderson and John Cavanagh, "Top 200—The Rise of Corporate Global Power," December 2000, online document available at http://www.ips-dc.org/reports/top200text.htm; accessed October 2004.
** Paul De Grauwe and Filip Camerman, "How Big Are the Big Multinational Companies?," January 2002, online document available at http://www.econ.kleuven.be/ew/academic/intecon/degrauwe/PDG-papers/Recently_publishedarticles/How%20big%20are%20big%20multination-al%20companies.pdf; accessed October 2004.

Annual recorded inflows and the stock value of FDI both increased more than tenfold from 1982 to year end 2004, a rate far in excess of the three and a half-fold growth of world output and the fivefold increase in world exports. If educated guesses about the value added of MNCs in their home countries are combined with the estimated value added of their overseas subsidiaries, companies having a multinational presence probably accounted for between 50 and 80 percent of the world's industrial output in the early 2000s.[26] As seen in figure 3.2, two key indicators of FDI increased their share of world GDP by a significant amount in the relatively brief span between 1990 and 2004. The amounts, value added, sales, and exports of the overseas operations of the world's MNCs in years to come will, more likely than not, continue to grow at a faster rate than world GDP and trade, a trend that would further enhance the perceived importance of FDI in the world economy. In view of this growth, critics of FDI/MNCs believe that they have become excessively important (see chapter 13).

"Why do we focus on FDI?" asked a report prepared for the World Trade Organization. "The answer is very simple—FDI has become an increasingly more important factor of economic growth."[27] The stimulus given to domestic economic growth by the relatively rapid increases in FDI comes from three

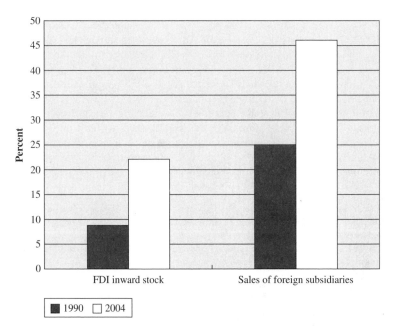

FIGURE 3.2. Growing importance of Foreign Direct Investment to world economic production, 2004 versus 1990: Key FDI indicators as a percent of global GDP (in U.S. dollars). *Source:* UNCTAD.

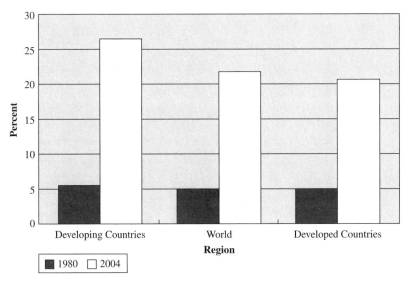

FIGURE 3.3. Inward FDI stocks as a percent of gross domestic product, by country category, 1980 and 2004. *Source:* UNCTAD.

directions. An indirect link between inward FDI and economic growth is the long-term increase in the share of country GDP attributable to inward FDI as measured by historic, or book, value (see figures 3.3 and 3.4). Figure 3.5 depicts the growth of inward FDI flows as a percentage of a second important economic benchmark, domestic investment (gross fixed capital formation).

The growing share of foreign-owned or -controlled subsidiaries in the industrial production of many countries is a third means of their providing stimulus to domestic economic activity. By way of example, in most Western European countries, the percentage of industrial production accounted for by FDI in 1998 was in the range of 25 to 30 percent; the figure rose to 70 percent in Ireland and Hungary.[28] Elected politicians also are aware of the contribution incoming FDI can make to the universal political priority of seeking full employment. MNCs probably provide work, usually at or above prevailing average salaries, for as many as 200 million people worldwide in host countries.[29] This figure presumably would generate an annual worldwide payroll in excess of $1.5 trillion.

The importance of FDI and MNCs also can be demonstrated in the corporate world. Production and sales in more than one country to increase sales and profits and reduce production costs on a per unit basis has become an essential part of the business strategy of most large and medium-sized companies. A statement by a well-known business consultancy speaks pointedly about international production being something between a priority business strategy and literally a

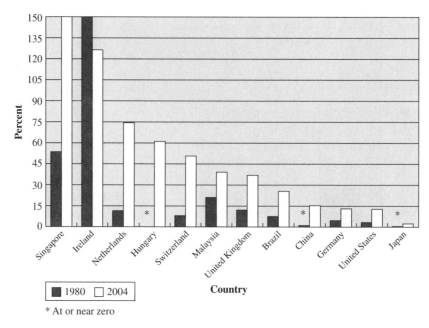

FIGURE 3.4. Inward FDI stocks as a percent of country GDP, 1980 and 2004.
Source: UNCTAD.

means of corporate survival: "Globalization is no longer merely an option but an imperative."[30] A scholarly study reached a similar conclusion: "For the major MNCs . . . overseas activity is no longer (if it ever was) marginal to corporate operations . . . but rather is increasingly central."[31]

The importance of FDI/MNCs to economic development (see chapter 8) is demonstrated by the statistic that FDI has been the largest single source of external finance, that is, access to hard currency, for the more advanced developing countries since the early 1990s.[32] (Foreign aid and workers' remittances are more important for poorer, relatively less developed countries.) Estimated net capital flows to LDCs in 2002 were $175 billion; of this amount, $147 billion, or 84 percent, was FDI, an amount far in excess of net official development assistance (foreign aid) flows of $21 billion.[33] Looking at aggregates in this case is misleading because of asymmetries. The poorest, least developed countries receive disproportionately little FDI inflow, whereas China, at about $50 billion annually, receives a disproportionately large share (it can be as much as one-third) of annual FDI flows going to all countries classified as developing.

The importance of FDI/MNCs to international trade can be quantified in several ways. MNCs and their subsidiaries account for about two-thirds of the world's trade in merchandise.[34] Large firms use FDI more than they use

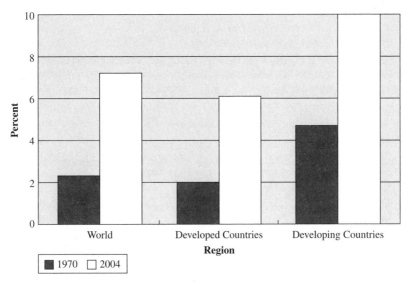

FIGURE 3.5. Inward FDI flows as percent of gross fixed capital formation, 1970 & 2004. *Source:* UNCTAD.

exports—by a factor of 1.5 (half again as much)—to sell to foreign markets.[35] At an estimated $17.6 trillion in 2003, sales of foreign subsidiaries worldwide were almost twice as large as world exports of goods and services and almost one-half the size of world GDP.[36] In many countries, the volume and product composition of exports has been radically altered thanks to overseas shipments by foreign-owned companies (see chapter 9).

Finally, FDI/MNCs are at the core of the very big and very controversial process of globalization (see chapters 5 and 13). Their importance in this case can be summarized with the observation that the process of FDI and the proliferation of MNCs are second to none as a leading cause of the globalization of economic activity and all the good and bad things—real and perceived—that flow from this trend.

Notes

1. Geoffrey Jones, *The Evolution of International Business* (New York: Routledge, 1996), p. 23.
2. John H. Dunning, *Multinational Enterprises and the Global Economy* (Wokingham, UK: Addison-Wesley, 1993), pp. 133, 132.
3. It can be argued that the Medici Bank, which established branches in several European countries in the fifteenth century, was the first MNC.
4. Dunning, *Multinational Enterprises* p. 99.

5. Ibid., p. 603.

6. Jones, *Evolution of International Business* pp. 29–32.

7. Dunning, *Multinational Enterprises* p. 118.

8. The Colt firearms company established a subsidiary in Britain in 1852 to make guns, technically making it the first American-owned overseas manufacturing subsidiary. However, it did not become profitable and within a few years was sold to local interests.

9. John Micklethwait and Adrian Wooldridge, *The Company* (New York: Modern Library, 2003), p. 169.

10. Source: http://www.kodak.com; accessed February 2005.

11. Source: http://www.unilever.com; accessed February 2005.

12. Jones, *Evolution of International Business* pp. 41, 44, and 124.

13. Data sources: Medard Gabel and Henry Bruner, *Global Inc.—An Atlas of the Multinational Corporation* (New York: New Press, 2003), pp. 2, 3; and UNCTAD, *World Investment Report 2006*, p. 10, available online at http://www.unctad.org; accessed October 2006.

14. Data source: UNCTAD, *World Investment Report 2005*, p. 14.

15. See, for example, Robert Gilpin, *U.S. Power and the Multinational Corporations* (New York: Basic Books, 1975), pp. 3–19; Theodore H. Cohn, *Global Political Economy*, 2nd ed. (New York: Longman, 2003), p. 326; Dunning, *Multinational Enterprises* chap. 5; and Jones, *Evolution of International Business* pp. 23–24.

16. Previously, U.S. investment in Canada was probably the largest single flow of FDI.

17. Data sources: Stephen Thomsen, "Investment Patterns in a Longer-Term Perspective," April 2000, available online at http://www.oecd.org; accessed February 2005; and Yu Ching Wong and Charles Adams, "Trends in Global and Regional Foreign Direct Investment," August 2002, available online at http://www.imf.org; accessed February 2005. FDI going into LDCs increased to an annual average of $20 billion during the 1980s.

18. UNCTAD, *World Investment Report 2004*, p. 336.

19. UNCTAD, *World Investment Report 2002*, p. 4.

20. Robert Gilpin, *Global Political Economy* (Princeton, NJ: Princeton University Press, 2001), p. 288.

21. Volker Bornschier, "Multinational Corporations in World System Perspective," in *Imperialism and After—Continuities and Discontinuities* (London: Allen and Unwin, 1986), pp. 243, 242 emphasis in original.

22. Robert Gilpin, *Global Political Economy—Understanding the International Economic Order* (Princeton, NJ: Princeton University Press, 2001), p. 290.

23. David Held, Anthony McGrew, David Goldblatt, and Jonathan Perraton, *Global Transformations* (Stanford, CA: Stanford University Press, 1999), p. 282.

24. UNCTAD, *World Investment Report 1997*, p. xvi.

25. Data calculated from table 1.3, UNCTAD, *World Investment Report 2005*, p. 14.

26. See, for example, Raymond Vernon, Louis Wells Jr., and Subramanian Rangan, *The Manager in the World Economy*, 7th ed. (Upper Saddle River, NJ: Prentice Hall, 1996), p. 28; and "The World's View of Multinationals," *The Economist*, January 29, 2000, p. 21.

27. Zdenek Drabek and Warren Payne, "The Impact of Transparency on Foreign Direct Investment," World Trade Organization Staff Working Paper ERAD-99-02, November 2001, available online at http://www.wto.org; accessed November 2004.

28. OECD, *Measuring Globalisation*, vol. 1, 2001, p. 13.

29. This guesstimate was derived by multiplying the 700,000 foreign subsidiaries estimated to exist in 2004 by a rough guess of an average of 300 workers per subsidiary.

30. Boston Consulting Group, "Capturing Global Advantage," April 2004, available online at http://www.bcg.com; accessed December 2004.

31. Held et al., *Global Transformations* p. 271.

32. Linda Goldberg, "Financial-Sector Foreign Direct Investment and Host Countries: New and Old Lessons," Federal Reserve Bank of New York Staff Report no. 183, April 2004, available online at http://www.newyorkfed.org/research/global_economy; accessed October 2004.

33. World Bank, *Global Development Finance 2004* p. 8, available online at http://www.worldbank.org; accessed January 2005.

34. UNCTAD, *World Investment Report 2002*, p. 153.

35. UNCTAD, *World Investment Report 1998*, p. 5.

36. UNCTAD, *World Investment Report 2004*, p. 9.

4

HETEROGENEITY

*The Many Kinds of Foreign Direct Investment
and Multinational Corporations
and Their Disparate Effects*

The heterogeneity and diversity of foreign direct investment (FDI)
and multinational corporations (MNCs) are not compatible with
the generalizations that dominate the conventional wisdom about them. This
chapter begins with a defense of this transcendent theme by arguing that FDI
and MNCs can be divided into so many distinct formats that they cannot
conform either to a single model of behavior or to a uniform checklist of effects.
Emphasis is placed on the importance of their multifaceted and variable nature.
The second and third sections of the chapter consist of a straightforward exercise
in disaggregation. The common tendency of those speaking about FDI and
MNCs to give them a universal persona, good or bad, has blurred the real nature
of these phenomena behind a fog of generalization.

Viewed as a whole, the chapter also seeks to defend a second transcendent
theme: the balance between costs and benefits of FDI and MNCs should primarily
be calculated on a disaggregated basis to adjust for the different forms that they
take. The relatively lengthy discussion that follows of the many different kinds of
international business phenomena lays out their distinctive behavior patterns and
mixed record of effects on countries' economies, people, companies, and the environment. A methodology based on making an all-inclusive pronouncement on
what are portrayed as homogenous entities is inadequate and misleading.

The Implications of Diversity

The terms *FDI* and *MNC* for the most part appear in the public domain at
relatively high levels of generalization. It is common for people to form a pro or con

view of them on the basis of a generalized judgment, declaring that "they are what they are." This is oversimplified reasoning sustained in large part by the continuing failure of government officials, business executives, nongovernmental organizations, scholars, and journalists to explicitly recognize the seemingly obvious points that these phenomena are not all alike and that important implications flow from this reality. Deep insights into the nature and impact of FDI and MNCs will not be forthcoming if they are treated as generic terms for a kind of investment strategy and a kind of business entity, respectively. Neither FDI nor MNCs as entities are monolithic. As a group, foreign subsidiaries share only two major traits. Physically, they all transact business in at least one country outside the one in which they are headquartered. Strategically, they all have been established to strengthen the parent company in some way and to avoid being a financial failure.

Making the assumption that all forms of FDI and all kinds of MNCs are homogenous is to take a wrong turn in the journey to an accurate understanding of their diverse nature and effects. Their intrinsic heterogeneity means that, if evaluated separately, the 77,000 multinational companies that operate 770,000 individual foreign subsidiaries and affiliates mentioned in the previous chapter would be scattered along two vast continuums. One would be for home countries and the second for host countries. Each would measure a range of effects from very positive to very negative, with a large gray area in between. If we can get more and better data than currently exist, an elaborate matrix could be constructed in which the vertical axis would portray the distinctive kinds of FDI and MNCs described in the next two sections. The horizontal axis would portray the quality of various behavioral patterns of inward direct investment; the main criteria for judging quality are the ripple effects on the host country's economy, financing arrangements, level of job skills, propensity to export and import, likelihood of technology transfer, and environmental impact. Because every investment has some distinguishing features, when the many possible kinds of investments and multiple levels of quality are factored in, an individual overseas subsidiary could have any of dozens of profiles.

Unfortunately, the magnitude of the depth and breadth of heterogeneity is usually underemphasized or ignored outright by opinion makers of all political persuasions. Sometimes failure to give appropriate weight to this factor reflects a speaker or author's narrow frame of reference, for example, implications of multinationals for unions and the impact on less developed countries (LDCs). In other cases, people with their minds firmly made up about MNCs being good or bad things may not wish to be bothered with nuance and details. Overgeneralization may also reflect unfamiliarity with the ever expanding kinds of services being offered on a transnational basis. Accountants, brewers of beer, restaurant chains, discount retailers, and employment agencies were not part of the early wave of MNCs that set the terms of the debate that still exists. The large number of industrial sectors engaged in transnational operations is suggested by the twenty-two specific types of manufacturing industries and twenty-six specific kinds of services industries listed in the United Nations Conference on Trade and Development (UNCTAD) industry guide to its FDI data.[1]

The often oversimplified processing of information has been a contributing factor to a debate waged since the 1970s that is at once spirited, fascinating, and frustrating. Admittedly, the dividing line is blurred between excessive generalizations and the proper level of specificity when analyzing FDI and MNCs. The problem remains, however, that on balance, past efforts to bridge the perceptions gap have generated far more heat than light. A single, one-size-fits-all pronouncement on the net positives or net negatives of all MNCs in every country opens itself to suspicion that it is more the outcome of selective data collection in support of a preexisting value judgment than a painstaking, open-minded exercise in inductive reasoning. In any situation, different inputs can be expected to produce different outputs. The bottom line is that the *quality*, that is, the net economic benefits to the host country, of a foreign-owned subsidiary will vary on a case-by-case basis (this argument is developed in detail in chapter 14). The behavior and effects of any given foreign investment project may warrant effusive praise, strong condemnation, or the label of a wash between good and bad. This is the result of the inevitability of heterogeneity and the fallacy of generalization. The proper answer to the question of whether an individual foreign subsidiary is of high quality or low quality is: "it depends." Too many pronouncements on the advantages and disadvantages of FDI and MNCs have been made after looking at them as undifferentiated wholes.

The logic of a gray-area conclusion about net desirability is consistent with the underlying fact that corporations per se are idiosyncratic. Corporate culture really does vary from company to company; it is not a theory only found in readings assigned by business school professors. Large companies do not adhere to a single standard operating procedure beyond the most basic legal and regulatory guidelines and the financial imperative of avoiding perpetual losses. Every company has created a unique mosaic of priorities, procedures, traditions, and standards that mirrors its weaknesses, strengths, successes, failures, operating philosophies of past and present senior managers, product mix, and so on. Corporate culture will reflect the extent to which it has grown from within or been built by mergers and acquisitions (M&As). A study, conducted by the MIT Industrial Performance Center, of how MNCs compete added a number of additional variables that individualize corporations' strategic and tactical approaches to business: the institutions and values in a company's country of origin; the aggregate learning experience derived from customers, suppliers, and rivals; and the know-how and skills gained from solving problems of survival, renewal, and growth. The report added that the history of a company shapes the way the owners and managers structure their organization, and it influences corporate strategies and the way they are implemented. In some cases, a corporation's operational DNA reflects "accidents of history."[2]

The existence of so many variables allows for a very large number of variations as to how a company goes about establishing and then reviewing its degree of decentralization, guidelines on personnel evaluation and promotion, lines of communication between different layers of hierarchy, importance attached to current profits versus long-term growth and community service, marketing strategies, optimal extent of product diversification, and so on. Tolerance for risk and the premium placed on continuous product development vary from company to company. Dissimilar corporate cultures also account for variations in two key international areas of decision making: (1) where and how much to invest overseas, and (2) the degree of control exerted over overseas subsidiaries by headquarters-based executives.

Additional data and improved methodology would permit a more complete and accurate understanding and evaluation of FDI and MNCs, a desirable goal given their status as increasingly powerful global forces. A big step in this direction is to distinguish between the many kinds of overseas business production and examine their (usually) distinctive mix of beneficial, disruptive, and neutral qualities. The method of disaggregation employed in the next two sections cannot demonstrate absolutes because the subject matter cannot be reduced to absolute, irrefutable facts and figures. The taxonomy that follows represents an imperfect effort to differentiate between the two components of international business production, FDI and MNCs. Airtight compartments cannot always be constructed within and between these two symbiotic, often overlapping phenomena. Some readers may perceive occasional arbitrary or incorrect classifications in the sections that follow. Occasional disagreements and author error need not damage the creditability of the larger, more important ideas about heterogeneity to be developed here.

Identifying and Classifying Different Forms of FDI

FDI is defined as a financial phenomenon that takes place whenever a company acquires 10 percent or more of the voting stock in a commercial entity incorporated in a foreign country. A key assumption is that this magnitude of involvement will allow the investor to actively participate in management decisions on a long-term basis. Beyond this solitary universal requirement, FDI is anything but a uniform process having uniform results. Diversity can literally be cross-referenced. The various criteria by which different kinds of FDI can be identified and classified are presented roughly in the order of most general to most specific.

The former need to be further disaggregated to identify important second-stage variables, which influence and occasionally determine the idiosyncratic behavior and effects of individual foreign subsidiaries.

By Objectives of/Motivations for Establishing a Foreign Subsidiary

All of the different kinds of FDI share a common genesis: the decision by corporate executives that prospective financial rewards outweigh the projected costs of launching an overseas subsidiary. The means to achieve this common end differ according to the nature of each individual company. Each of the four subcategories of business objectives that follow tends to demonstrate distinctive characteristics and effects. Each has a distinctive set of likely assets and liabilities. Will a new subsidiary engage in strip-mining or operate a sophisticated research and development (R&D) facility with highly paid, skilled workers? A perceptive host government should be able to anticipate with reasonable accuracy many of the trade-offs associated with an incoming FDI project simply by looking at what path it will take to produce financial rewards for the parent company.

Resource-Seeking FDI   The first sustained, wide-scale FDI materialized in the second half of the nineteenth century. The dominant players were natural resource-seeking enterprises that extracted minerals and metals, such as oil, gold, and copper, or harvested tropical commodities, such as bananas and rubber. Resource-seeking FDI accounted for a majority of worldwide FDI until after World War II. Decisions on country locations of these kinds of investments were and still are determined in the first instance by geology and climate: the physical questions of where minerals and metals are located and where are the most favorable climactic conditions for crop growth. Secondary factors in MNC decisions on where to extract natural resources include the quality of the transportation infrastructure, accessibility of the raw materials, and the extent to which political officials accommodate foreign companies by providing good governance, favorable tax and regulatory policies, and the rule of law.

Relative to manufacturing and services, the reputation of MNCs in the primary sector is poor, to say the least. Their alleged callous disregard for the peoples of host countries has attracted a disproportionately large share of the total criticism and negativism leveled against FDI as a whole. Part of the explanation for this is the geographic fact that the vast majority of extractive FDI has taken place in LDCs, virtually all of which were colonies at some point in their history (many until the 1950s and 1960s). The resulting North-to-South investment axis partly explains why companies in the primary sector often have been labeled as neoimperialists. In addition, they have a long record of being accused (often for good cause) of such misdeeds as preferring collusion to genuine competition, trying to bypass or undermine host countries' governments when they got in the way, conspiring to minimize royalty payments to governments for raw materials extracted and sold abroad, and polluting the environment (see chapter 13).

Another distinguishing characteristic of resource-seeking FDI is the lack of intention to sell its output in the host country's market. The underlying business objective is to export the extracted raw materials to feed the North or to fuel its industrial machine. A third commonality within this sector has been the absence of any measurable damage to the economies of the countries in which resource-seeking MNCs are headquartered. The nature of the latter's output precludes the losses of either jobs (hence, the absence of significant barriers to the import of raw materials in the major consuming countries) or exports in these home countries. The debates about the net trade-off between costs and benefits for primary sector investment are directed solely to its impact on host countries in the South, not on rich home countries in the North. Among the few certain answers about that trade-off is that it is has differed over time and on a product-by-product and country-by-country basis. More assertive governments, intensified threats of expropriation, and more media attention given to criticisms of corporate behavior explain the trend toward LDCs gradually but steadily increasing their overall share of the financial benefits from resource-seeking investments.

The gross benefits to host countries can be assessed with relative precision; they equate to the foreign exchange income obtained from oil companies, mining companies, and the like. In many cases, these earnings have been considerable both in absolute terms and relative to GDP size. Efforts to calculate net benefits are clouded by variables on the other side of the equation that cannot properly be answered with generalizations. To what extent have these revenues been spent to directly benefit the public well-being? Has a "fair" price been received for a nonrenewable resource? Has there been a fair mark-up between the price of a raw material, such as coffee beans, and the final retail price in Northern markets? Has environmental damage resulted from mining, drilling, or farming operations, and if so will the MNCs responsible fully pay for cleanups?

Market-Seeking FDI Establishing an overseas subsidiary to protect or expand a foreign market is an example of market-seeking FDI. The typical sequence of events is that this kind of investment is the second phase of marketing strategy that follows an initial effort based on exports. The rapid post–World War II growth of direct investment inside the industrialized countries can largely be linked to a geometric increase in corporate perceptions that export-based marketing strategies had peaked or were at risk because of changing conditions in the foreign market. In sum, the dependence by major corporations on exporting as the primary means of selling to foreign customers has diminished, presumably on a permanent basis.

The core assumption behind market-seeking FDI is that for both defensive and proactive reasons, the best way to sell to existing and potential customers in a foreign country or region is by having production facilities physically close to them rather than by exporting from thousands of miles away. Defensive considerations include rising competition from locally owned producers, the arrival of subsidiaries from third-country MNCs, erection of new import barriers, and projections of a steady appreciation in the exchange rate of the home country's currency. Proactive reasons begin with the potential for reductions in transportation time and costs, an especially attractive option for large, bulky, or heavy products. In addition, "being there" improves the likelihood that the investing company will be better attuned to sensing how and when to modify a product to accommodate changing tastes of local consumers and to anticipating future changes. Being there also aids a company's efforts to portray itself as a home-grown operation that is providing jobs and economic stimulus to the local economy.

The geographic focus of market-oriented FDI is large, affluent, and growing markets. The inherent logic of adding production facilities in lucrative markets explains why FDI since the 1960s has mainly flowed into the relatively few rich industrialized countries (see chapter 7). Market-seeking FDI is exhibit number one in contradicting the antiglobalization camp's contention that venal multinationals naturally gravitate to countries with the cheapest, most exploitable labor and the least enforced environmental protection regulations. The average consumer goods–producing MNC wants customers. The average capital goods–producing MNC needs skilled labor. The best place to find both is in the industrialized countries. Nevertheless, it is still necessary to heed an often repeated theme of this book that evolutionary change in FDI is a constant, and it cannot be ignored. Industrialized countries are in the process of losing their virtual monopoly on incoming market-seeking FDI. China is the prime example of an emerging market with sufficient current and future consumer buying power to convince hundreds of MNCs to expand beyond an export strategy for that country and move up to the next phase.

Market-seeking FDI has the potential to provide more benefits to host countries than any other form of incoming direct investment. Market-seeking MNCs typically bring with them much more than the capital needed to build and equip a factory. They also will bring, in various degrees depending on circumstances, advanced production technology, marketing know-how, and most likely, the environmental protection technologies used in their plants elsewhere. Furthermore, a market-seeking subsidiary tends to do well in creating relatively high-skilled jobs and generating additional tax revenue. It tends to be above average in forging links with the local economy to fulfill needs for components and business services. Market-seeking MNCs might force competing local companies to produce more efficiently, improve product quality, and lower prices. Alternatively, incoming foreign manufacturers might bankrupt local competitors, increase unemployment, and allow foreign-owned companies to acquire a near or full monopoly on certain goods and services. Which will it be? It depends on individual circumstances.

The effects of market-seeking FDI on the *home* country further exemplify the appropriateness of the "it depends" response. Negative effects would be inconsequential *if* one accepts as true the long and often repeated corporate assertions that this strategy is overwhelmingly defensive in nature. Outsiders seldom, if ever, have presented a convincing case that they knew better than experienced corporate officials that for any of various reasons (see chapter 6), their ability to serve a market by exporting had peaked and faced a clear and present danger of steady decline. If exporting is destined to lose its viability as the primary overseas marketing strategy for a particular company, the home country in such a case presumably would at least benefit from remittances of profits from newly established overseas subsidiaries. Conversely, if the danger of declining overseas market share was exaggerated, the home country might well have unnecessarily lost jobs and export revenues in that instance. Establishment of a new foreign subsidiary may result in *increased* net exports from the home country in the form of components, assembly line machinery, and models of the product that won't be produced in the new subsidiary. However, this rosy scenario will materialize only in some cases.

Efficiency-Seeking FDI   A third common motivation to invest overseas revolves around the quest to reduce costs of production. Efficiency-seeking FDI is quite distinct from the two previously discussed business motivations and therefore produces distinctive behavioral patterns and economic effects. The first of two principal rationales for this kind of FDI involves establishing a subsidiary in a low-wage country. Relatively low-paid workers tend to be low-skilled workers. However, if they possess a work ethic, they can be and are cost-effective when producing low-tech, labor-intensive goods (apparel and footwear, for example) or assembling goods having a mature, that is, standardized and unchanging technology (radios and analog television sets, for example). The second major rationale for efficiency-seeking FDI is to achieve economies of scale. As will be discussed in chapter 6, pressure to minimize per unit costs of capital-intensive goods having very high upfront development and manufacturing costs explains the urgency that high-tech MNCs attach to successfully selling these goods in every national market of any significant size.[3]

Efficiency-seeking direct investments are a close proxy for a debate on the virtues of free markets. They have the potential to provide significant benefits by increasing the efficiency of global resource allocation. Yet this kind of FDI and free markets also can inflict hardship on specific groups in what some regard as the overly aggressive drive to provide financial rewards for corporate executives and the relatively few owners of capital. The number one grievance against FDI/ MNCs by unions in industrialized countries has been the allegedly growing tendency of employers to reduce labor costs by shutting down production in the home country and moving it to LDCs—or threatening to do so. Job shifts to foreign subsidiaries in lower wage countries have been most lambasted in the United States, but they also have occurred in Japan (mostly to other Asian countries) and Germany (mostly to Central Europe). No data exist to definitively test the standard corporate riposte that their ability to remain in business would have been put at risk if they continued relying on relatively high-priced labor in a globalized world of efficiency-seeking competitors. Nor are there conclusive data to validate labor's claims that significant increases in aggregate unemployment can be linked directly to outward FDI.

MNCs seeking to cut production costs are attracted by differences in factor endowments, most notably an ample labor supply. In such cases, incoming FDI will tend *not* to raise the overall skill or income levels of the labor force. The benefits will come in providing additional jobs, at or above prevailing wage levels, to countries likely to have relatively high rates of unemployment and underemployment. Cheaper labor, however, is not always the main objective. If a subsidiary is turning out state-of-the-art high-tech goods, relatively high-wage jobs will be created in host countries.

Whether the objective is highly skilled labor, very cheap labor, or strategic geographic location, this form of FDI has an above-average likelihood of generating increased foreign exchange earnings for host countries. An efficiency-seeking subsidiary is not ordinarily established to serve a single national market. Many are specifically designed to be export platforms. The statistic that U.S.-owned subsidiaries in Ireland export more than 95 percent of their output in that country epitomizes the export-platform/efficiency-seeking model of overseas investment.[4] One study of the overall impact of FDI on LDCs found that in addition to increased foreign exchange, efficiency-seeking FDI "is more likely to bring in technology and know-how which is compatible to the host countries' level of development, and enables local suppliers and competitors to benefit from spillovers through adaptation and imitation. . . . As a result, one would expect a relatively strong growth impact of . . . efficiency-seeking FDI."[5]

Strategic Asset-Seeking FDI A relatively specialized and infrequent motivation for engaging in FDI is to acquire some or all of the assets of a foreign company to enhance the purchasing corporation's competitiveness, either through increased synergy or less competition. The business objective in this case is not to reduce costs or protect specific markets. Instead, it is to acquire assets that are perceived to be capable of strengthening the overall competitive position of the acquiring company or weakening that of competitors.[6] Acquisition of strategic assets may allow a company to swallow a competitor, broaden its product line, upgrade the technology embedded in its products, or prevent a third company from acquiring the purchased assets. This form of direct investment has no inherent advantages or disadvantages (except possibly to reduce competition) of significance for either the host or home countries as a whole. If this kind of transaction successfully achieves its commercial goals, the main beneficiaries most likely will be the shareholders of the acquiring company.

By the Role in the Parent Company's Global Production Strategy

A second kind of FDI can be defined in terms of which of two broad production strategies a foreign subsidiary is designed to contribute. In the manufacturing sector, the most common form of FDI is characterized as *horizontal*. This term refers to a horizontal transfer of a portion of home country production to overseas subsidiaries for the purpose of strengthening the firm's global competitive position. The potential benefits to the host country's economy would be similar in most cases to those previously attributed to market-seeking FDI.

An initial reduction in exports of the finished products whose manufacture has been shifted out of the home country is the norm. But in the medium to long term, the home country's total exports would not automatically decline by the amount of production that had moved overseas. Given the sharp increases in intracorporate trade experienced by the two biggest MNC home countries, the United States and Japan, the chances are good that the initial export loss will be partly or totally offset by increases in exports of other products from the home country. As already noted, overseas subsidiaries can trigger increased shipments of components of the product now being made overseas, capital equipment and replacement parts to be used on the new subsidiary's assembly line, and complementary models manufactured only in the headquarters country that will be marketed by the overseas subsidiary. In a similar vein, some domestic jobs will be eliminated when production lines are shifted overseas, yet the aggregate number of unemployed workers need not necessarily rise. The affected workers might simply be assigned to making other goods produced by the same company. Alternatively, they might find comparable or even better jobs elsewhere, a relatively common occurrence in a growing economy. The closing of a given production line (for any reason) may or may not result in a net loss of jobs on a nationwide basis; total employment depends mainly on the business cycle.

Vertical FDI has been the faster growing subcategory of production strategy since the 1980s. This is due to the increasing technical complexity of a wide range of manufactured goods, most notably automobiles and information technology hardware. Advances in communications, data transmission, and transportation have allowed the business strategy known as *global production networks* and *vertical integration* to thrive and operate at high rates of efficiency. Technological progress is responsible for the growth of vertical FDI beyond its original phase in which oil and other resource companies extracted raw materials and exported them to company-owned facilities for processing.

The most common version of vertical FDI is dividing the manufacturing process into segments in which various parts of a finished product are made by two or more subsidiaries in two or more countries anywhere in the world. For example, as components become more numerous and more complicated to design and manufacture, automakers increasingly designate individual subsidiaries to specialize in making engines, transmissions, and so on. Geographic specialization exploits cost advantages in different countries for different products. In economic jargon, companies are minimizing production costs by taking advantage of international factor-price differentials, a core concept of the law of comparative advantage. Capital-intensive goods and high-skilled services mainly will be produced in capital and skilled labor-rich developed countries. Labor-intensive, low-tech products and simple assembly work will be assigned to subsidiaries in poorer countries with relatively low labor costs. The spread of global production networks is praised in some quarters as elevating the efficient use of the world's resources to a new level.

Vertical FDI is inherently trade-creating. Intracorporate trade blossoms as intermediate goods are exported from various countries either to the home country or to a third country for final assembly. As parts, components, and raw materials move back and forth in a highly complex global production network, the "traditional connection between production and market is broken."[7]

Export processing zones (EPZs; also referred to as free trade zones) are a common player in vertical integration. EPZs have been established almost exclusively by LDCs. MNCs operating subsidiaries in EPZs usually do so for the purpose of exporting labor-intensive goods to other subsidiaries of the parent company. Incentives to build a subsidiary in an export zone, which is usually physically separated from the rest of the country, include exemptions from import barriers, most business regulations, and some or all corporate income taxes.

Method of Establishing a Foreign Subsidiary

Another kind of FDI can be identified on the basis of how a foreign subsidiary or affiliate has been established. Once again, disaggregation is appropriate to designate the options available to MNCs. And once again, each of three distinguishable options has its own characteristics and brings its own cost-benefit ratio to the table. The vast majority of new FDI has originated either as *greenfield* investments or through M&As. The former involves incorporating and building a brand new local company, hypothetically involving construction of new facility on an open, grassy field. The latter involves acquisition by a foreign-based company of management control over an existing company in the host country; it does this through the purchase of voting stock in the local corporation. Alternatively, the transaction could involve a mutual transfer of stock to consummate a formal merger of equals located in two countries. M&As emerged only in the 1990s as a consistently significant percentage of new FDI, presumably because a growing number of companies were nearing the limits of further growth from within. The larger M&A deals thus far have mostly been between big European and American companies. (There is no way to know whether the relatively recent upsurge in M&As relative to greenfield investment is a temporary or long-term change in corporate strategy.)

The third means of establishing a foreign subsidiary is via *privatization*. The purchase of a government-owned industry, utility, transportation system, and so on is a by-product of the shift in the 1990s toward free market policies by developing countries in Asia, Latin America, and Africa, as well as in formerly communist countries in transition from command to private enterprise-based economic systems. In economic terms, privatization differs from M&As in that the seller is the government of what becomes the host country and the buyer acquires an entity for whom profits were not a priority goal (or necessity). Unless renationalized, an entity can only be privatized once. Any further transfers of ownership would be between two private companies and fall into the commercial M&A category.

The most important difference in economic impact between incoming FDI taking the form of greenfield plants and incoming FDI via M&As or privatization can be summed up in one word: *incrementalism*. A takeover of an existing business entity does not initially create the incremental economic activity, jobs, and tax revenue in host countries associated with greenfield investments. Mergers, takeovers, and privatization at the outset involve only a change in ownership. Though the foreign company may later decide to expand output in its newly acquired foreign subsidiary, it might first go on a cost-cutting offensive that reduces the local payroll by a considerable margin. This is the likely scenario when a foreign company acquires a poorly managed, money-losing company. The new property in such a case tends to be viewed as a candidate for a corporate "makeover" incorporating better management and more efficient production processes.

Although free-market economists praise any and all improvements in efficiency, political leaders prefer the benefits of incrementalism provided by greenfield investments—especially those that do not compete with local companies. Very few voters express happiness if a foreign firm is able to maintain the output of what previously had been a locally owned company while using only a fraction of the old workforce. Nationalists in all countries will be alarmed at the perceived loss of control associated with any extensive takeovers of local businesses by foreign interests. This was exactly the feeling voiced by some Americans in the 1980s as Japanese companies went on what was widely viewed as a buying spree in the United States (see chapter 7).

By Method of Financing a New Subsidiary

Absent an exchange of common stock, new FDI cannot occur without a capital outlay by a foreign-based company in a host country. The foreign MNC most likely will transfer hard currency, usually dollars, from its home country. For greenfield investments, these funds will be converted into the local currency to pay for the initial purchase of land, construction of buildings, equipment, and the hiring and training of workers. For most M&As, the capital outlay consists of purchasing equity from the existing owners of the targeted local company. Inflows of dollars or euros converted into local currencies have a favorable balance of payments impact of special importance to LDCs: They provide additional resources to pay for imports of goods and services needed to spur economic development and raise living standards. For many countries, FDI-related capital inflows have become a relatively stable and important source of financing trade deficits and therefore a valuable force for economic growth.

FDI can take place without international capital flows. New subsidiaries can be built and acquisitions of existing companies can be made by borrowing in the local capital markets. A foreign MNC may calculate that it can save money by using its superior credit rating to raise needed capital by borrowing from banks or selling bonds in the host country. Locally financed FDI has two drawbacks for the host country's economy. First, by definition, the host suffers the opportunity cost of forgone incoming foreign exchange from the foreign MNC's headquarters country. Second, there may be a *crowding-out* effect as domestic banks prefer to engage in relatively risk-free lending to blue-chip foreign companies rather than making loans to local businesses with lower quality credit ratings. The potential for crowding out is greatest in countries where the volume of borrowing by foreign investors is highest relative to the domestic availability of lendable funds.

By Extent of Foreign Ownership

When a foreign company owns at least 10 percent equity in a foreign-based company, it is considered to be FDI. However, it is not axiomatic that a relatively small percentage of ownership translates into an active voice in management decisions. The foreign company in such cases may be more interested in the financial rewards associated with investment in a growth company than having an active voice in the day-to-day operation of the company. A "hands-off" FDI would normally have no direct impact on the economies of either the host or home country. At the other extreme is the highly visible, attention-grabbing kind of FDI that takes place when large corporations establish major overseas subsidiaries that in almost all cases are 100 percent owned. Big, globe-spanning companies like ExxonMobil, Royal Dutch Shell, IBM, General Motors, Ford, Toyota, General Electric, Nestlé, and Siemens can have a significant impact on the economies of countries that host their investments. Their above-average size and ability to attract attention means that they are important but not necessarily the benchmark for assessing the behavior and impact of MNCs in general.

A discussion of how the variable of foreign ownership creates differences in FDI characteristics and effects would not be complete without an examination of international partnerships. They seek to facilitate the achievement of business objectives that would be financially burdensome, excessively time-consuming, or possibly unattainable if the two (and occasionally more) partnering companies acted independently. Partnership is attractive when a company has rejected acquiring or merging with another firm, perhaps due to the latter's being involved in business lines that are alien or unattractive to the potential suitor.[8]

International joint ventures and strategic alliances are the two most common and important forms of partnership between companies headquartered in different countries.[9] Imbued with at least two separate corporate cultures, jointly owned business entities tend to require more compromise and consultations than a subsidiary of a company with a single set of priorities, executives, and shareholders. Joint ventures and strategic alliances have not demonstrated extraordinary or distinctive effects on national economies. They tend to be microeconomic phenomena best analyzed mainly at the company level.

The most important qualitative difference between these two arrangements is that a joint venture requires creation of a newly incorporated, jointly owned business entity in an agreed-on country (or countries). A strategic alliance consists only of formally specified areas of collaboration between cooperating companies who remain legally independent of one another. Otherwise, both have similar objectives and potential consequences. International partnerships between two already powerful, well-managed companies can represent a healthy step forward in achieving greater efficiency and better products. Alternatively, a mutual strengthening of two ostensible rivals and an increase in their market shares can reduce competition, deliberately or unintentionally, by squeezing existing competitors and discouraging new entrants.

Collaboration between companies in different countries is nothing novel. "What is new is their current scale, their proliferation and the fact that they have become *central* to the global strategies of many firms rather than peripheral to them. Most strikingly, the great majority of strategic alliances have been *between competitors.*"[10] According to an OECD study, companies that "have long shunned joint ventures or close collaboration with other firms in their core business areas are increasingly entering into such co-operative arrangements."[11] By one measure, international strategic alliances, including joint ventures, increased more than fivefold to 4,440 between 1989 and 1999. The study also found evidence that recent international partnerships had become "far larger in scale and value terms than earlier partnerships." It concluded that the two-to-one ratio between international and domestic strategic alliances illustrates that globalization "is a primary motivation for alliances."[12]

Arguably, the search for synergy is the most common rationale for strategic alliances and joint ventures. *Synergy* in this case can be defined as "additional economic benefits (financial, operational, or technological) arising from cooperation between two parties that provide each other with complementary resources or capabilities."[13] In particular, an international partnership can promote economies of scale for the partners in the various stages of manufacturing: raw materials acquisition, production, marketing, and distribution. Another common inspiration for formal international cooperation among even the largest corporations is the need to pool capital to spread financial risks. The multibillion-dollar pursuit of a breakthrough technology (new generations of semiconductor chips are an excellent example) may be too expensive to be borne by just one company. Business alliances can reduce the absolute size of each participant's R&D outlays, and they can reduce potential losses in expensive and risky efforts at innovation that are long shots to produce a commercially viable product.

Strategic partnerships and joint ventures are used sometimes to enlarge the pool of scientific and engineering talent needed to successfully develop an especially challenging new technology. This is yet another reason to mutually learn from and draw on some aspect of the superior intellectual capital or marketing know-how of the other company. New United Motor Manufacturing, Inc. (NUMMI) is a joint venture established in California in 1984 whose origin is generally attributed to different needs of two automobile giants. General Motors reportedly wanted to observe firsthand the lean production techniques of Toyota. The Japanese company reportedly wanted to observe firsthand GM's expertise in dealing with the regulatory and marketing nuances of manufacturing and mass retailing automobiles in the United States. The NUMMI partnership supports the contention that any given FDI project can be mutually advantageous and that an injured party is *not* inevitable.

Joint ventures are typically the partnership vehicle of choice if a foreign company is uncertain about the vagaries of an especially "exotic" foreign market it wishes to enter and sees virtues in piggybacking on the domestic expertise and the commercial and political connections of a savvy local company. A foreign company may opt for a joint venture with a local company to project an image of a domestic business and reduce perceptions that it is an outsider. Government restrictions may make joint ventures compulsory. Until the Japanese government was pressured into genuine liberalization beginning in the 1970s, nearly all incoming FDI took place through joint ventures with foreign ownership capped at 50 percent. (Even if it was a 50/50 partnership, in most cases there was no doubt that the Japanese partner had the upper hand and would manage the company in conformity with that country's unique business culture and equally unique government-business relationship.)

Identifying and Classifying Different Kinds of MNCs

To the casual observer, the term *MNC* invariably conjures up the image of the usual suspects: big oil companies, big manufacturers of consumer goods, big banks, and so on. The 100 largest MNCs, as measured by UNCTAD, do indeed account for a statistically significant percentage (roughly 15 percent) of the annual sales and employment of the approximately 700,000 foreign-owned or -controlled subsidiaries doing business around the world.[14] None of these indicators, however, suggest that it is valid to define the behavior and effects of *all* MNCs in terms of the largest, most visible, and often most notorious companies. Because size itself is an important variable in determining behavior and effects, an objective analysis cannot logically declare the behavior of a numerically small sample of corporate behemoths to be representative of the much larger statistical universe.

As with FDI, MNCs can be divided into a number of distinctive kinds, most of which have their own unique subsets of identifiable qualities. Also like FDI, differences in business objectives, relationships to the host country's economy, financial structure, propensity to export, and so on will produce two continuums, one for host and one for home countries, on which MNC activities can be charted from very favorable to very unfavorable. Even within the same industrial sector and among companies of comparable size from the same home country, the heterogeneity factor prevails. Given the large number of variables, an individual foreign subsidiary should not be stereotyped through a one-size-fits-all ledger of positive and negative trade-offs. With the chance of identical results so slim, it is not a big exaggeration to advocate disaggregation down to a subsidiary by subsidiary review as the ideal means of avoiding the fallacy of generalization when evaluating the overall FDI and MNC phenomena.

By Economic Sector

Economists divide national economies into three broad sectors based on their distinctly different outputs and characteristics. The *primary* sector extracts raw materials and harvests commodities. The *secondary* sector equates to manufacturing. The *tertiary* sector encompasses services. MNCs within each of these sectors share a number of common traits and effects that tend not to be found in companies operating in the other sectors.

Primary Sector   As noted, natural resource-extracting companies led the first wave of modern FDI. Being first has done nothing to enhance their image. As also noted, for a number of reasons, fear and loathing have long been directed at them to a degree that is disproportionately high to their numbers relative to MNCs in the manufacturing and services sectors.

The questions of ownership and control over natural resources production schedules assume maximum significance in the frequent instances where the producing country is relatively poor. Most overseas subsidiaries of mining and oil companies were and are located in former colonies, most of whom have lingering fears about neocolonialism in general and concerns about the power of foreign-owned companies in particular. The dependency of countries in the South on MNCs to deliver hard currency payments in exchange for overseas sales of their natural resources is especially sensitive when dealing with nonreplenishable resources. By definition, such a mineral or metal eventually will be exhausted, as will the income flow derived from selling it. For this reason, noncorrupt governments of resource-rich countries cannot be pleased when foreign companies dominate decisions on production levels and price.[15]

Oil is the most important example of powerful control over LDC-based natural resources by carpetbagger MNCs. For decades, the large international oil companies collectively set terms for royalties received by host countries, determined volumes of drilling, and effectively controlled worldwide prices of that commodity. However many billions of dollars in potential royalties have been forgone by LDC governments, a dramatic about-face begun in the early 1970s revolutionized the relationship between countries belonging to the Organization of Petroleum Exporting Countries (OPEC) and the oil companies. The eruption of accumulated anger in the oil-producing countries of the Middle East, North Africa, and in Venezuela triggered a classic case study in the ultimate power of sovereign governments, even in small countries, over the largest, most economically powerful MNCs. In the 1970s, one OPEC country after another nationalized local operations of foreign oil companies and began dictating to them financial terms and levels of output. In his seminal study of the history of oil in world affairs, Daniel Yergin eloquently explained the legitimate but conflicting claims that formed the two sides to the story of host country-oil company relations:

> The host country [has] sovereignty over the oil beneath its soil. Yet the oil was without value until the foreign company risked its capital and

employed its expertise to discover, produce, and market it. The host country was, in essence, the landlord, the company a mere tenant, who . . . [paid] an agreed-upon rent. But, if through the tenant's risk-taking and efforts, a discovery was made and the value of the landlord's property vastly increased, should the tenant continue to pay the same rent as under the original terms . . . ?

[Producing countries saw the companies as] "exploiting" the country, stifling development, denying social prosperity, . . . and certainly acting as "masters"—in a haughty, arrogant, and "superior" manner. . . . [Oil companies felt] they had taken the risks . . . and they signed laboriously negotiated contracts, which gave them certain rights. They had created value where there was none. They needed to be compensated for the risks they had taken—and the dry holes they had drilled.[16]

A second lightning rod for criticism of primary sector MNCs is the relatively limited degree to which the typical extractive project is commercially integrated with the local economy, especially in developing countries. Most mines, oil wells, plantations, and so on are largely self-contained enclaves (sometimes fenced-in communities) located away from main population centers. The result is minimal linkage with host country economies in comparison with manufacturing direct investment, which often procures goods and services from indigenous companies. The local workers hired by natural resource companies tend to be relatively few in number and concentrated in the lower skilled or most dangerous jobs.

Another aspect of the separation between resource-seeking FDI and the host country's economy is that it has seldom provided transfers of technology that could be incorporated into the local industrial sector. Furthermore, it historically has established little value-added activity within LDCs. Processing raw materials such as petroleum or cut diamonds into finished products requires capital and skilled labor, both of which are in short supply in LDCs. The payoff from adding value is that industrialization and rising levels of productivity work hand in hand as the chief catalysts of increased wealth and higher living standards. Hence, a handful of wealthy countries prefers to retain dominance in the value-added process. Their success in doing so is suggested by the fact that facilities for processing raw materials into manufactured goods are located predominantly in the North.

The invaluable benefit provided by FDI in the primary sector has been provision of much-needed foreign exchange to governments that lack the indigenous technical and marketing expertise to act entirely on their own to cash in on the commercial value of their natural resources. For most LDCs, the money earned from the in-country activity of primary sector MNCs is a major source of revenue for the national government. These hard currency revenues typically are the major means of paying for imports of consumer and capital goods needed for economic development and poverty reduction. Saudi Arabia earned approximately $100 billion from oil sales in 2004. During the 1950 and 1960s, the copper produced in Chile by the Anaconda and Kennecott corporations ranged from 7 percent to 20 percent annually of Chilean GDP, 10 to 40 percent of government tax revenues, and 30 to 80 percent of all hard currency earnings from exports.[17] The most vexing problem for LDCs has been that even if a fair market price is the basis of their royalty earnings, capital flows alone have never been sufficient to guarantee economic prosperity and social stability.

Secondary Sector   A major milestone in the evolution of the international economy was reached in the 1960s with the onset of a numerical and geographic proliferation of FDI in the secondary, or manufacturing sector. The subsequently rapid growth in the output of the overseas subsidiaries of manufacturing companies relative to domestic output and exporting was a critical ingredient in the internationalization of economic activity. By the mid-1970s, manufacturing MNCs had eclipsed those in the primary sector to become the face of FDI and the focal point in the public debate about it. Critics usually cite the manufacturing sector when expressing their opposition to MNCs, be it exploitation of workers, increased pollution, reduced competition, crowding out of domestic businesses, or erosion in national sovereignty. Debates about the contribution of incoming FDI to economic development, poverty reduction, shifts in international trade flows, and the need for technology transfers also tend to be couched in terms of what manufacturing MNCs do or do not do.

FDI in the secondary sector is dissimilar to that of the primary sector in several important respects. First, it involves possible economic dislocations in the home country. The labor force might shrink in the short run (or longer during periods of economic stagnation) if domestic production lines are closed because overseas production has been selected as the means of serving customers in the host and/or home countries. Even if total unemployment does not increase, job losses due to foreign competition are always a politically sensitive issue for elected representatives of the people. Second, host countries find incoming manufacturing FDI to be particularly appealing because as a group, these companies have demonstrated a greater willingness to reinvest profits, expand operations, and increase jobs in host countries than the other sectors. Incoming subsidiaries of manufacturers that are market-seeking (see previous discussion) tend to be the most economically beneficial to host countries because of the near certainty that they will employ skilled workers (and train them if necessary) and pay them above-average salaries. A final difference is that unlike resource-seeking investments, the pioneers of manufacturing MNCs built foreign subsidiaries in other industrialized countries.

Companies in nearly every subsector of manufacturing have now become multinational, some to protect overseas markets, some to cut production costs, and some to do both. High-tech companies (information technology, semiconductors, pharmaceuticals, heavy machinery, and so on) are avid overseas investors because their need to amortize high fixed costs and hold down per unit costs requires achieving economies of scale through maximum sales volume. Manufacturing industries with more than $75 billion of inward FDI stock at year end 2003 were chemicals and chemical products; motor vehicles and other transport equipment; electrical and electronic equipment; processed food, beverages, and tobacco; metal and metal products; machinery and equipment; wood and wood products; and petroleum and fuels.[18] Not all MNCs in the secondary sector are traditional manufacturers. Like most large publishing houses, Oxford University Press, the publisher of this book, is a multinational, operating sales offices in more than 50 countries and printing facilities in 13 countries.[19] Three manufacturing sectors are noticeably absent from overseas investment: steel, textiles, and apparel. Not by coincidence, they are three of the most vociferous, long-standing seekers of import protection among all industries in the United States and elsewhere.

Tertiary Sector   The fastest growing segment of FDI since the beginning of the 1990s has been *services*, also known as the tertiary sector. Its relatively vigorous and sustained growth spurt was sufficient to propel this sector to the largest category of worldwide FDI. Reaching an estimated level of $5.2 trillion at the end of 2003, the worldwide value of inward FDI stock by services sector companies accounted for approximately 60 percent of the worldwide total, up from 25 percent in the early 1970s. (FDI in the secondary sector declined to a share of about 34 percent in 2003, and the primary sector accounted for about 7 percent of global inward FDI.)[20]

The relatively recent growth spurt in the tertiary sector was caused by a different mix of factors than those that acted as catalysts for increased direct investment by manufacturing and raw materials companies. Services have become the fastest growing sector by far within the GDPs of the wealthiest industrialized countries. One reason for this is the constant stream of new kinds of services that find a ready market among increasingly affluent customers with more leisure time.

FDI activity by tertiary sector companies has been given a major boost by technological advances, particularly in information processing and telecommunications, which have allowed a growing array of service industries to operate efficiently on a global basis. Relatively new entrants include data transmission, overnight freight deliveries, and back office support centers. A whole new subset of MNC that is increasingly making its presence felt on a global basis consists of

Internet-based companies like Yahoo!, Google, Amazon.com, and eBay, who have set up overseas subsidiaries to handle content, sales, customer support, and market research efforts. More recent entrants into multinational business are the U.S.-based gambling companies Las Vegas Sands Corporation and Wynn Resorts, who are building casinos in Macau and Singapore.

No limit is in sight for the kinds of innovative services that can be provided on a multinational basis. Foreign-based companies that manage regional water supplies and operate toll roads and bridges, once a curiosity, are becoming common. Press reports in 2005 noted that a U.S.-based operator of senior citizen housing complexes had opened facilities abroad and that Laureate Education had expanded the number of college campuses it owned overseas. This new wave of service companies joined long-established, still expanding MNCs in tourism, passenger and freight transportation, banking and finance, wholesaling and distributing, insurance, construction, and energy exploration and transmission services.

A third source of growth in services MNCs has been the need for and opportunities provided to banking, accounting, legal, advertising, and other business services to set up branches close to the proliferating overseas presence of their manufacturing sector clients. Another factor is the steady increase in consumers' discretionary income throughout much of the world that induced many retailers, restaurant and specialty food chains, health care providers, and cable networks to become MNCs. Finally, the expanding trend of privatization of government-owned enterprises post-1980s caused a surge in overseas investment by what had traditionally been the most home-bound of corporations: transportation and utilities providing electricity, water, natural gas, and telecommunications.

FDI in the services sector shares relatively few of the characteristics attributable to MNCs in the primary and secondary sectors. The tertiary sector has much less scope than manufacturers for traditional exporting. In some cases, such as in construction, resorts, and oil drilling, the services rendered personify the economic concept of nontradability, that is, services providers must physically be present in the place where their product is consumed. The prevalence of the nontradability syndrome has precluded controversy about services-oriented FDI displacing exports from home countries. Conversely, no claims can be made, as they are in the secondary sector, that overseas services subsidiaries generate a high volume of alternative exports from the home country in the forms of components, machinery, and models of goods not being produced abroad.

MNC critics traditionally did not accuse FDI in the services sector of causing substantial job losses in the headquarters country. Part of the reason was nontradability; another part was the propensity of service companies to send accountants, lawyers, advertising copy writers, and senior supervisory personnel from headquarters to serve a temporary overseas assignment. White-collar workers did not feel the same sense of vulnerability that workers on the factory floor did. No data exist to suggest that the former received the same threats from employers as did blue-collar workers that entire production lines would be transferred to low-wage countries if demands for increases in wages and benefits were not restrained.

The exemption long given to service sector FDI from criticism alleging losses in home country jobs came to an abrupt end in the early years of the new millennium. A heated backlash, mainly in the United States, erupted almost overnight against *international outsourcing* (a term that usually denotes an arm's-length transaction between two companies in different countries). More specifically, the target of heated finger-pointing has been *offshoring* (see chapter 13). Also lacking a single, precise definition, this term refers to a decision by a local company to shift service functions being performed in the headquarters country to a subsidiary located in a lower wage country or to a different company in a different country.[21] Advances in information and communications technologies have caused great distances to become irrelevant to a growing number of services sectors. An x-ray can be evaluated quickly and cheaply by a radiologist 10,000 miles from the patient, and software code can be written almost anywhere and transmitted quickly and cheaply to any other point on the planet. This trend has helped launch a new attack on the theory of free trade (see chapter 11). Some have agonized that if very high-skilled, high-income service jobs are going to be shifted overseas to further fatten corporate bottom lines, the irreversible unraveling of America's high standard of living has begun.

In the past, services companies established overseas subsidiaries solely as part of market-seeking strategies. The efficiency-seeking strategy (offshoring) is still in its infancy, and resource- and strategic asset-seeking are statistically irrelevant as foreign investment motives. Overseas subsidiaries of service companies have not been accused of being part of the alleged race to the bottom. They do not engage in activities that pollute the environment (think of accountants or executive job recruiters working in a modern office building). They seldom have been accused of exploiting local workers or imposing sweatshop conditions. Except for a few big retailers like Wal-Mart, service MNCs have not been loudly criticized for crowding out local business establishments. Foreign subsidiaries in the service sector are not associated with lost jobs and exports in the home country; in many cases, such as hotel chains, lawyers, journalists, and retailers, new positions for expatriates from the headquarters country would be created. An additional factor muting public criticism is that many service multinationals, for example, wholesalers, distributors, and trading companies, have a low profile and are largely shielded from public view.

McDonald's, Starbucks, MTV, and Disney exemplify the main criticism of the new wave of tertiary sector FDI: alleged threats to the integrity of local culture and lifestyles. This is a complaint seldom directed against MNCs in the primary and secondary sectors. Other service-related problems on the horizon are governments squabbling over how to collect sales taxes from international e-commerce transactions and further growth and expansion of multinational media conglomerates.

FDI by service companies is not so unique as to be exempt from the heterogeneity/don't generalize thesis. Some overseas subsidiaries are part of megacorporations (Citigroup, for example). Others are small cogs in relatively small companies that are partnerships or non-stock trading corporations (advertising, public relations, and architects, for example). They operate in a limited number of countries, have relatively few employees overseas, and have little need to subvert local laws and regulations. Some overseas subsidiaries of services companies generate relatively few new local jobs, for example, law and accounting firms. The tourism industry is a different story. The arrival of multinational hotels and resorts can create a flourishing tourist sector that needs thousands of jobs to give direct service to tourists and provide a variety of logistical support functions, such as food deliveries and all manner of hotel supplies.

Miscellaneous

MNCs have become so diverse that not all correspond to one of these three traditional categories. First of all, there are what can be called virtual MNCs, companies that design and market state-of-the-art information technology, electronics, and telecommunications products but do not actually manufacture them. Overseas subsidiaries of such companies would mainly be R&D and design operations that mostly employ engineers and scientists, not traditional factories employing blue-collar production workers. For example, Microsoft is more a multinational research and product development campus than a manufacturing company. It is almost totally reliant on outsourcing for the manufacture of CD-ROMs, video game machines, and other physical products bearing its name.

A growing number of major companies in the high-tech sector contract out—outsource—to specialized assemblers and manufacturers. This has given rise to a new industrial category, electronics manufacturing services. It consists of contracted manufacturers and distributors of information technology products developed elsewhere by familiar brand names (Cisco Systems, Dell, Hewlett-Packard, and Nokia, among others). All the large electronics manufacturing specialists are themselves MNCs because they need to respond quickly to orders and provide rapid deliveries in the dozens of markets in which their major clients are marketing their goods. Flextronics, a Singapore-based electronics manufacturing services provider, operates production centers in over thirty countries on five continents.[22]

Nike is a low-tech version of the virtual MNC. It does not own any of the dozens of licensed plants overseas that physically assemble the footwear that it designs, promotes, and sells on a global basis. Absent overseas marketing and distribution subsidiaries, it would not, strictly speaking, be an MNC.

Coca-Cola may be the most ubiquitous brand name on Earth, but the company does not fit the typical profile of a consumer goods multinational. It is more an intermediary supplier than a retailer. Coke has foreign subsidiaries in surprisingly few countries given the fact that its products are sold in more than 200 countries and territories. Its overseas manufacturing presence is concentrated in some twenty factories that prepare its proprietary syrup. These plants then sell the syrup to bottling companies and wholesalers throughout the world. Although some foreign bottlers are wholly or majority-owned Coca-Cola subsidiaries, most of the bottling companies operating in 478 licensed marketing districts worldwide are locally owned.[23] They are the ones that literally do the heavy lifting of selling countless millions of bottles and cans of beverages bearing the Coca-Cola logo. They also pocket the profits from doing so.

Singapore actively promotes itself as an ideal location for the Asian regional executive headquarters of MNCs. This kind of subsidiary ensures a strong local job market for office professionals, generates income taxes, and stimulates demand for upscale housing. Regional headquarters offices do not operate sweatshops, do not pollute, and pose no threat to domestic companies. But neither do they produce large numbers of jobs for local residents.

By Corporate Size

The popular view of MNCs is that they rank among the biggest, most powerful companies on Earth. Though literally true, this is only a small part of the picture. The largest companies are the ones most frequently discussed by critics *and* supporters of FDI/MNCs. The fact that a relatively small number of very large corporations accounts for a disproportionately large percentage of the worldwide economic activity of multinationals does not mean that they should define the nature and effects of *all* FDI and MNCs—even if they represented a homogeneous cohort. In numerical terms, the majority of MNCs are medium and small companies that lack the financial and market power of the elite minority of mega-MNCs. Lacking the clout of the giants, small firms provide another set of exceptions to challenge the generalization that FDI/MNCs inevitably have a major impact on host countries and inherently are monopoly-seeking phenomena that stifle competition and exacerbate the asymmetrical global distribution of income.

Small and medium-sized MNCs seldom have a perceptible economic, political, or social impact on either host or home country. "Most of the estimated 45,000 firms that operate internationally employ fewer than 250 people. It is commonplace to find service companies that maintain fewer than 100 employees operating across more than 15 countries."[24] A Conference Board study found that most small and medium-sized goods-producing companies had only one to three overseas plants, whereas big companies had an average of thirty-six plants in fourteen foreign countries.[25] Paris-based BVRP Software, with only $74 million in annual sales in 2003, became a multinational after acquiring two small California software firms, one of which had annual sales of only $8 million.[26]

By Degree of Multinationality

MNCs differ quite literally in their worldliness. An American company might have as its sole FDI presence one relatively small factory in Canada that sells only in that market. This modest operation does not fit the image of a gigantic globe-spanning company seeking to manage the world as an integrated unit and dominate all major markets for its products. Deutsche Post, Ford, Nestlé, and Royal Dutch Shell do fit that profile as each has facilities in more than ninety host countries.[27] The most widely cited quantitative estimate of the degree to which corporations "gear their activities outside of their home countries" is the "transnationality index" (TNI) published periodically in UNCTAD's annual *World Investment Report*. The index is a composite of three ratios compiled for each of the top 100 nonfinancial MNCs: foreign assets to total company assets, foreign sales to total sales, and foreign employment to total employment. The average TNI for all 100 corporations increased by only 2 percentage points, from 51 to 53 percent, between 1990 and 1999. This suggests that the corporations with the largest foreign assets were not on average becoming more global in the 1990s.[28] Economic necessity correlates well with degrees of transnationality. Consistent with economic reason, countries with small domestic markets, most notably

Switzerland and the Netherlands, continue to account for an above-average number of the most globalized companies as measured by the index. U.S. and Japanese firms on average register well below the 50 percent mark on the TNI.

The degree of a corporation's multinationality is a factor in the way it organizes itself. A certain degree of decentralization is necessary to the extent that a large share of a company's assets, sales, and employment are located outside of its home country. A low degree of multinationality would facilitate a decision to exert tight control from corporate headquarters and could reduce the linkage between its overseas subsidiaries and host countries' business sectors.

By LDC-Owned MNCs

One of the harshest and longest running criticisms of FDI/MNCs is their alleged use of economic might and political leverage to exploit the poor countries of the South. The image of massive extraction of profits and minimal infusion of long-term benefits first emerged from the often controversial behavior of extractive companies already summarized. More recently, criticism was expanded by opponents of globalization to include allegations of a rush to the South by big manufacturing companies to exploit cheap labor and lax enforcement of environmental protection laws (see chapter 7). Viewing MNCs in this harsh light grew out of a valid generalization: Outward FDI historically had flowed in one direction—from the rich countries of the North mostly to other rich countries. This is another international business trend terminated by the constant of change. FDI and MNCs have not been and are not likely to become static phenomena.

A new trend that has yet to attract much public notice is the increasing number of prosperous, growing corporations in LDCs establishing overseas subsidiaries, that is, becoming MNCs. The old one-way, North-to-South axis of FDI is being reconfigured by the spread of market forces. Most of the companies headquartered in emerging market countries that have made the decision to become MNCs have done so largely for the same reasons that companies in industrialized countries went overseas according to UNCTAD, a UN agency whose mandate is to protect and enhance the economic interests of the South. LDC-owned companies recognize that "in a globalizing world economy, they need a portfolio of locational assets in order to be competitive internationally." This formula for long-term survival applies to both manufacturing and services companies and involves "complex as well as simple" industries.[29] Although motivations to invest overseas are similar, FDI by LDC-based manufacturing companies has mostly been in industrial countries and therefore does not raise the traditional concerns that giant foreign investors will dictate to relatively weak host countries.

The statistical significance of the emerging "new geography" of outward FDI can be demonstrated in several ways. UNCTAD statistics show that annual FDI outflows from developing countries grew at a faster rate in the 1989–2003 period than those from developed countries. Negligible until the early 1990s, outward FDI from emerging market countries accounted for about one-tenth of the world stock of outward FDI and about 6 percent of total world flows in 2003.[30] In some years, South-South FDI flows now grow at a faster rate than North-South direct investment.

When measured as a percentage of gross fixed capital formation, some developing countries invested more abroad between 2001 and 2003 than developed ones; by way of example, Singapore (36 percent), Chile (7 percent), and Malaysia (5 percent) topped the United States (7 percent), Germany (4 percent), and Japan (3 percent).[31] Other emerging market countries that UNCTAD considers to be current or soon-to-be factors in new outward FDI flows are Korea, Mexico, South Africa, Brazil, and India. Chinese enterprises were singled out as being "at the threshold of becoming major foreign direct investors in Asia and beyond" because of the country's rapid economic development and the government's avowed interest in encouraging outward FDI.[32]

Mexican-based Cemex has grown into one of the world's largest cement producers. As a result of newly established subsidiaries and acquisitions on five continents, about three-fourths of its revenues are generated outside of Mexico, including the highly competitive U.S. market. In 1987, a book by Louis W. Goodman titled *Small Nations, Giant Firms* looked at attitudes of MNC executives and economic policy officials in several Latin American countries to assess the impact of inward FDI from powerful foreign-based companies. Ironically, the title would be perfectly appropriate for a new book looking at the increased *outward* flow of FDI from large companies in emerging market countries.

It is not only the larger, more economically advanced developing countries whose companies have become multinationals. A number of companies headquartered in the relatively small and remote island country of Mauritius opened foreign subsidiaries. Apparel companies established subsidiaries in lower wage African countries to produce low-end garments, and some of Mauritius's more experienced hotel management companies expanded their operations to other countries in the region.[33]

Assuming the trend of increased outward FDI from emerging markets continues, the school of thought equating MNCs with exploitation of LDCs will face a quandary. The tendency to portray MNCs as oversized, capitalist villains will become increasingly incompatible with the growing numbers of LDC-based companies replicating the global business model conceived in the North. If the anti-MNC/pro-LDC faction retains a platform whose unequivocal message is the need for increased government-imposed restrictions on the growth of

BOX 4.2 Following in the Footsteps: Chinese and Indian
Companies Venture Overseas

One of the more optimistic pronouncements made by development economists in the 1970s was that the main difference between industrialized, rich countries and LDCs was a matter of timing, not economics, politics, or sociology. LDCs were said to be at an earlier stage of the development timetable and would gradually and inexorably follow the same path to prosperity taken by the developed countries. This claim was off the mark and is seldom heard today. However, it bears close resemblance to the recent propensity of MNCs based in emerging market countries (not the poorer LDCs) to invest abroad for reasons identical to those that many decades ago induced companies in the North to venture overseas, most notably to seek new markets for manufactured goods and new sources of natural resources.

The Haier Group, a Chinese conglomerate, opened a subsidiary in South Carolina in 2000 to produce refrigerators. Corporate officials stated that one of two primary reasons behind this move is to provide better and quicker service to its expanding sales base in the United States; in doing so, it hoped to increase its market share at the expense of domestic competitors. The second primary reason is to save on shipping costs: "When you ship refrigerators, you ship a lot of air, and shipping air is expensive," an American executive at the subsidiary told a reporter. Some observers have surmised that there was an additional factor. Government-owned Haier may have been willing to take a financial risk in return for reaping the prestige of being a pioneer in demonstrating that a Chinese company could prosper and build market share in the tough, highly competitive U.S. market. Haier America is paying its assembly line workers at least ten times as much per hour as their Chinese counterparts.* This raises the unique possibility that workers in the home country feel exploited, not those working for a foreign subsidiary.

In purchasing IBM's personal computer unit for nearly $2 billion in late 2004, the Lenovo Group, a computer producer partly owned by the Chinese government, risked a lot of money in an effort to become a global player. Economies of scale are of particular importance to a product like personal computers. They have become a commodity sold mainly on the basis of price, not brand loyalty or promises of superior performance.

An even more striking example of FDI by LDC-based companies was the purchases during 2004 of several U.S. and Canadian call centers and forms-processing centers by Indian-owned business services companies. These are probably the first examples of what could be dubbed reverse offshoring. Among the public reasons given by the Indian companies for this strategy was the belief that a global presence will be necessary to further expand their customer base, expertise, and geographic reach. An unstated reason may be that the striking success of Indian companies in attracting labor-intensive back office work from companies operating in higher wage countries enabled them to buy some of their battered U.S. and Canadian rivals at deep discounts. A second unstated reason for Indian companies to establish a U.S. presence and employ a limited number of Americans is to defuse the political furor in the United States associated with offshore outsourcing by American companies, most of which has gone to India.**

* "When Jobs Move Overseas (to South Carolina)," *New York Times*, October 26, 2003, p. C1.
** "India's Outsourcers Turn West," *BusinessWeek Online*, available at http://www.businessweek .com; accessed July 2004.

multinational firms, they leave themselves open to being ostracized for a callous attitude toward the long-term competitiveness of companies owned and managed by citizens of the South. The paradigm critical of big business will have to give greater effort to disaggregating FDI flows to categorize those going from South to North as being unlikely to seriously threaten the political, economic, and social fabric of the industrialized countries. Outward FDI from the South is likely to create another conundrum: How should the pro-South faction deal with the almost inevitable rise of claims that some MNCs headquartered in the emerging market countries are exploiting workers in subsidiaries they operate in poorer, lower wage LDCs?

Postscript

This is a long chapter because of the large body of (underutilized) data relevant to the thesis that generalizations cannot be applied to something that comes in as many forms as do FDI and MNCs. The heterogeneity factor is incompatible with any simple declaration that they are good or bad, desirable or undesirable. It is also incompatible with a single theory as to why they exist and what their effects have been. Finally, the heterogeneity factor precludes any easy formulation of multilateral policies to regulate the flow of FDI and operations of MNCs.

Notes

1. The URL for the industrial and geographical breakdown is http://www.unctad.org/ Templates/Page.asp?intItemID=3149&lang=1.
2. Suzanne Berger and the MIT Industrial Performance Center, *How We Compete— What Companies around the World Are Doing to Make it in Today's Global Economy* (New York: Currency-Doubleday, 2006), pp. 44–45.
3. An example of the relatively infrequently used efficiency-seeking model of FDI is the effort to employ an additional level of highly skilled, relatively high-paid foreign workers in strategic foreign markets to design and manufacture sophisticated high-tech goods.
4. Frank Berry, "Export-Platform FDI: The Irish Experience," European Investment Bank, *EIB Papers* no. 2, 2004, p. 9.
5. Peter Nunnenkamp and Julius Spatz, "Foreign Direct Investment and Economic Growth in Developing Countries," Kiel Working Paper no. 1176, July 2003, pp. 6–7, available online at http://www.uni-kiel.de/ifw/pub/kap/2003/kap1176.pdf; accessed September 2004.
6. John H. Dunning, *Multinational Enterprises and the Global Economy* (Workingham, UK: Addison-Wesley, 1993), p. 60.

7. Peter Dicken, *Global Shift* (New York: Guilford Press, 2003), p. 248.
8. Andrew Inkpen, "Strategic Alliances," in Alan Rugman and Thomas Brewer, eds., *Oxford Handbook of International Business* (Oxford: Oxford University Press, 2001), p. 407.
9. Some textbooks categorize joint ventures as a specialized form of strategic alliance, not as separate phenomena.
10. Dicken, *Global Shift*, p. 258; emphasis in original.
11. Nam-Hoon Kang and Kentaro Sakai, "International Strategic Alliances: Their Role in Industrial Globalisation," OECD Directorate for Science, Technology, and Industry Working Paper 2000/5, July 2000, p. 6, available online at http://www.olis.oecd.org/olis/2000doc.nsf/linkto/dsti-doc(2000)5; accessed September 2004.
12. Ibid., p. 7.
13. Oded Shenkar and Yadong Luo, *International Business* (Hoboken, NJ: Wiley, 2004), p. 315.
14. Data source: UNCTAD, *World Investment Report 2005*, p. 15, available online at http://www.unctad.org; accessed October 2005.
15. Pricing strategy for nonrenewable resources is a highly complex, ongoing search for prices that will maximize total long-term revenues to the country owning the resources. Too low a price is akin to selling one's birthright too cheaply. However, too high a price can encourage a permanent switch by consumers to other raw materials or synthetic substitutes. In the case of oil, for example, oil producers would not find it in their long-term interests to have oil prices reach and remain at levels so high that the development and use of alternative fuels becomes commercially feasible.
16. Daniel Yergin, *The Prize: The Epic Quest for Oil, Money, and Power* (New York: Simon and Schuster, 1991), pp. 432–33.
17. Theodore H. Moran, *Copper in Chile* (Princeton, NJ: Princeton University Press, 1974), p. 6.
18. Data source: UNCTAD, *World Investment Report 2005*, p. 260. Inward FDI stock of all manufacturing totaled $2.9 trillion at year end 2003.
19. Source: www.oup.com/about/worldwide.
20. UNCTAD, *World Investment Report 2005*, p. 260.
21. Both of these terms informally crept into the economics lexicon. Neither has been standardized to refer to only one kind of international transaction. Hence, they can either refer to an intrafirm transaction between two subsidiaries in different countries or to an arm's-length outsourcing to a different company in a second country.
22. Data source: http://www.flextronics.com; accessed June 2005.
23. Corporate information came from the company's 2004 10-K report and a telephone interview with a corporate spokesman, October 2004.
24. John Stopford, "Multinational Corporations," *Foreign Policy*, winter 1998/1999, p. 14.
25. As quoted in Shenkar and Luo, *International Business*, p. 119.
26. "The Rise of 'Small Multinationals,'" *Business Week Online*, February 1, 2005, available online at http://www.businessweek.com; accessed February 2005.
27. Data source: UNCTAD Investment Brief, no. 4, 2005, available online at http://www.unctad.org; accessed October 2005.

28. UNCTAD, *World Investment Report 2001*. The consistency of this data series is limited by constant changes because companies are dropped and new ones added.

29. UNCTAD, "FDI from Developing Countries Takes Off; Is a New Geography of Investment Emerging?" Press release dated August 10, 2004, available online at http://www.unctad.org; accessed September 2004.

30. Ibid.

31. UNCTAD, *World Investment Report 2004*, pp. 5, 7.

32. UNCTAD, "China: An Emerging FDI Outward Investor," e-brief, December 4, 2003, available online at http://www.unctad.org; accessed September 2004.

33. UNCTAD, "Investment Policy Review of Mauritius," available online at http://www.unctad.org; accessed December 2004.

5

PERCEPTIONS AND
ECONOMIC IDEOLOGIES

Attitudes toward multinational corporations (MNCs) and foreign direct investment (FDI) tend to be outgrowths of beliefs associated with larger issues. A predictable progression of value judgments flows from broad to specific. This chapter takes a brief detour into the realm of political philosophy to suggest how people are predisposed to endorse or condemn FDI and MNCs in their entirety based on their larger attitudes about income distribution and the relative merits of free markets versus government regulations.

If you, the reader, believe that economic progress and a country's standard of living tend to be inversely related to the extent of government management of economic activity, there is a near 100 percent certainty that you will agree with the idea that entrepreneurs and corporations should largely be left alone to make invaluable contributions to society at large by creating jobs and regularly introducing new goods and services produced with maximum efficiency. It logically follows that on balance, you view MNCs in positive terms and are not anxious to have a sweeping array of new regulations and international agreements enacted to curb what is viewed as their largely beneficial behavior.

Conversely, you may believe that the soul of a country should be defined by more than materialism and a just, stable society is incompatible with unregulated markets that give priority to the quest by businesses to maximize profits. If so, there is a near 100 percent certainty you will agree with the idea that government should redress the balance of power that has tilted too far in favor of protecting the interests of capital instead of serving the needs of ordinary people. It logically follows that on balance, you view MNCs in unfavorable terms and support implementation of new regulations and international agreements to curb their excessive domination of markets and political influence.

This chapter examines how and why there is a close correlation between one's attitudes toward the core dilemma of economic policy, fairness versus efficiency, and positive or negative perceptions of MNCs. The purpose is decidedly *not* to take sides on economic ideology or multinationals. Instead, two broad assumptions are made: First, there is no clear-cut right or wrong associated with personal beliefs about an intangible; second, no single economic ideology has cornered the market in wisdom. The chapter is designed to lay the foundation for understanding an essential theme: There is compelling logic, not inconsistency, in accepting the principle that each of the two irreconcilable viewpoints on FDI and MNCs exhibit both truths and fallacies. Neither demonstrates irrefutable logic or clear intellectual superiority.

The first section of the chapter consists of an overview of the role of perceptions in the study of our subject and a summary of the perceived differences between governments and markets. Specific arguments used to advocate an economic order based on the market mechanism are presented in the second section, and the third part advances the arguments made in favor of a system based on extensive and intensive governmental control. The antimarket critique is followed up with a separate, more specific analysis of the role played by MNCs in fomenting the worldwide backlash against globalization. The fifth and final section offers an explanation as to why a broad consensus exists for a middle ground approach between the two extreme versions of organizing the economy and why it is the most reasonable option, both academically and policy-wise.

Perceptions, Subjectivity, and the Separate Worlds of Governments and Markets

The ultimate reason MNCs as entities and FDI as process are viewed in two starkly dissimilar ways is that human nature has long meant that people can look at the same thing and come away with different, irreconcilable perceptions of the object under scrutiny. The aphorism that perceptions define reality assuredly applies in this case. Contrasting perceptions are easily understood if one accepts the theme of chapter 4 that pervasive heterogeneity has produced examples of all manner of MNC behavior—good, bad, and indifferent. Everyone has the option of embracing whichever category is most in accordance with his or her biases. Hard data can be assembled that empirically measure the behavior and effects of a control group composed of a limited number of corporations sharing similar characteristics. However, the behavior and effects of MNCs *as a whole* constitute an enormous abstract mass that cannot be scientifically weighed or measured. Even though companies exist in a physical sense, the determination that collectively they are a positive or negative force is a value judgment that is usually derived from and shaped by larger beliefs.

The larger philosophical debate over how strongly or loosely to manage the market mechanism effectively establishes the intellectual borders within which the debate over the relative merits of FDI and MNCs takes place. Because they are far more real than abstract economic theories, MNCs are an ideal proxy for casting either support for or opposition to capitalism. Selection of one of these two mutually exclusive views is the inevitable result of a thought process that channels images of MNCs through two dissimilar ideological prisms. People who embrace free market values are predisposed to see the merits of companies operating under the discipline of having to be profitable and seeking the most cost-efficient means of production. If companies are good enough to dominate the market for a given product in 100 or more countries, so be it; people must like their products because no one is forcing them to buy. Critics of free markets are predisposed to see the merits of government-imposed limits to reduce the antisocial behavior of corporations.

The free market versus government regulation debate is also sustained by pointed disagreements on assigning a priority between creating wealth and distributing it. A nation's income can take the form of a growing pie that is unevenly sliced among income groups or a smaller, slower growing pie that is sliced into roughly equal-size pieces. Those who prioritize the economic logic and benefits of creating wealth before worrying about how to distribute it tend to be to the right of the political center. They favor leaving markets relatively unburdened by official dictum to maximize efficiency and minimize waste. Those who prioritize the social benefits of distributing wealth more evenly and maintaining a generous, all-inclusive social safety net favor aggressive government presence and perhaps government ownership of some or all major producers of goods and services to relegate profit seeking to a secondary goal. Determination of what constitutes a fair distribution of income is a subjective political and ethical decision, not an economic one.

The value-laden issues of how evenly income should be distributed and how best to maximize the public's standard of living provide fertile soil for cultivating two rational but incompatible beliefs that likely will never be fully reconciled. A market system based on greed that may or may not debase the quality of life is pitted against an economic order guided by a relatively small number of government officials whose judgments may or may not slow growth and impede innovation. The unsurpassed ability of free markets and MNCs to generate output in an efficient manner must be weighed against their propensity to disproportionately distribute the financial bounty of an incentives-based system to a relatively few shareholders and entrepreneurs. True, the latter supply the capital and ideas and take the financial risks necessary to provide goods, services, jobs, and rising standards of living to the majority. However, many question whether they deserve or need unlimited incomes and vast tax loopholes when a large percentage of most countries' populations is living below the poverty line. Determination of how and how much a government should use the tax system to *re*distribute wealth is another highly subjective political question. The line beyond which entrepreneurs are discouraged from innovating and taking risk is invisible for all practical purposes.

A similar dichotomy exists on the issue of how good or bad a job MNCs do in providing goods and services at the cheapest possible prices. One side believes they do a good job because they respond quickly to market signals and are able to overcome governmentally imposed market imperfections, such as regulatory red tape and import controls. This view praises multinationals "as an integrating force in the world economy, surmounting national barriers, circumventing high transaction costs and improving the allocating of resources."[1] The contrary view asserts that MNCs, rather than being a means of overcoming market imperfections, are in fact a major distorting force in the global allocation of resources. This is partly because they operate mostly in oligopolistic markets and partly because of their ability to bypass market mechanisms and/or government regulations. Far from promoting competition, MNCs are said to engage in restrictive practices, raise barriers to entry, and thereby freeze existing production patterns.[2]

The ability of governments to enact laws transferring a politically determined percentage of wealth from the rich minority to the less affluent majority must be weighed against bureaucrats' propensity to wreak economic havoc by distorting prices and imposing barriers to the efficient use of resources, maximum returns to capital, and risk taking in the name of promoting group equality. Government regulation, even if deemed socially necessary, can result in disincentives to entrepreneurs who might otherwise start new companies and create new jobs. Regulation can also diminish incentives for existing companies to commit capital to develop new products, new technologies, and new cost-cutting production techniques. Although there is universal agreement that the goals of economic policy are increased incomes, rising living standards, and an improved quality of life for all people, there is no consensus as to the best and quickest *means* of achieving these objectives. No economic "ism" is foolproof. Winston Churchill put it this way: "The inherent vice of capitalism is the unequal sharing of blessings; the inherent virtue of socialism is the equal sharing of miseries."[3]

Conflicting perceptions also shape the debate on corporate social responsibility. Should the interests of shareholders or stakeholders (see chapter 2) have the greater say in guiding corporate behavior? Are managers of domestic and multinational corporations simply employees whose job it is to serve the financial interests of the owners, or do they have a larger obligation to serve society at large? Has emphasis on the profit motive worked against the overall public interest, or has it allowed corporations to fully justify their existence through their contribution to the material well-being of billions of the world's people? Is the pursuit of profits so inherently destructive and exploitive that government must tightly rein in companies and proactively protect the populace from their wickedness? Have corporations so badly fallen short in serving the larger public good that they must redeem themselves by financially supporting charities and social causes?[4] The response to all these imponderables should start with "It depends." It depends on one's larger political philosophy, mainly whether one prefers the official or the private sector to have the upper hand. It further depends on whether one realizes that there is no single pattern of behavior by MNCs as a whole, owing to substantial differences in corporate cultures, management and organization, size, product line, relationship with the host country's economy, and so on.

Governments and corporations live in different worlds. Their formulas for the proper ordering of human relationships diverge so much that some level of tension between them is inescapable. In Robert Gilpin's view, the state is based on "territoriality, loyalty, and exclusivity," whereas the market is based on the concepts of "functional integration, contractual relationship, and expanding interdependence of buyers and sellers." National governments need territorial boundaries as the basis of national autonomy and political unity. Markets want to minimize political obstacles to the operation of the price mechanism. To quote Gilpin again,

> Whereas powerful market forces in the form of trade, money, and foreign investment tend to jump national boundaries . . . [and seek to] escape political control, the tendency of government is to restrict, to channel, and to make economic activities serve the perceived interests of the state and of powerful groups within it. The logic of the market is to locate economic activities where they are most productive and profitable; the logic of the state is to capture and control the process of economic growth and capital accumulation.[5]

Bottom line: The transcendent issue is deciding which is the more desirable, or at least the lesser of the evils: free markets or government regulation. The first of two answers that I would offer is "it depends" on what specific issue is being examined. Broad generalizations are not the right framework to determine how to rank the net desirability of states and markets. Second, despite a lot of strong feelings in favor of one over the other, it is by no means obvious that it should be necessary to select the black or white option to the exclusion of the other. The viewpoint underlying this study is that neither a pure private sector nor a pure public sector model is indisputably more effective in all circumstances in all countries at all times. If one accepts the logic of a mix of free markets and regulations falling in some indeterminate spot between the two extremes, the logical progression is acceptance that MNCs are not always so magnificently beneficial economically as to merit nearly total freedom of action and blanket praise, nor so blatantly corrosive socially as to justify comprehensive government regulation and blanket condemnation.

The substance of discussions about governments versus markets and about the net desirability of FDI and MNCs should be less a manifestation of the ideological leanings of writers and speakers and more a dispassionate investigation of the multiple truths inherent in a subject as multifaceted and heterogeneous as this one. The larger but seldom recognized truth is that "there is no possibility of a 'value-free' assessment of foreign direct investment." Readers of articles and books on the subject "are left with the problem of identifying the values underlying any analysis of [MNCs], given that these are rarely defined and stated explicitly."[6] Chances for a significantly clearer understanding of the multiple layers of truth about FDI and MNCs would improve if there was less advocacy and more effort to methodically synthesize the many legitimate views embedded in all but the most exaggerated, simplistic, and demagogic assessments of these phenomena. Identifying which assessments meet these criteria is, of course, a value judgment.

The discussion that follows analyzes the ideas that sustain the two principal economic ideologies—free markets and governmental regulation. The overused, black-and-white alternatives of the "good society" and the "efficient economy" are offered as a simplified template for analysis. One-sided arguments on behalf of both ideological perspectives are presented for illustrative purposes as they might be in a debate, not necessarily on the basis of verifiable accuracy; neither is endorsed by the author as the preferable policy prescription. The intent is to defend the conclusion that these opposite belief structures have only enough validity to provide fragments of the whole truth, and only enough precision to provide a partial road map to the optimal design for managing national economies, shaping the international economic order, and regulating FDI and MNCs. There needs to be balance between government's implicit capacity to look out for the interests of the majority and business's explicit drive for efficiency and innovation to increase sales and keep customer loyalty.

Thesis: Follow the Invisible Hand, Curb Government Obstructionism

The first ideology to be summarized is known as the market, noninterventionist, and liberal (*not* the counterpart of political liberalism) economic model. It espouses what it perceives as the demonstrable benefits of allowing the private sector to operate on a relatively unregulated basis, both domestically and internationally.

This approach is rooted in the belief that markets by far are best able to make the infinite number of decisions necessary every day to allocate resources domestically and internationally in the most efficient, quickest manner. The discipline of risking one's own capital plus enlightened self-interest (a euphemism for the pursuit of profits) is deemed the natural means of ensuring maximum economic output, minimum costs, and maximum economic welfare. To best keep supply and demand in equilibrium, prices must respond in real time to changing market forces, not be set according to government fiat. This kind of economic order is most compatible with the philosophy that consumption is the number one purpose of economic activity.

The intellectual origin of this perspective is Adam Smith's epic work, *The Wealth of Nations,* published in 1776. By directing industry to perform in such a manner that its products are of greatest value, he wrote, the business community seeks its own gain. Yet in being forced to provide customers with goods and services that they want and can afford, each business owner is, often unconsciously, "led by an invisible hand" to promote the interests of society. "I have never known much good done by those who affected to trade for the public good. . . . it is not from the benevolence of the butcher, the brewer, or the baker, that we can expect our dinner, but from their regard to their own interest."[7] If private companies do not give consumers good products at competitive prices, or if they invest their capital in unprofitable endeavors, they face extinction—unless rescued by government bail-out. This sense of mortality seldom applies to government agencies; they just keep on spending the unending inflow of taxpayers' money.

Effusive praise for the modern corporation comes from two British business journalists who called it "the basis of the prosperity of the West." Among other benefits cited: "Companies increase the pool of capital available for productive investment. . . . And they provide a way of imposing effective management structures on large organizations."[8] The promarket ideology points to the steady stream of product and technological innovations spurred by the self-interest of increasingly large corporations. These advances are cited as being the major contributing factor to unprecedented rates of increase in material well-being and quality of life experienced over the past 100 years by much of the Earth's population. Guided by hard-nosed number crunching that takes them to the lowest cost locations anywhere on the planet and strengthened by economies of scale, globalized companies have taken efficiency to the ultimate level.

Skepticism and at times outright disdain for government is the other part of a belief structure that favors maximum freedom of maneuver for and minimum regulation of private corporations. One need only have a rudimentary knowledge of history to be aware of the countless physical and spiritual gulags imposed by hundreds of dictatorships on a populace deemed undeserving of personal freedoms and the right to choose their leaders. When viewing the past, Martin Wolf sees "corrupt, incompetent, brutal, and, depressingly often, murderous governments everywhere. A big part of the history of the twentieth century is a story of the crimes inflicted by those in power upon an innocent people."[9]

The extent to which corruption by government officials has impeded economic development is beyond calculation. Many billions of dollars have been diverted from the masses into the offshore bank accounts of political rulers and the pockets of lower level civil servants. The World Bank identifies corruption as being "among the greatest obstacles to economic and social development." Dishonesty by government officials, it says, undermines economic development by "distorting the rule of law and weakening the institutional foundation on which economic growth depends. The harmful effects of corruption are especially severe on the poor, who are...most reliant on the provision of public services, and are least capable of paying the extra costs associated with bribery [and] fraud."[10] Correlation between lack of development and official corruption can be seen in the annual report by Transparency International, a nongovernmental organization (NGO) that coordinates efforts worldwide to identify and reduce the corruption in the public procurement process, which it estimates siphons off at least $400 billion annually from the development effort. Its 2004 Corruption Perceptions Index identified sixty countries suffering from "rampant corruption." All of them are either among the world's poorest countries or middle-income, oil-rich states (Nigeria, Venezuela, Russia, and Iran) failing to realize their potential for raising incomes and living standards.[11]

The U.S. Congress faced one of the largest waves of congressional scandals in a generation during 2005 and 2006. Republican Majority Leader in the House, Tom DeLay, was forced to step down from his post after being indicted on charges of criminally conspiring to inject illegal corporate contributions into Texas state elections. Then a California representative was sent to jail for accepting the equivalent of more than $2.4 million in bribes. The guilty plea by big-time lobbyist Jack Abramoff to charges of tax evasion, conspiracy to bribe public officials, and fraud requires him to cooperate in a comprehensive investigation of his illegal dealings with members of Congress, members of their staffs, and Executive Branch officials. The potential for a major domino effect of indictments was signaled when the chair of the House Administration Committee "temporarily" relinquished his post after his involvement with Abramoff leaked. The bribery investigation of an obscure Louisiana Congressman probably would not have made headlines amidst these events had it not been for the FBI finding $90,000 of alleged payoffs in the freezer at his home and then raiding his congressional office in search of further incriminating evidence. Nonbelievers in congressional integrity received no surprises at ensuing events that repeated an old pattern: Resolute congressional promises to quickly remedy the ethics crisis resulted in watered-down reform language by subcommittees in both houses, and that was followed by studied inaction (as of mid-2006) by the joint conference committee charged with reconciling differences in the two bills. Few expect a serious dent in the influence and largesse of lobbyists. Voters were not expressing outrage and a determination to punish unethical incumbents. Maybe voters "expect lawmakers to be dishonest," mused one journalist.[12] A look at the record will show that in an average year, more elected politicians in the United States are charged with criminal wrongdoing than are senior corporate executives. According to one estimate, more than 1,000 U.S. government employees were convicted of corrupt activities in the 2005–2006 period, with the FBI investigating hundreds more.[13]

The combination of enlightened government and a free, prosperous, and egalitarian country has been all too infrequent throughout history. Communism claimed to serve the masses, but it disdained political freedom and created an equal distribution of income by making everyone poor, except for the top echelon of the party. James Madison wrote in the *Federalist Papers* that it is necessary to place controls on government because "if men were angels, no government would be necessary. If angels were to govern men, neither external nor internal controls on government would be necessary."[14]

Critics of the market mechanism feel threatened by it, wrote Johan Norberg, not because they think it results in a genuine loss of democracy but by the absence of the policies they want democracies to pursue. Many of those policies involve greater governmental power over society's economic decision making. "But saying that the market threatens government control of our economic actions is less exciting than calling it a threat to democracy. Why should it be 'more democratic' for a democratic government to have more powers of decision-making over us? . . . Democracy is a way to rule the state, not a way to rule society."[15]

The theory of *public choice* (sometimes referred to as rational choice) casts doubts on the benefits to be gotten by giving more power to any government, even a democratic one. This is a theory of recurring governmental failure that is fully comparable to the economic theory of private market failure, according to James M. Buchanan, the principal architect of the public choice approach.[16] Governments do not make decisions, elected officials and bureaucrats do, and therein lies the problem. This theory holds that it is a pipe dream to consider political decision makers as altruistic seekers of the public good. Instead, like everyone else, they put their own self-interests first, for example, reelection, a well-paying job after leaving government, or simple bribes. A corollary is that democratic governments more often than not support policies and programs that favor loud, well-organized, and well-financed special interest groups. This is most likely to happen when an official decision can prevent major harm to such an interest group without inflicting substantial harm that is clearly felt by the public at large. The Bush administration's imposition of higher tariffs on steel in 2002 arguably is an example of this scenario.

Public choice theory does not say that self-enhancement always results in corrupt, undesirable, or harmful official actions (special interests sometimes have a good argument). But it does argue that there is no incentive for government officials to give priority to the interests of a general public that is usually ignorant of, or not concerned with, noncosmic government actions and has a relatively short memory span—especially when confronted with demands from a committed minority with reasonable requests and a lot of cash.

The theory makes no pretense of being the definitive guide to government behavior or denying that many elected officials and civil servants are committed to doing the right thing. However, this paradigm does help explain such foibles as the enthusiasm of all members of U.S. Congress—past, present, and of all political persuasions—for championing the funding of even the most dubious pork (public works projects) because constituents want and are made happy by new projects in their localities, no matter how unnecessary. The frequency with which members of Congress insert funding for pet projects into unrelated legislation has spiked dramatically higher since the mid-1990s—despite a nearly equal increase in negative publicity and outright derision from those not on the receiving end.[17] Public choice theory also explains the equally long-standing history of U.S. regulatory agencies giving the benefit of the doubt to the industries they regulate rather than to the interests of society as a whole.

Acceptance of the hypothesis that politicians seldom act like selfless statesmen who put the long-term interests of their country before their political careers or ideological beliefs makes it easier to understand the endless bumbling and corruption in Washington, DC. There is not nearly enough space to provide an extensive review of the foibles of the U.S. government just in the 2004–2005 period; a few examples will have to suffice. President Bush's phrase "Brownie, you're doing a heck of a job" has entered the language as ironic comment on government incompetence. The shocking if not outright inhumane ineptitude exhibited by the Federal Emergency Management Agency in responding to flood-ravaged New Orleans in fall 2005 is suggested by the first sentence of a front page article in the *New York Times* on June 27, 2006: "Hurricane Katrina . . . produced one of the most extraordinary displays of scams, schemes and stupefying bureaucratic bungles in modern history, costing taxpayers up to $2 billion."

Members of the so-called 9/11 Commission were so alarmed at the failure of the federal government to act on its recommendations to lessen the chances of another major terrorist attack that they took the unprecedented step of continuing as a private group to lobby for more effective security efforts. Much attention but little action resulted when the members gave low to failing grades in late 2005 to the federal government's actions on its forty-one recommendations. One of their sharpest criticisms was aimed at congressional insistence on distributing state antiterrorist grant money on a "pork barrel" basis, whereby a significant percentage of appropriated funds are disbursed in even amounts among the states, not prorated on the basis of risk, vulnerability, or consequences of a terrorist attack.[18]

The premise that politicians and government officials have a high propensity to put their own interests on par with (if not ahead of) the public's interest is applicable to the actions of other governments. It explains, for example, the heavy burdens imposed on the Japanese people long after World War II by their government's economic policies. High food prices were the cost of rewarding the ruling party's strong farm base by restricting agricultural imports. Individual incomes, living standards, environmental protection, and interest on personal bank deposits were systematically curtailed to promote the bureaucrats' and politicians' fixation with creating world-class manufacturing companies at the fastest possible pace. Big business's interests uniformly were given higher priority than the public good. Elsewhere in Asia, the endemic corruption in China's state-owned banking system is another reason to challenge the notion of public servants as protectors of the public commons. Buchanan counseled those who wanted to reform the political process to do so by changing its rules and institutions, not waiting for a new crop of politicians and civil servants to be the first to see the light and become uncompromising defenders of the majority's interests.

Antithesis: Protect the Majority, Curb Corporate Avarice

As seen from a different perspective, the relentless pursuit of profits and an unregulated business sector produce a society marred by excesses of inequality, exclusion, and environmental degradation. This assessment is part of the political-economic ideology that sees capitalism producing unacceptably skewed results that fall well beyond the boundaries of fairness or logic. A small minority of the population reaps a large majority of the economic benefits in a winner-take-all pursuit of wealth that leaves a bare minimum to trickle down to working-class families. Capitalism can produce an abundance of goods, services, and material wealth; the problem is that it is intrinsically unable to distribute them on an even or "fair" basis. Production based on profit maximization produces too many antisocial distortions. Free markets perpetuate poverty in a large have-not class of people within a country and a large have-not class of countries internationally.

Have-not people and have-not countries face an uphill battle to break out of a vicious circle of poverty and inadequate education while the relatively few rich continuously get richer.

The capitalist international economic order allegedly is structured to protect and enhance the relative wealth of industrialized nations by preserving their domination of high value-added goods. Developing countries are shunted to the periphery, perpetually dependent on the North for advanced technology and capital. The systemic inequities of the old international economic order are sustained in part by holding the economic futures of developing countries hostage to decisions made in the headquarters countries of large MNCs, where the priority is most decidedly not promoting growth and higher living standards in host countries.

Heads of large U.S. corporations typically are paid millions of dollars in salary, bonuses, and stock options (on average, Chief Executive Officers (CEOs) in the United States were paid 300 times as much as rank-and-file workers in the early 2000s).[19] Furthermore, they seldom have their pay packages reduced even if corporate profits decline. Corporate CEOs also earn tens of millions of dollars more in severance packages and retirement benefits; at least eight current ones reportedly will be eligible for retirement benefits exceeding $3 million *annually*.[20] Michael Ovitz received a severance package valued at about $140 million after being ousted in 1996 as president of the Walt Disney Company *after fourteen months in office*. In the meantime, tens of millions of Americans lack health insurance.

Rather than giving business free rein to do whatever it takes to fatten the bottom line and raise dividends, fairness-driven, left-of-center ideology calls for economic institutions and laws to ensure that economic activity primarily serves the interests of society at large, not the relatively few owners of capital. This kind of economic order is most compatible with the philosophy that elevation of the human spirit is the number one purpose of economic activity. Those to the left of the political center are alarmed at what they see as a growing tilt in the balance of power in favor of companies and against the incomes and job security of labor, especially the relatively less skilled. Workers are viewed as disposable parts, easily shed whenever necessary to boost corporate profit margins. The rewards of capitalism, in short, are distributed on an unjustifiably unequal basis.

A much published American philosopher decried a "global overclass which makes all the major economic decisions" and makes them independently of the legislature and the will of the voters in any given country. "The absence of a global polity means that the super-rich can operate without any thought of any interests save their own."[21] "Never before in modern times has the gap between the haves and the have-nots been so wide, never have so many been excluded or so championless," claims a British academician. Those at the lower end of the pay scale continue to lose ground in both political and economic terms. "Jobs and incomes in rich and poor countries have become more precarious as the pressures of global competition have led countries and employers to adopt more flexible labour policies, and work arrangements that absolve employers from long-term commitment to employees."[22] Voltaire may have been the first to decry the plight of the many against the enrichment of the few when he reputedly said that the comfort of the rich depends on an abundant supply of the poor.

"Enron syndrome" is a recent addition to a long list of reasons to distrust corporations, the engines of capitalism. Employees, in the eyes of corporations, are interchangeable parts, not human assets deserving of special respect. Customers, in the eyes of corporations, are materialistic purchasing units meant to be manipulated into wanting your product. To people of the political left, anything with such traits cannot be left to its own devices. The parade in recent years of corporate chieftains on trial in the United States for various criminal offenses has added credibility to the view that private corporations are illegal and immoral actions waiting to happen. To some, it cannot be otherwise because companies are intrinsically amoral institutions, devices to serve and enrich their owners without regard to the well-being of everyone else. By one hard-edged reckoning,

> The corporation's legally defined mandate is to pursue, relentlessly and without exception, its own self-interest, regardless of the often harmful consequences it might cause to others. As a result, ... the corporation is a pathological institution, a dangerous possessor of the great power it wields over people and societies. Today, corporations govern our lives. . . . And like the church and the monarchy in other times, they posture as infallible and omnipotent. . . . Increasingly, corporations dictate the decisions of their supposed overseers in government and control domains of society once firmly embedded within the public sphere. . . . As a psychopathic creature, the corporation can neither recognize nor act upon moral reasons to refrain from harming others. Nothing in its legal makeup limits what it can do to others in pursuit of its selfish ends, and it is compelled to cause harm when the benefits of doing so outweigh the costs. Only pragmatic concern for its own interests and the laws of the land constrain the corporation's predatory instincts, and often that is not enough to stop it from destroying lives, damaging communities, and endangering the planet as a whole.[23]

In short, the critical school of thought thinks corporations need parental supervision. The author of this critique, a Canadian law professor, recommends that society and its elected leaders challenge corporate rule "in order to revive the values and practices it contradicts: democracy, social justice, equality, and compassion."[24]

Profit-making corporations are attacked for their economic shortcomings as well as their alleged moral and aesthetic deficiencies. Some have suggested that a reason that the invisible hand is invisible is that it does not really exist. "Even in the very developed countries, markets work significantly differently from the way envisioned by the 'perfect markets' theories." Markets have limitations that sometimes are too significant to ignore.[25] The existence of what economists call market failures is an integral part of ideology favoring strong, activist government regulation to limit corporate-induced distortions. Examples of market failures include the inability or refusal of companies to produce goods the public wants; external costs, such as pollution, that are not included in prices; and absence of price competition because a market is dominated by one (monopoly) or a few (oligopoly) large companies. The latter situation is of direct relevance to the study of FDI and MNCs in the international economy. Vladimir Lenin wrote in the early twentieth century that "Imperialism is capitalism in that stage of development in which the domination of monopolies and finance capital has established itself; [and] in which the export of capital has acquired pronounced importance." A major long-term decline in competition was in progress, he wrote. It "was creating large-scale industry and eliminating small industry, replacing large-scale industry by still larger-scale industry, finally leading to such a concentration of production and capital that monopoly has been and is the result."[26]

Lenin believed that imperialist expansion abroad allowed capitalism to postpone the inevitable crisis of having nowhere to expand sales and profits. The vehicle for this expansion was MNCs, though the term had not been invented in Lenin's day. Perhaps he was just ahead of his time. The drive to maximize economies of scale in the high-tech era have produced just the kind of business concentration in the hands of a relatively few, relatively large global corporations, just as Marx and Lenin had prophesied. Discussions of oligopolies and monopolistic competition are not confined to radical treatises; they are standard fare in the international trade theory chapters of contemporary textbooks on international economics. Indeed, it is now assumed that market forces encourage the emergence of a relatively few dominant companies in industries characterized by economies of scale; the result is a growing number of markets characterized by oligopoly, that is, three or four giant MNCs that influence if not control prices.[27] The best guess answer to the question of whether this situation on balance helps or hurts the world's peoples depends on which ideology one embraces.

MNCs and the Antiglobalization Movement

The nature and impact of the process known as globalization is arguably the most contentious new issue in international political economy. In the final analysis, the dispute is about the relative costs and benefits of the internationalization of capitalism. More specifically, it is about the costs and benefits of an international economic order that some believe has moved much too far in favor of protecting corporate assets and promoting profits and too far away from protecting the rights of workers. A central irony here is that the absence of consensus on a general definition or on a framework of analysis has not interfered with the heated arguments about it. Globalization remains an all-inclusive buzzword capable of generating great emotion but containing little intellectual precision. One of the more incisive assessments is that it is "a myth, a rhetorical device, a phenomenon, an ideology, a reality, [and] an orthodoxy."[28]

The most commonly used definition, increased economic interdependence, is short and to the point but does not do justice to the broad scope of what is involved. Globalization is much more than a greater interconnectivity of national economies in the wake of faster growth rates in foreign trade, international capital movements, and FDI relative to the growth of world domestic output (GDP). Those in favor of globalization argue that it was, is, and always will be the indispensable factor in stimulating economic growth and rising living standards. Conversely, countries that have not integrated themselves into the international economy have lagged behind. Criticism is leveled at globalization on a multidisciplinary basis: economics (income gains and losses are distributed in a very uneven, unfair manner); national politics (the alleged diminution of national sovereignty, discussed in chapter 10); local politics (concerns that people are increasingly losing control of their destinies to all-powerful global forces); and culture (principally, the perceived effects of excessive Americanization).

As the most visible symbol of what people like and dislike about globalization, FDI and MNCs are inextricably intertwined in the dispute between its advocates and critics. The core economic criticism of globalization is the same as that of capitalism—an increasingly unequal distribution of benefits—just on a broader geographical scale. Because corporations are the principal bête noire of critics of capitalism, it follows that MNCs are the principal bête noire of critics of globalized capitalism. It has been argued that "a major feature of globalization is the growing concentration and monopolization of economic resources and power by transnational corporations." Investment resources and modern technology are concentrated in the few rich countries, and a majority of developing countries are excluded from the positive aspects of globalization. The resulting international income imbalance "leads to a polarization between the few countries and groups that gain, and the many countries and groups in society that lose out or are marginalized."[29] Another concern is that the budgetary costs of providing incentives—subsidies and reduced rates of corporate taxation being at the top of the list—to attract and retain incoming FDI have inflicted financial harm on the populace of a growing number of countries in two ways. First, many governments have become more willing to reduce business tax rates in response to demands by country-hopping corporations, presumably with the result that the tax base needed to support the social safety net has shrunk. The second alleged source of harm is that some governments are partially offsetting lower business taxes by disproportionately increasing the tax burden on workers' incomes.[30]

Democracy deficit is the term used to describe the belief that size and wealth allows MNCs to bully governments into giving them concessions that are not desired by, or in the interest of, the majority of the local population. Those who adhere to this argument see governments as having abandoned priority commitment to social justice and assistance to the most disadvantaged citizens in favor of pursuit of an economic and political environment pleasing to business interests. To Noreena Hertz, "Governments once battled for physical territory; today they fight for market share. . . . The role of nation states has become to a large extent simply that of providing the public goods and infrastructure that business needs at the lowest costs."[31]

The anti–free market school of thought believes that MNCs enjoy an intolerable advantage in mobility, namely, the ability to move production to subsidiaries in foreign countries far easier than workers can move from country to country. This power allows management to issue ultimatums to host governments and their own workforce to accede to its demands or watch a factory move to a more economically attractive country. One does not read reports of companies who had forced give-backs from their workers subsequently raising wages when profitability returns.[32] Skeptics are concerned that globalization is solidifying class divisions between the haves and the have-nots, that is, those who have the work skills and mobility to flourish in global markets and those who do not. The danger is that international economic integration will contribute to domestic social *dis*integration.[33]

The perception that MNCs are engaged in a race to the bottom is another plank in the antiglobalists' platform. Though not documented, belief persists that profit-maximizing companies scour the planet to construct factories in countries where the wage scales are the lowest and the enforcement of antipollution laws is the least. Countries therefore would face the dilemma of choosing between losing out on industrial production or reducing their labor and environmental protection standards.

A critic of international capitalism concluded that the world economy is "running downhill—a system that searches the world for the lowest common denominator in terms of national standards for wages, taxes and corporate obligations to health, the environment and stable communities." The international economic order allegedly is evolving into a "kind of global feudalism—a system in which the private economic enterprises function like rival dukes and barons, warring for territories across the world and oblivious to local interests" inasmuch as local governments are no longer strong enough to govern giant global corporations.[34] Although no data have been produced to demonstrate any significant correlation between inward FDI and low wages or low environmental protection efforts in host countries, anecdotal evidence can be used to depict a more limited ratcheting down of manufacturing to progressively lower wage countries. For example, by one unofficial estimate, 200,000 assembly jobs were lost in Mexico's maquiladora sector in 2002 as the result of more than 300 companies, mainly foreign-owned, shifting production to lower wage China.[35]

Synthesis: Somewhere between the Market and the State Is the Least Bad System

Unconditional reliance on either the social benevolence of government or the efficiency-maximizing invisible hand of the marketplace is not something that generates widespread support in most countries. A hybrid economic philosophy appeals to Joseph E. Stiglitz, a Nobel Prize winner in economics, because he believes that "Both the left and the right have lost their bearings." Both sides need to update their economic agenda to make them relevant for current realities, and they need to accept that there is no "single set of policies which will make all of us better off." Unconditional faith that markets by themselves inevitably lead to efficient and fair economic outcomes "has been stripped away." At the same time, the collapse of communism has effectively ended support for socialism even in those countries that previously embraced it. The big challenge today is to find the right balance between the state and the market at the local, national, and global levels.[36] Stiglitz wrote that

> as economic circumstances change, the balance has to be redrawn...we cannot escape the issues of democracy and social justice in the global arena....Economies can suffer from an over intrusive government, but so too can they from a government that does not do what needs to be done— that does not regulate the financial sector adequately, that does not promote competition, that does not protect the environment, that does not provide a basic [social] safety net.[37]

Fundamentalists who put complete faith in either totally free markets or comprehensive government planning and regulation seem oblivious to the long empirical record of market failures and government failures. Acknowledging the shortcomings of markets does not logically lead to the conclusion that reliance on government is essential and vice versa. It does seem logical that both have an important role to play, in part to offset the shortcomings and vices of the other.

As one study put it, "an unbridled economic role for the government in the name of distributive justice is often a recipe for disaster in the long run, but, on the other hand, market solutions are often ruthless to the poor."[38] Selecting the ideal course for economic policy requires some very difficult choices.

Speaking cynically ("realistically" may be more accurate), the Marxist-radical and the free market perspectives have it half right at best when accusing the other's model of woolly thinking and disgraced policies. Each side has it totally wrong to think that the public sector, the business sector, or nonprofit groups perform in the noblest manner in the service of the public interest and don't need to be subjected to constant oversight. Neither government, nor private business, nor nonprofit organizations have anything close to a spotless record for effectiveness, honesty, and competence.

Institutions are run by people, and history clearly demonstrates that individuals act in reprehensible ways with frightening frequency no matter for whom they are working, what their salary is, or how noble the cause for which they are working. Questions about the need for adoption of more vigorous and effective accounting standards by nonprofit groups were raised by the 2004 imprisonment of the chief executive of the United Way's Washington, DC, branch after he pled guilty to embezzling nearly $500,000 from donations and the charity's pension fund. (The image and fundraising efforts of this particular charity received another setback over the next two years, when accusations were leaked that the new CEO was receiving overly generous salary increases. The new CFO subsequently resigned because, among other things, she was angered that exaggerated fundraising totals had been publicly reported.)[39] The Nature Conservancy, one of the largest conservation groups in the United States, was the target of a series of stinging criticisms in the *Washington Post* in May 2003. The articles questioned the propriety of property sales made by the organization to its major supporters on favorable terms, its relationship with corporations, and other issues. The Nature Conservancy subsequently admitted it had made errors in judgment and needed more comprehensive executive oversight.[40]

The Senate Finance Committee of the U.S. Congress, having been told by the Internal Revenue Service that abuse by charities and nonprofits of their tax-exempt status was not uncommon and increasing, announced in April 2005 that it would investigate the extent to which these groups were "excessively" compensating their executives and spending on public relations.[41] Later in the year, Senator Charles Grassley, chair of the Finance Committee, began an inquiry into the governance and effectiveness of the saintly Red Cross. He also demanded hundreds of documents from American University, where this author teaches, to shed light on how the oversight function in a tax-exempt, nonprofit institution failed to contain the unusually generous salary and benefits provided the then recently deposed university president.[42]

People with unshakable faith in either the public or private sector as champion of their values and material well-being should consider the fate of whistle-blowers who expose unethical or criminal behavior by their employers. Their commitment to honesty and protecting the public's welfare has not resulted in awards or promotions from admiring companies whose bottom line has been hurt. The usual result is harassment or being fired and finding little demand in the job market for ex-whistle-blowers. That federal agencies exhibit the same high propensity as private enterprise to intimidate and fire those who would air institutional dirty linen is suggested by the U.S. government's having enacted no fewer than thirty-five separate statutes to protect civil servant whistle-blowers.[43] The Clinton Administration felt compelled to issue a presidential directive in 1997 ordering the Justice Department to implement regulations protecting whistle-blowers in the Federal Bureau of Investigation, an organization that one would think is unequivocally committed to truth and honorable behavior. It cannot be assumed that nonprofit NGOs or even charities would take a more enlightened and benevolent stance if one of their own went public with charges of dishonesty or malfeasance after being unable to affect change from within. Rare is the government agency or private sector business or nonprofit organization that places the desire to reveal and halt internal wrongdoings above protecting its public reputation and the jobs of its leaders.

Even with improved supervisory and enforcement measures, human nature is such that there will always be a few people who reach the upper echelons of any organization, even humanitarian and law enforcement groups, who will violate the trust put in them because of urges for self-enrichment and power, a lack of ethics and personal discipline, an out-of-control ego, or terrible personal judgment. As will be suggested in chapter 15, government, the corporate sector, labor unions, and NGOs should all have a voice in setting policies regulating FDI and MNCs; in part this is because they deserve it and in part because that is the most effective way that each can keep a close eye on the others.

Notes

1. John H. Dunning, *Multinational Production and the Multinational Enterprise* (London: George, Allen and Unwin, 1981), pp. 36–37.
2. Ibid., p. 37.
3. Speech to the House of Commons, 1952, as quoted in *Bartlett's Familiar Quotations* (Boston: Little, Brown, 1980), p. 746.
4. Many of these questions are based on issues raised in "The Good Company—A Survey of Corporate Social Responsibility," *The Economist*, January 22, 2005, special section, pp. 6–16.

5. Robert Gilpin, *The Political Economy of International Relations* (Princeton, NJ: Princeton University Press, 1987), pp. 10–11. The author cited Robert Heilbroner, *The Nature and Logic of Capitalism* (New York: Norton, 1985) in connection with the final portion of the block quotation.

6. Neil Hood and Stephen Young, *The Economics of Multinational Enterprise* (London: Longman, 1979), p. 353.

7. As quoted in *The Concise Encyclopedia of Economics,* available online at http://www.econlib.org; accessed March 2005.

8. John Micklethwait and Adrian Wooldridge, *The Company* (New York: Modern Library, 2003), pp. xv, xxi. The authors' praise of the corporation included the following quote attributed to Nicholas Butler: "The limited liability corporation is the greatest single discovery of modern times."

9. Martin Wolf, *Why Globalization Works* (New Haven, CT: Yale University Press, 2004), p. 70.

10. "Anticorruption," available online at http://www.worldbank.org/publicsector/anticorrupt/index.cfm; accessed March 2005.

11. Data source: Web site of Transparency International, http://www.transparency.org; accessed January 2005.

12. Jeffrey Birnbaum, *Washington Post,* May 29, 2006, p. D1.

13. Source: Michael Josephson, "Character Counts," May 12, 2006, available online at http://www.charactercounts.org.

14. James Madison, "The Structure of the Government Must Furnish the Proper Checks and Balances Between the Different Departments," Federalist Paper no. 51, available online at www.constitution.org/fed/federa51.htm; accessed March 2005.

15. Johan Norberg, *In Defense of Global Capitalism* (Washington, DC: Cato Institute, 2003), p. 273.

16. James M. Buchanan, "Politics without Romance: A Sketch of Positive Public Choice Theory and Its Normative Implications," in James Buchanan and Robert Tollison, eds., *The Theory of Public Choice II* (Ann Arbor: University of Michigan Press, 1984), p. 11.

17. The Congressional Research Service counted 13,000 "earmarks" costing a total of $67 billion in the first half of 2006. Source: *New York Times,* May 28, 2006, p. IV 4.

18. See, for example, "Security Loses; Pork Wins," *New York Times,* July 14, 2005, p. A26.

19. Data source: Web site of United for a Fair Economy, http://www.faireconomy.org; accessed March, 2005.

20. *New York Times,* April 3, 2005, p. III 6.

21. Richard Rorty, *Philosophy and Social Hope* (New York: Penguin Books, 1999), p. 233.

22. Noreena Hertz, *The Silent Takeover—Global Capitalism and the Death of Democracy* (London: William Heinemann, 2003), pp. 8, 46.

23. Joel Bakan, *The Corporation—The Pathological Pursuit of Profit and Power* (New York: Free Press, 2004), pp. 1–2, 5, 60.

24. Ibid., p. 166.

25. Joseph E. Stiglitz, *The Roaring Nineties* (New York: Norton, 2003), p. 13.

26. V. I. Lenin, *Imperialism: The Highest Stage of Capitalism* (1916), as quoted in David N. Balaam and Michael Veseth, *Introduction to International Political Economy* (Upper Saddle River, NJ: Prentice Hall, 2001), pp. 68, 77.

27. See, for example, Thomas A. Pugel, *International Economics* (Boston: McGraw-Hill/ Irwin, 2004), pp. 96–98, and Paul R. Krugman and Maurice Obstfeld, *International Economics—Theory and Policy* (Reading, MA: Addison-Wesley, 2000), pp. 125–26.

28. Arie M. Kacowicz, "Regionalization, Globalization, and Nationalism: Convergent, Divergent, or Overlapping?" 1998, available online at http://www.ciaonet.org/wps/ kaa01.index.html; accessed October 2004.

29. Martin Khor, "Globalization and the South: Some Critical Issues," UNCTAD Discussion Paper 147, April 2000, pp. 4, 7, available online at http://www.unctad .org/en/docs/dp_147.en.pdf; accessed September 2004.

30. See, for example, Dani Rodrik, *Has Globalization Gone Too Far?* (Washington, DC: Institute for International Economics, 1997), p. 6.

31. Hertz, *The Silent Takeover*, p. 8.

32. See for example, a story about the poststrike revitalization of Caterpillar Corporation that resulted in a monetary rewards for executives but not for rank-and-file production workers. *Washington Post*, April 19, 2006, p. D1.

33. Rodrik, *Has Globalization Gone Too Far?*, p. 2.

34. William Greider, "The Global Marketplace: A Closet Dictator," in *The Case against Free Trade* (San Francisco: Earth Island Press, 1993), pp. 195, 213.

35. "China's FDI Boom Brings Benefits to Neighbours," *FDi* [sic], February/March, 2005, available online at http//www.fdimagazine.com; accessed January 2006.

36. Stiglitz, *The Roaring Nineties*, p. xii.

37. Ibid., pp. xii–xiii, 318.

38. Khor, "Globalization and the South," p. 51, citing A. Bhaduri and D. Nayyar, *The Intelligent Person's Guide to Liberalization* (New York: Penguin Books, 1996).

39. *Washington Post*, May 22, 2006, p. B1.

40. *Washington Post*, May 4, 5, and 6, 2003; and the Nature Conservancy's Web site, http://www.nature.org/pressroom.

41. *Washington Post*, April 6, 2005, p. E1.

42. He was forced to resign on grounds of excessive and legally questionable expenditures of university funds.

43. Data source: National Whistleblower Center's Web site, http://www.whistleblowers .org/html/nwc_publications.html; accessed March 2005.

PART II

The Strategy of Multinationals

6

WHY COMPANIES
INVEST OVERSEAS

At first glance, the answer to the question implied by the title of this chapter is simple and straightforward: a company establishes value-adding production facilities overseas to increase profits. Because no chief executive has publicly proclaimed that a desire to lose money and court bankruptcy was the reason for his or her firm's engaging in foreign direct investment (FDI), this answer is incontestable. The problem is that it explains only a small part of a big story. It is the truth, but not the whole truth. Profit maximization is too general a concept to provide deep analytical insight into the variety of differentiated motives behind a process as complex as this one.

Given the many variables associated with different kinds of multinational corporations (MNCs) operating in different industrial sectors, following different business strategies, and investing in different host countries, it is naive to expect a single reason to provide a meaningful, comprehensive answer to the question of why all FDIs have taken place year in and year out. Significant differences exist in the motivations behind natural resource, market, efficiency, and asset-seeking direct investments. The situation is further complicated by the fact that in business and economic terms, it is by no means axiomatic that producing overseas is the only, or even the shortest path to profit maximization. Feasible alternatives exist. A better but nondefinitive answer to explain why FDI takes place and why MNCs have proliferated is, predictably, "it depends" on relevant circumstances.

This chapter seeks to provide an appropriate level of disaggregation and detail on the heterogeneous forces behind corporate decisions to establish or purchase overseas subsidiaries. The diversity of the motivations behind this commitment has frustrated academicians' efforts to develop a single all-purpose model to explain and predict the establishment of overseas subsidiaries. Implicit in the analysis that follows is the belief that this is an inevitable and acceptable state of affairs. After an initial examination of how FDI and MNCs relate to general economic theory, the three major academic theories concerning these phenomena are examined. The chapter's third section consists of what is intended as an extensive checklist of real-world reasons for FDI. In some cases, they track theory, but more often they do not. Many of the motivations cited in this section are ignored by mainstream economic theory for a variety of reasons. The fourth and final section uses the automobile industry as a case study in support of the argument that multiple factors served as catalysts for the hundreds of thousands of individual foreign subsidiaries operating today.

Fundamentals of Economic Theory and the FDI Process

In the beginning, economic theorists made no efforts to explain why companies establish overseas subsidiaries. FDI was treated as a nondifferentiated international capital flow, that is, it was generically the same as any other kind of cross-border money movement. MNCs were viewed as being just another variant of capital arbitrage. It was assumed that companies shifted funds from one country to another for the same reason as any bank or individual investor would: to get a higher rate of return than could be obtained in the home country.

FDI has no place in the pure world of neoclassical economic theory. "Perfect" competition is assumed in an environment where "atomistic firms all enjoy equal access to technology and markets, with none large enough to influence inputs or outputs."[1] With perfect international markets (roughly synonymous with the colloquialism "perfectly level playing field") for technology, management, labor skills, components, and other material inputs, national markets would be controlled by local firms. Stated slightly differently, "in a world of perfect competition for goods and factors [land, labor, and capital], direct investment cannot exist."[2] MNCs in the manufacturing and service sectors would be few and far between in view of insurmountable competitive advantages bestowed on indigenous companies relative to carpetbagging foreign competitors. Local businesses would be more familiar with the economic, social, legal, and cultural aspects of the home market, have better political connections, possess closer relationships with wholesalers and retailers, and so on. Foreign companies would have to pay dearly for the insights native business managers either already learned or could find out on a relatively quick and cheap basis.[3] If firms everywhere manufacture essentially similar products and sell them at comparable prices, no company has dominant market power. In a pure textbook world, companies would not grow beyond the size of a single efficient plant and would have negligible problems of logistics and coordination. Any sales to foreign customers would be in the form of exports. The traditional theory of free trade unrealistically assumes that technology and production techniques are open-sourced and available to all.

Trade theorists paid little attention to the forces underlying FDI and MNCs. Their attention was directed to the Heckscher-Ohlin theorem (see chapter 9) whose assumption of perfect competition, constant returns to scale, and so on meant that the issues of ownership, proprietary technology, and corporate size mattered little or not at all. Relative factor endowments of a country were all-important for global economic efficiency. The transfer of manufacturing technology and other corporate assets to production facilities in foreign countries was not considered a "matter requiring analysis."[4]

Academicians could also ignore FDI on the grounds that it was and still is merely one of several options for selling in foreign markets available to nonextractive companies, not a priority business strategy. FDI is absolutely essential only for extractive companies who must conduct business where raw materials are physically located and where climatic conditions are favorable for growing agricultural commodities. In principle, any internationally competitive manufacturing company and companies providing certain services (e.g., education and data transmission, but not hotels) can successfully sell to foreign customers without opening subsidiaries in other countries. Exporting may have long ceased to be the only method of selling abroad, but it is still used to ship trillions of dollars worth of goods and services across national borders every year. Exporting has not lost its ability to allow some companies to increase production in their main manufacturing facility to levels that reduce average per unit production costs to a minimum (see discussion of economies of scale, to follow).

Partnerships of various kinds with local companies are another alternative to FDI as a means of generating profits from foreign markets. Licensing is the most common variant of this strategy. In lieu of the major financial commitment and risks associated with creating foreign subsidiaries, a manufacturer, retail chain, or service company can simply transfer, under predetermined contractual terms, basic know-how to an overseas firm that will then produce and market the good or service. The two main benefits to the foreign company of this option are first, the local licensee's greater knowledge of the domestic business scene and cultural patterns, and second, the licensee uses its own capital to start and operate the new sales effort. If it is successful, royalty fees provide a steady cash flow to the foreign company with no expenses or exposure. If the project should fail, the licensor suffers no out-of-pocket loss. High on the list of disadvantages to licensing is the need to share business secrets, such as proprietary technology, assembly techniques, and marketing strategy, with a potential rival. The RCA Corporation's licensing of its color TV technology to Japanese TV producers in the 1960s is the classic case study of how licensees can reverse teacher–student roles and take major market share away from the original innovator. Other drawbacks for the licensor include ceilings on profits; absence of control over pricing, sales volume targets, and quality control; and uncertainty as to the licensee's level of commitment to the project. These same advantages and disadvantages apply to two other common forms of partnership: joint ventures (consisting of co-ownership of a newly formed corporation) and international strategic alliances in which two corporations agree to specific forms of cooperation but do not create a new business entity (see chapter 4).

It was only in the 1960s that economic theory finally resolved its curious disinterest in the details of a phenomenon clearly growing in size and importance to the international economic order. Sooner or later, economists were going to have to come to grips with the discrepancies between the proliferation of MNCs and what was then a wholly inadequate conceptual framework about what exactly motivates companies to produce in multiple countries. Treating FDI simply as just another form of international capital flow seeking higher returns was a gross oversimplification; the fact that the literature defined higher returns mainly as higher interest rates further undermined the relevance of this concept in explaining direct investments. According to economic theory, capital should flow mainly from capital-intensive countries to capital-poor countries having low capital-output ratios; capital would be more valuable in this environment and garner higher yields. One obvious inconsistency was that the vast majority of U.S. corporate direct investment after World War II was going to relatively capital-abundant, high-labor cost West European countries. In addition, construction of a number of foreign subsidiaries was being financed within the host country; in these cases, no capital flows exited the capital-rich United States. More important, as increasingly sophisticated overseas factories hired and trained well-paid workers to manufacture increasingly high-tech goods and occasionally became one of the host country's largest exporters, the notion that FDI involved nothing more than a simple cross-border transmission of money became progressively untenable.

Even today, mainstream theory suffers from an inadequate degree of disaggregation when analyzing the myriad motivations of corporations to expand overseas. For example, when larger companies build overseas subsidiaries, it may be at the initiative of only one corporate division among many. Hence, a given decision to invest overseas might reflect calculations by specialists wanting to increase their relative contribution to the collective bottom line, and that *might* differ from the calculus of a company-wide decision.

FDI flows represent an extraordinary package of corporate physical resources and intellectual property—the source of both praise and condemnation. The opening of foreign subsidiaries poses potential short- and medium-term risks and prospective long-term benefits to host and home countries as well as to the companies involved. Transfers of manufacturing from one country to another raise the specter, among other things, of lost jobs in home countries and diminished sovereignty in host countries. FDI also holds out the promise of access to well-paid jobs, technologies, and management systems that otherwise would be beyond the reach of some host countries. The widening gap between the growing importance of MNCs and the static understanding of their effects created a pressing need by the 1960s to examine the more "qualitative attributes" and impact of MNC activity in host countries, namely, their sectoral distribution and technological content, along with the nature of the linkages to the local economy.[5]

A Survey of the Major Academic Theories

The academic literature dealing with the twin questions of why FDI takes place and how companies can successfully produce goods and services in distant and unfamiliar foreign environments is dominated by three theories.[6] How well they succeed in explaining these things is a value judgment.

It was not until the 1960s that the innovative ideas of Stephen Hymer provided the first meaningful insights into the theoretical underpinnings of FDI and MNCs. He was the first to expound on how these companies were different from purely domestic enterprises and why nonextractive companies could successfully compete in foreign countries, a task fraught with dangers and problems. The revolution in thinking in fact emerged as a slow evolution; Hymer's groundbreaking doctoral dissertation completed in 1960 made no immediate impact and was not published until 1976.[7] He dismissed as irrelevant the generic theory of differential returns on capital to explain FDI. In its place, he used industrial organization theory to explicitly outline for the first time why success in operating overseas subsidiaries was contingent on parent companies possessing advantages that overrode the daunting and costly process of producing goods and services in distant, perhaps inscrutable business environments.

Hymer's core thesis begins with the assumption that companies are motivated to move overseas as a second stage of efforts to maximize profits, "rent" in economic terms, derived from their monopolistic control over what they produce. However, management could project a comfortable profit margin from overseas production only if the company enjoyed an adequate mix of product innovation, low production costs, managerial excellence, or marketing advantages unique to the company and not easily duplicated by competitors. The now-familiar concept of *ownership advantage* (also called firm-specific advantage) had been born. Before opening a foreign subsidiary, Hymer said, management needed to make two specific determinations. The first is that ownership advantages were sufficient to outweigh the disadvantages and risks incurred when competing head to head with foreign companies on their home turf (as opposed to exporting or licensing deals).[8] Later theorists provided a list of specific ownership advantages: cutting-edge technology; superiority in management, production, marketing, and distribution know-how; advanced organizational techniques and information management capabilities; sufficient size to ensure economies of scale in production and maximum advertising; and the ability to parlay a blue chip credit rating into lower cost financing. The second requisite determination is that direct investment will produce better long-term results for the company than exporting, licensing, or joint ventures.

A second core assumption of Hymer's theory, initially disseminated by well-known economist Charles Kindleberger, is that ownership advantage works on a global basis only in the absence of perfect competition and perfect markets. (These concepts allude to the increasingly rare situation in which companies compete on a totally equal footing.) For FDI to thrive, there must be some imperfection in markets for goods or factors such as technology differentials or some interference in market competition by government or by firms.[9] Business practices causing market imperfections include technological exclusivity protected by patents, superior managerial and marketing know-how, product specialization (differentiation), collusion on pricing, and preferential access to borrowed capital. Governmental policies such as tariffs, quotas, and subsidies to favored industries constitute a second category of market failure.

Economies of scale is, in economic theory terms, a market imperfection that has become a critical applied factor leaving essentially all large producers of capital-intensive, high value-added goods no other option than to produce and market on a multinational basis. The theorists of Ricardo's day lived at a time when entrepreneurs could start and maintain a cloth or wine business for a minute fraction of the cost of starting and growing a high-tech company in the twenty-first century. The Heckscher-Ohlin theorem's assumption of constant returns to scale in measuring a country's relative competitiveness is completely at odds with the absolute requirement for today's advanced technology companies to achieve increasing returns to scale. Size matters in amortizing (spreading) fixed costs which consist mainly of R&D, factory preparation, and worker training. In all cases, these are expenses that a company incurs before it makes the first sale of a new product—assuming that massive R&D expenditures did in fact produce a commercially viable product. More than $3 billion is now required to develop a new generation of semiconductor chip and build and equip one factory for producing it.

Fixed costs, which must be recovered if a company is to maintain long-term financial health, remain the same (i.e., they are fixed) no matter how low or high the ensuing volume of sales. Selling limited numbers of new chips after a multibillion-dollar investment would impose either a prohibitively high price tag on each unit offered for sale or a crushing financial burden on the producer.[10] Conversely, maintaining the largest possible sales base, which is planet Earth, could help keep per unit costs to a minimum. Maximum volume equates to multinational marketing strategies. No single national market is large enough to allow for scale economies in the contemporary high-tech sector. The drive for maximum sales volume relative to current and potential competitors explains why it is de rigueur for the strategies of aggressive high-tech companies to maintain production and marketing operations in the consumer-rich Triad (Western Europe, Japan/East Asia, and the United States).

Much FDI now gravitates to high-tech business sectors where major competitors are so few in number that the market can be characterized as oligopolistic or even monopolistic. The pharmaceutical industry epitomizes this kind of market. Seeking to recoup an estimated $800 million in development and clinical test costs now needed to bring the average new medicine to market,[11] drug companies jealously protect their intellectual property and maximize their sales base. New market entrants are obviously limited by the extraordinary costs involved. The end result is that successful innovators possess a temporary global monopoly on products that in some cases generate billions of dollars in annual sales. Unsurprisingly, pharmaceuticals is an industry dominated by a relatively few, very large MNCs, many of which have grown in size through cross-border mergers. These companies are worldwide price makers, not passive price takers. Conversely, perfect competition exists in the novelty T-shirt industry. Unlimited new entrants are possible in a low-overhead business with simple technology, limited production runs sold by street vendors or small retailers, intellectual property consisting of a small design or a few cleverly chosen words, absence of government interference, and so on. These characteristics explain why there is no public record of a major MNC in the specialized T-shirt sector.

The related concepts of oligopoly and corporate size led Hymer to a theme that attributes sinister traits to MNCs. His later writings emphasized the Marxist principle that private corporations are inexorably driven by the *law of increasing size*. Executives were presumed to believe that steady increases in profits can come only through constant expansion, first domestically and then, after market saturation occurs, globally. A second Marxist tenet in Hymer's theory is the *law of uneven development*. It predicted that the size, mobility, and monopolistic power of MNCs maturing in the industrialized countries of the North would bestow these companies with sufficient economic power to control and exploit the whole world to their own financial advantage.[12] The implication of this thesis is that globalization of production is more a malevolent effort to expand corporate power over prices and preempt the entry of new competitors than a benevolent response to competition and a laudable quest for efficiency. The result, said Hymer, would be a hierarchal world economy literally separated into two hemispheres where above-average national affluence and influence would be determined by whether a country was a headquarters country to powerful MNCs. Host countries would have relatively little wealth or power. The North would grow richer, and the South would struggle under the burden of structural poverty, ostensibly all in the name of a more efficient utilization of the world's resources.

The second widely heralded academic explanation of why manufacturing companies chose to become MNCs is the *product life-cycle theory* of Raymond Vernon. First advanced in the mid-1960s, it emanated from the premise that the United States possessed a comparative advantage in product innovation; the theory therefore focused on the experiences of American companies in that time period. Vernon's core thesis was that products and production processes move through a three-stage cycle culminating in the need to invest overseas. (A tangible frame of reference for the conceptual description to follow is the competition dynamics that followed Xerox's introduction in the 1960s of the modern photocopying machine.) During the first phase, the one immediately following innovation and initial sales, the product is produced in limited amounts—the ultimate market potential and optimal assembly techniques are still unknowns— by skilled labor at relatively high costs. Retail price is of limited importance at this point due to the innovator's initial monopoly, the product's novelty and limited supply, and the relatively price-inelastic demand of initial users. Manufacturing at this stage is confined to the company's home base. Foreign sales initially are handled through exporting.

The second phase of Vernon's cycle is product maturation. The key change here is the start of sustained downward pressures on price. Imitators begin producing their own versions of the innovation, some of which will have more features and/or lower prices. Competition forces the innovator to improve its original product and trim costs. Consumers begin to comparison shop and become cost-conscious. Price reductions are facilitated by declining costs brought about by the product's being mass produced by better designed machinery and by the learning curve's effect: a more efficient assembly line operation. In this intermediate stage, an export surge has caused some countries to pressure the major foreign exporter(s) to produce locally. Somewhere in the transition between the second and third cycles, the innovating company and some of its major competitors determine that market-seeking and market-protecting FDI is necessary to replace sole reliance on exports. The latter no longer appear capable of protecting existing overseas market shares or allowing for expansion. At the time Vernon first articulated this theory, American wages were the world's highest, so investments in any other country presumably meant lower labor costs.

Product standardization represents the final stage. The technology to produce the product has reached its zenith, no major design or production changes are anticipated. Engineers and scientists are no longer tweaking the product or the assembly process. Less skilled workers far from headquarters can now be trained on a one-time basis and put to work on the assembly line. The product has become a commodity (like an analog television set), where price is a more important selling point than the name of the company making it. Market-seeking FDI is gradually replaced by efficiency-seeking FDI in relatively low-cost, low-wage countries where subsidiaries are designated as export platforms. Some of their exports may be destined for the home market where production of the now standardized product is being phased out in favor of manufacturing newly developed goods.

Most scholars have concluded that the product cycle theory itself has passed through a life cycle and descended into obsolescence. It was a good guide to and predictor of MNC strategy from the 1950s until the early 1970s when a lot of FDI took the form of American manufacturing companies setting up overseas subsidiaries to produce goods becoming susceptible to price competition. However, the theory does not explain most of the more recent developments that have introduced major alterations and additions to the FDI process. These include increased numbers of mergers and acquisitions, vertical FDI where companies produce components in a number of countries for final assembly elsewhere, and the growing numbers of companies, including those based in LDCs, engaging in market-seeking FDI in countries with higher labor costs than those in their home countries.

The *eclectic paradigm* introduced by John H. Dunning is an amalgam of three separate explanations of why overseas subsidiaries are established. His approach incorporates the theory of industrial organization (how a company can achieve competitive advantage over other firms); the theory of the firm (why does a company choose one organizational mode over another to create, use, and enhance its competitive advantages, the so-called transactions cost perspective); and the theory of location (to explain how firms choose where to locate overseas value-adding activities). The end result is a broad framework asserting that at any given moment, the "extent, ownership, and pattern" of MNC activity depends on the configuration of three variables/conditions being satisfied.[13] The requisite preconditions for management determining that overseas production is the best business strategy are commonly abbreviated as the O, I, and L advantages.

Ownership advantages are intellectual property and other intangible assets exclusive to a firm that can be transferred in full from the home country to overseas facilities. They include products and manufacturing processes protected by patents, trademarks, copyrights, and trade secrets; superior marketing and organizational skills; and the advantages of "common governance." The latter, according to Dunning, consists of size and established reputation of a company that affords it favored access to labor, natural resources, finance, and other inputs; economies of joint purchases by worldwide subsidiaries; and so on. Ownership advantages, whatever their exact mix, must provide a company with market power and/or cost advantages sufficient to outweigh the costs of setting up one or more subsidiaries in foreign countries and the burdens of succeeding there.

An *internalization advantage* exists when management determines its ownership advantages are sufficiently formidable or sufficiently sensitive that it does not need to rely on sources external to the company or should not risk sharing proprietary assets. In such cases, licensing assets to another company or sharing them in a joint venture arrangement are ruled out. Ownership advantages are best exploited internally within the company. Sales and profits presumably are maximized by retaining sole control of foreign production.

Assuming the first two conditions are satisfied, a company will opt to build and operate its own subsidiaries abroad if it also determines the existence of *location-specific advantages.* When existing in sufficient magnitude, these advantages designate a foreign country as the production site most likely to maximize profits from overseas sales. Location advantages can exist in the form of such simple market imperfections as import barriers that rule out exporting, prohibitive transportation costs, or overly long shipping times. In addition, they can take the form of pull factors like cheap real estate and labor, financial incentives for incoming FDI, and abundant endowments of key natural resources.

The three main theories are not the final word on corporate motivations to become multinational. Dunning suggested that a changing world economy had somewhat left behind the ideas of Hymer and Vernon (e.g., foreign trade barriers were reduced considerably since the early 1970s). They were "scholars of their time, and their explanations were strongly contextual. Both tended to deal with first-phase—rather than sequential—U.S. direct investment." Similar limitations, he added applied to the other FDI theories put forward in the 1960s and 1970s.[14] Above and beyond the limitations of the academic theories advanced is the fact that they overlook several relatively simple and specific business strategies. A second line of analysis as to why firms invest abroad is therefore necessary. The applied, real-world reasons are the subject of the next section.

Real-World Motivations for Direct Investments

If something works in practice, it is unclear how important it is that it also works in theory. The emphasis in this study on the heterogeneous nature and effects of FDI and MNCs is inconsistent with the premise that three thirty- to forty-year-old theories can provide a complete understanding of why these phenomena take place and why their growth has accelerated since the 1980s. For a number of reasons, the theories are insufficiently disaggregated and too limited in scope to do justice to the diversity of FDI and MNCs. They implicitly assume that firms in traditional manufacturing sectors (like chemicals and office equipment) represent a more or less standardized form of MNC. Even if this had been a reasonable assumption in the 1970s, it clearly is no longer valid today. And even if new forms of MNCs were not constantly evolving, a single theory of why FDI occurs is unlikely to be applicable to all foreign-owned subsidiaries, regardless of their product, business objective, size, mindsets of senior management, and so on. It cannot be taken for granted that corporate decisions to invest overseas are so consistent and coherent that as a group that they can be blended into a comprehensive economic model.

Another error of commission is the naive assumption of conventional theories that a decision to invest abroad is always a rational end result of meticulous research and coldly objective calculations of risk/reward trade-offs. Decisions to build foreign subsidiaries ultimately are based on the perceptions of a small group of senior managers, not a scientific formula. Sometimes these perceptions are formed under unique circumstances that follow no previous script. On occasion, the commitment to expand overseas might be the result of an impulse by a strong-willed executive, for example, a new subsidiary opened by an arch-competitor cannot go unanswered. Dunning, one of the giants of FDI theory, believes that "it is not possible to formulate a single operationally testable theory that can explain all forms of foreign-owned production any more than it is possible to construct a generalized theory to explain all forms of trade or the behavior of all kinds of firms."[15] In a literal sense, that overstates the case. All FDI technically can be explained by the single postulation that a judgment has been made, for any one of a variety of reasons, that a new foreign subsidiary eventually will positively contribute the parent company's bottom-line performance. This explanation, however, is so broadly constructed that the insight it provides is somewhere between irrelevant and useless.

The ability of the major academic theories on FDI to illuminate is further diminished by serious omissions. A few very basic business strategies and objectives are missing entirely, possibly a reflection of the paucity of social science academicians who have worked as managers in an MNC. In addition, minimal attention has been given to several major changes in business economics that have added new motivations for corporations to expand overseas. Textbook theory arguably has not kept full pace with changes in the international marketplace.

Relatively simple real-world explanations are therefore necessary to supplement the purported substantive shortcomings of basic academic theories. A second round of answers to the why question is also necessitated by the author's belief that much of traditional theory is written in an overly arcane manner; many of the specific inspirations behind the opening of foreign subsidiaries are relatively simple and concise. In the interest of brevity, the various real-world explanations of FDI are presented in the form of an annotated list divided into five classifications with, unavoidably, occasional overlaps.

Marketing 101 Strategies

There are very basic reasons why companies find FDI to be attractive. Economists tend to ignore the simple fact that corporate executives of countless companies see overseas expansion as an essential part of meeting the relentless demand from shareholders for growth. Increased sales and profits can come disproportionately from foreign subsidiaries because the domestic market where the company started may be saturated and because the rest of the world always contains more potential consumers than the home country.

Economic policy throughout history has focused on the core dilemma of trying to satisfy infinite demand with limited resources. It was not until late in the twentieth century that overcapacity and market saturation became a reality for some of the goods (e.g., steel, cars, and fiber-optic cable) and some of the services produced in the industrialized countries. Expansion overseas became the only feasible expansion route for companies so affected. Speaking more broadly, FDI for many successfully established companies represents the greatest opportunity for growth of sales and profits. Diminishing opportunity to expand in its home market was the deciding factor for McDonald's bold commitment many years ago to a global presence. One of the early architects of the restaurant chain's growth strategy explained that having ruled out diversification into other business activities, the only growth path for the company "was to do what no American retailer had ever done—successfully expand its service worldwide. . . . The rationale for going international was as simple as determining that the market was there."[16] Validation of this strategy is visible in the 66 percent of the company's total revenues of $20.5 billion in 2005 that came from its nearly 32,000 owned and franchised restaurants in more than 110 countries outside the United States.[17] Decades later, Starbucks is following the same growth strategy and finding the same favorable foreign reception to a "fun" product representative of the American lifestyle.

Citigroup, one of the world's largest diversified financial institutions, believes it has "largely accomplished the strategic build-out in the U.S., and [is] now ready to project our products and services globally." With the maturity of the consumer-finance market and credit card saturation in the United States, Citigroup's goal over the next decade is to increase the contribution of non–North American earnings to total earnings from an already respectable one-third to one-half.[18]

The second most common fundamental reason for manufacturing companies to invest overseas is the frequent assessment that it is essential to protecting and expanding an existing export market or to developing a new overseas market. Overseas manufacturing sites can reduce production costs and delivery times; they can also tailor products to local tastes and needs and respond more quickly to changes in consumers' preferences. The cell phone is a product that epitomizes a constant progression of new models with additional features geared to pleasing localized tastes, characteristics not conducive to exclusive reliance on exporting. "Make it where you sell it" has become a mantra among business executives, chanted so often that it is now accepted as a rule of business strategy. Being an insider is increasingly perceived as being critical to sales success in major markets around the world.[19] An executive from Intel, a true high-tech global titan, told a congressional committee that "to optimize global competitiveness, it is important to locate manufacturing and other facilities around the world."[20] The claim has to be taken on faith because he provided no explanation why this is so.

The constant of change in international business has added new wrinkles to the traditional goal of going overseas to lower production costs. "The China price" as an incentive to engage in FDI is an increasingly important variable. It occurs when an American or European supplier of manufactured goods is warned by important customers that they will go elsewhere if the company fails to match the significantly lower prices offered by China-based companies. Unable to do so from their factories in high-wage countries, the most feasible alternative to a potentially serious loss of business is to establish their own subsidiaries in the low-cost manufacturer, China.[21] India, China's neighbor to the south, has taken the lead in convincing American and European companies that for competitive reasons, they should set up foreign subsidiaries to engage in a variety of service sector activities. Offshoring (see chapters 4 and 13) was created and is sustained by the combination of lower salaries abroad for skilled service workers and the growing speed, sophistication, and efficiency of international telecommunications links.

As stated in the location theory discussed earlier, tariff jumping is a classic reason for companies to produce in foreign markets; tariffs literally are taxes designed to reduce or eliminate the price advantages of imported goods. In some cases, quotas or other prohibitive nontariff barriers leave foreign companies no alternative to FDI as a means of gaining market access for high volume sales. One of the most important impetuses for the surge in FDI in EU countries by U.S. companies that began in the 1960s was the widespread perception that their top foreign market would best be protected by avoiding the newly instituted Common External Tariff applied to goods from nonmember countries. The "voluntary" export restraints on textiles and clothing that many developing countries were pressured by industrialized countries to administer from the 1970s through 2004 encouraged direct investments in less developed countries (LDCs) that had not signed such an agreement. The loophole gambit explains why Chinese textile and apparel companies opened subsidiaries in Cambodia and Nigeria, two low-wage countries that did not agree to annual export quotas to the United States and the EU.[22]

Efficiency-seeking direct investments are pursued for cost-cutting purposes and are not designed to sell their output in the host country. Being export-oriented, they search for and invest in relatively low-cost labor in countries having efficient economic systems and accommodating political environments.

Finally, to repeat, companies in the primary sector are forced to seek out multiple overseas sources of minerals and oil resources since few exist in adequate supply in just one country.

Finesse Marketing Strategies

Generalized offensive and defensive efforts to preserve and grow foreign markets comprise only the outer, highly visible layer of MNCs' marketing strategies. Companies seriously committed to sales growth in foreign markets tend to have more subtle and sophisticated objectives and tactics that go beyond reducing costs or circumventing import barriers. Ambitious overseas sales targets often inspire efforts to display deep roots in the local market. Finesse marketing strategies were described in a letter to shareholders by the chairman of General Electric. It said economic reality "requires us to view the world as our market." However, the company's overseas growth strategy "requires more than simply shipping products. You must be equally committed to developing capabilities and relationships in the markets where you want to succeed."[23]

Practitioners of finesse marketing strategies cultivate the image of a company that is an integral part of the local landscape, a business with deep ties to the host country, a benefactor to its economy, and a philanthropist for local causes. One author suggested that IBM's decisions to construct overseas subsidiaries during the three decades beginning in the late 1960s were not primarily determined by the quest for cost efficiencies. Instead, the company allegedly selected locations mainly "to limit imbalances in its trade between its main markets and to ensure that in most markets it was a big employer as well as a big seller. Why? Because IBM felt it had to keep relationships with governments friendly. It needed to avoid regulatory attacks on its market dominance."[24]

Risk diversification is accomplished by geographical dispersion of production facilities to hedge against unforeseen events, such as labor strikes, natural disasters, unfavorable changes in legislation and regulatory procedures, and plant fires or sabotage. Desire to hedge against risk would seem to be an important motive for Intel's commitment to overseas operations. Although preferring FDI to having to worry about new trade barriers in key markets like the EU and

BOX 6.1 Toyota's Americanization Strategy

Toyota has literally become too successful selling cars in the United States to rely solely on exports to service the market. After Japan was unceremoniously advised by the Reagan administration and Congress in 1981 that rapidly rising exports of Japanese cars to the U.S. market had become disruptive and excessive, Toyota accepted the fact that its ambitious plans to expand sales and market share required a major manufacturing presence within the United States. Good product is not enough. To nurture its steadily growing U.S. sales (about 2.2 million cars and trucks in 2005) and market share (exceeding 13 percent in 2005 and poised to overtake Daimler-Chrysler for third place in the U.S. market), Toyota Motor Sales, U.S.A., is actively cultivating the image of a domestic automobile producer and a de facto American company. Many statistics are quoted in this effort. Cumulative direct investment in the United States in 2005 was approaching $14 billion, and purchases of parts and goods and services from U.S.-based companies (linkage personified) were $25 billion annually. Full-page advertisements appearing in many American magazines emphasized that the company's ten vehicle manufacturing and assembly plants; marketing, research, and design facilities; suppliers; and dealers accounted for more than 386,000 jobs in the United States.* Toyota's "American-ness" strategy centers on producing domestically more than 60 percent of the vehicles (including Lexus) that it sells in the United States.** Data on the company's Web site confirm that roughly 60 percent of total U.S. vehicle sales in 2004 were domestically produced.

As the result of extensive and still growing manufacturing presence in the United States, the president of Toyota Motor Corporation proclaimed in a speech that it could keep growing in the U.S. market without arousing "trade or political friction."***

*Data source for Toyota's U.S. FDI: http://www.toyota.com and http://www.toyota.com/about/usa/usdata/by_numbers.html; accessed December 2005.
**Wall Street Journal, November 12, 2005, p. A3.
***Fujio Cho, as quoted in the Dollar Morning News, January 12, 2005, Web site of the American International Automobile Dealers Association: http://www.aiadalists.org/default.asp; accessed November 2005.

anxious to discourage its competitors from establishing lucrative overseas subsidiaries, it still retains a picture-perfect profile of a company presumably able to prosper by manufacturing, assembling, and testing its main product, microprocessors, exclusively within the United States. It does not seem urgently in need of foreign plants. With an estimated 80 percent share of worldwide unit sales of mass market microprocessors and a 90 percent share by revenue,[25] Intel is a global oligopolist and is considered by some to have monopolistic power. It manufactures a capital-intensive, physically lightweight product that can be cheaply air-freighted overnight anywhere in the world. Production workers are a relatively small factor in its total cost of doing business.

A separate set of motives fits under the rubric of outmaneuvering or matching the international moves of your competition and having to choose between being the leader and following the leader. The advantage of being first to market either in geographic or product terms is one of the oldest business stratagems. Being the first to establish brand identity, distribution networks, and retail outlets often allows the first mover to permanently stay one step ahead of competitors. The latter then find themselves engaged in a second-best situation of playing catch-up and having lower market shares. A large and efficient market-seeking subsidiary in a medium-sized economy might well limit competition by creating disincentives for any further foreign entrants. Companies deprived of the FDI option in such a market may be forced to suffer the third-best practice of ceding a lucrative foreign market to a competitor, something archrivals like Coca-Cola and Pepsi are especially loathe to do.

Yet another foreign investment motivation related to head-to-head competition is building a subsidiary to launch a full-scale marketing effort in a major competitor's home market. The objective of this strategy is to force the competitor to lower prices and profit margins to protect its home turf and ideally distract the competitor's attention away from sales efforts in the first company's home market.[26] Lincoln Electric Company, a successful American-based manufacturer of arc welders, watched with increasing discomfort in the 1980s as ESAB, a Swedish company it considered to be its only real competitive threat, began acquiring European arc welder manufacturers. Concerned that ESAB was planning to establish a fortress on its home ground and then attack the U.S. market, Lincoln took preemptive action. In a relatively short time, it expanded from five plants in four countries to twenty-one plants in fifteen countries, mostly in Europe.[27]

Post-Theory Innovations in MNCs

Beginning with banks, a growing number of companies in the services sector became MNCs, not so much for O, I, or L reasons as the perceived need to follow and serve their important home market clients who were building major manufacturing facilities overseas. Companies providing accounting, legal, advertising, and public relations services began establishing a worldwide presence in the late 1970s, mainly in response to the overseas initiatives of their major clients. An often overlooked service industry that has become prominent in FDI is wholesale distribution subsidiaries established to expedite sales of exports from the parent company, goods made by local subsidiaries, or both.

Internet companies and cable TV networks present a new business model, one that can operate multinationally with little more than secure servers and a satellite link. They can sell their services to literally billions of potential new customers for a nominal capital outlay, the result being a very favorable leveraging of capital.

BOX 6.2 Why Did eBay Feel the Need to Become a Multinational?

eBay provides a Web site that users can access from any Internet-connected computer in the world. The servers that support the platform enabling electronic buying and selling of merchandise around the world are located at its headquarters in California. From a technical point of view, overseas subsidiaries are unnecessary for this company to conduct its business on a global basis. Location has a different connotation in cyberspace. But the potential rewards of doing business on a global basis are the same for all companies. Non-U.S. revenue has been growing much faster than eBay's home country revenue, and in 2004 overseas transactions revenues accounted for more than 40 percent of total corporate income. Given the company's relatively young, still-expanding international operations (including China), the overseas share of income could eventually rise above 70 percent.

The corporate strategy to establish wholly owned overseas subsidiaries to provide country-specific Web sites is based overwhelmingly on marketing considerations. (The demand by some governments that it have a locally domiciled business operation is a secondary reason.) The assumption is that revenue growth and the introduction of new services outside the United States cannot be maximized by having Americans living in California running an evolving "people" business still in its infancy. Foreign subsidiaries are managed by nationals of the host countries who understand the pulse of the local Internet market. Local nationals are presumed to be in the best position to gauge current needs and evolving desires of the individuals and companies who are buying and selling merchandise on eBay's overseas Web sites. They also are presumed best qualified to know how to structure and advertise each site to attract a maximum number of customers. If the company's larger task is bringing buyers and sellers together, a geographically decentralized organization makes sense for reasons that include understanding cultural nuances; creating local language Web sites and responding in the local language to customers' questions and complaints about unfilled orders or nonpayments; and acting on customers' requests for new services (e.g., fixed price sites and the ability to reconfigure the Web site's welcome page). In sum, the company believes steady increases in revenue and market share are best assured by giving people in different countries exactly what they want and need on their local eBay site—things not best recognized from headquarters.

The company's overseas subsidiaries are not factories or even repositories of high-tech equipment. Instead, they consist of twenty to sixty office workers, almost all of whom are local hires. They include a country manager, a marketing team, and financial and legal specialists. The company's strategy for wholly or majority-owned foreign subsidiaries (twenty-three in 2005) is to hire talented people, give them the resources they need, and hold them accountable for servicing the needs of customers and increasing revenues in their country of responsibility.

Sources: Telephone interview with Matt Bannick, president of eBay International, September 2005, and eBay's 2005 Form 10-K, available online at http://www.ebay.com.

Companies like Yahoo!, Google, and eBay have established relatively spartan value-added facilities overseas; they have no need to erect $2 billion factories like their counterparts who produce semiconductors. Nor do their overseas facilities require a large workforce. Another compelling reason for these companies to become multinationals is the utility of communicating with customers in the local language and in a format compatible with local tastes.

For defense contractors, a local manufacturing presence may be a legal requirement to actively sell in foreign markets. With European defense budgets relatively stagnant, some of Europe's largest defense contractors have become enamored with gaining a toehold in the fast-growing, mega-billion-dollar U.S. market for military procurement. But before being eligible to secure a major U.S. government defense contract bid, a foreign-based company needs to manufacture or at least assemble weapons and equipment in a U.S.-based subsidiary. For national security reasons, the Pentagon does not import major purchases of military matériel. A prime example of this kind of FDI motivation is BAE Systems of Great Britain. Its aggressive contract bidding and facilities and offices in thirty states allowed it to move into the ranks of the top ten Pentagon contractors in dollar terms.[28]

Post-Theory Changes in the International Economic Order

The international monetary system in general and sustained exchange rate swings in particular were not major issues to the first generation of MNC theorists. What few exchange rate changes took place under the Bretton Woods system of fixed exchange rates were almost all currency depreciations needed to offset a country's declining competitiveness. The advent of a floating exchange rate regime in 1973 meant that chronic surplus countries might—and some did—experience chronic appreciation of their currencies, a move that, all things held constant, makes their exports more expensive to foreigners. Anticipation of a continuing erosion in price competitiveness from large-scale yen appreciation (and rising labor costs) lead to unprecedented flows in the early 1980s of outward FDI by Japanese manufacturing companies. Cost-containment efforts centered on off-shore production of components and labor-intensive finished goods in relatively low-cost Southeast Asian countries with currencies unlikely to appreciate. After the follow-the-leader syndrome kicked in, the magnitude of the FDI exodus was so large that fears of an impending hollowing out of the Japanese industrial sector were heard with increased frequency. Should the Chinese yuan ever face prolonged appreciation, Chinese manufacturing companies might someday need to duplicate the Japanese strategy of containing costs by establishing a massive sourcing operation in low wage Asian and African economies with weak currencies.

Another source of structural change in the international economic and business environment affecting FDI was the information technology revolution that began in the United States in the early 1990s. One immediate effect was an upsurge in strategic asset–seeking direct investment in the United States. Foreign companies, mainly European, were responsible for record amounts of acquisitions and mergers with U.S. companies, often those possessing advanced technology or proven marketing prowess. Much of the buying of American companies was attributed to the desire by foreign firms to offset their own shortcomings, and some was motivated by the growing conventional wisdom that a major presence in the vast U.S. market was the sine qua non of corporate success and staying power. This merger and acquisition (M&A) boom cannot be explained by the theories of monopolistic designs and the product cycle or by the eclectic paradigm. When asked why his relatively small software company had made two U.S. acquisitions, a French executive said that being part of the "Silicon Valley world" was the major reason. An innovative European software firm "cannot become a global player without being strong in the U.S. market. It puts you in a situation to understand the market and have relationships with suppliers," he said.[29] An executive of a small Austrian software company used similar phraseology to explain his company's opening of a southern California subsidiary: the necessity to tap into informal networks and to be close both to distributors and customers and, equally important, to develop a feeling for the market. The "positive image" the company would project by operating in California also was a factor in the final decision to invest there.[30]

The size and growth of the U.S. and Chinese markets have made these countries the main destinations for foreign companies using FDI as a stimulus to sales and profits. Consider the financial reports on two companies issued by the brokerage arm of Morgan Stanley. Analyzing the growth and profit outlook for Yum! Brands, a multibrand restaurant chain (Pizza Hut, KFC, and Taco Bell, among others), a 2004 report described the "international market as the core growth engine" for the company. While this market contributed 35 percent of the company's profits at that time, Morgan Stanley's analyst estimated that overseas restaurants would deliver 60 percent of the growth in earnings over the next three years.[31] All but ignoring the U.S. market, another Morgan Stanley report on Yum! Brands concluded that the company's first mover advantage in China, its significant potential for expansion in that populous country, and strong acceptance by Chinese consumers are "primary reasons to own the stock in our view." Between 2005 and 2008, the estimate was that "China alone will contribute 35 percent of Yum's earnings growth."[32] A similar growth scenario was given for the payments services of Western Union. China was projected as the key growth driver of the company on the basis that in the second half of 2004, its business in China was "growing at a rate in excess of 100%."[33]

China is the source of another new variant of perceived need to establish overseas subsidiaries. The Phoenix Electric Manufacturing Company, a medium-sized producer of electric motors for power tools, kitchen appliances, and other products, opened a second subsidiary in China in 2005. The strategy was "a matter of survival" because the company's customer base has been moving there, explained its chairperson. Many of its biggest clients had shifted most of their consumer electronics production to China to cut costs.[34] Proximity of Phoenix's subsidiaries to its customers' Chinese subsidiaries preserved a critical portion of its business.

Regional free trade agreements are a major catalyst of FDI not given sufficient attention by the main academic theories on MNCs. The early success of what is now called the European Union encouraged two international economic trends. The first was the subsequent decision by every major trading country to pursue economic benefits through free trade with neighboring countries. The contemporary surge in regional free trade areas is measured by the existence in 2003 of more than 265 agreements, more than half of which had been created after 1995.[35] Second, the proliferation of these agreements has encouraged direct investments by foreign companies establishing a subsidiary in one member country to take advantage of unrestricted market access to all other members. This strategy is the number one reason for the attractiveness of Ireland to most foreign companies; it is also the number one reason for the above-trend growth of FDI in Mexico as soon as a free trade agreement with the United States appeared to be in the offing.

Two recent events in the international economic order had the effect of making acquisitions of existing corporations in the South uncommonly appealing to financially strong companies in the North. Privatization of government-owned enterprises in LDCs and former communist countries provided a one-time opportunity for well-managed foreign companies to buy potentially valuable assets at relatively low prices. Later, the financial crisis that hit much of East Asia in the late 1990s pushed many companies in Korea, Indonesia, and Thailand into de facto bankruptcy, making them available to foreign rescuers at what some called fire sale prices.

A new pragmatic reason to invest overseas is the growing concern about the international security of supply for oil and other critical commodities. The anxiety over the issue of control is keenly felt in China. Hence the official policy encouraging a growing number of Chinese corporate acquisitions of and bids for foreign-based natural resources companies whose output would help feed the country's voracious appetite for industrial raw materials (see box 8.1 in chapter 8).

"Thinking outside the Box" Motivations

Academic theory does not openly pay attention to the possibility that executives may approve opening a foreign subsidiary based on faulty assumptions or pressure to conform to a current management fad. The "make it where you sell it" strategy has taken on a life of its own. Although appealing in principle, it has not categorically been proven to be necessary, in part due to the impossibility of knowing the consequences of a subsidiary's *not* being established. A knee-jerk presumption that to ignore this guideline is to suffer diminished market share may sometimes be a substitute for hard data making an overwhelming case for FDI over exporting or licensing. Gut feelings can substitute for hard-nosed demonstrations of ownership, internalization, and location advantages. Exaggerated fears about the need to grow and to match the overseas moves of competitors appear to have been the motivating force to invest overseas in more than a few cases, one of which was automobiles in the 1990s (see following discussion). "An unsettling possibility is that foreign direct investment may to some extent reflect irrational follow-the-leader behavior." It might prove to be a temporary business fad like the overdone acquisitions and leveraged buyout craze that had a limited life span in the United States during the 1980s.[36] The ambivalence associated with conventional wisdom is evident in the following passage from an analysis by McKinsey and Company, a business consultancy:

> Most investors and executives want a piece of the booming Asian market for the right reasons.... And for many sectors, such as high technology and manufacturing, the advantages of going to Asia, particularly China, have so changed the competitive dynamics that there's little choice but to join the rush.
>
> But the decision to go to Asia can be unsound as well. Many executives who invest in China or India believe that these markets will suddenly kick-start stalled growth at home, reviving their companies' sagging prospects. On that score, we think caution is in order...the returns from investment in Asia just aren't going to be that large—at least over the next decade.[37]

On a personal note, I still remember what a friend who worked for a lobbying group representing a number of large MNCs said to me back in the 1970s. He was convinced that some major overseas subsidiaries owed their existence to the personal prestige factor. A few executives, he surmised, did not want to be branded "provincial" for keeping their companies domestic, and some others did not like staying home while their counterparts were regularly flying off to consult with their affiliates in glamorous European settings.

Another reason for overseas investment not found in textbooks is the principal motivation for the establishment of one of Intel's first overseas subsidiaries. A design and development center in Haifa, Israel, was opened in the mid-1970s partly due to a traditional reason: the ready availability of skilled engineers and scientists.

But the main impetus was management's decision to accommodate one of the senior researchers at headquarters, a native Israeli who was planning to resign because of the desire to return to his homeland. Rather than lose his valued talents, Intel established a research center in Israel under his supervision.[38] The success of this initial enterprise later led to extensive investment in manufacturing facilities.

A chain of Austrian pastry and ice cream shops became multinational when it opened a restaurant–ice cream parlor and a company-owned franchise operation in Santa Monica, California. The owner of this relatively small business said his decision to open the restaurant was very spontaneous and made without consultations. He asserted that none of the traditional factors influenced his decision, as his intention to invest in the United States originated solely from his personal experiences during a vacation the previous year in California. While there, two thoughts had a major impact on his thinking. He did not find any place selling ice cream freshly made on the premises, as was the case with his shops in Austria. In addition, he realized he was very fond of the Los Angeles area and wanted to visit regularly. He told an interviewer that the investment decision was purely a matter of personal preference and the desire "to make a dream come true."[39]

Because the Dublin-based law firm of Matheson, Ormsby, Prentice deals only with Irish law, its decision to open subsidiaries in Silicon Valley and New York City made for an unlikely MNC. It expanded across the Atlantic for the counterintuitive reason of supplying the previously overlooked market for providing counseling on Irish law and regulations to U.S.-based executives of MNCs who have invested in Ireland or are preparing to do so. The firm attributes part of its success in attracting as clients blue-chip U.S. MNCs like Microsoft, Hewlett-Packard, and Xerox to its distinctive ability to provide lawyers for person-to-person consultations with senior executives at their U.S. headquarters.[40]

Case Study: What Drives the Multinationalization of the Automobile Industry

The automobile industry provides an excellent case study in the incentives and pressures that sometimes encourage and sometimes force industry consolidation into a relatively few globe-spanning companies. It is also an excellent case study of what can go wrong when companies become too enamored with bigness and too eager to seek global reach. The trend to fewer and bigger competitors in the automobile sector by no means has been accompanied by uniform success and profitability, nor has it generated universal shareholder happiness. If anything, the world's major carmakers suffer from the same negative syndrome that has befallen the dwindling number of U.S. airlines: A consistently profitable, financially sound company is the exception, not the rule.

In the early years of the twenty-first century, every large-volume, mass-market automobile maker is an MNC. The perception that only the very large global players will survive in this industry has become so strongly ingrained among automobile executives that it was elevated to a presumed truth many years ago. Increased global market share has become the ultimate test of an automaker's success and survival. The advantages of being a multinational carmaker are not imaginary; they are rooted in the economics of the business. Major companies spend billions of dollars on nonstop R&D efforts, redesign of existing models and development of entirely new ones, and factory retooling expenses. Very high fixed costs are inescapable. The end product is now a capital-intensive collection of hundreds of technologically sophisticated components, yet car models below the luxury names must vigorously compete for the approval of price-conscious consumers.

No single national market is currently large enough for a major car company to amortize fixed costs and offer competitive pricing. Consequently, all top-tier companies have assembly plants in at least two countries; hence, they are MNCs. Substantial sales to foreigners are no longer an option in the industry. To maximize sales, be close to customers, and avoid the threat of import barriers, the high-volume automakers no longer rely on exports as the sole or major vehicle for foreign sales to anywhere other than relatively small markets with no indigenous car industry. The one exception to this rule is continued reliance on exporting by very limited-edition luxury brands, such as Porsche and Ferrari. Toyota, the world's most profitable automaker and perennially at or near the top of the list of increased annual sales, operated fifty-one overseas manufacturing plants in twenty-six countries in 2005 to meet its sales, growth, and cost-containment goals.[41]

World car and truck production of more than 60 million units in 2003 was dominated by twelve large MNCs. General Motors, Ford, Toyota, Volkswagen, DaimlerChrysler, PSA Peugeot, Nissan (controlled by Renault), Honda, Hyundai-Kia, Renault, Fiat, and Suzuki (partly owned by General Motors) produced more than 48 million units, or 80 percent of world output; the remaining 20 percent was split among more than forty other companies.[42] The current degree of consolidation in this industry is starkly different from the early part of the twentieth century, when nearly 200 companies were producing cars in the United Kingdom and almost 100 were operating in the United States.[43] Following the demise of MG Rover in 2005, the United Kingdom was left with no locally owned mass-market automakers. All are foreign-owned.[44]

The global automobile oligopoly has been strengthened since the 1990s by a spate of cross-border M&As plus an expanding web of minority ownerships, joint ventures, and strategic alliances. With more than a tinge of the follow-the-leader syndrome, Daimler-Benz merged/took over Chrysler; Ford acquired Volvo, Jaguar, and Land Rover; GM's acquisition of Saab and a minority stake in Daewoo (Korea) added to its longer-standing ownerships of Opel and Vauxhall and minority stakes in Japanese companies Suzuki, Isuzu, and Subaru. Even BMW, a mid-sized producer of luxury cars, added to its offerings by acquiring ultra-luxury Rolls Royce. The most surprising cross-border acquisitions were the minority stakes taken in three ailing Japanese companies (Nissan by Renault, Mazda by Ford, and Mitsubishi Motors by DaimlerChrysler). In the 1980s it would have been considered ludicrous to predict that a country with a seemingly unstoppable automobile industry would be left with just two fully independent producers at the turn of the century. The two, Toyota and Honda, have been unique among the major producers in refusing to pursue growth through acquisitions or joint ventures.

In addition to the match-the-overseas-expansion-of-your-major-competitors model, automakers have been inspired to act over the past three decades by all the other leading reasons why nonextractive companies invest in other countries. High fixed costs have compelled the world's major automakers to pursue economies of scale via sales in all major markets as a core business strategy. The rise in prominence of strategic asset–seeking direct investments and alliances is clearly demonstrated by the surge in major cross-border acquisitions designed to gain entrée to new markets, acquire new product offerings, or gain access to new technologies or assembly techniques. Efficiency-seeking FDI in the automobile sector thus far has mainly taken the form of vertical supply networks, with subsidiaries making parts in relatively low-wage countries like Thailand, Indonesia, China, and Mexico.

The need to cater to varied local preferences has become an important factor encouraging production in foreign markets in lieu of exporting. An idea gained traction a few years ago that companies could mass produce a single "world car." It made great financial sense; designing and assembling essentially the same vehicle for worldwide sale was potentially one of the greatest ever applications of economies of scale. The concept has been dramatically downsized, however. It was the victim of consumers around the world stubbornly demonstrating an incompatible mix of preferences for a product associated with differences in lifestyle, road conditions, disposable incomes, and so on. Americans are in a category by themselves in their insistence on multiple cup-holders in their vehicles. The larger automobile producers demonstrate sensitivity to accommodating local tastes not only by producing in multiple countries but also by maintaining facilities engaged in product design, R&D, and technical evaluation on a regional basis. Hyundai's decision to open a billion-dollar assembly plant in the United States despite incurring significantly higher wage costs reflects the priority of being able to provide car buyers with what they want when they want it. A senior corporate official explained the move in these terms:

> Our decision to build this facility in . . . Alabama underscores our commitment to the U.S. market. . . . Hyundai is in the process of doing more

design and engineering in the United States so that our products will be even better adapted to the American consumers' needs and tastes. Our new plant will allow us to build more vehicles for this growing market and get them to our customers more quickly.[45]

It is highly probable that the decision also reflected the growing article of faith that sales success in the United States is a prerequisite for being a world player among automakers, as well as the desire to avoid a protectionist backlash down the road.

Avoidance of trade barriers has attracted major commitment to foreign-owned auto assembly facilities in the United States, Western Europe, and more recently, China. The automobile assembly sector has an extraordinary impact on all national economies in which it operates. Not only is it among the largest industries by sales and jobs, it also affects a vast supplier network in parts, steel, rubber, glass, electronics, plastics, and textiles. Governments covet auto assembly plants and ferociously oppose the loss of any locally owned producers to import competition.

At the onset of the 1980s, Japanese automakers were still categorically dismissing repeated exhortations by the U.S. government and the United Automobile Workers to begin serving the American market through local assembly facilities. The universal attitude among Japanese manufacturers at the time was that exports of made-in-Japan vehicles were essential for cost and quality considerations. They unanimously perceived American workers as overpaid and lacking the skills, discipline, and dedication to emulate the fastidious, hardworking, relatively low-paid, and strike-averse Japanese workers who were major cogs in the production of high-quality, price-competitive cars. Large, sustained increases in U.S. imports of Japanese cars, together with the falling market share and rising financial problems of Detroit's Big Three producers, lead to a showdown in the first year of the Reagan administration that changed the policy equation. The opposition of Japan's automakers to establishing facilities in the United States eroded in the face of escalating pressures in Washington. Congress intensified threats to pass highly protectionist legislation as it became increasingly apparent that U.S. automakers needed breathing room from further import increases while they borrowed and invested tens of billions of dollars to retool to make better quality, more energy-efficient cars (the second oil shock had peaked in 1980). Japanese government officials prevailed on executives of the auto companies to go the FDI route when the new administration sternly warned that uncapped increases in U.S. car imports would trigger protectionist legislation in Congress that it could not derail by veto.

The subsequent "voluntary" export restraint adopted by an agreement between Japan's government and auto industry marked a radical shift in the latter's overseas business strategy. Henceforth, increased market share in countries with an indigenous automobile industry would be pursued mainly through local production. Once the Japanese companies found that carefully selected foreign workers could adapt quite well to the advanced assembly line operations that had been so successful at home, the internationalization of the larger producers was off and running.

Three decades later, Toyota, Honda, and others proudly celebrate in the U.S. media how Americanized their companies have become. Responding to continued strong increases in U.S. sales and increased concern for a backlash against its growing prosperity in the midst of GM's and Ford's sales and financial stability problems, Toyota assiduously advertises its local roots and intentions to build additional manufacturing and assembly plants in North America (see box 6.1). Honda's booming overseas sales base led to a corporate philosophy of "glocalization," defined by the company as a commitment to manufacture products "in areas close to the consumer."[46]

For the three major companies, Toyota, Nissan, and Honda, steadily increasing foreign sales have offset sluggish domestic sales caused by the stagnation in the Japanese economy that persisted from the early 1990s to 2005. Toyota was selling more than twice as many cars overseas than domestically in 2003; for Honda, the foreign-to-domestic ratio was more than three to one in 2004.[47] About two-thirds of both companies' profits in 2003 were derived from the highly lucrative, no-need-for-discounts American market.[48]

China is the hottest new FDI destination for the automobile industry. Eleven of the twelve major foreign producers already mentioned (financially troubled Fiat is the exception) had opened subsidiaries in China by 2002.[49] Massive FDI inflows resulted from foreign companies wanting to produce within what is projected to remain the fastest growing national market, but one still protected by high tariffs on imported cars. It is also a market that lacks the buying power to easily tolerate transportation costs being added to retail prices. Foreign subsidiaries in China are also appealing as a means of keeping close tabs on the kinds of cars and accessories that will appeal to China's emerging middle class. Skilled but low-wage Chinese labor makes the country a natural to produce cheap small cars for export.

The compelling logic and widespread practice of major automobile makers to increase their global presence through new subsidiaries and acquisitions obscure the deep potholes on the MNC highway. GM had to pay the Fiat car division $2 billion in 2005 to extricate itself from an unusual contractual obligation to buy the 90 percent of the company that GM did not already own. It seemed like a good deal in 2000 when the commitment was made, but the Italian company subsequently began suffering large losses and incurring surging debt. Given GM's own financial problems, the last thing it needed was to be saddled with the purchase and management of perhaps the only automaker with worse troubles than its own.[50]

A second jolt in 2005 to the auto companies' globalization model came in the form of the decision by the CEO of DaimlerChrysler to bow to long-standing criticism by stockholders and securities analysts and take early retirement. Jürgen Schrempp's plan to transform Daimler-Benz, a middle-sized maker of luxury cars with a sterling reputation for advanced technological prowess, into a world-spanning company selling a full line of models was compelling on paper, but a resounding failure in application.[51] Shortly after it acquired Chrysler, the latter began suffering declining sales and heavy losses. Serious differences in corporate cultures added to the problems of trying to shore up the Chrysler division. DaimlerChrysler's purchase of a minority stake in Mitsubishi Motors, the would-be Asian pillar of its global presence, proved a worse investment. The Japanese manufacturer soon after went into a sales and earnings tailspin, accelerated by scandals over hiding defects in its cars to avoid a massive recall. Schrempp's plan in 2004 to shore up the ailing Mitsubishi Motors with a multibillion-dollar capital infusion was overturned by an incredulous management board. The ongoing failure of top management to get the gears of DaimlerChrysler's worldwide empire to mesh came full circle by 2005. Chrysler began turning a small profit at the same time that sales of the flagship Mercedes nameplate suffered a major decline amidst well-publicized quality control problems.

Earlier examples of global overreach included BMW's ill-fated takeover of Britain's Rover. After capital infusions in excess of $3 billion could not stanch the steady stream of red ink at what cynics dubbed "the English Patient," the German company jettisoned its Rover division in 2000. Volkswagen planned to capitalize on earlier success in exporting its famous Beetle model by producing the new Golf model in the United States. It failed. "Nearly disastrous quality control problems and lack of cost competitiveness in the face of Japanese competition" caused it to be shut down in 1989 after only a decade of operation. As such, it is one of the rare failures of a foreign-owned consumer goods–making subsidiary in the large, affluent U.S. market.[52]

Part of the explanation for the numerous failures in automobile companies' globalization strategies is that on occasion, invalid or irrelevant reasons seem to have been the driving factor in overseas investments and acquisitions. The possibility exists "that managers are driven to seek bigness as a goal itself. They may do so for private material benefits, such as higher salaries, or for the less tangible glory of empire building." Because it is difficult to find categorical evidence that increased size has bestowed auto companies with greater long-term efficiency and profitability, "size maximization remains as a residual category of explanation . . . after all the more conventional explanations" of mergers have been considered and dismissed.[53] The mixed record of the automobile makers' globalization strategy notwithstanding, GM's largest individual shareholder advanced a dramatic proposal in mid-2006. To get the auto giant's restructuring efforts on the fast track, he suggested that GM enter into some firm of three-way partnership-alliance with the already existing Renault-Nissan partnership.

Notes

1. Rachel McCulloch, "New Perspectives on Foreign Direct Investment," in Kenneth Froot, ed., *Foreign Direct Investment* (Chicago: University of Chicago Press, 1993), pp. 39–40.
2. Charles P. Kindleberger, *American Business Abroad* (New Haven, CT: Yale University Press, 1969), p. 13.
3. Richard E. Caves, "International Corporations: The Industrial Economics of Foreign Investment," *Economica*, February 1971, p. 5.
4. Geoffrey Jones, *The Evolution of International Business* (New York: Routledge, 1996), p. 7.
5. Ibid., p. 6.
6. For a detailed survey of the various theorists and the ideas that made more limited contributions to the evolution of MNC theory, see chap. 1 of John H. Dunning, *Explaining International Production* (London: Unwin, Hyman, 1989).
7. There are two inconclusive theories why this is so: (1) Hymer's ideas were so groundbreaking that they were incapable of immediate acceptance, and (2) his Marxist ideology caused him to be ignored by mainstream economists.
8. John H. Dunning, *Multinational Enterprises and the Global Economy* (Wokingham, UK: Addison-Wesley, 1993), p. 69.
9. Kindleberger, *American Business Abroad*, p. 13.
10. Although Boeing does not meet the criterion for being an MNC because it produces planes only in the United States, it presents one of the clearest examples of the high fixed cost/need for economies of scale syndrome. The unit price of a new generation of Boeing aircraft—which cost $8 billion and up to develop and build—would be astronomical if the company sold planes only in the U.S. market. The high price tag associated with a relatively small sales base for amortizing the company's enormous fixed costs would place it at a severe disadvantage against its archrival, Airbus. The latter would price its planes at a much lower level by being able to allocate fixed costs over a much greater sales volume thanks to the potential for selling aircraft to every major airline in the world.
11. Data source: "Pfizer Shows the Way," Economist.com Global Agenda, July 15, 2002, available online at http://www.economist.com; accessed July 2002.
12. Robert Gilpin, *Global Political Economy—Understanding the International Economic Order* (Princeton, NJ: Princeton University Press, 2001), p. 287.
13. John H. Dunning, "Globalization and the Theory of MNE Activity," in Neil Hood and Stephen Young, eds., *The Globalization of Multinational Enterprise Activity and Economic Development* (New York: St. Martin's, 2000), p. 26.

14. Ibid., p. 21.

15. Dunning, *Multinational Enterprises and the Global Economy*, p. 68.

16. Fred Turner, quoted in John F. Love, *McDonald's—Behind the Arches* (New York: Bantam Books, 1986), p. 417.

17. Data source: McDonald's Corporation, 2005 Financial Report, available online at http://www.mcdonalds.com; accessed June, 2006.

18. "Citigroup Looks Abroad for Its Future Growth," *Wall Street Journal*, March 15, 2004, p. C1.

19. Joseph Quinlan and Marc Chandler, "The U.S. Trade Deficit: A Dangerous Obsession," *Foreign Affairs*, May/June 2001, pp. 88–89.

20. Statement of Sean Maloney before the Senate Finance Committee, June 23, 2005, p. 2, available online at http://finance.senate.gov/sitepages/hearings.htm; accessed December 2005.

21. See, for example, "Big Three Outsourcing Plan: Make Parts Suppliers Do It," *Wall Street Journal*, June 10, 2004, p. A1, and "Increasingly, American-Made Doesn't Mean in the U.S.A.," *New York Times*, March 19, 2004, p. C1. The latter article featured the man tapped by President Bush to be his coordinator of efforts to strengthen the U.S. manufacturing sector but quickly dropped when his company's outsourcing to China was revealed.

22. UNCTAD, "China: An Emerging FDI Outward Investor," December 4, 2003, p. 8, available online at http://www.unctad.org; accessed January 2005.

23. General Electric Corporation, *2003 Annual Report*, available online at http://www.GE.com; accessed December 2004.

24. "Survey on Multinationals," *The Economist*, March 27, 1993, p. 9 of the survey.

25. Data source: "AMD Files Antitrust Suit against Intel," Associated Press, June 28, 2005, available online at http://www.macnewsworld.com; accessed July 2005.

26. Unable to pursue this invest-in-your-competitors'-backyard strategy, a number of American companies were especially bitter about being blocked from establishing subsidiaries in Japan in the 1970s and 1980s. They perceived the need to bring price competition there because of widespread belief that a Japanese market largely impenetrable to imports of goods made there allowed domestic companies to inflate domestic prices and profit margins, something acceptable to the stoic Japanese populace. This in turn allegedly enabled them to offset the rock-bottom export prices used to maximize sales and market shares in foreign markets.

27. *New York Times*, September 7, 1995, as quoted in Raymond Vernon, Louis Wells Jr. and Subramanian Rangan, *The Manager in the International Economy*, 7th ed. (Upper Saddle River, NJ: Prentice Hall, 1996), p. 27.

28. More recently, to be eligible to win Defense Department contracts for aerial refueling tankers and other military aircraft, the European Aeronautic Defense and Space Corporation (the maker of Airbus) opened an aircraft engineering center in Mobile, Alabama, in 2005. The company announced it would add an assembly plant if and when it is awarded a major defense contract.

29. "The Rise of 'Small Multinationals,'" *BusinessWeek* Online, February 1, 2005, available online at http://www.businessweek.com; accessed February 2005.

30. Gerhard Apfelthaler, "Why Small Enterprises Invest Abroad: The Case of Four Austrian Firms with U.S. Operations," *Journal of Small Business Management*, July 2000, p. 94.

31. "Yum! Brands," Morgan Stanley, *U.S. Investment Perspectives*, May 5, 2004, pp. 25–26.

32. "Yum! Brands," Morgan Stanley, *U.S. Investment Perspectives*, May 11, 2005, p. 60.

33. "First Data," Morgan Stanley, *U.S. Investment Perspectives*, December 1, 2004, p. 67.

34. "It's Getting Hotter in the East," *BusinessWeek*, August 22, 2005, p. 81.

35. Data source: "Regionalism: Friends or Rivals?," available online at http://www.wto.org; accessed June 2005. The WTO believes that the growing enthusiasm for regional free trade agreements may push the total well beyond 300 within a few years.

36. Edward M. Graham and Paul R. Krugman, "The Surge in Foreign Direct Investment in the 1980s," in Froot, *Foreign Direct Investment*, p. 30.

37. "The Scrutable East," *McKinsey Quarterly*, November 2004, available online at http://www.mckinsey.com/ideas/mck_quarterly; accessed January 2005.

38. Not for attribution interview with a former Intel employee, summer 2004.

39. Apfelthaler, "Why Small Enterprises Invest Abroad," p. 95.

40. "Ireland: Pluck of the Irish," *Lawyer* (London), October 20, 2003; accessed on the ABI/Inform database, August 2004.

41. Data source: Toyota's corporate Web site, http://www.toyota.com.

42. Data source: Ward's Communications, *Ward's Motor Vehicle Facts & Figures, 2004*, p. 15.

43. John A. C. Conybeare, *Merging Traffic—The Consolidation of the International Automobile Industry* (Lanham, MD: Rowman and Littlefield, 2004), p. 1.

44. Data source: U.K. Department of Trade and Industry, in email message to the author, May 2005.

45. "Hyundai Motor Company Announces It Will Build Its First U.S. Manufacturing Plant in Alabama," press release dated April 2, 2002, available online at http://worldwide.hyundai-motor.com; accessed May 2005.

46. See, for example, Honda's 2004 Annual Report to Stockholders, available at http://www.Honda.com.

47. Data sources: Toyota's Form 20-F submission to the U.S. Securities and Exchange Commission, June 2005, p. 42, available online at http://www.toyota.com; accessed July 2005; and "Overview of Honda's Financial Information," available online at http://www.world.honda.com; accessed July 2005.

48. Data sources: "Toyota Triumphs," *Newsweek International*, May 9, 2005, available online at http://www.msnbc.msn.com; accessed July 2005; and Honda's Form 20-F submission, May 2005, p. 41, available online at http://www.honda.com; accessed July 2005.

49. Data source: Ministry of Commerce of the People's Republic of China, "2003 Report of Foreign Investment in China," available online at http://english.mofcom.gov.cn/column/report.shtml; accessed May 2005.

50. Michael Hastings, "Stuck with a Lemon," *Newsweek International*, January 17, 2005, available online at http://www.msnbc.msn.com; accessed July 2005.

51. Investors and analysts greeted Schrempp's surprise retirement announcement with something approaching euphoria; the stock immediately rose more than 9 percent, the biggest single-day increase in more than six years (data source: *New York Times*, July 29, 2005, p. C1).

52. Conybeare, *Merging Traffic*, p. 13.

53. Ibid., p. 138.

7

WHERE MULTINATIONAL
CORPORATIONS INVEST AND
DON'T INVEST AND WHY

Not even the largest multinational corporations (MNCs) can afford to invest everywhere or accept the risks inherent in choosing overseas production locations in a random, cavalier manner. An important phase of the foreign direct investment (FDI) cycle is the decision that follows a company's making a commitment to overseas expansion: *where* the planned foreign subsidiary(ies) should be situated. Due diligence is required to avoid costly and embarrassing mistakes in site selections. One of the few valid generalizations about MNCs is that they invest in countries where their inquiries and calculations indicate a relatively high probability that financial rewards will exceed costs and risks by an acceptable margin in an acceptable time frame. The dynamics of those decisions are among the least subjective and least emotional aspects of the FDI/ MNCs phenomena. Value judgments and controversy appear in far greater amounts *after* subsidiaries open for business.

Viewed in a narrow sense, the geography of FDI is a simple statistical exercise in counting buildings around the world controlled by foreign companies. In a larger sense, insight into the MNC location evaluation process enhances the heterogeneity theme by showing how different kinds (market-seeking, efficiency-seeking, etc.) of direct investment each have a distinctive set of priorities when looking for a site to build an overseas subsidiary. An understanding of where FDI is and is not going serves to debunk the widespread myth that companies are moving abroad in a race to the bottom. The "where" factor also provides valuable lessons on the supply side: how countries, intentionally and otherwise, go about making themselves appealing or unattractive to foreign companies.

The purpose of this chapter is to integrate these themes. It begins with a straightforward review of the statistics showing the geographical distribution of MNCs, that is, where FDI is going. The chapter then takes a conceptual approach to examine the reasons FDI gravitates to some countries and avoids others. The second section examines the fundamentals determining the national climate for FDI, the thing that causes countries to win or lose the popularity contest that is corporate site selection. The third and fifth sections, respectively, focus on the specific market characteristics that MNCs do and do not want to find when evaluating overseas locations. Sandwiched in between, the fourth section reviews the debate over the "choose me" governmental tactic of offering lucrative financial incentives to attract preferred foreign companies.

Which Countries Attract FDI and Which Do Not

Statistics on FDI location can be used as a proxy for gauging the popularity of the four basic reasons that companies establish subsidiaries in foreign countries: obtaining natural resources, protecting or expanding sales in lucrative markets, seeking low-cost production for an export platform, or acquiring strategic assets. Geographic location is related to business objective. Countries with known reserves of raw materials or attractive corporate targets for acquisition become the locale for the first and fourth objectives. Large, thriving economies, regardless of labor costs, attract market-seeking subsidiaries. Poor countries with assets above and beyond relatively low wages attract mostly (if not entirely) efficiency-seeking factories.

Until World War II, FDI consisted mainly of companies extracting raw materials in colonies; as a consequence, most of it was located in what are now called less developed countries (LDCs). Natural resource extraction ceased being the largest form of direct investment after the relative surge of market-seeking investment began moving into Western Europe and Canada in the 1950s (see chapter 3). Many of the conveyers of conventional wisdom still seem unaware of the fact that a significant majority of the world's FDI has been moving into wealthy industrialized countries for more that half a century. UNCTAD data show the North's share of recorded worldwide incoming FDI flows averaged 58 percent annually from 1992 through 1997 and again in 2004.[1] These percentages bear no resemblance to the high-income countries' small share of the world's population: below 17 percent. However, this FDI share does correlate to their 80 percent share of world GDP.[2]

Firms moving to countries having the lowest paid workers and the least enforced environmental protection regulations are, given the absence of any proof to the contrary, rare exceptions rather than the rule. The data repeatedly and unequivocally show the vast majority of manufacturing and services-oriented FDI is capital moving from one affluent country to another. Low wages (excluding China) are inversely related to the volume of incoming FDI. Direct investment in LDCs, remember, excludes locally owned, sweatshop-like factories producing apparel, footwear, and other low-tech, labor-intensive goods. Claims by the antiglobalization movement that FDI is a greed-based race to the bottom are inconsistent not only with the data as to where it is going (Haiti and Afghanistan have rock-bottom wages, but foreign companies are not building factories there) but with basic economics as well. Labor costs are only one of several components of total production costs; raw materials, parts, and transportation are some of the others. Moreover, wages and benefits only partly determine total labor costs. Unskilled, undisciplined workers with spotty attendance records are seldom a bargain even if paid only a few cents an hour. The real cost of labor is mainly determined by productivity—output per unit of input used, usually measured as labor's output per hour worked—not their hourly wages. Relatively high and fast-growing levels of output per hour of work explain why companies can pay much higher wages in industrialized countries than in LDCs, where worker productivity is typically lower.

The Triad of the United States, the European Union, and Japan has been the main source and recipient of the world's FDI for more than half a century. From 1998 through 2000, it accounted for 75 percent of global FDI inflows and 59 percent of inward global stock (cumulative book value of original invest-ments).[3] Those Triad countries with the world's best-paid workers—the United States, Canada, Germany, France, the United Kingdom, the Netherlands, and Switzerland—dominate the list of largest recipients of FDI, whether measured as percentage of GDP or in absolute terms. Two other major host countries, Ireland and Spain, have only slightly lower labor costs. These countries are the principal actors in what is a virtuous economic cycle: high but noninflationary wage levels, rising productivity, increasing consumer buying power, and robust economic growth. Relative efficiency, prosperity, and incoming FDI go hand in hand. Not by happenstance, the poorest LDCs suffer from a radically differ-ent, vicious circle of economic trends culminating, as will be noted below, with negligible receipt of direct investment. Statistically, the number one rationale for choosing where to invest in another country is exploiting the present and pro-jected strength of foreign consumers' buying power, not the weaknesses of the host country.

The dominant North—North axis of direct investment contradicts the eco-nomic principle that capital seeks the highest rate of return. Because the marginal productivity of capital and therefore the marginal return theoretically are higher in labor-intensive, capital-scarce developing countries, the bulk of FDI should flow mainly from North to South. It doesn't, and the result is what Deloitte Re-search has called the "high-wage paradox." Corporate executives are obviously following a different set of metrics to determine optimal destinations for new or expanded foreign subsidiaries. Probably it is because they know better than anyone that no positive statistical correlation has been demonstrated between poverty in a host country and profits of manufacturing or services-providing MNCs.

The most consistent theme in the where-FDI-is-going and where-it-is-coming-from statistics is that in both directions it is concentrated in a relatively few countries. The 2001 edition of *The World Investment Report* pointed out that "Despite its reach,...FDI is unevenly distributed. The world's top 30 host countries account for 95 per cent of total world FDI inflows and 90 per cent of stocks."[4] Asymmetry is especially prominent in the data for sources of outward FDI, that is, the home countries of overseas subsidiaries. In 1980 and again in 2003, the countries classified by UNCTAD as developed accounted for 89 percent of the outward stock of FDI; if nearly developed Hong Kong, Taiwan, South Korea, and Singapore are added to this total, the share of the affluents jumps to 95 percent. Geographic concentration is also evident when the share of developed countries is disaggregated. Just nine countries (the United States, the United Kingdom, France, Germany, the Netherlands, Switzerland, Japan, Canada, and Italy) accounted for 84 percent of the $7.3 trillion in total outward FDI stock owned by developed countries in 2003.[5] About 90 of the world's 100 largest nonfinancial multinationals were headquartered in the Triad countries.

The geographic concentration of MNCs has created an FDI divide between haves and have-nots. Aggregated data do show a continuous and relatively sizable increase in MNCs moving to developing and in-transition countries since 1990; however, this is an exercise in statistical misdirection. A true depiction of FDI going to developing countries requires disaggregation to reveal another case of major geographic concentration. In a word, the most advanced LDCs, often referred to as the emerging markets, account for a disproportionate share. With recorded direct investment inflows exceeding $50 billion in the early 2000s, China alone has been taking more than 30 percent of the annual LDC total. The share of China and just the next four largest recipients (Hong Kong, Singapore, Mexico, and Brazil) is 58 percent of all FDI flowing in 2003 to what UNCTAD classifies as developing countries (nearly unchanged from their average 55 percent share in the 1992—97 time span). Inclusion of countries and territories that fall between emerging market and developed country status—South Korea and Israel, for example—further obscures numbers showing just how little the lower middle and lowest income LDCs receive in FDI. The approximately 50 countries classified by UNCTAD as least developed reported just over $7 billion in inflows in 2003, a trifling 1.25 percent of the world total (as bad as this performance was, it represented a doubling of their negligible share of average annual world inflows from 1992 through 1997).[6] If yet another statistical distortion caused by large investments by oil companies to develop newly discovered reserves is circumvented, FDI in Africa, Central Asia,

TABLE 7.1. FDI Inflows to Developing Countries* and Countries
in Transition, by Region (in millions of U.S. dollars)

	Annual Average	
	1992–97	2004
Total	130,000	268,100
Africa	6,000	18,100
Latin American & the Caribbean**	38,200	67,500
(of which: South America)	(22,100)	(37,900)
Asia, Pacific, and the Middle East	74,500	147,600
(of which: East, and Southeast Asia)	(69,600)	(130,700)
Eastern Europe and	11,500	35,000
Commonwealth of Independent States		

*As classified by UNCTAD in its annual *World Investment Report*.
**Includes Mexico.

Source: UNCTAD, *World Investment Reports, 2004 and 2005*; Annex Table B.1

and the Middle East has been minimal. The old adage that "it is better to be exploited than ignored" suggests that big MNCs are doing a disservice to the poorest, neediest countries, but not in the way that critics contend. Table 7.1 shows how closely the magnitude of FDI flows reflect the differentiated economic progress of East Asia, Latin America, and Africa.

Fundamentals of a Country's Climate for FDI

Two considerations sit atop the hierarchy of factors determining where manufacturing FDI does or does not go. The first is the company's best quantitative guesstimate what the difference will be between projected total production costs at a subsidiary and projected prices that can be charged for its output. Companies focus on net profits—margin—not on individual items such as gross labor costs, the need to comply with environmental protection regulations, and cost of utilities.

A second transcendent element of corporate decisions on where to invest is the qualitative judgment as to how business-friendly or -unfriendly the investment climate is in a potential host country. Though lacking a single, specific definition, this term refers in general to the myriad factors (discussed in the sections to follow) that are taken into consideration when companies balance risks and uncertainties against expectations for positive returns. Investment climate is not a quantifiable hard truth. It consists of perceptions by foreign enterprises about how attractive or unattractive a country looks relative to other countries as a place to make a long-term commitment of capital, personnel, and prestige.

The collective results of attitudes, actions, and inactions by the national government is the most decisive determinant of whether an investment climate attracts or repels nonextractive MNCs. Depending on whether government policies are overtly accommodating, neutral, mildly discouraging, indirectly negative, or proactively hostile, over time they will affect the volume, quality, size, and composition of incoming FDI. Quality of governance, political stability, and presence or absence of rule of law cannot be ignored by any foreign investor. Nor can macroeconomic policies that affect all phases of a country's economy. Fiscal policy includes corporate tax rates, and monetary policy includes setting the cost of borrowing (interest rates) in a country. Intermediate, or meso-economic factors are one small step below macro factors in importance when businesses evaluate foreign locations. They include the breadth and depth of industrial policies that provide various forms of assistance to targeted industries (direct subsidies, tax breaks, exemption from antitrust laws, protection from import competition, etc.), intensity of regulation of the business community, quality of physical and human infrastructure, import barriers, and regulation of capital outflows.

Michael Dell, founder of Dell, alluded to most of these factors when he summarized what attracted his company to Ireland in 1990: It has industrial and tax policies that are "consistently very supportive of businesses, independent of which political party is in power. I believe this is because there are enough people who remember the very bad times to de-politicize economic development." Transportation and logistics are very good, and Ireland has a "good location— easy to move products to major markets in Europe quickly."[7] Hungary's success in attracting FDI is closely correlated with political stability and its early commitment to a reformist, liberalizing policy path. Soon after it was freed from Soviet domination, the government set out to quickly free prices, liberalize foreign trade, reduce domestic subsidies, privatize state-owned enterprises, and improve the position of the private sector in general.[8]

Since the 1980s, the trend has clearly been for changes in official FDI policies to move in the direction of encouraging investment inflows. The regulatory changes classified on the UNCTAD Secretariat's annual scoreboard as more favorable toward FDI accounted for 95 percent of the total between the starting year of 1991 and 2003, meaning that changes categorized as less favorable to FDI accounted for a mere 5 percent. In 2003, 154 countries had an international promotion agency or a government entity assigned an investment promotion function.[9] One simple litmus test of investment climate is how aggressive and well-financed this agency is. Another is whether the promotion function is overshadowed by another domestic agency that conducts exhaustive, time-consuming screenings of applications for FDI that put the burden of proof on interested investors to prove their value.

UNCTAD's annual *World Investment Report* contains two indices designed to serve as a more accurate guide to calculating a country's success in attracting incoming FDI than an unadjusted total of its annual inflows or cumulative stocks. The Potential Index is based on several quantitative indicators (other than size of GDP) that produce an index number for the extent to which a country's assets should in principle attract FDI. The Performance Index is the ratio of a country's share of global FDI inflows in a given year to its share of global GDP, a more precise measurement than a simple FDI to GDP ratio. If a country's ranking in the Performance Index is significantly above (below) its ranking in the Potential Index, it presumably is doing something right (wrong) in making itself attractive to MNCs.[10] Of some 140 countries examined, only Japan consistently ranks among the leaders in potential at the same time it ranks among the laggards, that is, the bottom decile, in performance. This is the result of a booming economy being walled off for many years from incoming majority-owned FDI by formal barriers and more recently the continued presence of informal hurdles to foreign companies.

The first of four broad and partially overlapping FDI strategies that a government can adopt is a passive open-door policy with few or no proactive programs to support it. This is largely a laissez-faire approach, open to the idea of incoming MNCs but not linked to any industrial policies. The United States at the federal level is one of the few practitioners of a posture declaring that government will leave it to the market mechanism (except in extraordinary circumstances to reject proposed inward investments) to decide the amounts and kinds of FDI that do or do not enter. The second option is an open-door policy backed up by official programs designed to maximize incoming investment. This is by far today's most widely used policy model and comes in various degrees of intensity. The most aggressive governments will target certain companies and sectors as particularly attractive additions to the local economy, court them, and offer major financial incentives (see following discussion) to avoid losing out to another country.

Moving to the other side of the spectrum, a negative set of government policies can be off-putting to companies looking for overseas investment sites. This third policy strategy springs from innate suspicion of the motives of large foreign corporations and is characterized by different degrees of disincentives. Typically, a mandatory screening process created by statute will put foreign companies through differing degrees of inquisition to determine if their proposed investment meets the host government's tight or flexible criteria for protecting what is defined as the national interest. Countries with intense doubts that "acceptable" amounts of FDI benefits will naturally spill over into the domestic economy can use take-it-or-leave-it demands in seeking an adequate share of the economic gains from foreign subsidiaries. A fourth option, indirect in nature and usually unintentional, is for a government to manage domestic policy so poorly or to pursue a political agenda so extreme that nonextractive MNCs refuse to seriously consider investing in it. The resulting dearth of FDI (and likely poor domestic economic performance) in such cases is seldom considered serious enough to force the political system to alter the policy status quo.

Some variables remain outside governmental control, for example, a country's endowments of raw materials and the number of its consumers. Incoming FDI is not always determined (or repelled) by the conscious behavior (or misbehavior) of governments in would-be host countries. The quality of domestic suppliers and the aggressiveness of local unions are just two possible swing factors linked to the private sector. Sometimes, a government in power is burdened with decades of deep-rooted mismanagement and investment-retarding conditions created by predecessors. Furthermore, the best intentions of senior politicians do not guarantee immediate change if other parts of the government are not on board. The legislative body may oppose reforms and delay passage of enabling legislation; skeptical career civil servants might drag their feet on implementation and enforcement of new regulations. As a 2005 World Bank report states: "Investment climate improvements are a process, not an event." Everything cannot and does not have to be fixed at once.[11]

What MNCs Want in a Host Country

The academic and business literature is rich in descriptions of which economic, political, and social criteria corporate officials consider to be important when they consider overseas investment sites. Their ultimate goal is simple: finding a location that will allow them to make the most money in the shortest time with the least amount of adversity. Finding such a place is more complicated. No standard set of attributes, each with an assigned relative weight of importance, exists in the many lists of what matters in location published by business groups, international organizations, and scholars. Determining where to invest is a case-by-case decision. No single formula exists because specific strengths and weaknesses of a country or region might receive high priority by one team of corporate evaluators and be ignored by another, depending on what kind of investment is contemplated, which in turn will determine a subsidiary's objectives and operational needs. Furthermore, individual corporate cultures will assign different relative importance to what attributes they require in a country, what they would like to see, what negatives they can work around, and what is unequivocally unacceptable. Calculating trade-offs between positive and negative country characteristics is an art, not a science. In short, to understand why MNCs go where they go, it is once again necessary to acknowledge the heterogeneity factor, disaggregate, and accept a modicum of uncertainty and inconsistency.

Only resource-seeking investments retain a short, simple, and unchanging list of priorities for choosing where to invest. The top three priorities are: reasonably easy access to an abundant supply of a sought-after raw material, physical infrastructure that will permit it to be transported out of the host country at an acceptable cost, and less than crushing corruption and environmental protection regulations. A company looking to establish a subsidiary to drill for oil will have a checklist whose contents and order bear little resemblance to that of a services company or a manufacturer of goods looking to use a new subsidiary as an export platform or as a vehicle to maximize sales in a foreign market.

Market-seeking investment is drawn to large economies with strong consumer purchasing power and good records of growth, countries with above-average human capital and physical infrastructure, and members of a major regional free trade agreement. Most countries matching this profile are located in the Triad. Efficiency-seeking investments go to carefully screened countries, usually LDCs in which a relatively low wage scale will not be swamped by unproductive workers and other high production costs, such as inadequate infrastructure, intrusive and inconsistent regulation, and pervasive corruption. Priorities in labor force characteristics differ between efficiency-seeking investors trying to minimize costs of producing labor-intensive goods and market seekers trying to increase sales of high value-added goods in prosperous markets. Finally, a decision to make a foreign investment for the purpose of acquiring a strategic asset by purchasing or merging with a foreign company presumably means that corporate-specific attractions outweigh country-wide factors, such as labor costs.

Negative factors also will be weighted differently depending on the objective of a planned investment. Prohibitive import barriers should not be a major concern to what was designed to be a tariff-jumping, relatively self-sufficient, local market—seeking subsidiary. The same prohibitive barriers will preclude plans for a plant whose task is to assemble components made in other countries with machinery that also is imported. China has been so extraordinarily attractive as a growth market and a low-cost production site that foreign companies have flocked there despite numerous negative conditions, especially the lack of rule of law, which would be deal-breakers in virtually any other country. A booming market with relatively low production costs can hide a lot of ugly blemishes.

Surveys asking corporate executives how they evaluate foreign locations arguably provide the best insights into what matters most in the selection process (it can only be assumed that anonymous responses genuinely reflect company thinking). Unfortunately, only sporadic efforts have been made to systematically collect and publicly disseminate this information. The only widely cited survey of executives' opinions on this subject that I found in my research was conducted in 2001 by the firm Deloitte & Touche.[12] Relatively few companies returned completed questionnaires, either unwilling to take the time or reluctant to provide proprietary information. This survey therefore represents only a minute fraction of the world's MNCs that may or may not be a representative sample of the thinking of the much larger MNC universe.

Consistent with the theme of FDI/MNC heterogeneity, no one factor—even in a limited number of replies—was unanimously rated as critical when corporations choose or reject countries. Different objectives, needs, and strategies have caused companies to design distinctive evaluation templates. There apparently is no such a thing as a single criterion (except perhaps the absence of ongoing major military hostilities) or minimum evaluation score that is unconditionally required by all companies at all times in all potential host countries. Unanimity might have appeared if the survey had disaggregated corporate responses and collated them by the categories of resource, market, and efficiency-seeking investors. Of the top twenty critical location factors, the one most frequently cited as very influential in selecting a location was access to customers; it was mentioned by 77 percent of the 191 responses received.

Other widely cited influential factors, in descending order of importance, were a stable social and political environment, ease of doing business, reliability and quality of physical infrastructure (transportation, telecommunications, and utilities), ability to hire technical professionals, ability to hire management staff, level of corruption, cost of labor, crime and safety, ability to hire skilled laborers, corporate tax rates at the national level, costs of utilities, and quality of roads. Identified by less than 25 percent of respondents as very influential factors were access to raw materials, availability and quality of university and technical training, available land with connected utilities, local taxes, access to suppliers, labor relations and unionization, and air freight and passenger service.[13]

Anecdotes of real world situations provide additional insights into the business world's approach to the question of where. The speed and rigor with which countries in transition embarked on structural reforms to create a fully functional market economy—liberalization, privatization, and regulatory and institutional reforms of the economy—was especially important to the first wave of foreign investors in Central Europe.[14] When considering possible sites, Ericsson, the Swedish-based multinational telecom equipment maker, has said it attaches greatest weight to market size, quality of the bureaucracy, quality of infrastructure (including customs clearance procedures), the tax system, trade policies, level of political risk, production costs including labor, and the availability of suitable contractors and suppliers.[15] Intel's brief public recitation of its site selection process for new factories inside and outside the United States lists the quality of the local technical workforce, utilities, transportation capability, construction and supplier capabilities, and regulatory and investment conditions.[16] A General Electric business development officer introduced additional factors when listing the criteria he would use to compare Mexico's and China's strengths as sites for new manufacturing operations: labor and electricity costs, supplier base, transportation costs and transit time, skill level and productivity of labor, international telecommunications costs, protection of intellectual property, and transparency in business regulations.[17]

A few more qualities need to be mentioned or expanded on to assemble a comprehensive record of what corporations, especially in the secondary and tertiary sectors, want in a host country. Good logistics mean that goods, people, and communications can quickly, cheaply, and dependably be moved into, through, and out of the host country. Companies want to go into markets where reasonably transparent, predictable, nondiscriminatory, and honest legal and regulatory systems are in place. A desirable rule of law also enforces clearly enunciated rules at the national and local levels, enforces commercial contracts, and defends property rights, be they buildings, financial assets, or patents, copyrights, or trademarks. The host country's legal system should also establish and follow clear ground rules for settling disputes between the government and foreign subsidiaries. MNCs prefer countries committed in law and spirit to the policy of national treatment, whereby the host government is obligated to treat foreign-owned companies at least as favorably as it does local companies in like circumstances.

A government will make itself more attractive to MNCs if political leaders and the bureaucracy make it known that they are genuinely committed to facilitating business development on a priority basis. Corporations look favorably on absence of a large bureaucracy enamored with red tape and cheerfully keeping itself powerful by requiring official approval of all manner of business activity. Clear lines of authority among federal government agencies and between the national and provincial governments further add to the appeal of a potential host country. Other selling points are reasonable land prices and construction costs, a local financial system willing and able to lend to foreign-controlled subsidiaries, and a lifestyle attractive to expatriates from the parent company.

The "what's already in place" syndrome can be sufficiently powerful in three different ways to attract foreign investment. The first involves supplier—customer relationships in the age of just-in-time delivery. A maker of intermediate goods may feel compelled to build a factory near a major overseas subsidiary opened by an important client, lest more nimble competitors push it aside. *Agglomeration economies* are another potential determinant of location decisions. This concept refers to a company's being able to enjoy what economists call positive externalities by setting up business in a particular place. In plain English, a locale may be compelling simply because companies in the same or related fields are already there. These so-called clusters (best illustrated by Silicon Valley) arise because a region offers an ample supply of skilled labor, excellent physical infrastructure, availability of raw materials, proximity to research institutions and universities, and so on. As a cluster grows, so do the numbers of businesses supplying raw materials and intermediate goods and providing specialized services (lawyers, venture capital, consultants, product designers, specialized advertising agencies, etc.). The burgeoning community of interests becomes an important source of support to existing companies and new entrants alike. Furthermore, executives value physical proximity to competitors and complementary businesses because it is helpful in recruiting new personnel and provides an ideal observation post for staying informed about new products, technologies, and business deals.

The third variant of the "what's already in place" syndrome is the demonstration effect, considered by some as an offshoot of agglomeration economies. Often a growing stock of inward FDI is itself sufficient to attract more foreign subsidiaries; in some respects it is a corollary of Say's Law that supply creates its own demand. A countryside teeming with prospering and expanding MNCs demonstrates an excellent investment climate far better than self-promoting claims and statistics. Risk-averse companies, small firms with limited financial resources, or larger companies with tight budgets sometimes choose to piggyback rather than making expensive in-person inspections of various countries. In such cases, a country is selected as the site for a new overseas subsidiary on the basis that world-class companies with methodical site selection procedures made major investments there, all of which thrived. Singapore and Ireland exemplify the old adage that nothing succeeds like success (see discussion in next section).

Some countries have taken unilateral policy initiatives that propelled them to the top of destinations lists maintained by foreign companies previously having had no interest in them (see the discussion of Costa Rica and Intel in chapters 9 and 12). Creation of export processing zones, also called foreign trade zones and special economic zones, has enabled some developing countries to make MNCs an offer they could not resist. These cordoned-off districts offer attractive inducements to foreign-owned factories built solely for the purpose of manufacturing goods for export or to process, test, or repackage goods for reexport. Incentives include duty-free entry of all imports, reduced or deferred corporate income taxes, below market prices for land, and relaxed regulatory controls. A second initiative that has put some countries on the FDI map is announcement of privatization of government-owned businesses and utilities on attractive terms. Neither of these two initiatives has been as controversial or costly as financial incentives given to MNCs, to be discussed later.

Case Studies: Countries That Attract FDI

Why Ireland and Singapore Are Masters of the Art of Attracting FDI
Ireland and Singapore exhibit a surprising number of similarities. They are both island countries with populations of about four million. Both have had their

economies and standards of living transformed for the better by relatively large inflows of FDI. Success in attracting MNCs was not left to chance or the invisible hand of the marketplace by either country. It was generated by high-priority, popularly supported industrial policies crafted to create a probusiness milieu that virtually shouted world-class reward-to-risk ratios for foreign investors. Both countries created investment promotion agencies that have sufficient authority and personnel to act as one-stop shops able to single-handedly help a foreign company with all of the commercial, administrative, and legal details associated with opening a subsidiary.

The book value of Ireland's and Singapore's cumulative FDI, valued at $229 and $160 billion, respectively, in 2004 put them at the top of the list of inward FDI on a per capita basis (if Hong Kong and special situations like bank-laden tax haven Caribbean islands are excluded). The two countries are also among the world's leaders when inward FDI is measured as a percent of GDP (126 and 150 percent in 2004, respectively).[18] In absolute terms, Ireland had the sixth largest and Singapore the thirteenth largest inward flow of FDI funds in 2003.[19]

Their economic histories are similar in that through the 1970s, both were down-and-out, underperforming economies by almost any measure. With no prospects in sight for internally generated improvement, attracting large volumes of high-quality FDI was designated a high-priority government objective. Market-oriented economic policies, attractive political and legal environments, financial incentives, aggressive marketing specifically aimed at foreign companies in high value-added sectors, programs to boost education and technical training, and geographical advantages made their shared quest a resounding success. Foreign companies were accounting for about one-half of employment in the two countries' manufacturing sectors by the turn of the century. The evidence is compelling that Ireland's and Singapore's success in attracting quality FDI was the number one cause of subsequent higher GDP growth rates, reduced unemployment, and rising standards of living. Good domestic economic policies were an important number two cause.

For more than 100 years prior to the 1960s, one of Ireland's principal exports was its own people. Emigrants in search of a better life reduced its population from roughly 8 million in the 1840s to a nadir of 2.8 million in 1961.[20] In what was a near overnight accomplishment for a national economy, Ireland became one of the world's major exporters of highly sophisticated technology goods, all but entirely due to the massive presence of high quality FDI. More than 1,000 foreign companies had established operations there by 2005, and they accounted for one-quarter of total economic output.[21] In roughly a decade beginning at the end of the 1980s, it rose from low-income status within the European Union (EU) to parity with the average per capita income of member countries. And it went from being one of the slowest growing to one of the fastest growing EU countries.

The Industrial Development Agency did a superb job of getting out the message on Ireland's many selling points as a host country: unrestricted export access to the markets of other EU members, the lowest corporate tax rates in the EU, and low labor costs (reflecting the union-government social partnership calling for wage restraint), yet a relatively well-educated and high-skilled workforce. It erected a first-class physical infrastructure, much of which was financed by grants from EU structural and cohesion funds earmarked for aiding less developed regions within the Union. The agency could also trumpet the government's providing tax holidays on profits earned from exporting and providing grants to defer start-up costs of new subsidiaries. Given the additional bonus of its being an English-speaking country, a who's who of U.S. high-tech firms selected Ireland as their main export springboard to the massive EU market.

Singapore is a city-state with very little land mass and no natural resources. It also was host in 2005 to some 7,000 MNCs, a total that includes many shipping companies, small firms, and companies maintaining only R&D and regional headquarters facilities.[22] Like Ireland, the dramatic and rapid up-market shift in the composition of its exports from labor-intensive to skill- and technology-intensive can be traced directly to the Singaporean government's highly successful FDI strategy of attracting companies that produced progressively higher value-added goods. The Economic Development Board's Web site boasts of world-class physical, legal, and social infrastructure; a relatively low corporate tax rate; tax deductions and grants for preferred business activities such as R&D expenditures, start-up ventures, and establishment of regional headquarters offices; a highly skilled, motivated, and disciplined workforce; a central location in the booming East Asian market; an expanding network of free trade agreements and bilateral investment guarantee agreements; the best quality of life in Asia; and a university system whose curriculum by design was shifted to an emphasis on technology and science.[23]

Why Foreign Capitalists Still Like China Better than India   Troubled by prolonged slow growth and widespread poverty amidst fast-growing populations, China in the early 1980s and India a decade later set about partially and gradually decontrolling their heavily regulated economies. The process is still unfinished as political factors demand a measured pace despite overwhelming data pointing to a link between economic liberalization and higher growth rates and reduced poverty rates. Market-oriented reforms in both countries included an opening of their previously closed economies to international trade and capital flows. Despite the fact that the histories of China and India encouraged them to associate MNCs with Western imperialism, step-by-step relaxation of controls on incoming direct investment remained an important part of their deregulation programs. Both were in great need of the capital, technology, and business know-how that FDI can bring. Until the mid-1980s, only small amounts of FDI chose to locate in China and even less flowed to India (an average of a token $62 million annually between 1980 and 1985). Now, having at least partially embraced market-based reforms, both countries (on paper) are attractive candidates to host foreign subsidiaries. Both offer overseas companies a seemingly inexhaustible supply of extremely cheap labor and in numerical terms, the two largest consumer markets in the world. The similarities end there.

China remains a political dictatorship and officially retains a communist, largely state-owned economy. Its rule of law standards fall far short of Western practices. Its officialdom is accountable only to each other, and its regulatory system is still opaque. These conditions encourage official corruption. The country holds the reputation in the United States and elsewhere of being the world's most prolific and brazen violator of foreign companies' intellectual property rights. Some foreign companies have discovered partners illegally selling counterfeit versions of products produced by their joint ventures. In the early years, it was common for Beijing to demand that foreign companies team up with a local partner and transfer up-to-date technology. Yet another negative factor is China's banking system being insolvent by Western standards because of extensive nonperforming loans.

India, on the other hand, is a democracy with a capitalist economic system. Its growth rates have been above the world average for several years. Its legal system and capital markets both function much better than those of China. India's average wage rates are only slightly higher. Many Indians are fluent in the international business language, English. And the country has direct access to sea routes, just like China.

Ironically, China is miles ahead in attracting FDI. China's $280 billion of aggregate FDI inflows from 1998 through 2003 were more than fifteen times greater that that of India—$18 billion.[24] At year end 2004, the book value, or cumulative stock of China's FDI had passed the $500 billion mark,[25] a figure well above India's $39 billion. (A data disaggregation is necessary here: China's FDI inflow can be called inflated because much of it is not "foreign" in the strictest sense of the term. Consensus estimates suggest that in a typical year, 60 percent or more of the value of FDI inflows come from investors in Hong Kong and Taiwan and from mainland Chinese firms engaging in round-tripping to take advantage of tax breaks given only to foreign investors.)

China, as already noted, is by far the largest recipient of FDI among emerging market countries and in most recent years has been the second largest destination (after the United States) for direct investment flows. Ultimately, the reason for this improbably big and quick success is that China wanted FDI badly, needed it badly, and eventually created an extremely attractive environment for both efficiency-seeking and market-seeking investments. Leaders of the Chinese Communist Party continue to believe that a major MNC presence is an indispensable part of history's biggest social contract: 1.3 billion people consenting to the Party's continuing to monopolize political power in return for a stronger economy capable of raising living standards on a sustained basis for large numbers of people.

China first stuck its foot into the waters of attracting FDI by establishing special economic zones (discussed in the next section) in the early 1980s. Pleased with the success of what was a bold experiment for Beijing, not an official embrace of a new economic ideology, the government added more zones and designated "open" coastal cities for relative policy autonomy in recruiting FDI. The physical separation of the special zones allowed the Chinese government to radically depart from socialist philosophy and provide a genuinely business-accommodating environment. Foreign-controlled subsidiaries were given a wide variety of tax concessions, including reduced rates and deferred taxes for several years, an ultra low-wage but relatively educated and disciplined workforce, excellent infrastructure that was constantly upgraded, low cost power, duty free or low tariff imports of capital equipment and intermediate goods, promises of expedited regulatory procedures, and last but not least, absence of unions.

By the second half of the 1990s, China's partial acceptance of market economics had unlocked its enormous economic potential. In terms of attracting FDI, the equivalent of a perfect storm resulted. Few major manufacturing companies anywhere in the world could ignore the incredible combination of China's rapid growth, the perception that China was becoming the world's low-cost producer of thousands of labor-intensive and medium-technology goods, the potential size of its consumer market, and the growing number of foreign companies setting up subsidiaries there. Fears of the potentially lethal consequences of being marginalized in such an incredibly attractive market led to spreading boardroom chants of "we cannot afford not to be producing in China" and to annual FDI flows of $40 to $50 billion.

India chose a different path. Politicians and civil servants could not shake deeply held beliefs dating back to the country's independence. The most important were the virtue of achieving economic self-sufficiency, the vices of unregulated markets, and the unfairness and indignity of being taken advantage of by big Western companies. Thanks to democracy, mass discontent was only a threat to the tenure of ruling parties, not a threat to trigger civil war as in China. The Indian government for much of the 1970s and early 1980s became a case study of how rightly or wrongly to antagonize foreign companies with unusually intrusive demands and regulations. Some disinvestment resulted as several companies, including IBM and Coca-Cola, shut down their operations in frustration and literally locked the doors.

A big remaining problem for India is that good intentions, for good reason, have fallen well short of convincing foreign corporate executives that the real advantages of choosing the country as a site for a manufacturing facility now outweigh the perceived disadvantages. A kind of perfect storm in reverse prevails. India's regulatory burden and the paperwork that goes with it are viewed as excessively time-consuming, expensive, and unjustifiable in a country trying to adopt a business-unfriendly mentality. What is needed, suggested *The Economist,* is a major reform of the "inspector Raj" and the "license Raj"—"a creaking edifice of central planning held together by miles of red tape."[26]

The country's physical infrastructure is viewed as being woefully inadequate— far behind that of China—with clogged roads, trains, and ports delaying shipments and causing unacceptable increases in production costs. According to the World Bank, India in 1980 had higher infrastructure stocks—power, roads, and telecommunications—than China. However, the latter has invested so heavily in infrastructure that it has overtaken India and is still widening the gap. Its lead in infrastructure stocks "is now so large that for India to catch up only to China's present levels of stocks per capita, it would have to invest 12.5 percent of GDP per year through 2015."[27] Financial incentives are still minimal in relation to comparable cost countries. Tax regulations are burdensome. Furthermore, labor laws are restrictive—even more restrictive than those of communist China. Foreign companies in the secondary sector have no use for the law prohibiting any manufacturing company with 100 or more workers from laying off employees without the seldom granted permission of the local or state government.[28] Contract labor is forbidden. Domestic investment is discouraged even more than foreign, as seen by the nominal effort of the Indian textile industry to increase production after termination of export ceilings imposed by the lapsed Agreement on Textiles and Clothing.[29]

A consulting company report provides a good summation: "When asked to describe what differentiated these two countries as investment destinations, most respondents considered China to be 'more business oriented' than India." The majority also were of the view that "China has more FDI-friendly policies."[30] That none of these weaknesses is insurmountable given adequate policy changes is suggested by India's impressive advances in the services sector, especially information technology. Government regulation is less intrusive, a skilled labor pool is available, and the telecommunications infrastructure has been adequate to the task of supporting a boom in the arrival of subsidiaries of foreign business services companies and outsourcing contracts received by Indian providers of business services from foreign companies.

The Thorny Issue of Government Incentives for MNCs

Corporate executives are like everyone else: They like to receive handouts from governments. A can't-miss stratagem to attract FDI, at least in theory, is for a government to provide millions of dollars (or the equivalent) in up-front grants to a foreign company that will reduce the costs, limit the risks, and increase the rate of return on its investment. However, corporate decisions on where to invest overseas are usually based on multiple factors; hence incentives in practice can be viewed as an expensive government program whose necessity and true value cannot be calculated with exactitude. It would be just another obscure unknown aspect of the FDI/MNCs phenomena if not for impassioned opposition by some to the idea of using tax revenues collected from middle and lower income people to the fatten the bottom lines of big, rich foreign companies. The act of shifting welfare from citizens to foreign multinationals becomes even more contentious if a poor developing country is making the transfer of financial wealth to a well-heeled MNC from the North.

Incentives to attract FDI are a component of industrial policy. The latter is an umbrella term for various government policies and programs used by government officials in the belief that they can create the best of all worlds by stuffing a very tangible fistful of money into the invisible hand of the marketplace. Assistance is provided to targeted companies or sectors, such as information technology or biotechnology, to influence the private sector to engage in investment and production activities to a greater degree than what they presumably would have done in a free market situation with no government intervention.

The mix and magnitude of FDI incentives included in the final package offered by a would-be host government to an interested MNC are determined on a case-by-case basis by the relative leverage and negotiating skills each party brings to the table. The standard benefits offered to foreign investors can be divided into three categories. *Fiscal incentives* reduce a foreign corporation's tax liabilities by means of any or all of the following: reduction in the standard corporate tax rate, tax holidays in which corporate income and property taxes are deferred for a fixed number of years, accelerated depreciation allowances, tax credits for domestic reinvestment of profits, and exemptions in the value-added tax for capital goods and raw materials purchases. Income derived from exports may be exempted indefinitely from corporate taxes or assessed at a preferential rate.

The second category, *financial incentives*, consists of direct grants that defray one or more of an MNC's expenses in getting a subsidiary up and running. These nonrepayable subsidies can reduce the costs of land acquisition, construction, worker training, and capital goods (factory equipment) purchases. Other financial incentives provided by governments are subsidized loans and loan guarantees. The third category of incentives is the catchall category of *other*. Modernized or expanded transportation and telecommunications infrastructure, subsidized power and water, exemption from import duties on raw materials and capital equipment, preferential access to government contracts, closing the domestic market to future direct investment by competing foreign companies, and preinvestment feasibility studies are included here. So, too, is official commitment to raise import barriers to protect the output of the new subsidiary from foreign competition. Although seldom used, this policy can puncture the generalization that MNCs are unwavering advocates of free trade.

Though the gross monetary outlays for incentives are fairly easy to calculate, determining their net costs/net benefits is not. At worst, incentives can be a total waste of government funds if a corporate recipient would have invested in a country without them, perhaps because it was judged to offer the best chance for long-term competitiveness of the new subsidiary.[31] At best, the short-term costs of inducements eventually will pale relative to long-term benefits. Increases in jobs and tax revenues may eventually exceed original estimates by wide margins. The financial success of a foreign subsidiary lured by generous incentives can trigger a positive chain of events that includes a major expansion of the facility's operations (e.g., Intel in Costa Rica), arrival of direct investments by suppliers, and a succession of minimally subsidized competitors and other companies.[32] Under this scenario, the latter are drawn in by the original investment's financial success and happiness with its governmental host, improved infrastructure, and the arrival of firms providing specialized business services. In other words, the demonstration effect and agglomeration economies just discussed come into play.

Estimating in advance the cost/benefit ratio of any given incentives package is a very imprecise art because one cannot predict its future effects, cannot know the well-being of a domestic or regional economy if an investment had not been made, and seldom can give precise answers to gray-area variables. For example, would a country or region have been better advised using taxpayers' money to create long-term economic strengths—better human and physical infrastructure—rather than dispensing short-term financial rewards to favored companies? On the favorable side, it is possible that part or all of the costs of incentives might be recovered in the form of social goods, that is, positive spillovers of superior knowledge and technology possessed by many MNCs (see chapter 12) that would not have occurred in a free market environment. Economic theory states that governmental assistance to a company can be justified *if* it is necessary to convince management to establish the kind of subsidiary that maximizes social benefits, for example, increases skill levels of workers, teaches domestic businesses to increase their productivity, and so on.[33]

Not surprisingly, consensus does not characterize inquiries into the overall merits of incentives. UNCTAD has concluded, "How to measure the cost and benefits of incentives is complex and problematic; even when this can be done, the implementation and administration of a calibrated incentives programme is often very difficult and can be distorted by political objectives." Also difficult to answer is the larger question as to whether national welfare gains enhance world welfare or come at the expense of other countries.[34] Because studies are based largely on interviews with a limited number of corporate executives, the selection of companies for the sample, and the willingness of the executives interviewed to be candid about a potentially touchy subject can skew the results in either direction.

Interestingly, there are indications that the importance accorded incentives differs according to what kind of investment is being considered and what its objectives are, a central theme of this study.[35] When a site is being selected for an efficiency-seeking export platform or for servicing a relatively small national market, incentives are likely to be more important than for a subsidiary intended to exploit a large, growing national market. Another reasonable conclusion is that the value of any incentive package is likely to be most decisive when a company has compiled a short list of two or three acceptable host countries relatively evenly matched in economic and political fundamentals—and therefore need something extra to stand out.

The desire to offer something extra has led to bidding wars in which national and regional governments of rich and poor countries alike sometimes go to dubious lengths as they seek to outbid one another to land attractive investment projects. Examples abound of incentive packages that came close to deferring all of a company's plant-opening expenses or equated to hundreds of thousands of dollars for every job initially created.[36] Dow Chemical received a $6.8 billion subsidy from the German government in 1996 to invest in a petrochemical plant in the depressed eastern region of the country; it set a still unequaled record of equating to $3.4 million for each job created.[37] Despite (or maybe because of) the absence of any FDI incentives from Washington, an economic war of the states periodically erupts in the United States. The most notable have involved Southern states aggressively vying for foreign-owned automobile plants. Alabama has won four of these bidding contests. One consisted of a reported incentive package worth $253 million to get a $300 million Mercedes-Benz plant in 1993, about $169,000 for every job promised; a comparable $253 million in incentives was given to Hyundai in 2002, about $125,000 per job promised.[38]

The monetary costs of these incentives need to be weighed against the German government's priority effort to revive the economy of the old East Germany, and Southern states need to offset the steady erosion of jobs in the declining textile and apparel industries that once were the mainstays of the region's economy. Expensive incentives, however, are not an absolute requirement even for an LDC with solid economic and political attributes to attract quality direct investment. This was the case with Costa Rica and Intel in the 1990s. The former granted the latter "no special favors . . . , no side deals or firm-specific concessions." The concessions they did make—schools, transportation enhancements, free trade zones, and so on, were "not unreasonable or capricious," all were "generalizable to other investors—and generally good for Costa Rica's economy."[39]

A negative or positive attitude toward FDI incentives as a whole is going to be linked to one's answer to a much larger question: How much good or harm do MNCs impart to host countries? Persons who believe they are exploitive likely would find no redeeming qualities in incentives to attract them. Those who believe MNCs surpass domestic companies in technology, management know-how, enhancement of worker skills, wages and benefits, and so on, likely would favor them. If one believes that the impact of MNCs on host countries depends on case-by-case company and country variables, the answer to the question of whether FDI incentives are wise or foolish, necessary or unnecessary is likely to be: *it depends.* In any event, in a perfect world the controversy over incentives could be easily resolved, and the bidding wars quickly ended. Governments need only sign an agreement to halt the process and let economic fundamentals be the selling points, and then not violate the spirit or letter of self-restraint (see chapter 15).

What MNCs Don't Want in a Host Country

The more successful economies do not lack for FDI. The more unsuccessful ones do. Dozens of moderately successful economies are dissatisfied with the quantity and quality of the direct investment they get and would like to upgrade on both counts. Before examining deliberate and inadvertent government behaviors that cause MNCs to write off countries as sites for their foreign subsidiaries, two overarching points need to be emphasized. First, a small amount of FDI in a country is not necessarily unequivocal evidence that its economic performance and policies are substandard. Whatever economic benefits MNCs might bring, the majority of citizens may place abstract values, for example, control over national destiny and a social status quo, ahead of material wealth and be happier without an influx of foreign companies. Second, by discouraging incoming manufacturing and services subsidiaries, however justified and admirable the motives, an individual country cannot stop the proliferation of MNCs, nor can it humanize their practices. The main result is generating gratitude by the countries where FDI is redirected. With more than 200 countries and territories to choose from, manufacturing and services corporations seldom have a problem finding locales where governing authorities roll out the red carpet and meet company demands to seal the deal.

The most effective policy to repel FDI is to ban it outright or at least in sectors where sensitivity to foreign control is especially acute. In democracies, this can be done either through constitutional amendments (as the Philippines did with mining) or national legislation. Nearly every country, from the richest to the poorest, has enacted statutes that specifically prevent foreigners from having controlling interests in a relatively few stipulated business sectors. An absolute, across-the-board ban on incoming FDI is a policy no longer being used. It has universally been judged prohibitively expensive, though this verdict is subject to change without prior warning. Not even North Korea has a total prohibition because it accepts investment from South Korea, which it perceives to be a foreign country.

Various federal statutes in the United States limit foreign participation in domestic airlines, radio and TV stations, nuclear energy, coastal and inland waterway shipping, and certain segments of mining, among others. States have their own series of restrictions, chiefly involving land ownership. A Congress alarmed at the putative selling of America passed legislation that resulted in establishment of an interagency Executive Branch committee that can stop foreign investors from acquiring or merging with U.S. firms if it determines the transaction threatens to impair U.S. national security.[40]

A very effective means of discouraging incoming FDI is for a government to engage in mass expropriation (nationalization) of foreign-held companies with inadequate or no compensation. This practice has largely been phased out from its peak popularity in the early 1970s as contemporary heads of government, except for the occasional bellicose dictator, have come to view it as a short-sighted and self-defeating.

Regulatory hassles are the most overlooked of the top reasons why MNCs are disinclined to invest in certain countries. Most business regulations tend to be obscure to everyone except those directly affected by them. Even if such burdens are imposed in equal measure on locally owned business, MNCs view onerous regulations, surprise announcements of new ones, and capricious, unpredictable reinterpretations of existing regulations as aggravation they most definitely do not countenance. Nor do they need to, with so many alternative destinations. The World Bank emphasized the perils of a burdensome regulatory regime in its *Doing Business 2005* report. Businesses in poor countries were found to face much greater regulatory burdens than those in rich countries: three times the administrative costs and nearly twice as many bureaucratic procedures and delays associated with them. Businesses in LDCs on average receive less than one-half the property rights protections provided to them by the industrialized countries.[41] Defined broadly, burdensome regulations also include import barriers that would restrict shipments between an MNC's subsidiaries and the need to pay bribes to expedite cooperation by officialdom.

Existing investments are not immune from regulatory and governance problems. Sony closed a major audio equipment plant in Indonesia in 2004, allegedly due to frustration with inconsistent regulation, corruption, and labor unrest. RWE Thames Water withdrew in the same year from a water treatment project that it had built and operated in Shanghai when the Chinese government changed the rules on the rate of return for such investments. Disinvestment has become common in countries achieving pariah status and becoming the target of official sanctions. A number of multinationals decided that discretion was the better part of valor and withdrew from South Africa, Burma, and Sudan when human rights groups loudly complained that their corporate presence helped repressive regimes stay in power.

Performance requirements are another means by which host countries make themselves less attractive to foreign investors. The term refers to any of several publicly announced operational limitations that a government can demand as the price of admission for a proposed foreign subsidiary. The economic objective of performance requirements is to constrain pursuit of profit in a manner that makes the foreign company's operations more compatible with a country's development goals and strategy. Some governments, mostly in LDCs, appreciate the potential value of FDI but do not subscribe to a pure free market philosophy that assumes a company acting in its own self-interest automatically promotes the national interest.

One of the most common stipulations in the past was a local content requirement that required a minimum percentage of the final value of a subsidiary's output be produced locally, thereby further increasing domestic production and jobs. The Trade-Related Investment Measures (TRIMs) Agreement concluded in 1994 at the Uruguay Round of multilateral trade negotiations bars member countries of the World Trade Organization from invoking this measure. The rationale is that local content requirements distort and interfere with market-directed trade flows. The occasionally invoked requirement that the annual value of exports be at least equal to a subsidiary's total imports (known as trade balancing) also was banned by the TRIMs agreement because of its distorting impact on trade. A still-used performance requirement requires a subsidiary to export a minimum agreed-on percentage of the value of its annual output (thereby guaranteeing foreign exchange earnings for the host country). Other examples of mainstream performance requirements are stipulated transfers of technology, agreement on how many local citizens will be placed in management positions, limitations on repatriations of profits, a minimum level of taxation, and demand that a factory will be built in a depressed, high-unemployment region of the host country.

Below-average rates of economic growth rank near the top of the list of things not wanted by companies scouting sites for overseas subsidiaries. A close statistical relationship has long existed between the LDCs having the lowest per capita incomes and relative absence of FDI (see previous discussion and chapter 8). This is a connection whose root cause in virtually every instance is economic policy mismanagement and poor governance, and in some cases, social unrest. Although economic malaise inflicted by governments is seldom intentional, it is a failing that extinguishes desire by nonextractive, risk-averse foreign companies to invest. When developing countries do abysmally in the widely read rankings of national economic and business performances, the odds are overwhelming that they have long been absent from the radar screens of major MNCs. A positive three-way statistical correlation frequently appears between countries with high and growing standards of living, good grades in these international comparisons, and high rates of FDI. The same three-way correlation exists in reverse for the poorest countries. Direct investments by oil and mining companies often have a strong financial incentive (and sometimes no alternative) to tolerate adverse conditions that would scare off manufacturing and services companies. The poorest countries typically have dysfunctional economies and an inconsequential number of foreign-owned factories. As the next section points out, the least developed countries do not have a monopoly on economic policies that scare off inward manufacturing investment.

Country Case Studies: Why Nigeria and Venezuela Are Masters of the Art of Repelling FDI

Nigeria and Venezuela live in parallel universes located many light years away from the Ireland-Singapore galaxy. They are in a class by themselves as serial underachievers in converting massive wealth earned from exports of their natural resources into sustained economic progress. In the thirty-three-year period from 1974 (the initial year of the first oil shock) through 2006, Venezuela earned an estimated $518 billion, and Nigeria earned an estimated $500 billion from oil exports.[42] Poor governance and economic policy mismanagement in both countries have resulted in a nearly total absence of incoming FDI in manufacturing or services for many years, their oil bonanza notwithstanding. This should not be the situation when a country on paper offers foreign companies relatively low-cost labor, a large domestic market, or both.[43] Nigeria and Venezuela both did poorly in the Heritage Foundation's 2005 Index of Economic Freedom (numbers 141 and 146, respectively, out of 155 countries evaluated). Interestingly, Venezuela ranked first and Nigeria third in the list of countries exhibiting the greatest decline in economic freedom over the eleven-year history of the index.[44]

Nigeria's noxious economic environment has caused steady deteriorations in per capita incomes and living standards since the late 1970s. A good clue as to how this happened is the World Bank's estimate that approximately 80 percent of the country's oil and natural gas revenues have gone to just 1 percent of the population.[45] A Nigerian government official, quoted in a 2005 International Monetary Fund publication, estimated that corruption and mismanagement, even after reforms, still swallowed as much as 40 percent of the country's annual oil income while nearly 75 percent of the country's population continues to live below the poverty line.[46] Most extractive companies operating there must provide their own electricity, water, Internet, and telephone facilities rather than rely on substandard and erratic public utilities.[47] The country's economic and political shortcomings and the resulting negative business environment are manifested in a perennially dismal showing in major rankings of comparative national economic performance:

- The bottom 10 percent of the 135 countries included in the World Bank's estimates of per capita gross national income in purchasing parity terms. At $900, Nigeria's per capita income in 2003 was well below the average of $2,190 for low-income countries.
- Number 98 out of 140 countries on UNCTAD's index for potential inward FDI in 2000–2002.
- The 144th most corrupt country out of 146 listed in Transparency International's (an NGO) Corruption Perceptions Index for 2004.
- Number 81 in the 103 countries included in the World Economic Forum's Business Competitiveness Index for 2004–2005.
- The eighth most risky (politically and economically) emerging market country in 2004 according to the Economist Intelligence Unit's rankings. "Nigeria is an insecure environment for commercial operations."[48]

Venezuela's per capita income has held steady at a higher level than Nigeria's, but its recent economic development has been woeful given its oil wealth. It was the third riskiest emerging market on *The Economist*'s 2004 list, the 88th country in the World Economic Forum's competitiveness list, and 114th in Transparency International's corruption perceptions list. Venezuela's current problem attracting manufacturing FDI is neither absence of prospective consumer buying power nor relatively high wages, but its mercurial political leader, Hugo Chavez. His anticapitalist rhetoric, the unremitting turbulence and political polarization that followed shortly after his inauguration in 1999, and decay of political institutions have devastated the atmosphere for nonoil FDI.[49] The Economist Intelligence Unit's assessment that "most non–oil FDI will continue to be put off by the uncertain legal and regulatory regimes" is classic understatement.[50] Disaggregated data (not available for Nigeria) show that FDI inflows in the manufacturing sector were effectively zero from 1994 through 2002, the latest year data is available. The country's accumulated stock or book value of FDI in the secondary sector was \$3.9 billion in 2002, exactly the same as it was in 1993.[51]

In contrast to the vicious cycles and poor rankings of Nigeria and Venezuela, the masters of attracting FDI fared much better. Singapore ranked 10th, 2nd, and 5th on the above-mentioned competitiveness, economic freedom, and (non)corruption perception indices, respectively. Ireland's standings in the same indices were 22nd, 5th, and 17th.

Notes

1. Data sources: UNCTAD, *World Investment Report 2004*, p. 370, and *World Investment Report 2005*, p. 303, both available online at http://www.unctad.org; accessed November 2005.
2. Data source: World Bank, Word Development Indicators database, statistics are for 2003, available online at http://devdata.worldbank.org/wdi2005/Cover.htm; accessed November 2005.
3. UNCTAD, *World Investment Report 2001*, p. 9.
4. Ibid., p. xv.
5. Data source: UNCTAD, *World Investment Report 2004*. I have ignored the large numbers for inflows into and outflows from Luxembourg because of the distortions caused by "trans-shipments" of FDI by holding companies and extensive investments in thinly regulated banking offices.
6. Data source: UNCTAD, *World Investment Report 2004*.
7. As quoted in Thomas Friedman, "The End of the Rainbow," *New York Times*, June 29, 2005, p. A23.
8. The Economist Intelligence Unit, "Hungary—Country Profile 2005," p. 31, available online at http://www.eiu.com; accessed September 2005.
9. UNCTAD, *World Investment Report 2003*, p. 29.
10. The UNCTAD Secretariat compares national performance in the two indices in detail by presenting a fourfold matrix of inward FDI performance and potential: (1) frontrunners: countries with high FDI potential and performance; (2) above potential: countries with low FDI potential but strong FDI performance; (3) below potential: countries with high FDI potential but low FDI performance; and (4) underperformers: countries with both low FDI potential and performance.
11. The World Bank, *World Development Report 2005*, p. 15, available online at http://www.worldbank.org; accessed May 2005.
12. The survey was conducted on behalf of the Multilateral Investment Guarantee Agency, an affiliate of the World Bank.
13. "Foreign Direct Investment Survey," January 2002, p. 19, available online at http://www.ipa.net/documents/WorldBank/databases/survey/FDIsurvey/fdisurvey.pdf; accessed April 2005.

14. Magdolna Sass, "FDI in Hungary—The First Mover's Advantage and Disadvantage," *European Investment Bank Papers*, 9(2), 2004, p. 72.

15. UNCTAD, *World Investment Report 2002*, p. 137.

16. Source: http://www.intel.com/pressroom; accessed March 2005.

17. U.S. International Trade Commission, "Industry Trade and Technology Review," July 2002, p. 19, available online at http://www.usitc.gov; accessed April 2005.

18. UNCTAD, *World Investment Report 2005*, Annex tables B.2, B.3.

19. Data source: Ibid., pp. 367–70. Data for 2003 are used here because Ireland and Singapore had unusually low and high FDI inflows, respectively, in 2004.

20. Eileen M. Doherty, "Evaluating FDI-Led Development: The Celtic (Paper?) Tiger," Working paper, Columbia International Affairs Online, January 1998, available online at http://www.ciaonet.org; accessed November 2004.

21. Data source: http://www.idaireland.com; accessed May 2006.

22. Singapore Economic Development Board, available online at http://www.edb.gov.sg; accessed November 2004.

23. The URL for the board's exhaustive Web site is http://www.edb.gov.sg.

24. Data source: UNCTAD, *World Investment Report 2004*, p. 370.

25. Data derived from http://www.uschina.org/china-statistics.html and various press reports.

26. "Can India Work?" *The Economist*, June 12, 2004, p. 67.

27. The World Bank, "India—Inclusive Growth and Service Delivery: Building on India's Success," May 29, 2006, p. 106; available online at http://siteresources.worldbank.org/SOUTHASIAEXT/Resources/DPR_FullReport.pdf; accessed July, 2006.

28. Business Week Online, "India's Manufacturers in Shackles," October 20, 2003, available online at http://www.businessweek.com; accessed February 2005.

29. "India Plays Catch-Up in Textiles," *Wall Street Journal*, December 1, 2005, p. A15.

30. A. T. Kearney, "FDI Confidence Audit: India," February 2001, p. 16, available online at http://www.atkearney.com; accessed June 2005.

31. This is no way implies that government officials can or should know at the time they are negotiating an incentives package that the company has made such a determination.

32. I could find no data or articles providing estimates on the extent of follow-up jobs created in the years after major foreign subsidiaries began production in various countries.

33. The theory is based on the concept that because a company does not consider the possibility of favorable spillovers to society at large in the home country when calculating returns on investment, social returns can exceed private returns. The rest of society in a host country can free ride on certain benefits provided by a new subsidiary. In theory, incentives can be formulated to convince an MNC to invest in a manner that maximizes positive externalities and social returns, that is, spillovers of knowledge and technology are maximized. Converting these variables into hard, convincing numbers is seldom possible.

34. UNCTAD, *World Investment Report 1995*, p. 299.

35. For a good survey of studies on FDI incentives, see Theodore H. Moran, *Foreign Direct Investment and Development* (Washington, DC: Institute for International Economics, 1998), pp. 98–104; also UNCTAD's *World Investment Report 1998*, p. 103.

36. For a scoreboard of the cost of incentives per job created in a number of major FDI projects, see UNCTAD, *World Investment Report 2002*, pp. 204–5.

37. Ibid.

38. Data sources: *Wall Street Journal,* April 3, 2002, p. 1, and *FDi Magazine,* December 2, 2002, available online at http://www.fdimagazine.com; accessed April 2004.

39. Debora Spar, "Attracting High Technology Investment—Intel's Costa Rican Plant," Foreign Investment Advisory Service Occasional Paper 11, April 1998, p. 23.

40. The so-called Exon-Florio provision was contained in trade legislation enacted in 1988. It has resulted in only one known direct rejection of a proposed takeover as of 2004. It may have discouraged some contemplated takeovers or mergers from moving forward.

41. "Removing Obstacles to Growth: An Overview," available online at http://www.worldbank.org/Documents/DoingBusiness/Intro.pdf#search; accessed March 2005.

42. Calculated from unpublished data provided to the author by the Energy Information Administration, U.S. Department of Energy, June 2005.

43. With a population well in excess of 100 million people, Nigeria was ranked as the world's tenth most populous country in 2003 by many estimates.

44. Heritage Foundation, "Executive Summary," *2005 Index of Economic Freedom,* available online at http://www.heritage.org; accessed May 2005. Venezuela ranked fifty-third and Nigeria fifty-ninth, respectively, in an evaluation of the business environment in sixty countries by the Economist Intelligence Unit's *World Investment Prospects,* 2001.

45. U.S. Department of Energy, "OPEC Revenues: Country Details," January 2005, available online at http://www.eia.doe.gov/emeu/cabs/orevcoun.html; accessed February 2005.

46. *IMF Survey,* February 7, 2005, p. 22.

47. The Economist Intelligence Unit, "Nigeria Risk: Risk Overview," June 2005, available online at http://www.eiu.com; accessed June 2005.

48. Data sources: http://www.worldbank.org, http://www.unctad.org, http://www.transparency.org, http://www.weforum.org, *The Economist,* May 29, 2004, p. 98, and the Economist Intelligence Unit, 2006, as quoted at http://www.tmc.met.com/usubmit/2006/06/14/1683314.htm; accessed June, 2006.

49. The Economist Intelligence Unit, "Country Report—Venezuela," May 2005, available online at http://www.eiu.com; accessed June 2005.

50. The Economist Intelligence Unit, Executive Briefing, "Venezuela: Foreign Investment," October 2003, and "Venezuela Risk: Risk Overview," June 2005, available online at http://www.eb.eiu.com; accessed June 2005.

51. Data source: UNCTAD, "FDI Country Profiles," available online at http://www.unctad.org/templates/page.asp?intItemID=3198&lang=1; accessed May 2005.

PART III

Impact on the International Order

8

EFFECTS OF FOREIGN DIRECT INVESTMENT ON LESS DEVELOPED COUNTRIES

Vagaries, Variables, Negatives, and Positives

The most contentious single point regarding the merits of foreign direct investment (FDI) and multinational corporations (MNCs) is whether on balance they help or hinder the economic development of less developed countries (LDCs). A resolution of the polemics is not in sight. Supporters of international business argue that the efficiency and know-how of private enterprise allow foreign subsidiaries to play a uniquely valuable role in accelerating economic growth and raising living standards and workers' skill levels in low-income countries. Critics maintain that venal efforts by foreign companies to maximize profits are so overwhelmingly detrimental to the economic and social fabric of LDCs that MNCs should be tightly regulated if not banned outright. A third assessment is that in some cases, economic and political conditions in a host country are the independent variables determining the effects of incoming direct investment, not the other way around. The absence of a clear answer leaves policy makers in LDCs with mixed signals in deciding how much or how little FDI they should allow to enter.

The structure of this chapter conforms to the integrating themes of this book—the importance of disaggregation, the fallacy of generalization, and the ability of perceptions to define reality. These themes are directly applicable to the many layers and manifold ambiguities of the LDC–FDI relationship. The first section discusses the context for the argument that uncertainties and conceptual obstacles are too great to allow a definitive, black or white—and accurate— answer to the contentious question of how well or poorly FDI has affected the economic well-being of LDCs. The remainder of the chapter discusses four credible answers. The second and third sections summarize, respectively, two mutually exclusive but plausible views on whether incoming FDI on balance has harmed or bolstered economic development in LDCs. These perspectives are presented in the form of two aggressive, conflicting legal briefs that aim to do justice to the pro and con sides without injecting any of the author's value judgments as to which is preferable and where the holes are in the arguments. (Neutrality in this case should come easily because the author is not enamored with either of these two sides.)

The fourth section is a lengthy examination of the many variables that justify yet another call for disaggregation. A number of credible assessments of the net impact of FDI on LDCs are possible; the facts depend on circumstances. Disaggregation is essential to control for the range of conditions that exist within host countries and for the diverse characteristics associated with the many forms of FDI and MNCs. The "it depends" mantra, repeated throughout this chapter, has the additional credibility of being consistent with the findings of a majority of widely cited academic studies produced over the past twenty years on the FDI–LDC interface. The chapter's last section argues that due to the pervasive murkiness of the issue, a fourth legitimate response is that we simply do not know for sure whether the cumulative net effects of FDI on LDCs as a group should be labeled positive or negative.

Eight Obstacles to a Clear-Cut, Definitive, and Accurate Assessment of the Effects of FDI and MNCs on LDCs

The much contested issue of how FDI and MNCs have affected the economic development, living standards, poverty reduction efforts, and growth rates of LDCs is arguably the single best validation of this study's thesis on how best to analyze and assess these international business phenomena. The ongoing emphases on complexity, heterogeneity, multiple versions of "the truth," uncertainty, and inconsistency apply to virtually all aspects of FDI and MNCs, but especially so in this case. Generalizations lacking qualifications about their effects on the economies of LDCs brazenly ignore the existence of very credible conflicting arguments. "Determining exactly how FDI affects development has proven to be remarkably elusive."[1]

The conflicting schools of thought on whether FDI is a meaningful catalyst of economic growth in LDCs are graphically displayed in a table appearing in a nongovernmental organization (NGO) monograph containing a review of the scholarly literature. Next to a list of fifteen published studies is a column that lists which of four different answers each gave to the overriding question of FDI

being an engine of LDC growth: yes, mainly yes, no, and maybe.[2] A second column summarizes the main variables cited by each of these studies as determinants of whether FDI promotes growth. No two sets of variables are identical!
Conflicting results should not be a cause for angst because they are natural outgrowths of studies examining subjects short on simplicity and hard facts. Eight
major obstacles to a single unambiguous, unassailable, and all-inclusive assessment of FDI's impact on lower income countries can be easily identified.

The first is agreeing on the best criteria to determine which countries to
designate as developing or LDCs. It is far from clear what countries this chapter
deals with. The terms *third world* and the *South* make sense only in political
terms. With the exception of Thailand, all countries designated third world at
some time were forcibly colonized or made spheres of influence (e.g., China) by
industrial countries, mainly in Western Europe. All of them believe, with different intensities of resentment, that the few rich countries exercise great power
in the international arena and account for a large percentage of the world's wealth
that in both cases are grossly out of proportion to their small share of the world's
population.

In the realm of economics, the terms *third world* and *South* lack substance. The
countries of Africa, East and South and Western Asia, Eastern Europe, and Latin
America and the Caribbean collectively share economic diversity. The only other
thing they have in common economically is the status of not being among the
twenty-seven sovereign countries (plus Taiwan and Hong Kong) classified by the
International Monetary Fund (IMF) as relatively wealthy industrialized countries, that is, the North. For purposes of economic analysis and comparison, the
countries colloquially designated as third world should be divided into six separate categories. Countries in each of these groupings share similarities in terms
of both their levels of economic prosperity and relationships with MNCs. The
six should be discussed as parts of two larger classifications. The first includes
two subgroups of countries that definitely meet the economic criteria for being
considered relatively poor and below average in terms of economic development.
The second classification consists of four subgroups whose statistical profiles
suggest that they have graduated to a status somewhere between intermediate and
low-level developed. The true LDCs can be divided between those that are
moderately well-off countries (e.g., India, Peru, and Mauritius) and the least
developed countries (a category including most Sub-Saharan countries and some
in South Asia and Central America, e.g., Afghanistan and Honduras).

Value judgments determine whether the other four subgroups of countries
truly belong in the LDC category and in this chapter. The first subgroup consists
of several oil-rich countries in the Persian Gulf region that are among the
countries having the highest per capita incomes. *Emerging markets* has become a
phrase applicable to countries that have unofficially graduated from developing

status by virtue of their relatively high standard of living compared to truly poor LDCs and their ability to attract considerable inflows of private capital, including FDI in the manufacturing sector. Emerging market countries account for two subgroups, one appropriately labeled *emerging* and the other *entry level developed*. Thailand, Brazil, and Malaysia exemplify the former, whereas Korea, Singapore, and Israel exemplify the latter category. The fourth subgroup consists of former communist bloc countries and former Soviet republics, plus China. Perhaps they have now passed the deadline for continued designation as countries in transition from communism to market-based economies. Given their wide range of economic development and standards of living in these countries, an argument can be made for eliminating this subgroup and reassigning them to the categories of least developed, moderately developed, emerging market (Russia, for example), or entry level developed (Central Europe).

A second formidable obstacle in constructing an accurate blueprint of the LDC–FDI relationship is an outgrowth of the first obstacle: finding consistencies among *heterogeneous* FDI/MNCs (see chapter 4) as well as consistencies within the *heterogeneous* economies of up to 160 countries. The domestic economies of the nonrich countries display no significant common characteristics. They epitomize heterogeneity. They are not even all poor in the conventional sense. Indicators of economic diversity begin with the wide arithmetic spread that LDCs display in basic development indicators such as per capita GDP, average level of education, and life expectancy. The developing country category includes countries with fabulous oil wealth and well above-average per capita incomes along with those having relatively sophisticated manufacturing and services sectors. The category also includes countries suffering pervasive and entrenched poverty that is literally life-threatening to a significant percentage of their populations. The relatively prosperous economies of countries like Kuwait (per capita income in excess of $16,000 in 2003) and Malaysia have nothing in common with the backwardness afflicting Ethiopia (per capita income of $90 in 2003), Afghanistan, or Malawi. China and India, each with populations equivalent to about one-fifth of humankind, stand in sharp contrast to several island countries in the Caribbean and Pacific having populations numbering only in the tens of thousands.

The hierarchal nature of economic performance and living standards among "LDCs" broadly defined creates a third conceptual obstacle to a hard-and-fast determination of how FDI affects them as a group. Statistics have long shown a very concentrated geographical distribution of FDI in the developing countries as measured by both amounts and kinds. This distribution closely correlates with relative economic performance. The result is that LDCs as a collective have registered a skewed set of experiences with incoming MNCs. Many of the least developed, resource-poor countries to this day have received negligible FDI and therefore have recorded no statistically meaningful effects, good or bad, from it. Other countries, principally in the Middle East and Africa, have mainly or exclusively attracted resource-extracting companies. Many of the latter have compiled a long historical record of acting in an imperious fashion and generating only a few jobs for locals but lots of under-the-table cash for local political leaders and power brokers. A second group of countries, most of which are in South Asia, possess large numbers of unskilled labor and consequently attract mainly or exclusively labor-intensive manufacturers needing relatively low-paid workers for relatively simple tasks. Finally, a third category is mostly composed of East Asian and South American countries where much of the South's FDI in sophisticated manufacturing and services is located, along with the relatively high wages associated with skilled labor.

The asymmetrical country-by-country distribution of FDI among LDCs/countries in transition creates a situation in which a single set of statistics can be interpreted in two different ways. On one level, it is factually correct to argue that inward FDI has become an increasingly important source, in relative and absolute terms, of much-needed convertible hard currency for LDCs.[3] According to UNCTAD data, FDI as a percentage of total capital flows to LDCs rose from 6 percent in 1980 to 60 percent in 2000.[4] The book value of FDI in developing and transition countries jumped from an estimated $302 billion in 1980 to $2.4 trillion in 2004. Annual inward flows in these countries grew at an even faster rate, from an estimated annual average rate of just over $13 billion in the years from 1981 through 1986 to an unusually strong $268 billion in 2004.[5] Annual inflows of FDI to LDCs now dwarf the totals for official aid flows; the former were ten times as large as the latter in 2000. As recently as the early 1990s, these two categories of capital flows were about equal.[6]

Although FDI is very important for developing countries in arithmetic terms as a means of earning hard currency, a disaggregation of investment flow data is essential to provide a better depiction of reality. The fact is that inward FDI is a major source of potential benefits (or costs) to a relatively small number of economically advanced LDCs. For many years, they have accounted for a disproportionately large percentage of new FDI in the South. One country, China, has typically accounted for about 30 percent of FDI flows to *all* developing countries since the mid-1990s. China together with the next four largest nonindustrial country recipients of FDI accounted for 50–60 percent of total flows in each year from the mid-1990s through the early 2000s. In 2001, the last year that UNCTAD published these numbers in their annual *World Investment Report*, the share of the top thirty host developing countries was 95 percent of the total. This means that more than 130 LDCs and countries in transition on the middle and lower rungs of the economic development hierarchy received minimal FDI. In 2004, identified FDI flows to the more than fifty countries in Africa were $18 billion, only 0.07 percent of flows to all developing countries and a mere 0.027 percent of world totals.[7]

One more clarification is needed to erase any and all obfuscation in the statistics on geographical concentration of FDI in LDCs. There is more symmetry than meets the eye when it is noted that the largest recipients of FDI have an approximately equally large share of the GDP, employment, and exports of all countries categorized as less developed. A less skewed picture results if UNCTAD's recently devised Inward FDI Performance Index is used; it calculates the ratio of a country's percentage of global FDI inflows to its share of global GDP. When absolute receipts of FDI are adjusted for a country's relative economic size, the results are surprising: Some relatively obscure developing poor countries rank near the top. The explanation is that a small number of high-cost incoming foreign subsidiaries can be statistically significant in a country with a small GDP. Because of booming foreign-owned oil drilling ventures, Azerbaijan, Angola, Gambia, and Brunei were among the top seven performers in UNCTAD's GDP-adjusted FDI Performance Index rankings for 2001–2003. (Another statistical anomaly is Luxembourg-Belgium's being ranked first since the performance index started, a consequence of extensive financial and holding company investments lured by minimal regulations; trans-shipped FDI capital flows; and a relatively small GDP.)[8]

A fourth obstacle arises from conflicting views on how to define *economic development*. The question in qualitative terms is whether in fact it is first and foremost an economic process. Some have made the case that a country's progression to advanced industrialized economy status must be preceded or at least accompanied by social modernization. Defining development in quantitative terms poses a separate set of dilemmas. "Per capita" data are averages of a statistical universe that can be distorted if a country's population is divided between a few extremely wealthy persons and a majority of very poor citizens.

The more narrow term *economic growth* is largely defined through commonly used quantitative indicators. However, a larger, more important question is what are the economic, social, political, and psychological forces that have elevated a limited number of countries to comparative affluence? Which of these forces are essential and which are optional? Is a separate configuration needed for every country to complement unique national characteristics? If we knew the correct answers, we would know what actions to take, and the number of poor countries would progressively shrink as would the more than one billion people currently living subsistence lives on incomes equivalent to $2 a day or less. Until and unless the abstruse wiring in the black box of economic development is fully mastered, it is safe to assume that no one will be able to devise a beyond-a-reasonable-doubt method of determining how diverse kinds of FDI and MNCs affect the economic well-being of a large number of economically, politically, and socially diverse developing countries.

The methodological difficulties of correctly identifying cause and effect and distinguishing between cause and correlation constitute a fifth obstacle to definitively assessing FDI's impact on LDCs. Knowing in which direction lines of causality flow in this case is problematic because they can run in two directions: inward FDI stimulating economic growth and economic growth stimulating incoming direct investment. A host country's internal conditions are a decisive factor in corporate decisions on where to invest and what kind of manufacturing facility to build. A demonstrable record of successful growth, most likely the result of a favorable economic and political domestic environment, in theory can "cause" FDI to be established in particular LDCs. The extent to which lines of causality run in this direction cannot be pinpointed with precision due to disagreement among researchers over the proper statistical means of controlling "endogeneity biases," that is, preexisting conditions in a host country or sector that encouraged or discouraged the arrival of FDI. If countries or sectors are ex ante relatively productive, then statistical observations of ex post high productivity are not proof that entry of foreign companies was the cause of above-average productivity.[9]

Dani Rodrik has argued that "much, if not most" of the correlation between FDI and superior economic performance seems to be "driven by reverse causality: multinational enterprises tend to locate in the more productive and profitable economies."[10] In cases where favorable internal economic conditions and strong growth rates persuade foreign-based companies to establish operations in a particular LDC, new FDI is a lagging indicator that a government has implemented an effective economic development and growth plan.

A convincing argument could be made in the early 2000s that in only two countries can inward FDI be clearly identified as being directly responsible for most of the accelerated rates of increases in a home country's GDP, national income, average per capita incomes, and technological sophistication. Singapore and Ireland are the major exceptions to the rule that no relatively low-income country has yet attracted the sheer volume of high-quality, nonoil FDI relative to population and GDP that the influx of foreign-owned factories can unequivocally be identified as the number one source of accelerated economic growth. For all other developing countries, the data are insufficient to assert categorically that FDI is the major cause of accelerated economic development and to proclaim that it produced results superior to what an equivalent amount of well-designed domestic investment could have accomplished.

Certain motives for FDI are more likely than others to exemplify reverse causality. Incoming subsidiaries are most likely to follow economic growth when they are market-seeking in nature (see chapter 4). By definition, they are attracted by the buying power of potential customers in foreign markets. When the subsidiary is resource-seeking, incoming FDI is least likely to be generated by a country's rate of economic growth because the presence and accessibility of natural resources are the most important variables. Efficiency-seeking, vertically integrated foreign subsidiaries would be somewhere in the middle in view of their need to weigh a number of variables, for example, labor costs, regulatory environment, and absence of trade restrictions. Finally, it is possible that in some cases causality is not unidirectional. New inward FDI and a host country's track record of economic success might equally induce increases in the other. The causal process is "bidirectional" if both incoming FDI and domestic economic growth are mutually reinforcing.[11]

Obstacle number six to a clear-cut assessment of how FDI affects economic development is the presumption that at least some of the researchers examining this sometimes emotionally charged question have been overly influenced by their conscious or unconscious ideological values (see chapter 5). One of the most respected academicians specializing in the study of MNCs, Richard E. Caves, was uncharacteristically blunt when writing that the empirical research on the effects of FDI on the LDCs' economic fortunes has suffered both from a lack of "theoretical guidance and in some cases from special pleading by the researchers. . . . The statistical studies of this issue, it must be said, bear strong imprints of their authors' prior beliefs about whether a negative or positive relationship would emerge."[12]

Yet another conceptual problem is the absence of proof inherent in counterfactual conjecture. Looking backward, it cannot be known how a host country's economy and social and political systems would have fared if some or all foreign subsidiaries had stayed away or acted differently. Similarly, when looking forward, forecasts about future trends in existing direct investment in LDCs are pure guesswork. There is no way of knowing if the positive growth effects of newly arrived FDI are temporary or long-term. It cannot be known if a given subsidiary will expand or by how much, and the extent (if any) to which its success attracts other companies to establish job-creating production facilities. Neither can it be known if foreign companies will get frustrated with the results of an investment, drop good-citizen strategies, and switch to a strict emphasis on self-serving, profit-maximizing actions that harm the interests of the host country.

The eighth and final impediment to a clear-cut assessment is that many if not most of the factors that shape the impact—favorable and negative—of foreign-owned subsidiaries are equally relevant in shaping their impact on wealthy, middle-income, and poor countries. The nature and business objective of a foreign subsidiary in most cases will be at least equal in importance to the average income and education levels in the host country. Consequently, it is not appropriate to consider LDCs in complete isolation as if they were a fully autonomous subset of the generic issue of the costs and benefits of FDI/MNCs on host countries. Accordingly, the next two sections, the first presenting the potentially deleterious effects and the second the potentially beneficial effects, are relatively brief. They will focus only on LDC-specific issues, not a broader discussion of praise and then of condemnation of incoming direct investment for all host countries as will be presented in chapters 12 and 13.

Potential Harm of FDI to Developing Countries

It is almost self-evident that some subsidiaries "can have an adverse effect on development."[13] MNCs can be harmful to developing countries for reasons proven and perceived, and both economic and social (see chapters 3, 4, and 13). Antipathy toward them was and is a natural reaction in countries trying to permanently erase memories of the colonial experience and still angry at the one-sided long-term deals that foreign-owned, raw materials-extracting companies negotiated with compliant local governments or colonial rulers. Attitudes toward MNCs are still affected by recollections of the United Fruit Company's imperious reign early last century as a kind of government within a government in some Central American countries. A classic case study of corporate misbehavior was the company's role in bringing about the U.S. government–engineered coup in 1954 that ended the elected presidency of Jacobo Arbenz in Guatemala and started a prolonged period of political unrest in the country. The illegal interference by ITT Corporation in Chilean politics during the early 1970s (see chapter 13) led to a barrage of negative publicity and a one-way downward spiral in the company's position in Chile.

These events sustain the mistrust that is a natural reaction for those who see the relatively fragile political and economic systems of LDCs as no match for the big money, power, and ruthlessness of MNCs, many of whom are adept at playing governments off against one another. The zeitgeist of the 1960s and 1970s portrayed multinationals as exploiters that removed far more wealth from developing countries than they added. Furthermore, multinationals were typically perceived in the third world as vehicles used by their home-country governments to project political power and influence in other regions.[14] A popular view in both developing and industrialized countries was that the average LDC on balance would be the victim of long-lasting economic harm by allowing foreign-controlled, monopoly-bent corporations to enter and dominate the undeveloped, imperfectly competitive domestic market. Hence the hypothesis that because MNCs operating in LDCs frequently mean increased unemployment, unequal income distribution, and capital outflows, there "can be little doubt" that the eventual impact of inward FDI "can only contribute to the further impoverishment of the poorest 60 to 80 percent of Third World populations." The "clear message" was that the continued and unchecked expansion of MNCs into the third world would increase the instability of these societies.[15]

What this study repeatedly refers to as low quality FDI (see chapters 4, 13, and 14) can inflict enough financial harm on a developing country that it could credibly be claimed that the host country would have been far better off without it. The heterogeneity of FDI and MNCs undermines the assumption that the inherent virtues of a foreign-controlled subsidiary mean net benefits automatically ensue. Locally owned companies in developing countries are especially susceptible to being crowded out in any of several ways by larger, wealthier, and more competitive foreign companies. MNCs' financial clout, for example, can give them priority access to loans from local banks and relatively low interest rates. They might also secure preferential access to locally held balances of foreign exchange, usually in critically short supply in an LDC, for use by the subsidiary to pay for imports and to repatriate profits. When FDI takes place in the form of an acquisition, wholesale eliminations of jobs may take place in connection with a restructuring by the foreign purchaser.

In the external sector, the balance of payments position of a host country can be adversely affected by incoming FDI. A low-income country could see an especially painful diminution of its already limited holdings of convertible foreign exchange that otherwise could be used to pay for needed imports of capital goods like factory machinery and telecommunications and transportation equipment. The costs of components and machinery imported by a foreign subsidiary could exceed its export earnings, assuming it has any. Profits repatriated over time by subsidiaries to their headquarters countries could be geometrically greater than the value of foreign exchange originally sent into the host country to build the subsidiaries.

The "curse of natural resources" is a relatively new phrase that refers to the growing body of evidence that a perverse relationship often exists between economic development and royalty payments to LDCs from MNCs who are extracting oil and mineral wealth. Endowments of natural resources in demand internationally "can be bad for growth and bad for democracy, since they tend to impede the development of institutions and values critical to open, market-based economies and political freedom: civil liberties, the rule of law, protection of property rights, and political participation."[16] Authoritarian political leaders in Iraq, Nigeria, and elsewhere have established an inglorious track record of siphoning off for their own use billions of dollars of royalties paid to their governments that otherwise could have been spent on development and poverty-reduction projects. In the words of Catholic Relief Services,

The gap between expectations and the dismal economic performance of oil-exporting countries is politically explosive. Because oil governments funnel petrodollars to their own friends, family, military and political supporters, social class, ethnic or religious groups, their populations see foreigners and favorites getting rich, but their own lot does not change. In the context of apparent oil riches, it may even get worse.[17]

This syndrome became so pervasive[18] that the World Bank initiated a novel arrangement in 2000 with the government of Chad, a destitute country with an old tradition of corruption and a windfall from new oil production. In an effort to break the pattern in other countries of oil riches gone astray, the World Bank designed an agreement intended to provide for public disclosure of the value of royalties paid by foreign oil companies to the government and to ensure that minimum percentages of these monies are allocated to economic development and poverty reduction. The long-term success of the plan was jeopardized early on when Chad's leaders demanded that they be given more money for current expenditures, mostly for military use.

In addition to being the main symbols of how inward FDI in the primary sector can be prohibitively costly to host countries, LDCs have been at the epicenter of loud protests that MNCs have unconscionably exploited third-world workers in their unceasing quest for larger profits. Human rights NGOs around the world have produced evidence of sweatshop conditions where workers, some of whom were children, experienced one or more of the following: long hours for relatively little pay; factories that were unsafe, unhealthy, and uncomfortable; and prohibitions against bargaining collectively or forming a union. The factories in question always are located in low-wage countries. They typically are part of a trans-border assembly line of apparel or footwear to be sold in affluent countries bearing the labels of retail chains or companies like Nike and Levi Strauss. Only credible threats of consumer boycotts forced these companies to respond to public demands with programs to provide better protection of workers' rights, which they largely administer by self-regulation.

The ongoing debate on the sweatshop problem raises three subjective questions, the uncertain answers to which are shaped by ideological beliefs. The first is how widespread are sweatshops. Insinuations by antiglobalization, prolabor forces that virtually all export-related factories in low-income countries shamelessly exploited their workers were exaggerated even when demands for the upgrading of working conditions first began in the 1990s. The second question is how culpable are foreign-owned companies for harsh working conditions—compared to Western standards—when virtually all of the most criticized factories are not subsidiaries of industrial country MNCs. Sweatshops were and are contractors operated by local owners who have contracted to be suppliers to foreign consumer goods companies. Nike, the company attracting the most negative publicity, does not formally meet the definition of an MNC: It does not partly or wholly own any of the factories abroad that make its athletic shoes. These plants are licensees. Finally, the most delicate question is the extent to which Western values and labor practices (including child labor) should be imposed on contractors to American or European companies when the former are foreign-owned firms doing business outside the jurisdiction of the countries in which the contracting companies are domiciled.

Potential Benefits of FDI to Developing Countries

By the early 1990s, the image of MNCs in the third world had undergone a radical makeover that gained momentum without planning or leadership. Official attitudes in most of the South had completed a transition from a mindset based on suspicion and tinged with implied threats of expropriation to one of desire and a sudden generosity anxious to offer financial incentives for multinationals to set up shop and help promote growth. As is the case with most great transformations, several factors were responsible for convincing decision makers in Africa, Asia, and Latin America that hostility to FDI had become too high a price to pay in an increasingly interdependent world economy. Implosion of the communist economic model encouraged an embrace of market-based economic practices. Instead of being viewed as a metaphor for neocolonialism, FDI became for many a symbol of hope in solving long-festering problems of low standards of living and lagging technological capabilities. The opening of the door to foreign companies and the adoption by LDCs of business-friendly policies led to a surge in FDI that can be viewed in two different ways, depending on one's value judgments. It can be characterized as a new pragmatism about what kinds of economic policies produce the best results. This policy turnaround can also be viewed as a sellout in which the relatively few owners of capital found new populations of workers to exploit on the road to further enrichment.

For better or worse, the pro-FDI stance eventually received the imprimatur of most of the development establishment, in particular the major international organizations whose primary mission is promoting growth and reducing poverty in LDCs. UNCTAD, the only major global economic organization controlled by the third-world countries, stated in its *World Investment Report* for 1999 that FDI "can play an important role in complementing the efforts of national firms" to improve a country's international competitiveness.[19] The so-called Monterrey Consensus of 2002 articulated the consensus of the attendees at a major conference held under UNCTAD's auspices. It proclaimed that "private capital flows, particularly foreign direct investment, along with international financial stability, are vital complements to national and international development efforts." FDI "contributes toward financing sustained growth over the long term."[20]

A research paper prepared by staff members of the World Bank typifies that institution's firm and often repeated conviction that incoming direct investment as a whole is far more beneficial than harmful to the development process:

> FDI is a key ingredient for successful economic growth in developing countries. This is because the very essence of economic development is the rapid and efficient transfer and adoption of "best practice" across borders. FDI is particularly well suited to effect this and translate it into broad-based growth, not least by upgrading human capital. As growth is the single-most important factor affecting poverty reduction, FDI is central to achieving that goal.[21]

Most of the relevant literature, including this study, emphasizes the *potential* for inward FDI to be more beneficial than harmful to LDCs. The notion of automaticity is mainly the province of passionate believers in the market mechanism. In any event, arguments have been repeatedly made that high-quality FDI usually brings with it a highly desirable series of state-of-the-art business practices. Without a competitive edge, companies are loathe to risk the money, energy, and reputation associated with investing in a foreign market (see chapter 6). By definition, most if not all large MNCs have achieved above-average success in their business category. Foreign companies possessing highly regarded products or services, creating relatively high-paying jobs, and bringing with them advanced levels of technology, management capabilities, and marketing acumen can be an attractive addition to economies at any level of development. Where star companies can shine the brightest and have the most dramatic results is in capital-short LDCs making the right policy moves to overcome economic backwardness. Leaving aside potential disadvantages, such as displaced local companies, the economy-bolstering benefits that an LDC potentially can receive from high-quality investments include the following:

- Investment capital;
- Additional jobs, many of which provide workers with higher levels of training and wages than those provided by local companies;
- Expanded sales and profits for local businesses as MNCs buy components, equipment, and services from them (sometimes MNCs provide technical and financial assistance to local contractors so that they can meet MNCs' high standards);
- Advanced technology to increase productivity, produce higher value-added goods, lower costs, and improve quality control;

- Advanced management techniques;
- Increased exports and foreign exchange earnings;
- Secondary effects: forcing local competitors to perform at higher levels of competitiveness; additional investments attracted by the success of the first wave of investment; trained workers leaving a foreign subsidiary and starting their own business or transferring their expertise to a local company; and improved environmental protection.

The potential benefits of inward FDI to LDCs are perhaps best described as an aggregate, not as individual items; in other words, the whole may be greater than the sum of its parts. Theodore Moran characterizes the contribution of foreign-controlled subsidiaries as "integrated packages—technology, business techniques, management skills, human-relations policies, and marketing capabilities—that place host-country plants on the frontier of industry best practices, and keep them there."[22] The package of benefits analogy was also used by two UNCTAD economists: "Not only can FDI add to investible resources and capital formation, but, perhaps more important, it is also a means of transferring production technology, skills, innovative capacity, and organizational and managerial practices between locations, as well as of accessing international marketing networks."[23]

FDI is widely cited as the most desirable form of private capital inflow for LDCs. Short-term capital flows, mainly portfolio investment (stocks and bonds) and bank lending, are volatile, which is why they are sometimes referred to as hot money. The several financial crises that disrupted emerging market countries in Asia and Latin America beginning in the 1980s can be succinctly described as stampedes of short-term capital out of these countries. FDI-related capital flows are different. They are based on business decisions involving a long-term commitment to the host country. This is partly because of the very large amounts of money involved and the fact that FDI takes the form of buildings and assembly lines that cannot be easily or cheaply removed at the first hint of trouble or shift in relative interest rates. FDI inflows have the additional advantage over bank loans of not creating debt. A Brookings Institution study examined the question of whether the benefits to LDCs from unregulated capital inflows were sufficient to offset the risks. It concluded, "The answer would appear to be a strong yes for FDI."[24]

Finally, the conventional wisdom that the economic benefits FDI can bestow on LDCs comes solely from investment flows *into* those countries is obsolete. It was previously argued (see chapters 1 and 4) that being dynamic phenomena, FDI and MNCs are constantly mutating into new kinds and shapes. A major new variant is the increased number of LDC-based companies becoming multinationals by establishing overseas subsidiaries or acquiring foreign companies.

They do so for the same long list of reasons that industrial country-headquartered companies go abroad (see chapter 6). As a result, their overseas subsidiaries now consist of all the major forms: resource, market, and efficiency-seeking subsidiaries in manufacturing, services, R&D, and so on. Negligible until the late 1980s, the estimated outward FDI flows from the developing countries of $83 billion in 2004 (an unusually high amount) accounted for about 11 percent of total world flows.[25]

As more LDCs see their home-grown companies expand production facilities in other countries, they increasingly will be on the receiving end of the advantages (stronger, faster-growing companies, increased exports, and growing repatriation of profits) as well as the disadvantages (declines in jobs and exports, and increases in capital outflows) accruing to home countries. If researchers subsequently determine that outward FDI is providing the same degree of benefit to them as it has had for industrial countries, an entire new aspect of MNC contributions to the prosperity of developing countries will be confirmed.[26]

"It Depends": Variables That Can Determine the Impact of FDI on LDCs

One of the most common themes in scholarly articles is that the economic impact of FDI on LDCs ranges from good to bad depending on circumstances. To use this study's terminology, it depends on the array of variables that present themselves in a particular country at a particular point in time. Although various authors identify different variables determining the multinationals' effects on economic development, they generally agree that there are compelling reasons to refrain from advancing a definitive, all-inclusive assessment of the FDI–LDC relationship. The equivocation inherent in the "it depends" approach derives from a two-pronged heterogeneity: (1) the idiosyncratic nature of 160 developing and in-transition economies, and (2) the distinctive objectives and operations of the various kinds of FDI and MNCs. Peter Nunnenkamp and Julius Spatz of the Kiel Institute in Germany put it this way: "The link between FDI and economic growth varies between different types of FDI and . . . host-country characteristics have an important say in this respect."[27] FDI has not been and cannot be a universal cure-all for LDCs, partly because of its inherent limitations and partly because its unique advantages are most likely to flourish only under supportive host-country conditions that are usually lacking in the poorer developing countries.[28]

The school of thought stressing the importance of these variables affirms only the *potential* for a net positive contribution by FDI to economic development in LDCs. This approach is skeptical that the arrival of direct investment *by itself*

BOX 8.1 China Expands Abroad: The Surprising Growth of Outward FDI from a Low-Wage Communist Country

While the spotlight has been focused on the tidal wave of FDI going into China, the country has quietly and surprisingly become one of the developing world's largest sources of outward direct investment. All signs point to a continuation of this trend because it has two strong forces behind it: the same business decisions that spurred Western companies to become multinationals and the active encouragement from a national government flush with a more than ample supply of dollars to finance the deals. "The Chinese government encourages local enterprises to 'make positive moves overseas' because the rise of China as a major economic power is dependent upon the evolution of Chinese companies into world-class enterprises," explained a senior Chinese executive.* China's outward FDI rose from an annual average of well under $1 billion during the late 1980s and early 1990s to an average of $3.7 billion in the three-year period beginning in 2001.** Most of this increase was in the form of overseas acquisitions by companies partly or wholly owned by the government. China's increasing outward direct investments have come in two forms: resource-seeking, mainly in developing countries, and market- and asset-seeking, mainly in high-wage industrialized countries.

Desire borne of insecurity led to aggressive investments in overseas oil, natural gas, and mining ventures, all of which were intended to secure future supplies of raw materials to meet the voracious appetite of China's burgeoning manufacturing sector. The government's policy of acquiring as many energy assets as possible led to direct investments in oil and natural gas fields in rogue states like Sudan, Burma, and Iran. Opportunities abound for China in these countries because they are either unofficially shunned by foreign investors in the industrialized countries or the targets of governmentally imposed U.S. and European sanctions.

Some Chinese manufacturing firms have felt that becoming an MNC is a prerequisite for long-term growth and survival. In part, their establishment of overseas operations has been and is motivated by traditional desires to assure continued access to foreign markets for their goods and to establish local distribution networks to support growing exports. But in addition, increased outward Chinese FDI reflects what likely will become a major new trend among big LDC-based companies: acquiring advanced technology, internationally recognized brand names, and marketing know-how by acquiring full or part ownership of companies in industrialized countries. As the product cycle in manufacturing shortens and the pace of technological change accelerates, the costs and time required to internally develop state-of-the-art technology and sought-after brand names are becoming increasingly burdensome to corporations aspiring to world-class status.

Some companies, like Haier (see chapter 4) have invested abroad to expand sales and build international brand recognition. Others are acquiring established companies and product lines, most notably Lenovo Corporation's $1.75 billion purchase in 2004 of IBM's personal computer business (which triggered Lenovo's decision to move its world headquarters to New York State). Earlier, the TCL Corporation acquired control of the television unit of the Thomson Corporation of France (which has rights to the RCA recording label). The most counterintuitive

(continued)

reason that Chinese enterprises invest overseas is the occasional need to relocate mature industries to lower wage countries, for example, bicycle production in Ghana. In the future, a growing impetus to Chinese overseas FDI is likely to be the need to circumvent mounting threats of import barriers by trading partners; this was the path followed by several Japanese companies in the 1980s in the wake of that country's export boom.

Even more ironic than the country thought to have the world's lowest production costs expanding its overseas direct investments is the growing number of investment promotion agencies from countries including Ireland, Denmark, Sweden, and Malaysia that have tried to capitalize on this trend by opening branch offices in China to court outward investors.

The future will also shed light on the interesting question of how well Chinese companies fare after acquiring foreign businesses with very different corporate cultures, staffed by workers of very different national cultures some of whom will be unionized, and operating in rule of law-based democracies.

*Dongsheng Li, chairman and CEO of TCL Corporation, "The Future of Asia," May 26, 2005, available online at http://www.nni.nikkei.co.jp; accessed July, 2005.
**Data source: UNCTAD, *World Investment Report 1996* and *2004*.

will generate significant and sustained boosts to host countries' economies. In fact, no conclusive proof exists that improved economic performance automatically follows in a country gaining foreign-owned subsidiaries. Context is all-important. FDI's ability to be a catalyst of positive change is contingent on existence of conditions favorable to economic growth in the host country and arrival of foreign subsidiaries meeting a minimum level of quality. A typical conclusion of econometric studies is that FDI inflows do not exert an influence on economic growth that is independent of other factors that contribute to growth.[29]

A survey of the literature concluded that "while substantial support exists for positive spillovers from FDI, there is no consensus on causality." However, it was noted that there is increasing conviction that FDI is positively *correlated* with economic growth.[30] In other words, "fast growth and large FDI inflows go hand in hand in many instances," but the line of causality is not always clear.[31] An econometric study of the interaction between FDI and economic growth concluded that "the causal relationship between FDI and growth is characterized by a considerable degree of *heterogeneity*."[32]

A widely quoted observation by Swedish economist Ari Kokko gets to the heart of the consequences when two heterogeneous forces dominate: "It seems clear that host country and host industry characteristics determine the impact of FDI and that systemic differences between countries and industries should be expected." The need to disaggregate is implied by the "strong evidence pointing to the potential for significant spillover benefits from FDI, but also ample evidence indicating that spillovers do not occur automatically."[33] Hence, "ensuring a large quantity of FDI alone is not sufficient for the objective of generating growth and poverty reduction."[34]

FDI having mixed results in advancing economic development is the inevitable outcome of the larger reality that not all incoming FDI is created equal. One study found that relatively substandard, low benefits–yielding performance is likely to be associated with a subsidiary that does not operate on a relatively free market, high-volume basis. A plant is likely to suffer diminished efficiency, for example, if it is operating in a country imposing burdensome, market-distorting regulations on incoming FDI, such as mandating domestic content requirements and minority ownership for local companies, or it is manufacturing consumer goods for sale only in a host country closed to imports.[35] Conversely, much greater efficiency and host country benefits should be expected from a wholly owned subsidiary operating in a market-oriented environment and producing sophisticated components for assembly into high-tech finished goods that will be sold by the parent on a global basis. Such circumstances encourage maximum emphasis on corporate best practices.

The sheer number of outcomes possible with so many variables in play makes it a mathematical certainty that over time and throughout the developing world, the effects of tens of thousands of foreign-controlled or -owned subsidiaries on economic development can fall anywhere in a span that begins with grievous harm and ends with stimulation to growth that exceeds other sources. Midway between the poles is a broad zone of irrelevance. Foreign-controlled subsidiaries might have had a negligible role in the acceleration of growth rates enjoyed in a given developing country. Incoming FDI could also be judged a nonfactor if no boost in growth rates was recorded after the arrival of several foreign subsidiaries. A third scenario where FDI might have negligible value added is if it was attracted by a host country's preexisting successful formula for economic success that would have performed brilliantly even without the arrival of MNCs.

The state of an LDC's domestic economy is always a variable in determining the extent and nature of the impact of incoming FDI; the only question is how important it is on a case-by-case basis. A close examination of the historical record will indicate that externally induced economic growth, be it from FDI or foreign aid, seldom occurs in a vacuum devoid of endogenous factors. The reason for this is the unrelenting importance of the host country's larger economic and political environments, which can range from highly conducive to brutally hostile to economic progress. The UNCTAD Secretariat's advice is that if countries want to achieve their development objectives, they cannot pursue FDI policies in isolation. "Instead, they must be inextricably linked with policies in core areas of economic development" (new business capacity and enhanced technological skills, for example).[36] Development policies need to be adapted that will be compatible with economic and political landscapes that vary from one country to another.

Hence, "There is no ideal development strategy with respect to the use of FDI that is common to all countries at all times."[37]

If a country is lacking the preconditions necessary for efficient operation of foreign subsidiaries, it is unlikely to experience significant FDI-induced growth and poverty reduction even if it throws its doors wide open to foreign companies. Inward FDI in such circumstances "may even be counter-productive."[38] A different study reached a similar conclusion: Generally it seems to be much easier for a developing country to attract FDI than to derive macroeconomic benefits from it.[39]

What, then, are the elements of a successful development strategy that must be in place in a host country for the odds to favor a demonstrably positive effect from incoming FDI? Once again, different econometric studies point to different causal factors. A relatively high level of *human capital,* a term for an estimate of the aggregate skills, training, and education of a county's labor force, is one of the most frequently cited. A typical finding is that FDI significantly contributes to a host country's economic development "only when a sufficient absorptive capability of advanced technologies is available in the host country: The higher the level of education of the labor force, the greater the gain in growth from a given FDI inflow."[40] The "most robust finding" of another study was that "the effect of FDI on economic growth is dependent on the level of human capital available in the host economy. . . . There is a strong positive interaction between FDI and the level of educational attainment" in a country. Furthermore, "it is likely that at very low levels of human capital, the contribution of FDI to growth is close to nil and that it rises rapidly at higher levels of human capital."[41] One tangible reason for this correlation is that the more sophisticated is a host country's labor force, the greater the likelihood that MNCs will transfer sophisticated technology to their subsidiaries, create relatively high-paying jobs, and buy parts, factory equipment, and services from local businesses.

Some studies qualify the importance of a highly skilled labor force by suggesting that it is a necessary but usually *not sufficient* factor in making incoming FDI an effective agent of change and growth within LDCs. Their ability to capture the maximum benefits of FDI has been linked to the presence of other favorable internal variables. FDI appears "most effective as an agent of change in economies that possess a threshold level of human capital and skills and in those economies that have attained a threshold level of growth."[42] Presumably, a strong economic performance is an outgrowth of an economic and political environment that has been accommodating to the local private sector and will likely interact positively with new foreign subsidiaries. The main pillars of an MNC-enticing environment, discussed at length in chapter 7, are limited government regulation of the business sector; rule of law; competent, honest government; a good educational and vocational training system; and good physical infrastructure.

The second mega-variable universally influencing the nature and degree of FDI/MNCs impact on LDCs is the foreign subsidiaries themselves. However good or bad is the host country's economic progress, the questions of which kinds of investments (see chapter 4) are involved and their levels of quality are always important if not critical variables. Unfortunately, the empirical literature usually fails to do analysis at the company level and thus is unable to determine if certain kinds of subsidiaries have a tendency to provide the host country with net benefits or net costs. The diverging results of studies about FDI's role in the development process are probably

> explained in terms of the varying quality of FDI inflows received by different countries. Companies are guided by different motivations when establishing overseas subsidiaries, and different business strategies lead to different forms of behavior and effects on host countries. The literature has, however, tended to treat FDI as a homogeneous resource benefiting the recipients in the same manner and has neglected any potential differences in the quality of FDI received.[43]

Efficiency-seeking subsidiaries that are vertically integrated into the global sourcing network of their parent company were found to be the most beneficial to the development process in a study conducted by Theodore Moran, an academic specialist in this field. He determined that the investments most favorable for host countries, what this study would classify as high-quality investment, are subsidiaries designed to be integral parts of the parent company's effort to maximize its international competitive strength. When this is the case, a high statistical probability exists that positive spillovers in the form of well above-average technology transfers, wages, and managerial and marketing techniques will ensue "far in excess" of what is commonly assumed.[44] At the opposite end of the costs-benefits spectrum, resource-seeking investments have had a dismal record of lifting poor countries (exclusive of Persian Gulf oil-producing states) to middle or higher income status, as discussed previously in this chapter and in chapters 4 and 13.

An additional variable determining how FDI affects the development of LDCs, one combining elements of the two mega-variables (local conditions and quality of subsidiary) is whether a foreign subsidiary faces significant competition, from within the host country and/or from imports. The productivity level, pricing policies, and innovation record of any enterprise, domestic or global, are functions of concerns, or lack thereof, for inroads by competitors.

Two recent case studies provide a clear illustration of how diametrically different developing countries' experiences with foreign-owned subsidiaries can

Notes

1. "Introduction and Overview," in Theodore H. Moran, Edward M. Graham, and Magnus Blomstrom, eds., *Does Foreign Direct Investment Promote Development?* (Washington, DC: Institute for International Economics, 2005), p. 1.

2. "Searching for the Holy Grail? Making FDI Work for Sustainable Development," March 2003, Appendix 1, available online at http://www.wwf.org.uk/researcher; accessed March 2005.

3. Inflows of dollars and other convertible currencies play an important financial role in the development process. The larger a country's net inflow of capital, the larger is its potential ability to pay for the imports needed to promote economic growth and rising living standards. By definition, an underdeveloped country has a limited export capacity but an overwhelming dependence on imported consumer goods, such as food and medicine, and capital goods, such as transportation and telecommunications equipment, factory machinery, computers, schoolbooks, and so on. For balance of payments reasons, the ability of countries to import is roughly limited to the combination of earnings of hard currency from exporting and net capital inflows. A trade surplus is a dubious achievement for a poor country striving to overcome the limits of an undeveloped economy. Despite the popular notion that a trade surplus is good and a deficit is bad, economic theory tells us that an LDC is materially better off being a net taker of growth-promoting and living standards–increasing, real economic resources (goods and services) from the rest of the world. It would finance the resulting trade deficit with capital inflows.

4. UNCTAD, *World Investment Report 2002*, p. 12, available online at http://www.unctad.org; accessed January 2005.

5. Data sources: UNCTAD, *World Investment Report 2004* and *2005*.

6. UNCTAD, *World Investment Report 2002*, p. 12, and *2004*, p. 5.

7. Data sources: UNCTAD, *World Investment Report 2005*, Annex table B.1.

8. Data source: UNCTAD, *World Investment Report 2004*, Annex table A.I.5.

9. Linda Goldberg, "Financial-Sector Foreign Direct Investment and Host Countries: New and Old Lessons," Federal Reserve Bank of New York Staff Paper, April 2004, available online at http://www.ny.frb.org/research; accessed January 2005.

10. Dani Rodrik, *The New Global Economy and Developing Countries: Making Openness Work* (Washington, DC: Overseas Development Council, 1999), p. 37.

11. Kevin Honglin Zhang, "Does Foreign Direct Investment Promote Economic Growth? Evidence from East Asia and Latin America," *Contemporary Economic Policy*, April 2001, p. 176.

12. Richard E. Caves, *Multinational Enterprise and Economic Analysis*, 2nd ed. (Cambridge: Cambridge University Press, 1996), pp. 235–36.

13. UNCTAD, *World Investment Report 1999*, p. 155.

14. Edward M. Graham, *Fighting the Wrong Enemy* (Washington, DC: Institute for International Economics, 2000), p. 168.

15. Ronald Müller, "The Multinational Corporation and the Underdevelopment of the Third World," in Charles K. Wilber, ed., *The Political Economy of Development and Underdevelopment* (New York: Random House, 1973), p. 146–47.

16. Nancy Birdsall and Arvind Subramanian, "Saving Iraq from Its Oil," *Foreign Affairs,* July/August 2004, p. 77.

17. Catholic Relief Services, "Bottom of the Barrel—Africa's Oil Boom and the Poor," June 2003, p. 23, available online at http://www.catholicrelief.org; accessed January 2005.

18. In its 2003 report on human rights practices in Equatorial Guinea, another newly oil-rich country, the U.S. State Department stated that "there was little evidence that the Government used the country's oil wealth for the public good. Most oil wealth appears to be concentrated in the hands of top government officials while the majority of the population remained poor. Most foreign economic assistance was suspended due to the lack of economic reform and the Government's poor human rights record." Available online at http://www.state.gov/g/drl/hrrpt/2003.

19. UNCTAD, *World Investment Report 1999*, p. xxiv.

20. "Monterrey Consensus of the International Conference on Financing for Development," 2002, available online at http://www.un.org/esa/ffd/aconf198-11.pdf; accessed April 2005.

21. Bita Hadjimichael, Carl Aaron, and Michael Klein, "Foreign Direct Investment and Poverty Reduction," World Bank Working Paper no. 2613, June 2001, p. 2, available online at http://www.worldbank.org; accessed October 2004.

22. Theodore H. Moran, *Beyond Sweatshops—Foreign Direct Investment and Globalization in Developing Countries* (Washington, DC: Brookings Institution Press, 2002), p. 162.

23. Padma Mallampally and Karl P. Sauvant, "Foreign Direct Investment in Developing Countries," *Finance and Development,* March 1999, p. 35.

24. Barry P. Bosworth and Susan M. Collins, "Capital Flows to Developing Economies: Implications for Saving and Investment," *Brookings Papers on Economic Activity,* 1, 1999, p. 165.

25. Data source: UNCTAD, *World Investment Report 2005*, Annex table B.1.

26. The traditional assumption that costs and benefits of FDI on LDCs accrue solely from *incoming* subsidiaries from the North is doubly obsolete. Not only are more companies that started in the countries of the South going multinational, but an estimated one-third of FDI inflows into LDCs at the start of the new century came from other LDCs. Data source: Dilek Aykut and Dilip Ratha, "South-South FDI Flows: How Big Are They?," *Transnational Corporations,* April 2004, p. 149, available online at http://www.unctad.org; accessed February 2005.

27. Peter Nunnenkamp and Julius Spatz, "FDI and Economic Growth in Developing Economies: How Relevant Are Host-Economy and Industry Characteristics?," *Transnational Corporations,* December 2004, p. 76, available online at http://www.unctad.org; accessed February 2005.

28. Peter Nunnenkamp, "To What Extent Can Foreign Direct Investment Help Achieve International Development Goals?," Kiel Working Paper no. 1128, October 2002, pp. 6–7, available online at http://www.uni-kiel.de/ifw/pub/kap/2002/kap1128.pdf, accessed January 2005.

29. Maria Carkovic and Ross Levine, "Does Foreign Direct Investment Accelerate Economic Growth?" May 2002, p. 13, available online at http://www.worldbank.org/research/conferences/financial_globalization/fdi.pdf, accessed December 2004.

30. Ewe-Ghee Lim, "Determinants of, and the Relations between, Foreign Direct Investment and Growth: A Summary of the Recent Literature," IMF Working Paper 01/75, November 2001, available online at http://www.imf.org; accessed March 2005.

31. UNCTAD, *World Investment Report 1999*, p. 315.

32. Abdur Chowdhury and George Mavrotas, "FDI and Growth: A Causal Relationship," WIDER Research Paper no. 2005/25, June 2005, p. 8, available online at http://www.wider.unu.edu/publications/rps/rps2005/rp2005-25.pdf; accessed June 2005; emphasis added.

33. Ari Kokko, "Globalization and FDI Incentives," paper presented to the World Bank ABCDE-Europe Conference, June 2002, p. 5, available online at http://www.worldbank.org; accessed April 2005.

34. Dirk Willem te Velde, "Policies towards Foreign Direct Investment in Developing Countries: Emerging Best-Practices and Outstanding Issues," March 2001, available online at http://www.odi.org.uk/iedg/fdi_conference/dwpaper.pdf; accessed January 2005.

35. Theodore H. Moran, "Foreign Direct Investment and Development: A Reassessment of the Evidence and Policy Implications," 1999, pp. 42, 45–47, available online at http://www.oecd.org/dataoecd/52/47/25555208.pdf; accessed January, 2005.

36. UNCTAD, *World Investment Report 1999*, p. 156.

37. Ibid., p. xxv.

38. V. N. Balasubramanyam and Vidya Mahambare, "FDI in India," *Transnational Corporations,* August 2003, pp. 45, 69, available online at http://www.unctad.org; accessed February 2005.

39. Nunnenkamp and Spatz, "FDI and Economic Growth," p. 80.

40. Peter Nunnenkamp, "Foreign Direct Investment in Developing Countries: What Economists (Don't) Know and What Policymakers Should (Not) Do!," 2002, p. 29, available online at http://www.cuts-international.org; accessed January 2005.

41. Eduardo Borensztein, Jose de Gregorio, and Jong-Wha Lee, "How Does Foreign Direct Investment Affect Economic Growth?," *Journal of International Economics,* 45, 1998, pp. 134, 126.

42. Balasubramanyam and Mahambare, "FDI in India," p. 63.

43. Nagesh Kumar, *Globalization and the Quality of Foreign Direct Investment* (New Delhi: Oxford University Press, 2002), p. 4.

44. Theodore H. Moran, "Foreign Direct Investment and Development: A Reassessment of the Evidence and Policy Implications," pp. 42–43.

45. The *New York Times* has reported extensively on the nature of the pollution problems that emerged near the mine site and the subsequent investigations and legal action taken by the Indonesian government against the company; see, among others, articles in the issues dated September 8, 2004; December 22, 2004; and March 28, 2005.

46. Theodore H. Moran, *Foreign Direct Investment and Development* (Washington, DC: Institute for International Economics, 1998), pp. 54–56.

47. Richard E. Caves, *Multinational Enterprise and Economic Analysis* (Cambridge: Cambridge University Press, 1982), p. 252. Interestingly, this critical comment seems to have been deleted from the second edition of his textbook.

48. Overseas Development Institute, "Foreign Direct Investment: Who Gains?," Briefing Paper dated April 2002, p. 1, available online at http://www.odi.org.uk/publications/briefing/bp_may02.pdf; accessed October 2005.

49. UNCTAD, *World Investment Report 1999*, Overview, p. xxv.

50. Caves, *Multinational Enterprise*, 2nd ed., pp. 235, 237.

51. Asian Development Bank, "Impact of Foreign Direct Investment," *Asian Development Outlook 2004*, p. 4, available online at http://www.adb.org/documents/books/ADO/2004/part030200.asp; accessed December 2005.

52. Theodore H. Moran, Edward M. Graham, and Magnus Blomström, "Conclusions and Implications for FDI Policy in Developing Countries, New Methods of Research, and a Future Research Agenda," in Moran, Graham, and Blomström, *Does Foreign Direct Investment Promote Development?* (Washington, D.C.: Institute for International Economics and the center for Global Development, 2005), p. 375.

9

WHY AND HOW MULTINATIONAL CORPORATIONS HAVE ALTERED INTERNATIONAL TRADE

The proliferation of foreign direct investment (FDI) and the rapid, sustained increase in the output of multinational corporations (MNCs) have irreversibly changed the determination of what individual countries do and do not import and export. Sometime in the 1980s, FDI unobtrusively passed foreign trade to become the primary vehicle by which large manufacturing companies sell their goods to customers in foreign countries. The reason for this transition is straightforward: A growing majority of companies for many reasons perceive overseas production as the superior business strategy. Dependence on traditional exports has been eroded by basic changes in the way international business is conducted.

This chapter examines the various ways in which the FDI/MNC phenomena created a new era in international trade relations. It examines from various perspectives why some analysts believe that competitive strengths of companies may soon surpass (if they have not already done so) national comparative advantage as the dominant factor determining the product composition of most countries' foreign trade. The first section surveys the data demonstrating the extent to which overseas production as a whole has displaced exports as the primary marketing vehicle for selling to foreign consumers. Next, a series of case studies examines the potentially dramatic impact FDI can have on country trade patterns. The third section examines the long-standing debate about the extent to which the shift by MNCs to overseas production has reduced—or more likely, increased—employment and exports in home countries. The final section investigates the degree to which FDI's effects on merchandise trade flows may have rendered traditional trade theory obsolete. After considering the failure of efforts to revise trade theory to explicitly consider the trade effects of MNC proliferation, the suggestion is made to include FDI as a basic factor determining the product composition of host countries' exports and, to a lesser extent, imports.

Measuring the Changing Foreign Trade-FDI Dynamic

The international trading system has outgrown being a straightforward exchange of goods and services between countries dictated by their relative economic strengths and weaknesses. In fact, the spread of FDI has made foreign trade into a much more complicated process. Depending on circumstances and market conditions, MNCs as a group can and do affect the volume of trade and alter the product composition of trade flows. Since the 1970s, a steadily growing percentage of trade has consisted of overseas shipments by large MNCs, often to a company's subsidiaries in other countries. A significant though incalculable amount of potential international trade flows no longer takes place because foreign markets are increasingly served by overseas production facilities of MNCs in lieu of exporting finished products from the headquarters country. The contemporary trading system can be fully understood only "in the context of the operations" of MNCs.[1] A noted scholar in this field, Edward M. Graham, wrote in 1996 that "foreign direct investment has by some measures become even more important than international trade."[2] Two Wall Street economists writing three years later were much less equivocal in making the case for the relative importance of FDI: "Trade is no longer the primary vehicle for global interaction and integration.... Foreign direct investment has become the primary means by which firms compete in markets."[3]

Ripple effects throughout the trading system from the boom in overseas production are more than abstractions of interest solely to academics. Output by foreign subsidiaries is large enough to have broad economic implications, among which are alterations in national patterns of industrial production, GDP growth rates, and the creation and loss of jobs. These shifts also have potential political consequences if changing economic conditions change voters' satisfaction with their government's performance.

Defense of the still contested argument that companies are close to or at the point of supplanting country characteristics as the principal determinants of international trade flows rests primarily on relatively hard data. Perhaps the most striking corroborative numbers appear in the first chapter of the UNCTAD's annual *World Investment Report*. Its estimate of global sales by foreign subsidiaries in all countries during 2004 was $18.7 trillion, an amount almost double the recorded total of $11 trillion in worldwide exports of goods and services. The relatively recent growth spurt in the value of overseas production can be seen in two additional numbers: The 2004 sales total was more than triple the figure for 1990,

sector's international presence tends to be inversely proportionate to its support for protectionist trade policies.

Two strikingly different forms of trade policy have at times served to encourage companies to invest overseas. Protectionist trade policies created the strategy of tariff jumping, that is, establishing foreign subsidiaries within countries to bypass import barriers (see chapter 6). Conversely, the process of trade liberalization has made vertical FDI feasible by allowing MNCs to freely ship parts and assembled final products from one country to another on the basis of market considerations.

Country Case Studies: The Impact of MNCs on National Trade Performance

Data excluding the role of sales by overseas subsidiaries "are increasingly partial and misleading as indicators of national competitiveness or fundamental trends in the world economy."[13] The limitations of considering only conventional trade flows are more apparent in some countries than others.

The United States

The possibility that a major American manufacturing company (outside of the aerospace and weapons sectors) enjoys sufficient competitive advantage to be willing to rely solely on exporting to sell its products in overseas markets has all but disappeared. Having a dominant global market share even in the high-tech sector is no longer sustained by exporting alone, even with a limited number of competitors and relatively cheap overnight air freight services. For example, Dell is widely considered to be the most efficient assembler of personal computers in the world today. It now takes a single worker in its state of the art factories about five minutes to assemble a PC; the total labor cost is at most 2 percent of the machine.[14] Textbook comparative advantage or no, once Dell decided to be a major global player (overseas sales accounted for 36 percent of net revenue in its 2004 fiscal year),[15] exports became irrelevant to the company's global strategy. "Dell is not an exporter of products from the U.S. to other countries."[16] Computer equipment ordered by customers in Europe, Asia, and Latin America is shipped from Dell's overseas subsidiaries in Ireland, Malaysia and China, and Brazil, respectively. A similar global marketing strategy is used by Intel and Microsoft, two other world giants in their fields that produce products that are easy and cheap to ship.

It has been argued that "U.S. exports and imports are increasingly dictated by the strategies of both U.S. and foreign multinationals."[17] Emphasis on FDI in overseas marketing means that the traditional goods and services trade balance no longer adequately measures the total ability of U.S. industry to sell in foreign markets. The more accurate gauge combines trade and FDI. Step one in constructing a broader "international sales" figure for the United States is to add together annual U.S. exports and annual sales of majority-owned U.S. overseas subsidiaries (a process that involves some double-counting, as explained shortly). The second step is to subtract from this figure the total obtained after combining U.S. imports with sales in the United States of majority-owned subsidiaries of foreign-based MNCs (which also involves some double-counting). On this basis, a net U.S. international sales figure would have been in surplus until the start of the new millennium owing to the fact that sales of overseas U.S. subsidiaries exceeded sales of foreign-owned subsidiaries in the United States. After that point, the U.S. goods and services deficit grew so large as to swamp the FDI sales surplus, and the combined trade/direct investment balance moved into deficit.

The impact of inward and outward FDI on overall U.S. foreign trade flows is of special significance because the United States is the world's largest home and host country for FDI; the book value (original cost) of each is in excess of $1.2 trillion. How inward FDI affects its two-way trade flows can be examined in some detail because the United States (at least in early 2006) was the only country regularly publishing comprehensive data on the role of MNCs in its exports and imports. The statistical relationship between conventional cross-border trade and production overseas by U.S.-owned MNCs is sufficiently clear that an economic study by the U.S. International Trade Commission asserted that sales by foreign subsidiaries are the "predominant mode of delivering both American goods and services to foreign customers."[18]

One measure of the growing role of FDI in U.S. trade is the U.S. Department of Commerce's disaggregated data showing the amounts of U.S. imports and exports accounted for by MNC activity. As seen in figure 9.1, roughly 78 percent of all exports of U.S. goods in 2003 can be linked to various sales transactions involving American MNCs, their overseas subsidiaries, and subsidiaries of foreign-owned MNCs operating in the United States. More than one-fifth of all exports were intrafirm transactions, that is, sales of components, raw materials, and finished goods by U.S. parents directly to their foreign affiliates (a synonym for *subsidiaries* preferred by the Department of Commerce). Exports by majority-owned foreign subsidiaries located in the United States contributed an impressive 21 percent of U.S. goods exports (up from 15.5 percent of total U.S. exports in 1987), a figure bolstered by large shipments from subsidiaries of Japanese trading companies. Some kind of MNC-related activity accounted for nearly two-thirds of total U.S. imports in 2003 (see figure 9.2).

Since the late 1970s, annual sales of goods and services produced by majority-owned U.S. foreign subsidiaries have been more than twice as large as U.S. exports (the ratio has been growing in recent years, the result of subsidiaries' annual sales growing faster than exports). Total sales of majority-owned U.S.

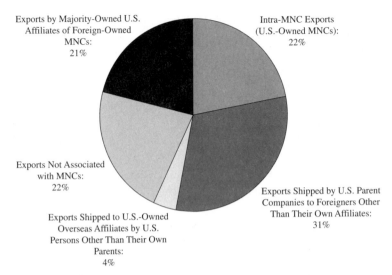

Exports by Majority-Owned U.S.
Affiliates of Foreign-Owned
MNCs:
21%

Intra-MNC Exports
(U.S.-Owned MNCs):
22%

Exports Not Associated
with MNCs:
22%

Exports Shipped by U.S. Parent
Companies to Foreigners Other
Than Their Own Affiliates:
31%

Exports Shipped to U.S.-Owned
Overseas Affiliates by U.S.
Persons Other Than Their Own
Parents:
4%

FIGURE 9.1. U.S. trade in goods associated with MNCs in 2003. MNC–associated exports (78%). Total exports: $725 billion. *Source:* U.S. Commerce Department, Bureau of Economic Analysis.

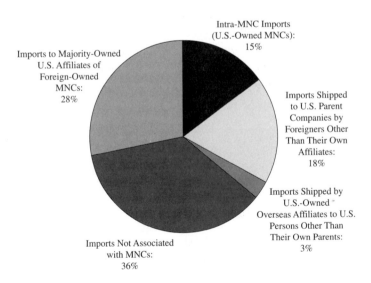

Intra-MNC Imports
(U.S.-Owned MNCs):
15%

Imports to Majority-Owned
U.S. Affiliates of
Foreign-Owned
MNCs:
28%

Imports Shipped
to U.S. Parent
Companies by
Foreigners Other
Than Their Own
Affiliates:
18%

Imports Shipped by
U.S.-Owned
Overseas Affiliates to U.S.
Persons Other Than
Their Own Parents:
3%

Imports Not Associated
with MNCs:
36%

FIGURE 9.2. U.S. trade in goods associated with MNCs in 2003. MNC–associated imports (64%). Total imports: $1,257 billion.

overseas operations in 2003 were $2.9 trillion,[19] as compared to goods and services exports of $1 trillion; this means that only 26 percent of "total deliveries" of U.S. goods and services to foreign customers in that year were in the form of traditional cross-border exports. However, these numbers somewhat overstate the role of foreign production in U.S. global commercial success probably by at least 20 percent. This results from the double-counting of some foreign subsidiaries' sales incorporating components imported from the United States and other sales consisting of exports from American-based companies to overseas wholesaling and retailing affiliates. In addition, the Department of Commerce's compilation of all sales by overseas subsidiaries includes oil extracted and sold abroad by U.S.-owned oil companies, not a true measure of American corporate competitiveness.

The ratio for sales to Western European customers is even more striking. Sales of majority-owned U.S. subsidiaries in Europe in 2003 (some of which would have been sold outside Europe) exceeded $1.5 trillion, compared to U.S. exports to Western Europe of only $166 billion. This is a nine-to-one ratio and means that 90 percent of all goods delivered by American companies to European customers in 2003 came from their local subsidiaries.[20]

European multinationals use exactly the same marketing priorities in selling to U.S.-based customers. Sales of majority-owned Western European subsidiaries in the United States were estimated at $1.3 trillion in 2003, five times greater than U.S. imports of $266 billion in that year. Germany surpassed the United States in 2003 as the world's largest, most successful exporting country, but its companies sold four and a half times more in the United States in that year through their majority-owned U.S.-based subsidiaries ($301 billion) than through exporting.[21] Despite the strong surge in U.S. imports since the 1990s, total sales of goods produced by foreign subsidiaries in the United States have grown steadily. Their $2.1 trillion of sales in 2003 were well in excess of total imports of U.S. goods and services ($1.5 trillion) and had grown to be five times larger than their U.S. sales in 1980.[22]

One final statistical note: U.S. FDI in China did not reach significant levels until the mid- to late 1990s, yet by 2003, sales by American-controlled enterprises in that booming market were nearly twice as large as U.S. exports to it.[23]

FDI's Radical Makeovers: Ireland and Singapore

Ireland and Singapore can both point to FDI as the most important factor in their highly successful, sustained, and largely export-led economic growth rates over the past two decades. The surge in sophisticated, capital-intensive exports by both countries was not home-grown: An estimated 90 percent of their exports of manufactured goods is accounted for by an impressive assemblage of world-class

MNCs operating there.[24] In other words, virtually none of Singapore's or Ireland's exports of manufactured goods has anything to do with domestic companies or the countries' relative endowments of land, labor, and capital. In the words of Robert Lipsey, "One could not have predicted the current comparative advantage of Ireland from its comparative advantage before inward investment was liberalized, which was that of an agricultural country."[25]

Within the span of a generation, Ireland went from one of the least developed and slowest growing economies of Western Europe to become a major exporter of microprocessors (it is the home to the largest Intel chip manufacturing operation outside of the United States, and Intel is the country's largest exporter), computers, pharmaceuticals, and medical equipment. Ireland claims to have surpassed the United States to become the world's largest exporter of software, 90 percent of which is shipped by subsidiaries of foreign companies.[26] Much of the impetus behind the rise of the Irish economy since the 1970s "can be explained in terms of the quite phenomenal growth of export-oriented FDI in manufacturing, from a zero base in the late 1950s to a situation where [in the late 1990s] almost 65 per cent of gross output . . . in manufacturing is in foreign-owned export-oriented firms."[27]

Within the span of a generation, Singapore made the transition from poor colony, whose economy had been heavily dependent on a British naval base, to affluent exporter of advanced electronics, precision engineering, and other high value-added goods. Here, too, the sophisticated composition of their exports does not reflect any conventional measure of relative endowments of land, labor, and capital. In fact, at the time it achieved independence in 1965, the political leadership concluded that the small island lacked the capital, market size, and natural resources to industrialize to the degree necessary to reduce unemployment and enhance living standards. An additional problem was the domestic business sector having had expertise in entrepôt trade, but not domestic manufacturing or exporting domestically produced goods. Lee Kuan Yew, the first prime minister and architect of Singapore's economic modernization, wrote of his belief that despite their poor image at the time, MNCs were the only answer to the new country's deep-rooted economic problems and bleak prospects. Economic development strategies revolved around the priority goal of making "it possible for investors to operate successfully and profitably in Singapore despite our lack of a domestic market and natural resources. . . . Had we waited for our traders to learn to be industrialists, we would have starved."[28]

The inferred linkage in these two countries between well above-average economic success and well above-average inflows of FDI raises one red flag. If trends were to dramatically change, both countries might find that they had gone too far in depending on foreign-controlled companies for sustaining their prosperity while doing little to foster their own world-class industrial companies.

Incoming FDI has been sufficient in a few countries to have had a dramatic effect on trade, but its long-term growth has been insufficient to directly boost GDP growth, national income, and the overall employment rate on a sustained basis to the extent it did in Ireland and Singapore. At first glance, an MNC-induced export boom is dramatic testament to the virtue of incoming FDI because in most cases, it is inconceivable that the kinds and value of manufactured goods subsequently exported would have been possible without the output of foreign-controlled companies. Like so much else that surrounds this subject area, however, a closer examination yields a more ambiguous story. Big MNC-induced increases in exports sometime are accompanied by nearly as large MNC-induced increases in imports. An increase in imports is a function of the extent to which a foreign subsidiary is producing goods from scratch for the local market as opposed to assembling components, mostly produced in another country, for reexport to other markets. Although a foreign subsidiary under normal circumstances exports at least slightly more than it imports, repatriated profits also may limit the net foreign exchange earnings produced by FDI in a host country. The extent of earnings retained in-country is based on decisions by individual MNCs in connection with plans to upgrade and/or expand their overseas subsidiaries and corporate tax considerations.

In theory, Costa Rica should not be exporting state-of-the-art microprocessors (also called logic chips and central processing units) because it is a middle-level developing country, lacking in capital and technological know-how relative to advanced industrialized countries. In theory, Intel, the world's largest maker of semiconductors, could rely solely on exports: It has a comfortable majority of the world market for the semiconductor chips that are the brains of computers and networking and telecommunications systems. These highly sophisticated integrated circuits are relatively capital-intensive to manufacture and relatively nonlabor-intensive to test and assemble. Plus they are small and light enough to be cheaply air-freighted by the tens of thousands.

In practice, the situation is different. Costa Rica's human capital, stable and competent government, and business-friendly economic policies bestow on it a comparative advantage in attracting certain kinds of FDI. Intel was interested in further geographic diversification to minimize unforeseen risks that could disrupt production or shipments of product to customers and to dilute the risk of new legislation that could increase production costs. The company's actions also suggested an interest in reducing labor costs in the testing and assembly phases of chip making and in receiving tax incentives to further lower production costs. Presumably, it does not believe its dominant market share makes it permanently invulnerable to price cutting and innovations by competitors.[29]

Costa Rica became a major exporter of what may be the world's most sophisticated manufactured product, not for traditional trade reasons but because of a foreign-owned facility built in 1997 to test and do the final assembly for the microprocessors whose design and ultra-complex circuitry had been produced in the United States. The approximate impact of the billion-dollar-plus annual overseas shipments by Intel's subsidiary is reflected in the increase in Costa Rica's exports from $4 billion in 1996 to $6 billion in 1999. A disaggregation of the country's exports for 2000 showed that Intel's overseas shipments of $1.7 billion accounted for about one-quarter of the country's total exports. Forty-four percent of its exports in that year were accounted for by the twenty largest foreign MNC exporters.[30]

This is only part of the story of the effects of the Intel investment on Costa Rica's balance of payments and foreign exchange earnings. As is the case with any foreign subsidiary, there are two potentially offsetting factors that in any given year can negate much or even all of the benefits of incremental exports. According to official statistics, Costa Rica exported microprocessor chips valued at $1.4 billion in 2003, but it was also *importing* unassembled chips valued at $1 billion, to which it was adding value, not making from scratch.[31] That virtually all of this two-way trade was accounted for by Intel is suggested by U.S. government trade data showing that U.S. exports of semiconductor chips to Costa Rica in that year were $1 billion.[32]

The second factor mitigating the positive impact on Costa Rica's overall balance of payments is the apparent profitability of the subsidiary; it can be assumed that in most years, Intel repatriates a varying amount of profits back to its California headquarters. This is suggested by the jump in the country's income payments remitted to other countries from $434 million in 1997 to $1.5 billion in 2000.[33] Confidentiality precludes a public breakdown of exactly how much of this total can be attributed to Intel. In any given year, the company's headquarters could be a net exporter of capital to Costa Rica as it presumably was in 1999, when it built a second plant there. Even if one were to make the probably incorrect assumption that this subsidiary provided minimal net foreign exchange earnings over an extended period of time, this would not negate the considerable internal benefits accruing from increased employment with relatively high wages, enhanced labor skills, local procurement, the showcasing of Costa Rica as a good place for FDI, and so on.

The big-export-increment/big-import-increment syndrome is also evident in Hungary, one of the premier success stories of Central and Eastern European countries making the transition from a government-owned command economy to a market-based order. Exports grew by a robust 300 percent plus between 1991 and 2003, but imports jumped by almost 400 percent. Both increases reflect the propensity of foreign subsidiaries to reexport goods assembled from components mostly made elsewhere. According to estimates, 80 to 90 percent of Hungary's exports are shipped by foreign-owned or -controlled subsidiaries.[34] Approximately 45 percent of total exports in 2000 came from just the fifty largest MNC exporters.[35] The country's top three export goods—telecommunications appliances, auto engines, and automobiles—are FDI driven; they accounted for 18 percent of total exports in 2002, up from virtually zero in 1992, the pre-FDI era.[36] The secretariat of the Organization for Economic Cooperation and Development (OECD) in 2004 attributed much of the strong growth of the Hungarian economy since 1997 to a "dynamic export sector largely made up of foreign-invested firms and rapid integration into European production networks."[37] MNCs, in the words of the UNCTAD Secretariat, "have been the main drivers of export growth in Hungary."[38]

Although there is no evidence of incoming FDI harming the economic development of Hungary, neither is there any convincing evidence that it has forged strong links with the domestic economic sector and created substantial numbers of jobs outside the export sector. Much of the work of foreign subsidiaries consists of assembling imported components for reexport to higher wage Western European countries. Local sourcing of intermediate goods to date appears to have been relatively limited. Some worry that the country has become too dependent on foreign companies, one result of which is a diminution of efforts to nurture domestic entrepreneurship.

Export Success without MNCs: Japan and South Korea

In keeping with the theme that avoiding generalizations is the best approach to studying the subject matter, Japan and South Korea represent clear-cut case studies of great export success being attained by countries without any meaningful boost from inward FDI (and with no meaningful endowments of natural resources). Japan's overriding priority after World War II was to rebuild its shattered economy without compromising its strong, unstinting historical drive to keep external influences at arm's length. Preservation of its much cherished 2,000-year-old culture was of utmost importance. Maintaining control over its economic destiny was incompatible with opening the doors to strong American companies at a time when the weakened Japanese economy was highly vulnerable to foreign competition. Profit-maximizing Western companies, unlikely to understand or comply with unique informal rules of the Japanese system (e.g., close cooperation between industry and government, collusion among big firms, etc.) would be far more trouble than they were worth. Restrictions—all FDI through the late 1960s was prohibited unless specifically approved by the government—kept majority-owned foreign subsidiaries to an absolute minimum until the 1990s. Even after controls were eased, relatively high land costs, difficulties in hiring skilled local personnel, continued prohibitions on unfriendly takeovers, and zoning hassles limited the number of foreign companies establishing a manufacturing subsidiary there.

The subsequent Japanese economic miracle, as it was rightly called, did not seem in any way hampered by the dearth of foreign-owned or -controlled subsidiaries. Superlative Japanese companies in sectors like electronics, automobiles, and precision instruments achieved world class status in a relatively short period of time. The country's record of export growth from the 1960s until the early 1990s was the best in the world. It long enjoyed the world's biggest merchandise trade surplus until being passed by China in 2005. Major production innovations such as just-in-time delivery, an unprecedented ability to seek out and license new foreign technologies and products, willingness to disregard profits in the short run, financial assistance from the Japanese government, and a nearly fanatical drive to succeed in foreign markets created a mighty export machine devoid of non-Japanese MNCs. Despite a much more welcoming environment for incoming direct investment since the late 1990s (particularly to rescue distressed domestic companies), Japan remains an outlier. The book value of inward FDI as a percentage of GDP is by far the lowest among industrial countries, only 2 percent in 2003; this is one-tenth the average percentage for developed countries as a group.[39]

South Korea was a less developed country (LDC) with rather bleak prospects at the start of the 1960s. It was recovering from a destructive civil war, lacked natural resources, and was heavily dependent on U.S. foreign aid. By the start of the millennium, steady economic growth and the emergence of a world-class manufacturing sector qualified it for membership in the OECD, the economic policy coordinating group open only to advanced industrialized countries. Korea was the twelfth largest exporter in the world in 2005, thanks mainly to technologically sophisticated products such as semiconductors and automobiles. Nevertheless, it, too, followed the Japanese model of barring most FDI because of acute sensitivity to foreign domination and confidence that it could succeed economically on its own. Korea, in the words of UNCTAD, "remains one of the few examples of a developing country that has become an export winner mainly by way of low-equity relationships" with MNCs.[40] The book value of its inward FDI was an unusually low 1.8 percent of GDP in 1995, the period just prior to its financial crisis, which forced a policy about-face. In fact, inward FDI in what is an attractive market for such investments was marginally lower as a percent of GDP than the percentage of Korea's *outward* FDI in that year.

The Debate over Displaced Exports and Lost Jobs

One of the few FDI/MNC controversies concerning their impact on the interests of the *home* country is the question of the extent (if any) to which overseas production causes the loss of exports and the jobs that come along with them. The debate was initiated in the United States in the early 1970s when the American Federation of Labor–Congress of Industrial Organizations (AFL-CIO) abandoned its liberal trade policy stance and switched to advocacy of new restrictions on imports and on FDI by American companies. The labor confederation's objective was to curb the alleged increase in the export of American jobs.

Critics of MNCs view the issue in terms of a commonsense argument: When a company switches its marketing strategy from exporting to serving foreign markets through production by overseas subsidiaries, workers in the home country that have been producing the affected goods or services are likely to lose their jobs. Those persons sensitive to the interests of workers are further incensed by the anecdotal evidence indicating that some companies threaten their workers with moving production facilities to another country if they do not accept management's offers of frozen or reduced wages and benefits or if workers declare their intent to unionize. Both of these scenarios add fuel to the fires of those who view globalization and MNCs as unfair, unjustifiable exploitation of the majority by a small minority.

There is, of course, the inevitable other side of the story and tinge of vagueness. Unequivocal proof is absent because of the counterfactual dilemma common to most FDI/MNC controversies: There is no way to know how well or poorly exports of specific goods from a specific company would have held up if individual overseas subsidiaries had not been established. Only turning back time and prohibiting specific overseas investment projects would allow an empirical measure of whether jobs and exports would have been preserved, increased, or lost in the absence of a move to overseas production.

The most appropriate answer to the conundrum of the impact of FDI on home countries' exports is this study's often repeated refrain: It depends. First, it depends on what exactly is being measured: *specific* jobs and exports or *aggregate* employment and exports. If the focus is on the former, it is probable that at least some companies will export less following the establishment of one or more foreign factories specifically designed as substitutes for exporting. In addition, some workers can be expected to lose their jobs. In the United States, the most vulnerable workers, as is usually the case, would be those having relatively low skills and education. The result is a question of fairness, a political and social issue, not really an economic one because only a small fraction of a country's total workforce is adversely affected by foreign subsidiaries coming online. The precise number of export sector workers who otherwise would have permanently retained their jobs in the absence of FDI has never been determined for any host country and probably never will.

Efforts to compile convincing evidence of direct causation between new outward FDI and job losses are further hampered by a number of possible mitigating circumstances. For example, there is no reason to assume that an outsider can know if a company shifting production overseas has truly exaggerated the need to preserve foreign markets through FDI. In the long term, a company's exports might shrivel because changing overseas market conditions would best have been addressed by FDI. Faulty strategy by a company mistakenly sticking to the marketing status quo, instead of shifting production overseas to maintain competitiveness, could in theory be the cause of diminished competitiveness and losses of jobs and exports in the home country. When overseas subsidiaries are established to skirt newly imposed import barriers, the case that a steady to growing level of exports would have continued in their absence is dubious at best.

Another microeconomic variable is the number of workers whose production tasks have been shifted to an overseas subsidiary of their companies but who do not lose their jobs. Rising *domestic* demand for the product they were assembling could leave production schedules unchanged in home country factories. In addition, workers may be switched to producing other corporate products that are enjoying growing sales at home or abroad. Furthermore, if a company regularly introduces new or improved versions of products, as successful exporters and MNCs tend to do, it may simply reassign the assembly line workers no longer producing the old line of exports to a newly opened assembly line elsewhere in the factory. Laying off workers is not necessarily the outcome of a dynamic, growing company's recourse to overseas production for a specific product.

If analysis is made at the macro level, the plight of the relative few who may have lost jobs becomes a secondary issue in economic terms. No universal, one-to-one relationship exists between jobs lost to FDI—or imports for that matter—and the aggregate size of a country's labor force. Even assuming some job losses from runaway plants and rising imports, the business cycle in a market economy is the critical variable determining overall demand for labor. Domestic economic conditions in turn are the main determinant of whether those unemployed (for any reason) can find new jobs and whether most of these jobs pay as much or more than those lost.

Similarly, even if some degree of lost exports is assumed after expanded overseas production, the home country does not necessarily suffer a loss in *aggregate* exports. Indirect statistical evidence exists to suggest that most overseas direct investment is *complementary* with exports, not a substitute. Establishment of overseas production facilities can be simultaneously trade-displacing and trade-creating. As previously demonstrated in this chapter, intrafirm trade has grown steadily in the wake of the proliferation of MNCs. There are data for a few countries indicating that exports of different products *increase* when domestic companies establish foreign subsidiaries. The new wave of exports includes raw materials, components, and capital equipment, that is, machinery for the assembly line. It is also common for overseas manufacturing subsidiaries to serve as distributors for models of finished products (some of which may not have previously known export success) that continue to be manufactured only in the headquarters country. Not every FDI venture generates a level of exports near or above those that have been displaced. It depends on the nature of the subsidiary. Vertical integration consisting of subsidiaries created for final assembly and re-export of intermediate goods manufactured at corporate headquarters is likely to have a robust effect on exports from the parent company and capital goods producers in the home country. Conversely, in cases of horizontal FDI where a subsidiary is tasked with manufacturing consumer goods for the local market, the likelihood of a fully offsetting increase in exports—assuming the parent company previously had been exporting to that market—is possible but less likely, especially if parts or ingredients can be obtained locally.

Two additional variables undermine the validity of generalizations about the negative trade impact of FDI on home countries. The first concerns the extent to which existing flows of exports are physically displaced. Overseas subsidiaries may be established to develop sales in a foreign market before significant export penetration has been achieved. China exemplifies a super-fast growing market that prior to the late 1980s was not an export destination for American companies. Profit potential, not preservation of an existing volume of exports, was the dominant motive for these companies to invest in that country. American workers might have suffered what economists call an opportunity cost when U.S-owned or controlled factories were opened in China. It is theoretically possible that U.S. exports and jobs would have grown dramatically in the absence of direct investments there. Once again, magnitude is a hypothetical; it cannot be known for sure by how much and for how long exports would have grown if FDI had not taken place. Moreover, as already indicated, a successful new subsidiary can result in a net *increase* in exports from the headquarters country. A final variable influencing the impact of outward direct investment on a home country's trade balance is the amount of goods foreign subsidiaries export back to it. This is not common in the case of the United States, although many U.S.-owned plants in Mexico were established to make goods for sale in the American market. Many Japanese companies shifted production of labor-intensive components to subsidiaries in lower labor cost Asian countries, a strategy that increased Japanese imports but helped sustain the global price competitiveness of a wide variety of domestically produced finished goods.

For the United States at least, FDI as a whole has not yet been shown to be an unequivocal cause of serious or sustained harm to aggregate exports or employment. The nonpartisan U.S. International Trade Commission issued a study in 2000 that stated, "The balance of evidence indicates that U.S. exports tend to be positively associated with U.S. direct investment abroad" and that the data indicate that "U.S. direct investment abroad is a complement to, rather than a substitute for, U.S. exports."[41] The 1991 report of the President's Council of Economic Advisers asserted that "*On a net basis, it is highly doubtful that U.S. direct investment abroad reduces U.S. exports or displaces U.S. jobs*" (emphasis in original). The gist of the reason for making this conclusion is that FDI helps American companies be more competitive internationally and allocate their resources more efficiently, both of which tend to create exports and jobs.[42] A comparative study of American, Japanese, and Swedish-based MNCs determined that parent companies' worldwide exports tend to be large, relative to their output, when the firms' overseas production is large.[43] Long-time FDI scholar Robert Lipsey posits, "There is probably no universal relationship between outward investment and home-country exports, and to the extent that any relationship is present, outward FDI is more often found to promote exports than to compete with them."[44]

UNCTAD, which is controlled by the developing countries, analyzed the trade-FDI nexus in a slightly different manner:

FDI and trade flows are determined simultaneously.... The issue is no longer whether trade leads to FDI or FDI to trade; whether FDI substitutes for trade or trade substitutes for FDI or whether they complement each other. Rather, it is: how do firms access resources—wherever they are located—in the interest of organizing production as profitably as possible for the national, regional, or global markets they wish to serve?... The decision where to locate ... is a decision where to invest and from where to trade.... It follows that, increasingly, what matters are the factors that make particular locations advantageous for particular activities.[45]

A discussion of the impact of outward FDI on exports is not complete without mention of the possibility of a reverse correlation between the two phenomena. A credible case can be made that the *absence* of majority-owned subsidiaries in a foreign market may *impede* a country's ability to export. Indirect support for such a thesis comes from a comparison of two statistical correlations that spanned more than thirty years beginning in the early 1960s. The first is the existence of a strong U.S. export performance and chronic U.S. trade surpluses with Western Europe (that lasted until the early 1990s when the U.S. trade balance began to deteriorate universally) despite the fact that a clear majority of large American exporting companies were mainly supplying European customers with products made by subsidiaries within the EU.

The second correlation is the relatively poor U.S. export performance that contributed to chronic bilateral trade deficits with Japan on the one hand, and the relative dearth of FDI by American manufacturing companies in that county on the other hand. Dennis Encarnation, a Harvard Business School professor, advanced the novel thesis that the main reason behind the long string of U.S. trade deficits with Japan was the fact that formal and informal Japanese barriers had severely limited the number of incoming majority-owned U.S. manufacturing subsidiaries, "long ... the principal sources of foreign sales" by these companies.

> FDI has moved national competition beyond simple bilateral rivalries to encompass multilateral contests among the far-flung (but closely linked) subsidiaries of multinational corporations. Today, these transformations must be acknowledged and regarded as fundamental; in their wake, old standards of international trade and bilateral relations have been rendered insufficient as fair measures of national success in economic rivalries among industrialized countries. ... In Japan, the lower incidence of majority [*sic*] U.S. subsidiaries has effectively denied to American multinationals the same access for U.S. exports that they have enjoyed in other industrialized countries.[46]

Is an "MNC-Centric" Trading System Compatible with Trade Theory?

Given the extent to which the global spread of MNCs has altered the composition of international trade flows, it logically follows that the two-centuries-old body of theory used to explain the underlying dynamics and results of trade might be totally out of date. Exactly how much FDI-induced change has devalued traditional (classical and neoclassical) trade theory[47] is another complex question having no single, universally applicable answer. Two different characterizations of the impact on trade theory can be given depending on which of two perspectives is used to evaluate the situation; the first looks only at traditional theory, while the other perspective incorporates efforts by a growing number of theorists to expand and modernize it.

The strongest case for devalued relevance can be made when examining the well-known core elements of classical and neoclassical trade theory. The long revered theory of *comparative advantage* has become part of popular culture, at least in the United States, in large part because it is in the curriculum of every university course dealing with the basic concepts of foreign trade. To say that the logic of comparative advantage has been repealed outright is to overstate the case. However, the cumulative impact of the spread of FDI and MNCs, together with other business and economic changes, has been to leave only the rudimentary concepts of classical and neoclassical theory in sync with current patterns of international competitiveness and trade flows. At the heart of David Ricardo's early nineteenth-century theory of comparative advantage is the assertion that if two countries specialize in the production of only those goods that each can produce relatively more efficiently and then exchange the goods with one another, both countries are better off than if they had not specialized and engaged in trade.[48] Utilizing limited resources in the most efficient manner is mutually advantageous because specialization of production followed by a maximum flow of trade (relatively efficiently produced goods in exchange for goods that would be relatively costly to produce at home) would expand output, reduce costs and prices, and increase the material well-being of both parties by allowing for increased consumption.

The most important reason that at least the essence of this premise remains valid is that countries still differ in terms of their relative abundance of capital, labor, land, and natural resources. It follows then that all things held constant, countries would tend to be relatively more efficient in producing and exporting goods that require relatively intensive use of their most plentiful and therefore relatively cheap factor. Comparative advantage is the intellectual lodestar for the pursuit of liberal trade policies in which governments impose a minimum of barriers and distortions to the flow of international commerce determined by free market forces. Free trade based on comparative advantage is consistent with the belief held by the vast majority of economists (at least those trained in the so-called Anglo-Saxon school) that in economic theory terms, the ultimate logic of foreign trade is the opportunity for countries to obtain goods that others can produce more efficiently and cheaply. Exporting, according to this theory, is merely the means to pay for the ends, i.e., imports.

Classical trade theory does not make reference to FDI because, for reasons discussed in chapter 3, it did not exist as such in the early 1800s. Still, the principle of comparative advantage is observable in the fact that MNCs establish overseas subsidiaries in labor-abundant, relatively low-wage LDCs for the purpose of minimizing the cost of making relatively standardized, labor-intensive goods, most or all of which will be exported. The theory is also consistent with the preponderance of relatively high value-added manufacturing FDI being located in industrialized countries with skilled, albeit well-paid workers and large, growing, and prosperous markets.

Once beyond these arguments, however, the specifics of traditional trade theory begin to unravel. Accusations of invalid assumptions and debilitating obsolescence are mainly aimed at a crucial follow-up to Ricardo's identification of comparative advantage. Two Swedish economists, Eli Heckscher and Bertil Ohlin, in the early twentieth century purported to explain *why* comparative advantage exists. Their theorem is traditionally explained by an oversimplified model consisting of two countries exchanging two products, one a light manufacture and the other an agricultural commodity—not the closest representation of today's sophisticated manufactured goods and complex trading patterns. A more serious shortcoming is that the theorem is based on a number of assumptions that even if they were valid 100 years ago, are clearly unrealistic in today's world economy. The conclusions of any theory are only as good as its assumptions, and the assumptions in this instance have problems. Some trade theorists, wrote John Dunning, "were less concerned with explanations of the composition of goods and factors actually traded across boundaries ... than with theorizing on what would occur if, in the real world, certain conditions were present."[49]

A clearly outdated assumption of neoclassical trade theory is immobility of capital (and labor) across national borders; if true, companies would be severely hampered in transferring production abroad to take advantage of cheaper labor. Among several other untenable assumptions are constant returns to scale (corporate size does not count in traditional trade theory, so incremental production was presumed not to reduce marginal costs and permit economies of scale), perfect competition (monopolies tend to distort the influence of factor endowments), ease of market entry to any new or existing company wishing to adopt new product lines, and comparable technological capability. Information about technology was presumed to be freely available to all interested parties in all countries. In the real world, technology is protected by patents. Heckscher-Ohlin's assumption of perfect competition conflicts with the new reality that high-tech firms face fixed costs in the billions of dollars to bring major new products to market. The result is that the arrival of new competitors is relatively infrequent; companies without vast financial resources face major barriers to market entry.

The traditional version of comparative advantage is inconsistent with two observable realities associated with the contemporary flow and composition of international trade. A large majority of trade takes place among industrialized countries possessing similar levels of technology and comparable factor endowments. A newer trend is the sharp increase in intra-industry trade, in which industrialized countries export and import the same general kinds of manufactured goods. Neither of these trade realities reflects specialization based on relative efficiency. Rather, they reflect two basic changes in business economics, specifically increasing product differentiation and specialization within many manufacturing sectors, e.g. automobiles, machinery, and chemicals; and secondly, the efficiencies accruing to big companies from economies of scale, or more specifically, increasing returns to scale.

Economies of scale occur when a company is able to reduce average unit production costs by increasing the amount of total output, i.e., output grows by a greater amount in proportion to increases in capital and labor inputs. Volume can bring lower unit costs in several ways. A company can amortize fixed costs over a larger sales base, enable production line workers to move more quickly down the learning curve by mastering assembly techniques and finding shortcuts, and stand a better chance of being able to demand lower prices from suppliers and contractors. With the more advanced industrial countries being fairly similar in their competitive strengths, intense pressure exists among world-class manufacturing companies to gain a competitive edge from better technology and lower production costs than rivals and would-be rivals.

The Heckscher-Ohlin theorem also can be faulted for implicitly assuming immutable differences in countries' relative endowments of land, labor, and capital, the three principal factors of production and the presumed main determinants of national competitiveness. Immutability in turn implies that a country's comparative advantage was effectively permanent. In other words, it would be difficult to impossible for a capital-poor, technology-deficient country to upgrade its productivity and know-how to catch up with the most technologically sophisticated countries in the manufacture of more sophisticated, up-market goods. The policy inference is that economic policy-makers should accept domestic production and foreign trade as being based on a presumably unalterable status quo. The theorem does not mention the MNC, despite the facts that it now regularly alters factor proportions of host countries and that relative levels of corporate technological sophistication obviously have become very important determinants of who exports and imports what.

The behavior of contemporary MNCs is inconsistent with traditional trade theory in several other ways. Most FDI consists of companies based in industrialized countries investing in other industrialized countries whose relative factor endowment is similar to their home country. Production costs therefore tend to be roughly comparable and occasionally even slightly higher. When MNCs from wealthy industrialized countries establish subsidiaries in similar economies, they in effect have issued a vote of no confidence in the ability of comparative advantage in the home country to ensure a desired level of sales to foreign customers. FDI has overtaken exporting because it has become the corporate method of choice to preserve and expand overseas markets for most manufactured goods.

The classical and neoclassical calculation of comparative advantage ignores the increasing importance of corporate entrepreneurship (as later articulated by Joseph Schumpeter) in producing innovations that can change a country's international trade profile. This is an acceptable omission in a nineteenth-century model in which two countries are trading wine and cloth, but not in a real world of multiple countries trading myriad technology-intensive and differentiated manufactured goods where being first to market can be critically important. "National prosperity is created, not inherited.... A nation's competitiveness depends on the capacity of its industry to innovate and upgrade," wrote Michael Porter.[50] "At best, factor comparative advantage theory is coming to be seen as useful primarily for explaining broad tendencies in the patterns of trade . . . rather than whether a nation exports or imports in individual industries."[51] While patterns of trade are still influenced by the skills and costs of labor in different locales, it is not comparative advantage in a literal sense that matters, but the overall productivity of a location in combining all inputs (including imported components) into finished goods.[52]

Traditional trade theory does not explain why a Finnish company, Nokia, began as a paper mill as befits its origins in a country with a rich endowment of forests, but eventually grew into a sprawling multinational enterprise after becoming the innovative force and world market leader in the manufacture of cell phones. Comparative advantage does not explain why research at Intel developed and still dominates the microprocessor field. This company and Advanced Micro Devices Corporation are solely responsible for the United States being the world's largest exporter of logic chips, while the country simultaneously is a large net importer of memory chips. The latter is also a member of the integrated circuit family, a differentiated product that American companies are hard-pressed to produce as cheaply as some East Asian countries. Neither can traditional theory explain why Intel has extensive overseas production to augment exports (see the first section of this chapter). The growing importance of company innovation relative to innate national comparative advantage is further suggested by the potential ability of a handful of bright software engineers in any of several dozen countries to get together in a basement, come up with a better antivirus or antispam program, and start a successful exporting company. "In today's integrated, knowledge-based, world economy, there is an international division of mental labor."[53]

FDI also has changed trade patterns by transferring technology and manufacturing capabilities that can reduce or eliminate the need for host countries to import goods that they previously were unable to produce themselves. By combining a parent company's proprietary technology, production techniques, and marketing savvy with relatively well-educated and dedicated workers, an overseas subsidiary may be able to create competitive advantage in a host country in very short order. The result is that market forces generated by a foreign-controlled or -owned company have trumped comparative disadvantage and created domestic production that is sufficiently efficient to reduce or eliminate imports of certain manufactured goods. Looked at from the opposite direction, establishment of overseas subsidiaries under certain conditions can terminate the exports of goods from home countries that they previously had produced on a relatively low-cost basis.

Conventional concepts of relative factor endowments would also fail to predict or explain how inward FDI in little more than a decade transformed a capital-, technology-, and management-challenged Slovakia from a relatively backward communist economy at the start of the 1990s into a major European center for the production and export of technology-intensive automobiles. Nor is the traditional construct of comparative advantage consistent with the role of foreign companies in transforming labor- and land-abundant China into a growing exporter of capital-intensive electronics and information technology products. Costa Rica's relative factor endowment does not explain how, on a nearly overnight basis, its single largest export item became state-of-the-art semiconductor chips (see following discussion).

A very malleable interpretation of the traditional tenets of comparative advantage, one emphasizing location and stretching the theory close to the point of being unrecognizable, can partially explain why these particular investments were made. The availability of relatively low-paid but reasonably skilled workers in these three countries was definitely a factor in attracting foreign subsidiaries. However, if these countries had exhibited below-average endowments of the new nontraditional factors of production like an accommodating economic environment (which would include financial incentives), good government, and adequate infrastructure, it is unlikely they would have been able to convince the foreign companies in these cases to invest.

Finally, it is difficult to reconcile the Heckscher-Ohlin theorem with internal transfer prices (see chapter 13) that do not accurately reflect the true costs of goods moving between two subsidiaries of the same company, one located in a high-tax country and the other situated in a low-tax country.

Academic economists of various ideological leanings have sought to close the disconnect between theory and an MNC-centric world trading system by amending and updating classical and neoclassical trade theory, for example, relating trade flows to increasing returns to scale rather than constant returns to scale. Their starting point is to assert that the ideas of Ricardo, Heckscher, and Ohlin do not represent the final, inviolate word for explaining why countries export and import as they do.[54] Paul Krugman wryly alluded to the inadequacies of the traditional precepts when he observed that

> Most students of international trade have long had at least a sneaking suspicion that conventional models of comparative advantage do not give an adequate account of world trade. . . . It is hard to reconcile what we see in the manufactures trade with the assumptions of standard trade theory. In particular, much of the world's trade in manufactures is trade between industrial countries with similar relative factor endowments; furthermore, much of the trade between these countries involves two-way exchanges of goods produced with similar factor proportions. Where is the source of comparative advantage?[55]

The "new" trade theories are not well known outside of a small group of international economic theorists and economics majors taking advanced courses in trade theory. Interestingly, some of the more widely cited of the new ideas overlap with major premises in this book. Both assert that differences between countries cannot be considered as the sole or even dominant basis of foreign trade when corporate differences (e.g., technological sophistication, product innovation, and proficiency in managing information and complex logistical systems) and intrafirm trade have become as important, if not more so, than country factor endowments. Another overlap between the new trade theory and the study of FDI/MNCs is found in the Krugman model that links successful exporting with the corporate pursuit of economies of scale that in turn leads to oligopolistic competition (a relatively few companies having a large percentage of the total market share for sales of a given product).

Despite their useful work, trade theory revisionists (used in the best sense of the term) have curiously failed to make a formal affirmation of the important impact that MNCs have in determining and explaining contemporary trade patterns. Every one of the many textbooks for the introductory international economics course examined by the author still discusses FDI in a separate chapter from the one reciting post–Heckscher-Ohlin trade theories. This arguably inappropriate separation fails to give proper weight to the important role that the proliferation of multinational production has had in making necessary the further evolution of traditional trade theory. A rare exception to this artificial dichotomy is Lipsey's assertion that "a country's exports depend not only on the conventional factor endowments and advantages of the country as a geographical entity, but also on the firm-specific advantages of the firms producing there."[56]

A widely used basic international economics textbook is by Paul Krugman and Maurice Obstfeld. Although stating that MNCs "play an important part in world trade," the authors argue that "multinational corporations probably are not as important a factor in the world economy as their visibility would suggest." This reasoning is based on the premise that "the factors that determine a multinational corporation's decision about where to produce are probably not much different from those that determine the pattern of trade in general." A company's decision to produce the same good in more than one country, the concept of location, is said to be "no different from ordinary trade theory. If multinationals were not there, the same things would still happen, though perhaps not to the same extent."[57]

I respectfully disagree. There is no factual basis for declaring that the same economic transactions "would still happen" in the absence of MNCs. Furthermore, there are far too many intricacies to the questions of why and where FDI takes place (see chapters 6 and 7) to dismiss them simply as subsets of trade theory. Failure to view FDI as a distinctive cause of trade flows instead of a synonym for trade theory is not consistent with a micro examination of the far-reaching effects on the trading patterns of various countries discussed in previous sections of this chapter. Viewing trade theory and FDI theory as coterminous cannot explain why "FDI flows into Ireland have not gone primarily into sectors in which the economy had a traditional comparative advantage. In fact, traditional measures of revealed comparative advantage are a very poor predictor of subsequent sectoral developments." The Irish experience clearly suggests that FDI manufacturing inflows go primarily into sectors in which there are increasing returns to scale for the company, not into those where there is a presumption of country "comparative advantage.[58] Another scholar had a similar conclusion about the Irish experience: "Once it opened up to FDI inflows, ... the missing link needed for manufactured exports was supplied by the foreign firms, and Ireland's comparative advantage was transformed."[59]

The best course of action to integrate FDI's impact on today's trading system into the new generation of trade theory is to introduce a new criterion for explaining (in part) the product composition of a country's exports. An explicit new element of comparative advantage should be *the ability of that country to attract and retain incoming FDI that produces more sophisticated, higher quality goods than the domestic sector would be capable of acting on its own.* Trade theory should explicitly accept that in the long run, decisions made for any number of reasons by senior executives in MNCs regarding where to produce what goods and services will be an increasingly important variable in determining the direction and composition of trade for many host and home countries. A new factor of production has been added to the equation.

Notes

1. Geoffrey Jones, *The Evolution of International Business: An Introduction* (London: Routledge, 1996), p. 247.
2. Edward M. Graham, *Global Corporations and National Governments* (Washington, DC: Institute for International Economics, 1996), p. 13.
3. Joseph P. Quinlan and Andrea Prochniak, "Whose Trade Deficit Is It Anyway? A New Perspective on America's Trade Gap," *Investment Perspectives,* Morgan Stanley Dean Witter report dated October 13, 1999, p. 9.
4. UNCTAD, *World Investment Report 2005,* p. 14, available online at http://www.unctad.org; accessed January 2006.
5. UNCTAD, *World Investment Report 2000,* p. 153.
6. Ibid., and World Trade Organization, *Annual Report, 1996,* volume 1, p. 44.
7. Testimony of Nicholas Lardy to the House Committee on International Relations, October 21, 2003, available online at http://www.iie.com; accessed November 2004. Taiwan's bilateral surplus with China in 2005 was the largest of any of China's trading partners.

8. Data source: Robert Zoellick, "China and America: Power and Responsibility," speech of February 24, 2004, p. 7, available online at http://www.ustr.gov; accessed November 2005.

9. See, for example, Ministry of Commerce of China, "2003 Report of Foreign Investment in China," chapter 6, available online at http://www.mofcom.gov.cn, accessed January 2005.

10. Data source: UNCTAD, *World Investment Report 2002*, p. 162.

11. "Filipino Direct, Export/Import Rankings," available online at http://www.filipino-directory.com/framesets/exportimportf.html; accessed January 2005.

12. World Bank, *World Development Report, 2005*, available online at http://www.worldbank.org; accessed January 2005.

13. DeAnne Julius, *Global Companies and Public Policy* (London: Royal Institute for International Affairs, 1990), p. 71.

14. "Who's Afraid of China? Not Super-Efficient Dell," *New York Times*, December 19, 2004, p. III 4.

15. Data source: Dell's annual 10-K report for 2004, available online at http://www.dell.com; accessed January 2005.

16. E-mail from Dell to the author, dated March 18, 2005.

17. Quinlan and Prochniak, "Whose Trade Deficit Is It Anyway?"

18. U.S. International Trade Commission, *Examination of U.S. Inbound and Outbound Direct Investment*, Staff Research Study 26, January 2001, p. 5-1.

19. Data source: U.S. Department of Commerce, Bureau of Economic Analysis, *Survey of Current Business*, July 2005, p. 25, available online at http://www.bea.gov; accessed December 2005.

20. Data derived from ibid., p. 25, for affiliate sales, and U.S. Department of Commerce, *U.S. Aggregate Foreign Trade Data, 2004 and Prior Years*, available online at http://www.ita.doc.gov/td/industry/otea/usfth; accessed January 2006.

21. Data derived from U.S. Department of Commerce, *Survey of Current Business*, August 2005, p. 214, for affiliate sales; and U.S. Department of Commerce, *U.S. Aggregate Foreign Trade Data, 2004 and Prior Years*; accessed January 2006.

22. Data sources: U.S. Department of Commerce, Bureau of Economic Analysis, *Survey of Current Business*, July 1994 and July 2005, available online at http://www.bea.gov; accessed January 2006.

23. Data sources: U.S. Department of Commerce, *Survey of Current Business*, July 2005, and *U.S. Aggregate Foreign Trade Data, 2004 and Prior Years*.

24. Data sources: Frank Barry, "Export-Platform Direct Investment: The Irish Experience," *European Investment Bank Papers*, 9(2), 2004, p. 9; and *Time Asia*, July 7, 2003, available online at http://www.time.com/time/asia; accessed October 2004.

25. Robert Lipsey, "Home and Host Country Effects of FDI," in Robert Baldwin and L. Alan Winters, eds., *Challenges to Globalization* (Chicago: University of Chicago Press, 2004), p. 366.

26. Data sources: IDA Ireland, available online at http://www.idaireland.com; accessed January 2005; and UNCTAD, *World Investment Report 2002*, p. 174.

27. Frank Barry, John Bradley, and Eoin O'Malley, "Indigenous and Foreign Industry: Characteristics and Performance," in Frank Barry, ed., *Understanding Ireland's Economic Growth* (London: Macmillan, 1999), p. 45.

28. Lee Kuan Yew, *From Third World to First—The Singapore Story: 1965–2000* (New York: HarperCollins, 2000), pp. 58, 66.

29. The wisdom of Intel's desire to "run scared" was demonstrated first when IBM, Toshiba, and Sony unveiled a revolutionary new microprocessor in early 2005, and again, later in the year when archrival Advanced Micro Devices began increasing its market share at the expense of Intel.

30. Data source: UNCTAD, *World Investment Report 2002*, p. 168.

31. Costa Rican Ministry of International Trade, available online at http://www.comex .go.cr; accessed January 2005.

32. Data source: "U.S. Commodity Trade with Top 80 Trading Partners, 1999–03," available online at http://www.ita.doc.gov/td/industry/otea/usfth; accessed January 2005.

33. International Monetary Fund, *International Financial Statistics*, various issues.

34. Data sources: Magdolna Sass, "FDI in Hungary—The First Mover's Advantage and Disadvantage," *European Investment Bank Papers*, 9(2), 2004, p. 64; Ben Aris, "Muddling through Deficit Troubles," *Euromoney*, April 2005.

35. UNCTAD, *World Investment Report 2002*, p. 170.

36. Sass, "FDI in Hungary," pp. 82–83.

37. OECD, "Economic Survey—Hungary 2004: Key Issues and Challenges," available online at http://www.oecd.org; accessed February 2005.

38. UNCTAD, *World Investment Report 2002*, p. 169.

39. UNCTAD, *World Investment Report 2004*, p. 399.

40. UNCTAD, *World Investment Report 2002*, p. 178.

41. U.S. International Trade Commission, *Examination of U.S. Inbound and Outbound Direct Investment*, pp. 2–6, 5–7.

42. *Economic Report of the President, 1991* (Washington, DC: Government Printing Office, 1991), p. 259.

43. Robert Lipsey, Eric Ramstetter, and Magnus Blomstrom, "Outward FDI and Parent Exports and Employment: Japan, the United States, and Sweden," National Bureau of Economic Research Working Paper no. 7623, March 2000, p. 1, available online at http://www.nber.org; accessed December 2004.

44. Lipsey, "Home and Host Country Effects," p. 369.

45. UNCTAD, *World Investment Report 1996*, p. 14.

46. Dennis Encarnation, *Rivals beyond Trade* (Ithaca, NY: Cornell University Press, 1992), pp. 5, 31.

47. Discussion of traditional trade theory in this case is limited to so-called free trade theory. Mercantilism, the theory that a country's wealth is enhanced by maximizing exports and minimizing imports, has been arbitrarily excluded because it does not reflect the stated trade policy preferences of the major trading countries.

48. The theory also asserts mutual gain if one country specializes in producing and exporting the good for which it has the smaller absolute disadvantage, that is, in cases where the other country has an absolute advantage in both goods.

49. John H. Dunning, *Explaining International Production* (Boston: Unwin Hyman, 1988), p. 13.

50. Michael E. Porter, "The Competitive Advantage of Nations," *Harvard Business Review*, March–April 1990, p. 73.

51. Michael E. Porter, *The Competitive Advantage of Nations* (New York: Free Press, 1990), p. 12.

52. E-mail sent to the author by Michael Porter of the Harvard Business School, December 23, 2004.

53. Bruce Kogut, "International Business: The New Bottom Line," *Foreign Policy*, spring 1998, p. 162.

54. I thank my colleague, Robert A. Blecker, for this observation.

55. Paul R. Krugman, "New Theories of Trade among Industrial Countries," *American Economic Association Papers and Proceedings*, May 1983, p. 343.

56. Robert Lipsey, "Discussion," in Heinz Herrmann and Robert Lipsey, eds., *Foreign Direct Investment in the Real and Financial Sector of Industrial Countries* (Berlin: Springer-Verlag, 2003), p. 210.

57. Paul R. Krugman and Maurice Obstfeld, *International Economics—Theory and Practice*, 5th ed. (Reading, MA: Addison-Wesley, 2000), pp. 172–74.

58. Barry, Bradley, and O'Malley, "Indigenous and Foreign Industry," pp. 48–49.

59. Lipsey, "Discussion," p. 210.

10

MULTINATIONAL CORPORATIONS VERSUS THE NATION–STATE

Has Sovereignty Been Outsourced?

Multinational companies (MNCs) have amassed sufficient collective muscle to reshape the international political and economic landscape. The problem is that the specifics associated with this megatrend are blurred by layers of uncertainty. Not enough hard data exist to definitively describe the nature and extent of the changes introduced by global companies into the nation-state–based international order. On the one hand, it is a plausible thesis that in the aggregate, sovereign governments have lost their historical monopoly to formulate and administer social and economic policies and to conduct international, that is, state-to-state relations essentially as they see fit. On the other hand, it is a contestable assertion that governments have been pushed aside by an MNC juggernaut. The bottom line question is this: Have the changes in the country-centric international political order been marginal or structural? Have governments involuntarily lost a *significant* degree of authority, power, and influence in both quantitative and qualitative terms?

Even if we accept the proposition that MNCs have indeed become equal to or more powerful than nation-states and thereby have "significantly" shrunk governments' power, two more questions arise that are equally difficult to answer. First, to what extent have the foreign direct investment (FDI)/MNC phenomena been a direct *cause* of the reconfigured balance of power? Second, is a diminution of national sovereignty a good or bad thing? Conceivably, a major dilution of governmental might by private enterprise is something to be welcomed, not condemned.

Once again, the familiar all-purpose answer to all the above is: It depends. And once again, the core methodology of this study's examination of the nature and impact of FDI and MNCs is fully applicable. When seeking an objective and accurate answer to the question of whether MNCs have seriously eroded national sovereignty, there are at least three legitimate, at least partially accurate answers: yes, no, and it's uncertain.

The first section of this chapter considers definitions; the "it depends" syndrome begins with the vagaries of exactly how to describe the nature and context of *sovereignty*. The next two sections present the arguments for and against the proposition that MNCs now are able to have their way with government officials. Belief that the private sector has overtaken the power and prestige of sovereign governments to determine the destinies of nations and peoples' economic well-being is one of the more dramatic criticisms of big business's impact. Belief that this shift has occurred, in turn, is the source of urgings in some quarters that the historical imbalance of power be restored, ensuring once again that the peoples' elected representatives hold sway over profit-seeking corporate executives. The fourth and final section makes the case for uncertainty, synthesis, and framing the debate in different, more relevant terms.

Traditional Definitions and Semantics

It is advisable to begin by affirming that I am not comparing *countries* with MNCs; the latter, in my opinion, are clearly not more important or more powerful than entire countries, especially large and powerful ones. A popular contention that is worth investigating holds that MNCs collectively have diminished the ability of governments to exercise their supreme powers within their countries' borders to unprecedented and presumably undesirable degrees. Allegedly, these companies have grown so big and economically powerful as to leave national governments with severely diminished power and different means of exercising it.

The big question is determining to what extent, if any, the proliferation of FDI can be linked to a "significant" decline in or dilution of *national sovereignty* in theory and practice. Linkage is suggested by circumstantial evidence; it cannot be proved by laboratory-proven facts. The search for at least a tentative answer begins with selection of the "right" definition of the term, a task more difficult than it appears on the surface. Sovereignty, like *FDI* and *MNCs*, is a complex abstraction that has inspired conflicting interpretations of what the term actually entails. Most persons who believe that MNCs have undermined sovereignty equate the term with the ability of a government to exercise absolute control— deferring to no other power center—to determine what constitutes acceptable behavior and standards within a country's borders and to ensure the public's compliance with designated behavior and standards. Those who believe in the continued dominance of the nation-state tend to use a narrower, more legalistic approach that equates sovereignty with the unchallenged ability to conduct affairs of state that include enactment and enforcement of laws, collection of taxes, articulation of policy goals, waging war, and so on. In keeping with this study's preference for an eclectic viewpoint, the working definition used here is Stephen D. Krasner's broad description of sovereignty as exhibiting four distinct characteristics:

- Ability to control activities within and across a country's borders, including the movement of goods, capital, and people;
- Possession of clear title to ultimate political authority within the state;
- Ultimate arbiter of internal behavior, independent of any external authority (Westphalian sovereignty); and
- Formal diplomatic recognition by other nation-states that a government is able and entitled to exercise sovereign control of its territory.[1]

In point of fact, it is not necessary for a state to simultaneously meet all four criteria to claim sovereignty. For example, ineffective governments in failed states whose control over domestic events is systematically disintegrating remain legally sovereign as long as they retain diplomatic recognition. Although Taiwan technically is sovereign by virtue of meeting the first three of the criteria, it enjoys only limited diplomatic recognition as a government of an independent nation-state.

Sovereignty has two dimensions: internal and external. Paraphrasing Max Weber, a government is internally sovereign if it enjoys a *monopoly* as the ultimate authority regulating a range of social activities, including economic policies, within its country's borders.[2] That may be overstating it a bit, given the historical fact that soon after nation-states emerged in their modern form in the mid-seventeenth century, they began an ongoing process of diluting their absolute authority by voluntarily signing a steady stream of bilateral and regional treaties, alliances, and agreements with other sovereign states as well as with international organizations. For more than 350 years, governments of modern nation-states have been willing to cede some areas of sovereignty and autonomy by committing themselves to observe international commitments, thereby reducing their freedom of action. This sacrifice is presumed to be offset by the increased likelihood that mutual cooperation with other countries will be instrumental in achieving larger policy objectives in the national security, economic, and other spheres. Although unrecognized at the time, the level of international economic interdependence had reached record high levels in the early years of the twentieth century, thereby marking the first stage of disconnect between an increasingly integrated world economy and the long-standing political system of differentiated nation-states. A 1930 article in *The Economist* warned of the consequences of economics and politics "falling out of gear with one another," the result of the world economy's evolving into a single "all-embracing" unit while the international political system remained arbitrarily partitioned into a mélange of sovereign nation-states.[3]

An assessment of the durability of external sovereignty also produces equivocal results. On one level, it is undiminished because it still can be measured in relatively finite terms: recognition of a government by other nation-states and all the negotiations and pomp that goes with it. On the other hand, as will be discussed, the conduct of all manner of international relations can no longer be characterized as the exclusive preserve of nation-states.

All things considered, the thesis that national sovereignty has been seriously undermined and bypassed by big, powerful MNCs is yet another issue whose complexity and abstract nature guarantee different perceptions and perspectives. To ask whether MNCs have hollowed out the sovereignty of nation-states is to invite three responses familiar by now to readers of this study: affirmative, negative, and indeterminate, the latter consisting of a gray area combining elements of the first two answers and emphasizing imponderables. These three answers, as usual, coincide with the three larger perceptions as to whether FDI and MNCs are positive, negative, or indeterminate forces.

Yes, Globalization and MNCs Have Substantially Diminished the Power and Role of the Nation-State

The proposition that MNCs have left governments with little more than titular sovereignty has been advanced by analysts on both ends of the political spectrum. The reasoning differs, and some analysis takes place at the higher analytical level of globalization rather than being MNC-specific. Still, the common bottom line here is that the rising market power of multinationals has allegedly placed them on a level either equal to or above governments as determinants of the economic and (in some ways) political destinies of nation-states. Another commonality in the analytic commentary associated with this thesis is that none of the underlying rationale is based on hard empirical data; it is, to borrow a phrase from the art world, abstract impressionism. The academic and public debate additionally suffers from the tendency to view the sovereignty question as an either/or proposition within a zero-sum game situation. In fact, it is an *and* situation. Many cases of private governance exhibit no actual shift away from public to private sectors. "Instead, firms have created a *new* transnational world of transaction flows that did not exist previously."[4]

One part of the case for the ascendancy of MNC power over national governments is that global corporate networks allegedly have structurally altered interactions between the official and private sectors. Global production and sales strategies are seen as having fused national markets and having created "an economic geography that subsumes multiple political geographies." A government no longer proactively calls the shots within its territory, as demonstrated by MNCs' record of successful solicitations of favorable tax and regulatory treatment. "While globalization integrates markets, it fragments politics."[5] Another part of the argument speaks of the growing divergence between economic and political space. Markets have outgrown national boundaries. As big corporations further expand their international operations, the gap continues to widen between the global sweep of MNCs and the jurisdictional reach of nation-state governments.[6]

The late Susan Strange, a respected centrist scholar of international political economy, argued that globalized, "impersonal forces of world markets," have been integrated since World War II "more by private enterprise in finance, industry and trade than by the cooperative decisions of governments." Transnational commercial activity has become "more powerful than the states to whom ultimate political authority over society and economy is supposed to belong. Where states were once the masters of markets, now it is the markets which, on many crucial issues, are the master over the governments of states."[7]

Distancing herself from the view that national sovereignty had been stripped of any meaning by MNCs, Strange argued it was more accurate to say that the nation-state was undergoing a metamorphosis. The latter was triggered by structural changes in the world economy stemming from technological and financial changes and the accelerated integration of national economies into a single global marketplace.[8] MNCs have encroached enough on the traditional "domains of power" of national governments to reduce them to "just one source of authority among several, with limited powers and resources." The center of gravity in world politics, in her view, had shifted in favor of multinationals, who, while not taking over from national governments, were nevertheless "increasingly exercising a *parallel authority* alongside governments" in matters involving the full spectrum of economic policy management.[9]

Kenichi Ohmae is the spokesman for a school of thought that says governments have lost their traditional role because the economic concept of nation-states has been rendered meaningless in an era when the international economy is so tightly integrated that a borderless world has evolved. His view is that antiquated efforts by governments to protect domestic economic interests against external competition wind up harming the economic welfare of their people to an unacceptable degree. Why? Because it is no longer national economies that are the main units of competition in today's globalized marketplace. What really matters in the contemporary world economy are regional manufacturing clusters (dubbed region states) whose boundaries have been drawn by transnational efficiency-seeking market forces, mainly MNCs, not by political fiat and historical happenstance. Region states, in Ohmae's vision, are "natural economic zones" that encompass two or more countries as often as they fall within a single state. They "follow, rather than precede, real flows of human activity."[10]

Traditional roles of governments are alleged to be as obsolete in political terms as arbitrarily drawn national borders are for commercial purposes. By implication, civil servants who try to interfere with market-driven international flows of goods, services, and capital are living in a bygone era, mistakenly believing they still possess unchallengeable control over economic forces within their borders. A widely published author while a senior partner in the Japanese office of the management consultants McKinsey and Company, Ohmae wrote that in a tightly globalized economy, the nation-state has become "an unnatural, even dysfunctional, unit for organizing human activity and managing economic endeavor.... It represents no genuine, shared community of economic interests." Nation-states obscure the "true linkages and synergies that exist among often disparate populations by combining important measures of human activity at the wrong level of analysis."[11]

Taking a political science approach, Harvard scholar John Ruggie reaches a similar conclusion. He describes a newly emerging global public domain that is intellectually and physically distinct from the traditional system based on nation-states. Instead, it has become an international order consisting of interactions among transnational nonstate actors at least as much as between states. The end result is that the process for making authoritative allocations of values in societies is one that increasingly "reaches beyond the confines of national boundaries" and where a growing percentage of norms is determined through transnational channels and processes. MNCs operate globally and "function in near-real time, leaving behind the slower moving, state-mediated inter-*national* world of arms-length economic transactions and traditional international legal mechanisms, even as they depend on that world for their licenses to operate and to protect their property rights."[12]

Others emphasize the point that MNCs now engage in activities previously reserved for governments, for example, building physical infrastructure and setting product standards; they see the result as a blurring of the lines between the public and private sectors. Big global companies "have acquired power and resources on a scale previously held only by national governments. In the exercise of these powers in the pursuits of corporate ends, the activities of MNCs ... are often comparable to or even surpass those of the action of governments."[13] The ability of sovereign nations to control the behavior and impact of MNCs increasingly is in doubt.

A totally different perspective on the sovereign state versus MNC power relationship holds that a major new economic era has begun. We again encounter the theme that the status quo is not forever and that the dynamic nature of the

FDI/MNC phenomena reduces analysis to a snapshot of a moment in time that has a limited shelf life. Stephen J. Kobrin of the Wharton Business School believes there is a point when "degree becomes kind, where the erosion of autonomy and control over an economy and economic actors renders the presumptive right of states as the supreme authority within their borders relatively meaningless."[14] That point appears to have been reached in recent years, he argues, with the full-blown emergence of the digital revolution as manifested in the Internet and electronic commerce. This is a trend capable of doing something unprecedented—undermining governments' trump card of being able to deny foreign companies access to their sovereign territory. Absolute geographic jurisdiction may not be viable in cyberspace. To the extent that markets continue to migrate there and digital transactions become more common, territorial sovereignty will be less able to provide the basis for effective or efficient governance, Kobrin claims. The continued rise of nontraditional MNCs doing business through computer servers located in the headquarters country is one of several reasons to question the ability of nation-states to remain the supreme authority domestically and the dominant constituent unit of the international system. He concludes that "This time around, sovereignty in terms of both domestic authority and mutually exclusive territoriality may really be 'at bay.'"[15]

Analysts on the left of the political spectrum have criticized the rise of MNC power relative to governments in blunter, more negative terms. "Stateless corporations have given rise to corporate states," said the head of a Canadian nongovernmental organization (NGO).[16] A task force claimed that "governments have been largely stripped of the powers and tools they once had to regulate the investments of global corporations."[17] A third view is that "increasingly, corporations dictate the decisions of their supposed overseers in government and control domains of society once firmly embedded within the public sphere."[18] Convinced that the nation-state faces a crisis of relevance, another author wondered, "What remains of its purpose and power if authority over domestic social standards is yielded to disinterested market forces? If governments are reduced to bidding for the favors of multinational enterprises, what basis will citizens have for determining their own destinies?"[19]

The most scathing assessment comes from Ralph Nader, who believes that MNC-induced globalization

> impinges deeply on the ability of any nation to control commercial activity with democratically elected laws. Globalization's tactic is to eliminate democratic decision-making and accountability over matters as intimate as the safety of food, pharmaceuticals and motor vehicles, or the way a country may use or conserve its land, water, and minerals, and other resources.

What we have now in this type of globalization is a slow-motion coup d'etat, a low-intensity war waged to redefine free society as subordinate to . . . big business *uber alles*.[20]

Governments have been "hijacked by corporate power, the multinationals mostly. They have their own people in government." The result, Nader claimed, is a "convergence, almost a phalanx, of business controlling government and turning it against its own people."[21]

No, Multinational Companies Have Not in Fact Eclipsed Nation-States

Reports of the death of national sovereignty have been frequent, but to many observers, they are premature. This section summarizes the school of thought that believes governments still have the clear upper hand in running their countries. At least two outstanding scholars did some hasty extrapolations and produced erroneous forecasts of the demise of governmental authority and relevance, the purported victim of increasingly powerful MNCs. Charles Kindleberger of MIT asserted in 1969 that the "nation-state is just about through as an economic unit."[22] Two years later, Harvard's Raymond Vernon started his classic book, *Sovereignty at Bay,* by asserting that nation-states "are feeling naked. Concepts such as sovereignty and national economic strength appear curiously drained of meaning."[23] Multinational enterprises were cited as one of the institutions primarily responsible for these changes.

"Sovereignty at bay" entered the language as the metaphor of choice to express the notion that the power of MNCs had reached extraordinary heights. However, according to Vernon, the phrase was not a fully accurate reflection of a conviction that state sovereignty had been eclipsed by multinational companies. He later wrote: "If you want to draw public attention to your opus, find an evocative title. But if you want readers to remember its content, resist a title that carries only half the message." He argued that he did not predict "the decline of nation-states and the emergence of a world of stateless global corporations" because he felt the public would appreciate the advantages of both large corporations and strong governments. "I saw two systems . . . each legitimated by popular consent, each potentially useful to the other, yet each containing features antagonistic to the other."[24]

Even the most ineffectual government has the unequivocal authority to physically block the entrance of a foreign subsidiary that is not welcomed. Once up and running, it is more common for foreign-owned or -controlled corporations to turn to the host government for assistance in advancing or protecting their interest than vice versa. A government can force a foreign subsidiary to leave by tightening regulatory controls, raising the cost of doing business, or threatening to arrest executives, among other things. A "multinational" company does not literally exist in legal terms. Its headquarters and overseas subsidiaries all must be incorporated in accordance with the laws of each country in which it operates. The EU Commission in 2001 effectively vetoed the proposed merger between two A-list U.S. companies, General Electric and Honeywell—despite prior approval by the U.S. Department of Justice, the ever-vigilant protector of the tough U.S. antitrust laws. The EU Commission's controversial final determination held that the market strength of the combined companies in aircraft components and leasing would violate the EU's dominant position principle in the aerospace sector. Given the importance of the European market, the two companies called off the merger after additional pleading and pressure from the companies and the Bush administration fell on deaf ears at the EU's headquarters.[25]

The argument that globalization in general and MNCs in particular have significantly eroded sovereignty over the past three decades ignores the fact that for centuries, both the control and authority of nation-states have been challenged on a regular basis. This is the inevitable consequence of an international system that is based on territorial states but lacks a universal authority structure. According to Krasner, it is an "anarchical system" in which the "interests of the strong will not necessarily coincide with accepted norms." He thinks the argument that the challenge to sovereignty is a post-MNC, late-twentieth-century phenomenon ignores another historical fact: At the start of the twentieth century, some measures of international economic interdependence, capital flows in particular, were as high as they were at the end of the century.[26] Contemporary technological change "has complicated state control in some areas, but there is no evident secular trend." The nation-state arguably has never retained full unilateral control over its domain, in part because of centuries of treaty making in which some national autonomy was yielded for the greater benefits accruing from international cooperation.[27]

The nation-state "is still the only universally recognized way of organizing political life." States have lost bits and pieces of their sovereignty "in terms of autonomy (if, indeed, they had complete or absolute sovereignty to start with...)... Yet this erosion of sovereignty does not signify that they have all become dysfunctional or obsolete."[28] David Fieldhouse has argued that the host government still has the upper hand and can set the rules of engagement.

At the macro-economic level it can adjust its policies in such a way that it is no longer possible for MNCs to make "excessive" profits.... At the administrative level, it is always possible to use anti-trust laws against excessive concentration, to impose quotas, limit prices, above all to insist on a minimal level of local participation in the equity and of nationals in employment.

The ultimate sanction of nationalization happens infrequently, allegedly because experience shows that even very large foreign corporations will normally accept hard-and-fast demands from small states.[29]

MNCs can be viewed as just one of several vehicles that nation-states can exploit to exercise national power.[30] The two are not necessarily independent power centers engaged in a zero-sum game of domination with governments. To the extent that MNCs serve as means for governments to exert and enhance national power, they are sovereignty affirming rather than sovereignty diminishing.[31] A main theme of Robert Gilpin's classic book on MNCs and national power was the role of American corporate FDI as one of the three pillars (along with nuclear superiority and the international role of the dollar) of U.S. global hegemony in the early post–World War II era. Overstating the case a bit, he wrote that if British economic hegemony earlier in the century had been based on the city of London's global financial might, America's "was based largely on her multinational corporations."[32] Repatriated profits from these investments, he noted, helped offset the balance of payments costs of the worldwide U.S. military presence and foreign aid—thus aiding and abetting achievement of governmental priorities, not undermining sovereignty.

Governments have used their authority to integrate their countries into the global economy and admit foreign-owned and -controlled subsidiaries because internationalization and strong national economic performance are statistically linked (see chapter 8), and strong economic performance strengthens the legitimacy of the state and the popularity of its leaders. "If integration is chosen, rather than imposed, it is impossible to argue that it renders states impotent." The real question, according to Martin Wolf, concerns the nature of individual trade-offs between domestic and international priorities that government leaders confront after embracing economic interdependence.[33]

Rephrasing the Question and Placing It in a Larger Context

The kind of absolute authority originally bestowed on the governments of sovereign countries by the Westphalian system that emerged in the mid-seventeenth century could not be expected to remain immune forever from the cumulative effects of changing conditions and circumstances, both inside and outside of their borders. National borders are mainly the results of accidents of history and political compromise. They were not configured as the result of careful planning aimed at ensuring self-sufficiency or optimal operating efficiency in the territory being carved out. Even if borders had been designed with that intent hundreds of years ago, increasingly complex manufacturing processes eventually would have outgrown the home market. No nation-state has ever come near to being permanently self-sufficient in economic resources, national security, or, more recently, protection of the environment, prevention of terrorism, and containment of drug trafficking. "Increasingly, resources and threats that matter . . . circulate and shape lives and economies with little regard for political boundaries. . . . Even the most powerful states find the marketplace and international public opinion compelling them more often to follow a particular course" of action.[34]

The question of whether sovereignty has been ceded to megacorporations is best analyzed by rejecting a simple yes-or-no approach, as is also the case for best assessing the overall merits of FDI and MNCs. In both cases, the soundest approach is synthesizing multiple factors. What is happening is more a case of governments—for several reasons—losing their once-upon-a-time claim to be the exclusive arbiters of public policy, regulators of behavior, and controllers of national destiny than the amoral snatching of state power by profit-driven MNCs. An effort to better comprehend the broad implications of the new challenges and obligations facing nation-states in an increasingly complicated world would be a useful line of inquiry. It surely would be a more productive intellectual pursuit than trying to keep a subjective score for an ill-defined supremacy contest between governments and MNCs. The main reason that the numbers and economic strength of MNCs rose steadily has been their ability to effectively address a major event in economic history: the end of national markets for production and sales of goods having high fixed costs. If their power and impact have nearly reached, equaled, or exceeded parity with national governments, it is mainly in the context of MNCs being an effect of larger structural changes in the economic and technological order, not a cause of diminished sovereignty as traditionally defined.

The twentieth century saw major challenges emerge to the exclusive power of governments. The first developed in the wake of the Great Depression of the 1930s. Governments simultaneously found themselves confronted with an economic crisis of unprecedented proportions and exposed to the breakthrough concepts of John Maynard Keynes that explained how activist/countercyclical fiscal and monetary policies could revive economic growth and cure recessions. Without any formal fanfare, a policy revolution was born: Political leaders accepted responsibility for providing a well-functioning economy. Economic policy joined national security to become the two major responsibilities of governments. National elections for the first time began to reflect the ability of politicians to deliver the three fundamental economic benchmarks—growth, full employment, and price stability.

Just how severely nation-states, especially the smaller ones, were becoming limited in unilaterally achieving these goals became patently obvious after World War II, when international economic interdependence reached and passed critical mass. Partial, voluntary surrenders of economic sovereignty became the price to be paid if national leaders were to provide their citizens a rising standard of living and maximize the international competitiveness of the domestic business sector. Specialization of production, global marketing, and relatively unrestricted, market-directed flows of trade and capital among countries became the lodestar of economic efficiency and prosperity. Access by domestic producers to large, affluent, and high-growth foreign markets was now a critical issue. Reciprocity became a currency of the international realm: Domestic markets were opened to imports and direct investment in return for access to other countries' markets, a mutually beneficial situation in which all participating countries enhance their economic efficiency.

The European Union, begun in 1958, remains the greatest example of the rationale for voluntary surrender of state sovereignty to achieve national goals to a degree otherwise unattainable. Politically, the EU has always been about preventing another major war among the European powers by tightly integrating the Continent's national economies. Membership is politically appealing because when speaking out in the international arena as part of a large, influential regional group, the small and medium-sized European countries have a much louder and more powerful voice than if speaking on their own. Economically, the EU is the prototype of regional cooperation where scale provides far greater economic efficiency and material benefits to member countries than they could hope to attain through go-it-alone efforts. Despite the requirement to cede authority over many aspects of traditional state prerogatives—monetary policy, currency exchange rates, international trade negotiations, agricultural policy, and so on—to EU institutions, countries have literally been lining up since the late 1960s to join this unprecedented venture in supranational government. Member governments have not so much been motivated by an aesthetic desire to shrink their sovereignty and renounce nationalism than by pragmatism. An old aphorism applies: Less is more. It is now taken for granted throughout Europe that EU membership is invaluable for delivering the economic benefits that voters demand and the prestige political leaders want. The common rules and regulations imposed on EU members have grown steadily in number, a trend that is counterintuitive until it is noted that many of the priority economic objectives and obligations assumed by the modern nation-state have moved out of its reach when acting alone as an independent agent.

Another late-twentieth-century challenge to sovereignty was the emergence of *transnational actors*, defined as groups, businesses, coalitions, organizations, and so on, that are active in multiple countries and operate independently of any government. Energized by technological and communications advances that encouraged and reduced the costs of international activities, transnational actors have played a leading role (along with international organizations) in reformatting the old system of exclusive, unchallenged governmental sovereignty into a power/influence-sharing arrangement. It is a fact of life that governments have ceased to be the *sole* entities capable of affecting the course of trends and events within and between countries. The influx of new movers and shakers has visibly made international public policy making a more inclusive process. How positive or negative is this trend remains a matter of subjective opinion, not universally accepted truth.

MNCs are the most frequently discussed and most visible category of transnational actor, and they have become the number one symbol of globalization. Nation-states and multinational companies have a symbiotic relationship of unique dimensions. Each has something the other needs to succeed in its mission; governments provide legitimacy and corporations provide jobs, exports, tax revenues, and so on. Yet the overall situation is too complicated to declare the two to be natural allies or to describe MNCs as docile contributors to government rule. Both possess such dissimilar goals and culture that the ensuing limits to mutual trust and understanding discourage both from wanting to get too close or dependent on the other. The result is a relationship that is "both cooperative and competing, both supportive and conflictual. They operate in a fully dialectical relationship, locked into unified but contradictory roles and positions."[35] Neither side has absolute dominance over the other on a day-to-day basis. This rule is not applicable when governments forbid a foreign company from establishing a subsidiary in its territory, expropriate one that is already functioning, or when MNCs refuse to invest in a country or shut down an operational overseas subsidiary.

NGOs (see chapter 11) are another powerful subset of transnational actors. Broadly defined, NGOs equate to civil society, that part of the social order that falls between individuals and their government, exclusive of profit-seeking entities. Their ranks are made up of a wide range of nonprofit, citizen-based organizations and volunteer groups that include public interest groups concerned with economic development, human rights, and environmental issues; labor unions; grant-giving foundations; and bands of armed revolutionaries. The relatively meteoric rise of the influence, numbers, activity, and budgets of NGOs has made them forces to be reckoned with in national capitals and global media attention. It would be a major error of omission not to name them, along with MNCs, as the major nongovernment actors responsible for erosion of some outer layers of sovereignty. Advocates of social equity and critics of profit-driven corporate activities applaud NGOs' conscious efforts to (1) wrest traditional prerogatives from government, and (2) influence public policy. A double standard is at work here inasmuch as they condemn MNCs for attempting to do the same thing on an indirect basis.

Both nonprofit and for-profit transnational actors engage in activities that sometimes complement and sometimes compete with governmental responsibilities. Private charitable groups, sometimes operating under government contract, regularly provide nonstate foreign aid, medical treatment, disaster relief, and refugee assistance to developing countries. Profit-seeking transnational actors are equally involved in quasi-governmental activity. Credit-rating companies can cost or save countries hundreds of millions of dollars annually in international borrowing costs, depending on how good or bad they rate the economic outlook for a country. Commercial banks in the second half of the 1970s supplanted governments as the main source of capital flows used by many Latin American countries to pay for imports, repay old debts, and finance capital outflows by the wealthy. Financial companies have crafted internationally accepted accounting and stock-clearing standards. Representatives of MNCs participating in the TransAtlantic Business Dialogue have facilitated official agreements to reduce testing and certification costs in several industrial sectors and have established industry-wide consensus on a number of uniform product standards accepted by EU and U.S. companies.[36] Jessica Mathews suggests that nation-states may "no longer be the natural problem-solving unit. . . . The new technologies encourage noninstitutional, shifting networks over the fixed bureaucratic hierarchies that are the hallmark of the single-voiced sovereign state."[37] This imputed dilution of national sovereignty and rise in private authority have been termed international *governance* without *government* by distinguished international relations theorist James Rosenau. Unlike government, *governance* refers to activities based on shared goals that do not necessarily derive from legal and formally prescribed responsibilities ultimately enforced by police powers. "Governments still operate and they are still sovereign in a number of ways; but . . . some of their authority has been relocated toward sub-national collectivities."[38]

International organizations are a third outside force that has diluted the historical potency of sovereignty. Nation-states' maneuverability is restrained after voluntarily joining international economic organizations and agreeing to abide by the detailed rules covering international trade and monetary policies set out, respectively, in the International Monetary Fund's and World Trade Organization's articles of agreement. Being part of a system that forces other countries to respect your economic rights is another situation where governments have judged a modicum of surrendered sovereignty to be a favorable trade-off.

The argument that national sovereignty has not been eviscerated by MNCs or any other challengers is not necessarily an assertion that it is business as usual for the power of national governments. *Loss of autonomy* is a more accurate phrase in describing what governments have visibly lost to globalization in general and the proliferation of FDI in particular. Inability to unilaterally chart the course of a country's economy exactly in accordance with the desires of political leaders is now an accepted reality; loss by government of the supreme power to write, interpret, and enforce rules and laws within a country's territory is a less than a unanimously held belief. Policy makers in some countries indeed feel beholden to large corporations, whether domestically or foreign-owned, for the boost they can give the domestic economy and the contribution they can make to the political popularity (and in some cases, campaign funds) of a country's top leaders. Although the latter officially retain ultimate legal authority to establish whatever economic policies they choose, many policy makers today perceive the cost of alienating existing and potential foreign direct investors as prohibitively expensive in practical terms and therefore a prerogative to be shunned. Acceding to MNCs' demands for favorable tax treatment, relaxed regulatory rigor, direct subsidies, or improved infrastructure is still not mandatory or inevitable, just more compelling than in previous decades.

Other facets of international economic interdependence can affect the performance of national economies and curtail the autonomy of economic policy makers on a much broader and more forceful basis than incoming FDI. Exogenous variables outside the control of governments have become at least as important as endogenous variables in determining national economic performance. Countries suffering inflation rates and current account deficits far higher the international norm are increasingly likely to be victims of what effectively is a vote of no confidence by the international investment community. As the many financial crises suffered in the 1990s by emerging market countries in East Asia and Latin America confirm, governments following what are perceived as "irresponsible" economic policies can expect severe retribution when foreign exchange traders and owners of local stocks and bonds investors begin a massive, recession-inducing sell-off of a country's financial assets. Countries dependent on export-led growth can and do suffer economic downturns—through no fault of the party in power—when their major trading partners slide into recession. Given deep economic interdependence in North America, Canadian policy makers cannot fully immunize their country against changing economics in the United States.

At a time when countries routinely criticize each other on policies previously considered internal matters off limits to foreign meddling, the demarcation line between domestic and international economics has all but vanished. Today, agricultural support programs, enforcement of antitrust laws, transparency of government procurement procedures, and so on are being modified to reduce their distortions to foreign trade flows. *The Economist* quoted a former chancellor of the exchequer lamenting that "the plain fact is that the nation state as it has existed for nearly two centuries is being undermined. . . . The ability of national governments to decide their exchange rate, interest rate, trade flows, investment and output has been savagely crippled by market forces."[39] Very little of this is attributable to FDI. Viewed in the larger context, MNCs are among the many effects of technological change on the world economy. They are not the main instigators of either global economic change or diminished national autonomy. They are coincident indicators.

An untested and perhaps incorrect assumption lies at the base of the hypothesis that Internet-oriented MNCs are candidates for being the straw that breaks the back of sovereignty. It is far from certain that of purveyors of e-commerce will become the typical MNC or that they will adopt a business model that refutes the need to accommodate all or most of the dictates (including paying sales taxes, not selling banned goods, censoring certain Web sites and search engine terms, and hiring locals as executives) of governments in countries where large numbers of their foreign consumers reside. There is also the question of cause and effect. It can be argued, but not unequivocally proven, that the revolution in information and telecommunications technologies, along with cheap overnight delivery services, is the culprit/hero responsible for inaugurating a genuinely new era in diminished governmental authority. The continued growth of business on a transnational basis may be just another effect of this revolution.

Finally, another often repeated thesis in previous chapters is applicable to the consideration of MNCs' impact on sovereignty: Disaggregate, do not generalize. Part of any analysis of gauging the ability of MNCs' economic power to trump national sovereignty is to take a country-by-country approach in lieu of sweeping statements about 190 individual nation-states. Large and affluent countries infrequently bow to the demands and tolerate the transgressions of MNCs. Economically distressed countries desperate to lure direct investments and countries whose leaders seek personal enrichment presumably have a higher propensity to customize policies, laws, and regulations as a means to curry favor with foreign companies even at the price of skimping on domestic priorities. If an LDC government is

> too weak or class-dominated, if its officials are too ignorant or corrupt to promote "suitable" policies, then sovereignty becomes no defence against the MNC. So, ultimately, our assessment of the probable and potential impact of MNCs on host countries must turn on how effectively the host state performs its role as maker of policy and defender of the "national interest."[40]

The more attractive a country is to foreign investors, the less intense the pressure should be on government leaders to compromise their values to attract and keep the subsidiaries of relatively wealthy foreign companies. The U.S. government is content to keep its hands off all dealings with foreign investors except where national security might be compromised (leaving the states to wave welcoming banners and incentive money). With foreign companies knocking down the door to get in, the government of China has felt little or no need to kowtow. Unless one categorizes the Chinese Communist Party's creation of an efficient, business-friendly environment as a sell-out, no case has been (or is likely to be) made that China's sovereignty has been eroded by MNCs pressuring the government to take actions it does not want to take. When senior Chinese officials demand technology transfers as a precondition for entry, they are seldom refused, even by companies as large as General Motors. When the government refuses to intervene to halt violations of intellectual property rights, big foreign companies have no recourse; it becomes a cost of doing business there.

Some leaders are not willing to curb their control freak proclivities to attract more direct investment. Vladimir Putin's preference to rule like a czar rather than implement an effective rule of law is a case of putting preservation of sovereign prerogative ahead of creating an attractive environment for inward FDI. Costa Rica's accommodation of relatively moderate demands by Intel, namely, improved physical infrastructure and expanded vocational training programs, as described in chapter 7, demonstrated that FDI can be attracted for moderate concessions that have no major adverse effects on the long-term economic interests of the local population. Even compliant governments with little leverage have the potential power to assert their ultimate authority over powerful MNCs operating within their borders. The classic example of this is the nationalization of big multinational oil companies' local subsidiaries by members of OPEC states in the 1970s. These acts grew out of decades of frustration over being powerless to determine production volumes and prices of their most valuable and nonreplenishable natural resource.

In sum, the role of the nation-state has been modified on a continuous basis for centuries by the constant pace of change in the international order, principally from progress in technology, communications, and transportation. A dispassionate look at the evidence suggests MNCs have played only an indirect role in diminishing the autonomy of nation-states and increasing the level of acceptance by government leaders that this decline is inevitable and advantageous. The idea of a serious diminution in sovereignty caused specifically by multinationals is a harder sell. In the final analysis, this conclusion reflects the author's perceptions; given a slightly different set of values, the conclusion would have pointed to an unfortunate sell-out of political sovereignty to cash-rich MNCs.

Notes

1. Stephen D. Krasner, "Globalization and Sovereignty," in David Smith, Dorothy Solinger, and Steven Topik, eds., *States and Sovereignty in the Global Economy* (New York: Routledge, 1999), pp. 34–42.
2. Wolfgang H. Reinicke, "Global Public Policy," *Foreign Affairs,* November/December 1997, p. 129.
3. As quoted in. Stephen J. Kobrin, "Sovereignty @ Bay: Globalization, Multinational Enterprise, and the International Political System," in Alan M. Rugman and Thomas L. Brewer, eds., *The Oxford Handbook of International Business* (New York: Oxford University Press, 2001), p. 186.
4. John G. Ruggie, "Reconstituting the Global Public Domain: Issues, Actors, and Practices," Harvard Faculty Research Working Papers Series, July 2004, p. 7, emphasis in original, available online at http://ksgnotes1.harvard.edu/Research/wpaper.nsf/rwp/RWP04-031/$File/rwp04_031_Ruggie.pdf; accessed August 2005.
5. Reinicke, "Global Public Policy," p. 130.
6. Kobrin, "Sovereignty @ Bay," pp. 186, 200.
7. Susan Strange, *The Retreat of the State—The Diffusion of Power in the World Economy* (Cambridge: Cambridge University Press, 1996), p. 4.
8. Ibid., pp. 14, 72–73.
9. Ibid., p. 65; emphasis added.
10. Kenichi Ohmae, "The Rise of the Region State," *Foreign Affairs,* spring 1993, pp. 78–79.
11. Ibid., p. 78.
12. Ruggie, "Reconstituting the Global Public Domain," pp. 32, 35, 7; emphasis in original.
13. Medard Gabel and Henry Bruner, *Global Inc.: An Atlas of the Multinational Corporation* (New York: New Press, 2003), pp. 120, 7.
14. Kobrin, "Sovereignty @ Bay," p. 191.
15. Ibid., pp. 200–201.
16. Maude Barlow, as quoted in Robin Broad, ed., *Global Backlash* (Lanham, MD: Rowman and Littlefield, 2002), p. 43.
17. The International Forum on Globalization, *Alternatives to Economic Globalization* (San Francisco: Berrett-Koehler, 2002), p. 143.
18. Joel Bakan, *The Corporation—The Pathological Pursuit of Power* (New York: Free Press, 2004), p. 5.
19. William Greider, *One World, Ready or Not—The Manic Logic of Global Capitalism* (New York: Simon and Schuster, 1997), p. 334.
20. Ralph Nader, "Introduction," in Lori Wallach and Michelle Sforza, *The WTO—Five Years of Reasons to Resist Corporate Globalization,* available online at http://www.thirdworldtraveler.com/WTO_MAI/WTO_FiveYears.html; accessed December 2005.
21. Ralph Nader interviewed by *LA-Weekly,* as quoted in Manfred B. Steger, *Globalism* (Lanham, MD: Rowman and Littlefield, 2002), p. 107.

22. Charles P. Kindleberger, *American Business Abroad: Six Lectures on Direct Investment* (New Haven, CT: Yale University Press, 1969), p. 207.

23. Raymond Vernon, *Sovereignty at Bay* (New York: Basic Books, 1971), p. 3.

24. Raymond Vernon, "Sovereignty at Bay: Twenty Years After," in Lorraine Eden and Evan Potter, eds., *Multinationals in the Global Political Economy* (New York: St. Martin's, 1993), p. 19.

25. Technically, General Electric refused to comply with the commission's demands for product line divestitures as a precondition for approval.

26. Krasner, "Globalization and Sovereignty," pp. 34, 37.

27. Ibid., p., 49.

28. Arie Kacowicz, "Regionalization, Globalization, and Nationalism," Kellogg Institute for International Studies, Working Paper Series no. 262, December 1998, pp. 39–40, available online at http://www.nd.edu/~kellogg/WPS/262.pdf; accessed June 2005.

29. David Fieldhouse, "'A New Imperial System'? The Role of the Multinational Corporations Reconsidered," in Jeffry [sic] A. Frieden and David A. Lake, eds., International Political Economy (Boston: Bedford/St. Martin's, 2000), p. 178.

30. C. Fred Bergsten, Thomas Horst, and Theodore Moran, *American Multinationals and American Interests* (Washington, DC: Brookings Institution, 1978), p. 333.

31. Kobrin, "Sovereignty @ Bay," p. 183.

32. Robert Gilpin, *U.S. Power and the Multinational Corporation* (New York: Basic Books, 1975), pp. 139, 161.

33. Martin Wolf, *Why Globalization Works* (New Haven, CT: Yale University Press, 2004), p. 251.

34. Jessica T. Mathews, "Power Shift," *Foreign Affairs,* January/February 1997, p. 50.

35. D. M. Gordon, as quoted in Peter Dicken, *Global Shift* (New York: Guilford Press, 2003), p. 274.

36. TransAtlantic Business Dialogue, "About the TABD," available online at http://www.tabd.com/about; accessed November 2005.

37. Mathews, "Power Shift," pp. 65–66.

38. James N. Rosenau, "Governance, Order, and Change in World Politics," in J. Rosenau and E. Czempiel, eds., *Governance without Government: Order and Change in World Politics* (Cambridge: Cambridge University Press, 1992), pp. 3–4.

39. "The Myth of the Powerless State," *The Economist,* October 7, 1995, p. 15.

40. Fieldhouse, "'A New Imperial System'?" p. 175.

11

THE INTERNATIONAL
REGULATION OF
MULTINATIONAL
CORPORATIONS

*Why There Is No Multilateral Foreign
Direct Investment Regime*

Government regulation and big business are inextricably linked. All governments regulate companies operating within their jurisdiction to ensure consistency with domestic goals and values. International economic relations are largely conducted on three levels: private sector commercial and financial transactions, national rules and regulations affecting the private sector's behavior, and international rules and regulations adhered to by governments for the common good. A clearly defined international trading order exists, as does an international monetary and financial order. A foreign direct investment (FDI) regime dealing with investment policy and the actions of multinational companies (MNCs) does not exist. This is an anomaly in view of the recognition by senior political leaders that MNCs have a significant impact, real and potential, on the performances of national economies.

Governments should be anxious to have a formal international framework in place to steer FDI activity into what are deemed to be desirable directions. This chapter seeks to explain this paradox in the context of previously developed themes: complexity, heterogeneity, and deep differences in perceptions on the net merits of MNCs. The first section addresses the core question of why progress toward meaningful multilateral rules in this field continues to languish (or, to use Raymond Vernon's phrase, progress is coming at a "glacial pace"). The inquiry proceeds on two levels. At the macro level is the larger debate over the optimal distribution of power between government and the marketplace, domestic and global. The micro level encompasses more specific procedural and substantive problems associated with an effort to negotiate a comprehensive multilateral agreement on FDI policy. The chapter's second section presents a selective survey of the major government agreements and nonbinding multilateral codes of conduct that collectively provide a rudimentary, decentralized regulatory system addressing governmental actions and MNC behavior. Next come two separate case studies of vehement disagreement on how to apportion rights and responsibilities between the official and private sectors. The conflicting attitudes toward the proposed Multilateral Agreement on Investment (MAI) and the existing Chapter 11 of the North American Free Trade Agreement (NAFTA) are analyzed in depth because they demonstrate many of the irreconcilable differences that have relegated a definitive multilateral agreement on FDI and MNCs to an occasionally discussed abstraction rather than a reality. Finally, a fifth section examines the relatively recent and rapid rise in the role of nongovernmental organizations (NGOs) as unofficial external influences affecting the behavior of both multinational enterprise and governments.

Why No FDI Regime Exists

"Regimes" are common objectives, norms (rights and obligations), rules, and procedures that establish a uniform set of standards voluntarily followed by governments. They play a central role in managing the international economic order. It is widely acknowledged that although growing international economic interdependence has created new opportunities for pursuit of economic prosperity, it also has shrunk the ability of governments to achieve economic goals and solve problems when acting alone. Recognition of this shrinkage is a major raison d'être of the European Union. Because the economic benefits of interdependence to countries continue to exceed the political costs of diminished national autonomy, governments allow their international trade policy and international monetary and financial policies to be circumscribed by the multilateral regimes governing them. By joining the International Monetary Fund (IMF) and the World Trade Organization (WTO), a country limits its right to impose proscribed discriminatory economic measures against other countries. However, a government joining these international economic organizations takes comfort in the knowledge that all other signatories are required to extend it the same nondiscriminatory treatment.

Even before World War II ended, the Allies began collective efforts to plan a new international economic system, one that would prevent a return to the disastrous, mutually harmful "beggar-your-neighbor" unilateralism of the 1930s. The ill-advised, short-sighted adoption of restrictive international economic measures by the major economies crippled international commerce and deepened and prolonged the Great Depression. The Bretton Woods Conference of 1944 established the outline of a regime to define the rights and obligations of countries in addressing balance of payments disequilibria, managing exchange rate policies, and regulating international capital flows. A 1947 conference in Havana produced international consensus on a protocol for trade policy behavior. In the same year, the first round of multilateral tariff-cutting negotiations was completed under the auspices of the newly created General Agreement on Tariffs and Trade (GATT).

The initial blueprints of both regimes were drafted in a matter of months, just a little more than a blink of an eye relative to many subsequent international economic negotiations. The international monetary and trade regimes are supervised today by the IMF and WTO, respectively. They interpret and enforce the rules their members are supposed to follow, and periodically they are the venue for negotiations aimed at expanding or refining their respective regimes. The two organizations have been instrumental in preserving the relatively liberal (open and market-oriented) international economic order.[1]

Economic coordination efforts within the Organization for Economic Cooperation and Development (OECD) are examples of what might be called subregime multilateralism. The industrial countries use it as a discussion forum mainly to stay in sync on the many domestic and international economic policies and trends that collectively influence growth rates, employment levels, and price stability in this highly interdependent group of countries. The developing countries have acted in a similar manner by giving permanence to and expanding the mandate of the United Nations Conference on Trade and Development (UNCTAD). It is the less developed countries' (LDCs) preferred forum to discuss means of restructuring the international economic order in ways that are supportive of their special economic needs, and it acts as an advocate for measures to narrow the North–South income gap.

Conspicuous by their absence are multilateral principles and an institution to regulate FDI and MNCs. The *economics* of these phenomena provide a compelling case in favor of having such a regime. The last section of chapter 3 presented statistics showing that by consistently growing faster than total domestic production (world GDP) and international trade, FDI has become an increasingly important variable determining national economic performance and for many countries is a more important means of selling to foreign customers than exporting. Senior economic policy makers cannot ignore these trends, nor can they suppress the desire to channel the economic power of MNCs in directions that serve the national interest.

Multilateral efforts perceived by governments to influence the behavior of MNCs would have a number of advantages over unilateral initiatives. First, most large manufacturing and services MNCs are well positioned to stay one step ahead of unwanted coercion by a single government. Many are so geographically dispersed in their production and marketing activities that they have become less dependent on the good graces of individual governments (except those in the headquarters country and in their largest overseas markets) for survival and financial success. They have achieved increased mobility that facilitates their moving subsidiaries to places governed by more business-friendly regimes, to places with lower production costs, or both. Second, a multilateral FDI agreement also would have the potential to impose ceilings on financial incentives offered to foreign companies. Such a restraint would save some governments a lot of money, but no one wants to go first because others might not follow. "In light of the increased significance of the MNC in every facet of the global economy, it is remarkable that there are not international rules to govern FDI." Political economist Robert Gilpin added that ample evidence exists to suggest that an international agreement governing MNCs and FDI would be "desirable" for charting good policies for countries and corporations.[2]

The *politics* of FDI are the principal obstacles to the creation of an international FDI regime. The continuing stalemate in the larger sense is about value judgments on the appropriate balance of power between governments and markets, and more specifically about how much freedom governments should grant MNCs. Articulation of a universally acceptable doctrine has been impossible in the face of some fiendishly difficult normative questions concerning the relationship between governments and markets. The different options and emphases for dealing with values and actors in an FDI regime are illustrated graphically in table 11.1. Given the absence of incontrovertible truths, none of these questions has an obvious first-best answer that is acceptable to all:

Whose behavior most needs to be restrained by multilateral rules: privately owned corporations or the governments of host countries? In other words, when it comes to FDI, is public sector interference or the private sector's self-centered pursuit of profit the greater threat to the interests of society as whole? Can it be determined whether big business or big government is the lesser of the evils, and if so, how? If it is not an all-or-nothing proposition, what is the right balance in an FDI regime between pursuit of a "just and stable" social order and reliance on the private sector to create wealth, raise living standards, and maximize efficiency? Should a code of good behavior be more vigorously applied to government officials responsible for protecting the public's welfare or to business executives responsible for advancing their corporations' self-interests by providing goods and services to consumers at affordable prices?

TABLE 11.1. Governance Trade-Offs

	Efficiency-Oriented Regime	Fairness-Oriented Regime
Obligations and Restraints	Maximum for Host Governments; Minimum for MNCs;	Maximum for MNCs; Minimum for Host Governments
Rights and Freedom to Act	Maximum for MNCs; Minimum for Host Governments	Maximum for Host Governments; Minimum for MNCs

Absent resolution of these quandaries, there can be no effective multilateral agreement on FDI that will be enthusiastically embraced by a majority of the world's countries. The virtues of reduced trade barriers and the need to correct structural balance of payments disequilibria are simple and straightforward when compared with the myriad substantive and technical issues associated with establishing universal standards for government and MNC behavior.

The odds are further stacked against implementation of a comprehensive regime by the improbability that all interested parties will soon be able to get past their many incompatible views. On the procedural side, no deadlines exist that would pressure the factions to cobble together a compromise. The international economic order can exist indefinitely without a multilateral agreement on FDI policy. On the substantive side, compatible desires, needs, and attitudes have not, do not, and will not come easily to the major factions: (1) host countries, (2) home countries, (3) MNCs and their shareholders, and (4) stakeholders (the public at large, company employees, the environment, and organized public interest groups). The first and fourth of the major actors want governments to systematically seek significant net benefits from foreign-owned subsidiaries. They feel it essential that host countries have authority to demand that foreign subsidiaries conform to local laws, values, and definitions of good corporate citizenship. Theirs is an emphasis on fairness. Conversely, the second and third actors see the greatest good for the greatest number of citizens coming from letting business operate relatively unencumbered by government restrictions. Home countries rail against host countries that hinder the freedom and financial success of their overseas subsidiaries. MNCs combine economic self-interest with free market ideology to preach their unique capacity to maximize global wealth and economic efficiency. Their between-the-lines message is that their substantial benefits will be denied to governments averse to creating and maintaining a favorable business environment for incoming direct investments.

Even if conceptual differences can be resolved, many procedural and practical hurdles would remain. Getting past them is another prerequisite for achieving consensus on what a multilateral system of FDI/MNC governance should look like. First of all, few governments have a clear, consistent, and unambiguous position on what they are seeking in an FDI regime. Most are unable to fully reconcile two distinctly different subsets of FDI policy, one to deal with issues associated with being a host country, the other to deal with issues associated with home-country status. A double standard is inevitable in formulating two distinct sets of policy positions to deal with different national self-interests. Government officials instinctively support maximum freedom of maneuver for their companies' subsidiaries operating in other countries. However, when considering how to deal with foreign-owned subsidiaries operating within their own jurisdiction, governments want the option of being able to ensure compatibility with national needs. Devising principles simultaneously compatible with the interests of home and host countries is no simple task.

Second, opinions on the right degree of regulation differ among countries. Some still view inward FDI with suspicion and distrust, whereas others have built their economic growth strategy around it. Attitudes toward international business are filtered through prisms uniquely sculpted by different historical experiences, different levels of economic development, and differing economic ideologies. Capitalism is practiced in many distinctive forms around the globe because no common agenda exists on the government–business relationship. In short, infinite nuances exist as to how 190 sovereign countries redirect the invisible hand of the marketplace through interventionist economic policies and intrusive controls on MNCs.

Although all countries accept the broad principle of the need to regulate the business sector, each has its own ideas about how much and what mix of regulation are called for. Japan and France exemplify countries with strong bureaucracies that have proactively promoted the development of targeted industries through favorable treatment and financial subsidies. In return, these governments expect corporate executives to be responsive to their suggestions and demands. At the opposite end of the spectrum is the adversarial relationship mutually accepted by business and government in the United States. An extraordinary burden of proof is imposed on Washington before it can use taxpayers' money to assist private companies. Where to draw the line, or a series of lines, amidst a nearly infinite number of variations on the business–government dynamic is among the most complex policy issues affecting decision makers.

Yet another source of government ambiguity standing in the way of a comprehensive FDI/MNC regime is the degree of regulatory autonomy nation-states are willing to surrender to it. Chances are slim that most countries would be willing to relinquish their right to refuse entry of foreign-owned subsidiaries in sensitive sectors like defense, culture/mass media, and transportation. Nor is it likely that all countries would agree to relinquish their right to offer financial incentives to prospective foreign investors. Developing countries would be reluctant to cede authority to regulate the activities of foreign-owned extractive companies or to dilute their right to demand transfers of advanced technology from incoming MNC manufacturers. Congress is unlikely to approve participation in an investment treaty denying the U.S. government's right to order overseas subsidiaries of American companies to refrain from exporting to countries targeted by U.S. export controls or trade sanctions.

Practical difficulties inhibiting consensus on FDI/MNC regulation do not stop there. Successful negotiations to create an FDI regime will require extreme consultations between government delegations and senior executives of domestically headquartered MNCs. Multinationals will be the most directly affected by the design and operation of the new regime—both in terms of how governments can regulate them and what rights and obligations will be extended to companies. Because every major phase of corporate operations potentially would be directly affected by a multilateral agreement, most governments would feel it necessary to get expert advice on the business consequences of proposals to regulate and protect MNCs.

A more specific problem is determining whether it would be both desirable and legal to allow representatives of MNCs to directly participate in the negotiation of a multinational FDI agreement. Some would argue that only authorized representatives of national governments accountable to their citizens have the legitimacy to negotiate that which will have the force of international law. The counterargument is that MNCs will be more affected by a regime than governments and therefore cannot be denied access to the policy-making process; failure to accommodate them risks an MNC backlash that would seek to defeat ratification of the pact in key countries. A middle-ground arrangement would allow business representatives to assemble in a room near the negotiators and provide immediate advice and feedback when invited to do so. Similar questions can be raised about the possible participation of the NGOs who have been outspoken in demanding that MNCs operate in a more socially responsible, ethical manner.

A whole new set of practical problems arises if it is decided to accredit representatives of MNCs and NGOs to the negotiations. What is a manageable number of private sector participants? It presumably would make most sense to keep the number small enough to prevent them from vastly outnumbering government officials. Once a number is agreed on by whoever is chosen to make that decision, it then becomes necessary to determine the criteria to be used for selecting a relatively small number of participants from a large statistical universe. The worldwide total of economically important MNCs and politically active NGOs in each case is in the tens of thousands. What would constitute a "representative" group? How would noninvitees be able to make their views known?

Agreeing on the identities and numbers of direct and indirect negotiators is hardly the end of the tough procedural and practical dilemmas discouraging realization of an FDI regime. Selection of an appropriate venue for global talks could be a major sticking point. Developing countries would not be keen to use the WTO or the OECD, forums where they fear being bullied by industrialized countries. The latter in turn would oppose talks under the auspices of UNCTAD for fear that the more numerous developing countries would use the one-country, one-vote rule to co-opt agenda-setting and decision making. If a regime is created and requires institutional oversight, should the WTO's trade jurisdiction be extended to include FDI, or should an entirely new international economic organization be created?

Even if the preconditions for producing a global FDI/MNC regime were not formidable, the basic question remains as to whether it is a good idea. If not, the international economic order has been well served by failure to create it. An unconventional thesis is that multilateral rules in this area "are not necessarily desirable, let alone achievable." Implementation of a multilateral agreement could result in at least some LDCs believing it unnecessary to take the economically vital but politically difficult steps of domestic regulatory and institutional reforms needed to attract quality FDI on a sustained basis. Getting the basics right, for example, macroeconomic stability, good governance, strong financial systems, and industrial policies to improve corporate competitiveness, is of utmost importance to attract high-quality direct investment.[3] To the extent the authors are correct in their assessment, an FDI regime is far from essential and its absence is of little consequence. Countries wishing to publicize their commitment to the basic property rights of foreign companies can sign bilateral treaties with countries having significant outward direct investment.

An Abridged Survey of Existing Efforts to Regulate FDI-Related Activities

In the absence of a formal FDI/MNC regime, an uncoordinated, narrowly written collection of government agreements and nonbinding, voluntary codes of conduct provide a limited number of rules and behavioral guidelines applicable to host governments and MNCs. None seeks a balanced approach by establishing a twin set of standards and obligations applicable to both businesses and governments.

Bilateral Treaties

Quantitatively speaking, the most prevalent kind of official accord in the FDI realm consists of thousands of agreements signed on a *bilateral* basis.

Efficiency-wise, the proliferation of piecemeal bilateralism is second best to a single uniform accord as the means of defining the parameters of FDI policy and MNC behavior. Bilateral investment treaties take one of two forms. The nearly 2,600 bilateral "double taxation treaties" in force at the end of 2004 are designed mainly to minimize the double taxation of MNCs' earnings.[4] This is what would occur if a foreign-owned subsidiary paid corporate income taxes to the host country and then, on repatriating those profits to headquarters, was forced to pay a full second round of income taxes to the home country.[5]

A total of 176 countries were signatories to at least one of 2,400 more broadly based bilateral investment treaties (BITs) signed between 1959, when the first of these treaties was concluded, and 2004.[6] They deal exclusively with protection of a foreign-owned or -controlled subsidiary's basic legal rights; they do not impose any obligations on companies. Bilateral treaties include most or all of a core group of policy guidelines aimed at restraining discriminatory or confiscatory government behavior against inward FDI. At the top of the list typically are the mutual obligations to apply "fair and equitable treatment" to local subsidiaries owned or controlled by companies headquartered in the other country and to provide "national treatment," that is, apply domestic laws and regulations to foreign subsidiaries at least as favorably as locally owned companies.[7] Other provisions typically included are the rights of entry and establishment in each signatory country by companies headquartered in the other (specified industrial sectors are often excluded for reason of political or social sensitivity), the right to repatriate profits, and standards for determining "fair" compensation in cases of expropriation. It is also customary to stipulate procedures for settling disputes that might arise between a host government and a local subsidiary owned by a corporation headquartered in the other signatory country. Investment accords embedded in regional free trade agreements tend to be broader and deeper than bilateral agreements. Countries committing themselves to regional free trade and common economic institutions cannot at the same time arbitrarily exclude open-door, nondiscriminatory policies toward incoming FDI from other member countries.

The first major set of binding *multilateral* rules on FDI policy appeared in the mid-1990s, following the successful completion of the Uruguay Round of multilateral trade negotiations. The Agreement on Trade-Related Investment Measures (TRIMs), subsequently incorporated into the WTO, was an important symbolic first step by governments in formally recognizing the increasing interconnectedness between FDI and trade (see chapter 9). In practical terms, the agreement's impact on government actions has been small, owing to the unwillingness of many developing countries to impose major new restraints on government prerogatives. The net result is that TRIMs does not introduce any new limitations on FDI policy actions; it merely bans specified investment-related measures considered to be inconsistent with the GATT provisions as updated in 1994. A limited prohibition list of trade-distorting measures includes local content requirements (which mandate that a minimum percentage by value of a foreign-owned subsidiary's output must be made of locally produced goods) and trade balancing requirements (these mandate that a foreign subsidiary's exports offset imports, and/ or its capital inflows must balance its capital outflows).[8]

Nonbinding Codes

Nonbinding codes of conduct applicable to MNCs comprise a second category of de facto regulation. Voluntary constraints on corporate behavior, a response to critics and suspicious LDCs, take the form of principles laid out in codes of conduct covering broad areas of business practices and values. The most common are human rights in general and labor rights in particular, environmental protection, full disclosure of business activity, and ethical behavior. Accession to these codes is based on pragmatic self-interest, not an altruistic desire by corporate chieftains to create a better world. Multinationals agree to comply with these guidelines mainly to enhance their public image as good corporate citizens. Additionally, by agreeing to self-policing, they hope to preempt passage of intrusive and mandatory controls by national legislation or international treaty. Corporate executives must walk a fine line between potential long-term benefits of having their firms practice corporate social responsibility and the immediate desire of their bosses, that is, the shareholders, for increased growth and profitability. The willingness to voluntarily follow standards of conduct that can modestly increase the costs of doing business came in two separate phases. Desire to placate the suspicions and antipathy of LDCs was the major catalyst in the 1970s and 1980s. Desire to defuse the public outcry from NGOs has been the major catalyst for corporate social sensitivities since the mid-1990s (to be discussed in this chapter's penultimate section).

An uncountable number of corporate codes of conduct exist worldwide inasmuch as most MNCs have adopted a company code applicable to social, labor, and environmental standards.[9] More than forty "open" codes subscribed to by multiple companies were identified in 2000.[10] Nearly all lack quantifiable criteria for determining corporate compliance and permanent monitoring mechanisms. One of the few exceptions is the code administered by Social Accountability International; companies adhering to its social accountability standard, known as SA8000, allow independent auditing organizations to verify compliance with a certifiable set of labor and human rights standards by on-site inspections of factories and farms.[11] Compliance with the provisions in all corporate codes is based on moral suasion because none are grounded in international law, and none have means to punish violations by signatory companies.

The two most influential voluntary codes of conduct, as measured by the amount of public and corporate attention attracted, are administered by the OECD and the United Nations. The OECD's Guidelines for Multinational Enterprises is the core instrument comprising the Declaration on International Investment and Multinational Enterprises adopted by the OECD'S member countries in 1976 and updated periodically. The guidelines are described as "one of the world's foremost corporate responsibility instruments" and the "only multilaterally endorsed . . . code that governments are committed to promoting." It expresses the shared values of the major FDI home and host countries (the thirty OECD members and seven nonmember countries, as of 2005) in the form of recommendations for responsible business conduct by MNCs operating in the "adhering" countries.[12] To achieve the end of encouraging the "positive contributions" MNCs can make to economic and social progress, the guidelines spell out general policies dealing with human rights, sustainable development, appropriate corporate disclosure, and the need to "take full account" of established policies in host countries; employment and industrial relations dealing with the specifics of child and forced labor and nondiscrimination, and so on; environmental protection; avoidance of bribery; respect for consumers' interests; promotion of technology and science transfers; competition policy, that is, a noncollusive and competitive business climate; and respect for "both the letter and spirit of tax laws." Responses to complaints of noncompliance with these principles are limited to informal efforts of government agencies to "encourage" MNCs based in their country to alter or stop practices considered inconsistent with the guidelines.

Disagreement surrounds assessments of the impact of the guidelines. The OECD cites a number of reasons, such as an improved procedure for NGOs to report allegations of corporate violations to governments, to claim that the guidelines "are becoming an important international benchmark for corporate responsibility."[13] However, a report issued in 2005 by OECD Watch, a multinational public interest group, expressed no confidence in the ability of this code of conduct to limit improper MNC behavior. "NGO experience with the Guidelines indicates that they are simply inadequate as a global mechanism to improve the operation of multinationals and contribute to a reduction in conflict between communities and investors in any comprehensive way."[14] The guidelines are "simply inadequate and deficient" as a means of improving the performance of multinationals. "Without the threat of effective sanctions, there is little incentive for companies to ensure their operations are in compliance."[15]

A second high-visibility set of advisory guidelines is the Global Compact, a set of values and a forum promoting ongoing discussions between MNCs and the many citizen groups comprising civil society. Administered by the United Nations, it "seeks to advance responsible corporate citizenship so that business can be part of the solution to the challenges of globalisation" and can contribute to a "more sustainable and inclusive global economy."[16] More than 2,300 participating corporations and some 400 participating NGOs, labor groups, and business associations from over 80 countries[17] make it the largest, and most geographically and functionally diverse of the nongovernmental instruments seeking to hold MNCs to a higher level of social responsibility. Because no part of the principles is binding, no legal action can be taken against noncomplying companies. The Global Compact relies on policy dialogues between, and the enlightened self-interest of, MNCs and stakeholders to promote adherence to its guiding principles. They are similar to the OECD Guidelines in that they articulate standards for business in four broad areas: respect for human rights, protection of workers' rights, protection of the environment, and refusal to engage in bribery or corrupt practices. Another similarity with the OECD code is criticism that the nonbinding, nonenforceable nature of the principles has at best a marginal effect in preventing abusive actions by MNCs that have indicated their intention to adhere to the principles. A letter jointly sent to the UN by four major NGOs in 2003 expressed their growing dissatisfaction with the lack of "tangible evidence of progress" generated by the Compact and their concern about the inadequacy of its compliance mechanism.[18]

Regulatory Rorschach Test: The MAI

The daunting challenge of determining the optimal trade-off between government obligations and rights on the one hand and MNC obligations and rights on the other hand is clearly demonstrated by the fate of the proposed MAI. Although never seeing the light of day, it serves as a unique case study in explaining how the failure to create an FDI regulatory regime stems from the deeply rooted differences in political and social values held by the champions and the critics of MNCs. Most government officials and corporate executives viewed the proposed pact's free market orientation as a step toward a more efficient and prosperous world economic order. Those who call for enhanced governmental oversight to curb what they see as the multinationals' excessive economic and political power had a different reaction. To them, the largely pro-FDI language was a brazen ploy to make the world safer for ever larger corporate profits and independence. When the dust kicked up by the ensuing contretemps had settled, the anti-MNC faction was triumphant.

Ironically, the effort to create a set of multilateral FDI rules began in the mid-1990s as a relatively unheralded effort having no intention of breaking new political ground. Most industrialized countries had long before lowered barriers to incoming FDI and extended nondiscriminatory treatment to existing foreign-owned or -controlled subsidiaries. The decision to convene the negotiations primarily reflected consensus among economic officials in industrialized countries that the time had come to consolidate into one document the restraints on government provisions common to the more than 1,500 BITs that were in force at the time. As explained by an OECD official, "Although investment regimes have become much more open and welcoming in the recent past, there is no assurance that they will remain so in the years to come. Even in the OECD area, foreign investors still encounter barriers, discriminatory treatment and legal and regulatory uncertainties." An MAI was needed to strengthen existing FDI policy guidelines by developing "a comprehensive agreement" that incorporated the strongest features of existing multilateral, bilateral, regional, and sectoral arrangements.[19] "The benefits of rules that prevent backsliding and encourage countries to become more investor-friendly are . . . obvious," wrote *The Economist*.[20] Countries not belonging to the OECD were invited to participate in the talks, and the announced intention was to have the finished treaty open to accession by all countries.

A run-of-the-mill negotiation was anticipated. Negotiators labored in obscurity behind closed doors for almost three years, attracting little media attention or public interest. This changed in late 1997 when an NGO with negative feelings about MNCs received a leaked copy of the draft text. (No finalized text was ever produced.) NGOs were appalled at what they considered to be the one-sided, proinvestor bias of the proposed agreement and were angry at being excluded from the drafting process. They soon went into full attack mode that included a Joint NGO Statement posted on the Internet and signed by more than 600 groups in more than 70 countries. It complained that the agreement as drafted was "completely unbalanced" in that it would greatly expand the rights of international investors "far above those of governments, local communities, citizens, workers and the environment."[21] A development specialist complained that the text of the treaty wrongly assumed "that there is no need to distinguish between different types of foreign investment [and] that all foreign investments bring only benefits but no costs. . . . Social, cultural, development, environmental and human rights concerns are also ignored in this approach."[22]

The more militant NGOs demonized the MAI as an effort "to multiply the power of corporations over governments and eliminate policies that could restrict the movement of factories and money around the world. It places corporate profits above all other values" and "puts our democracy at risk."[23] Public Citizen, a Ralph Nader advocacy group, warned: "Imagine an international commercial treaty empowering corporations and investors to sue governments directly for cash compensation in retaliation for almost any government policy or action that undermines profits. This is not the plot of a science fiction novel of future corporate totalitarian rule. Rather, it is just one provision" of the MAI. The latter was further described "as a slow motion coup d'etat against democratic governance."[24] The Council of Canada called it something that "could crush Canada" and a "bill of rights for investors only."[25]

Opponents of the proposed MAI were especially incensed by the provision that would have protected foreign subsidiaries from broadly defined expropriation. It said, "A Contracting Party shall not expropriate or nationalize directly or indirectly an investment in its territory of an investor of another Contracting Party *or take any measure or measures having equivalent effect*" unless four specific conditions were met (e.g., expropriation or its equivalent was in the public interest and was accompanied by prompt and adequate compensation.)[26] Opponents of the MAI repeatedly charged that this clause would be interpreted as barring any national law or regulation that impeded or would impede a foreign investor's right to make a profit. If true, this meant that environmental, health, or workers' rights legislation that in any way could threaten MNCs' profits were allegedly at risk because they could be interpreted as being incompatible with the prohibition against de facto expropriation.[27] Proponents never provided an effective counterargument to this charge.

The MAI negotiations were adjourned in late 1998, permanently as it turned out, before final agreement on the text could be reached. It was a familiar story: No consensus could be reached to reconcile bitterly contested views on the proper formula for apportioning constraints on the conduct of governments and on the operations of MNCs. The immediate cause of the treaty's demise remains a subject of controversy. The first of two conflicting postmortems concluded that negotiators lost confidence that they could bridge the differences that remained on several points. When the talks disbanded, the working draft contained many brackets with alternative wording for unresolved issues. Most prominently, an unwieldy number of proposals had been advanced by different delegations to exempt sensitive sectors from the proposed further liberalization of barriers on incoming direct investment, for example, cultural industries (mass media) in Canada and motion pictures in France.

The other explanation is that the opposition of a global coalition of NGOs brought down the MAI. They unquestionably mounted an unexpectedly vociferous, ferocious, and widespread media blitz that surprised and rattled the countries negotiating the agreement. At a minimum, the relentless criticism put agreement further out of reach by exacerbating tensions and frustration among the negotiators and their ministers. The effective grassroots attack on the MAI is "a cautionary tale about the impact of an electronically networked global civil society."[28] Perhaps the most accurate assessment is that either one of these two explanations had the potential to derail the talks; in tandem, internal and external pressures were inevitably fatal, especially in the absence of a strong push by the international business community to keep the negotiations going. In any event, the question of exactly what killed the MAI is far less important than the main lesson learned from its demise: The two irreconcilable perceptions of the FDI/MNC phenomena perpetuate irreconcilable visions of to how to construct an FDI regime. Consensus on a model of international corporate governance remains a long way off.

A persuasive case can be made that intent of the MAI was designed to be MNC-friendly; the only real debate is whether the OECD countries went overboard in the pursuit of this objective. An insight into the reason why even moderate critics were convinced that the industrial countries had gone beyond the pale comes from a comparison of the ideological leaning of the MAI's text with the very different approach embodied in another stillborn agreement: the proposed UN Code of Conduct on Transnational Corporations. After two decades of on-and-off effort, negotiations quietly dissipated in the early 1990s, partly the result of ongoing dissension among LDCs, but mainly due to the industrialized countries' hostility to what they viewed as its inadequate treatment of host country obligations to MNCs. Rightly or wrongly, the proposed UN Code was broadly constructed to include a wide array of issues that included political principles (e.g., respect for national sovereignty and human rights), development needs of LDCs (e.g., encouragement of technology transfer and discouragement of transfer pricing), and social goals (e.g., consumer, environmental, and cultural protection). The draft code explicitly recognized that FDI as a whole had favorable as well as negative effects and favored a menu of actions intended to maximize the former and minimize the latter.[29] The two proposed agreements were the products of contrasting paradigms. The balanced approach of the UN Code was preferable, claimed Martin Khor, because it took into account the rights and obligations of host countries and foreign investors, ensured that they were properly balanced, and was based on the primary objective of contributing to economic development and social and environmental objectives.[30]

No efforts have been made to resurrect negotiations toward a multilateral FDI framework (as of mid 2006). One reason is that MNCs came to "prefer the existing patchwork of BITs, and a low profile to escape NGOs' interest."[31]

Going Overboard? NAFTA's Chapter 11

One of the more incendiary disagreements about the regulation of FDI concerns the present and future impact of Chapter 11 of NAFTA. The debate encompasses the irreconcilable views that it is either (1) a socially harmful, excessively probusiness framework for regulating foreign investment; or (2) an overdue lever for MNCs to use against illegal government actions taken against them. Critics see the provisions of Chapter 11 as imposing unacceptably strong direct and indirect restraints on governments that hinder their ability to make public policy choices consistent with the public's health and welfare.[32] Corporations and free market advocates defend it as a fully justifiable means of providing investors with legal rights to challenge acts of governments that violate their international treaty obligations. It is another familiar story: Interested parties have looked at exactly the same thing (touched different parts of the same elephant, so to speak) and, guided by dissimilar philosophies, once more advanced two mutually exclusive interpretations of its nature and desirability.

Differences of opinion are also natural outgrowths of the fact that Chapter 11 is in one sense unique and in another sense nothing new. It was the first time that a regional free trade agreement provided a full set of legal rights and protections to foreign direct investors (from other member countries). U.S. trade negotiators are due much of the credit, or blame as the case may be, for this innovation. Their action was motivated by the desire to lock Mexico into a system ensuring a greater commitment by that country's government and court system to respect the rights of foreign investors than they had displayed historically.

Though unprecedented as inclusions in a trade agreement, Chapter 11's provisions introduced no new principles of international law.[33] The litany of foreign investors' rights was identical to the guidelines that had begun appearing many years previously in BITs. National treatment (treatment no less favorable than what is accorded to domestically owned businesses with regards to establishment, operation, expansion, and so on) is mandated, as are guarantees of "fair and equitable treatment and full protection and security," to subsidiaries owned by companies from the other NAFTA member countries. Echoing the TRIMs agreement (see previous discussion), Chapter 11 prohibits several governmentally imposed performance requirements on foreign-owned companies.[34]

NAFTA Chapter 11's two most contentious provisions also have roots in bilateral investment treaties. Article 1110 establishes rules on expropriation and dispute settlement. It stipulates, "No Party may directly or *indirectly* nationalize or expropriate an investment of an investor of another Party in its territory or take a measure *tantamount* to nationalization or expropriation" (emphasis added). The term *investment* is not limited by the modifiers "foreign" or "direct." The prohibition is waived if four contingencies are met: The expropriation must be done for a public purpose, on a nondiscriminatory basis, in accordance with due process, and followed by just compensation by the government taking the action.

The second super-charged lightning rod for criticism is Section B of Chapter 11, wherein private investors in NAFTA member countries are given the right to pursue monetary claims for grievances against either of the other two NAFTA governments. By following stipulated procedures, a corporate or individual investor has the right to compel the foreign government to participate in a three-member arbitration panel. The tribunal is charged with determining the validity of the investor's claim that it has incurred a financial loss from the foreign government's alleged breach of the obligations just summarized. The panel's ruling on the dispute is binding. Like restraints on indirect expropriation, the principle of investor-state arbitration had been a common feature in BITs for many years.

Impassioned criticism has charged that Section B's occasionally imprecise wording gives foreign investors excessively wide latitude and a potent weapon to challenge and demand compensation for almost any regulation, law, or proposed law of another NAFTA government that has nothing more than a small, very indirect negative impact on the financial well-being of a foreign subsidiary. Critics of MNCs and globalization intensely dislike Chapter 11 assigning no rights whatsoever—not even to protect public health or the environment—to governments. They equally dislike the absence of any assigned responsibilities or limitations imposed on investors. To them, the gross imbalance between rights provided to foreign companies and obligations imposed on governments creates an unacceptable bias in favor of one side in investor–state disputes, and once again the interests and needs of society at large take a back seat to business's single-minded pursuit of profits.

Dismissing such criticism as sensationalized hyperbole becomes more difficult as the list of corporations filing suits lengthens and the grounds for taking NAFTA governments to arbitration expand at the hands of aggressive lawyers. For example, the Canadian Cattlemen for Fair Trade filed a petition for recovery of economic damages of at least $300 million they attribute to the U.S. government's suspension of imports of Canadian cattle and processed beef after a discovery of mad cow disease in Alberta. The organization's case presumably will try to stretch the reach of Chapter 11 by contending that what ostensibly was a U.S. public health measure had the effect of harming investments made in Canada for the purpose of exploiting free trade with the United States.[35] The Canadian ranchers have no U.S.-based investments. Supporters of this complaint could not have been pleased when a Canadian activist was quoted as saying, "By entering into NAFTA, the United States no longer has the right to protect its domestic cattle industry from contamination."[36]

Opponents are also irked that the arbitration procedures established in the chapter ignore the doctrine of sovereign immunity that bars a government from being sued or taken to arbitration unless it agrees to such a process or the suit is expressly allowed by domestic law. Chapter 11 also ignores the principle that only the state has the right of standing in disputes arising from intergovernmental accords. Instead, critics charge, the provision implicitly recognizes a corporation, when acting in the capacity of investor, "as an equal subject of international law, on par with governments."[37] Public Citizen argued that the provision's language empowers foreign investors to sue the U.S. government for cash compensation for the alleged damage of federal, state, and local policies on profits and the value of assets—a right not allowed under U.S. law.[38] This is a form of discrimination against domestic investors in the NAFTA countries because they have no recourse to bring similar charges against their own government. The net effect is that the NAFTA treaty arguably bestows on foreign investors operating within the United States more favorable treatment than the Constitution requires be extended to American businesses.[39]

A joint report by the International Institute for Sustainable Development and the World Wildlife Federation argued that "the basic legitimacy of the process is challenged by the ability of foreign investors to bypass local laws and legal processes in favor of the international rights and processes domestic businesses do not enjoy." The dispute settlement procedure as currently designed and implemented was characterized as "shockingly unsuited to the task of balancing private rights against public goods in a legitimate and constructive manner."[40] An angry Mexican scholar complained, "If a foreign corporation can override the efforts of elected governments to protect the health of its citizens and the integrity of its environment, democracy itself is undermined."[41] Even an article in the stolid *New York Times* was anything but nuanced: "Their meetings are secret. . . . The decisions they reach need not be fully disclosed. Yet the way a small group of international tribunals handles disputes between investors and foreign governments has led to . . . justice systems questioned and environmental regulations challenged. And it is all in the name of protecting the rights of foreign investors."[42] Another negative view is that Chapter 11 has "created concern rather than value."[43]

One of the cases most often cited by critics had its roots in the 1993 purchase of a Mexican company by Metalclad, an American corporation. The transaction took place after the federal and the state governments in Mexico approved construction permits for the company to build an underground hazardous waste storage facility (described by opponents as a toxic waste dump). Construction proceeded despite absence of the local municipality's authorization for construction; the company and its supporters claimed that it was told that federal and state permits were sufficient. Prior to the site's official opening, local residents launched a series of heated protests, asserting that the soil at the site was too unstable to ensure that toxic waste would not leak into underground water sources (an assessment shared by some outside environmental groups). Faced with strong, unstinting local resistance, the Municipality of Guadalcazar formally denied the company a permit to begin underground storage of hazardous waste. The state governor shortly thereafter declared the site and adjacent land a special ecological zone protected from commercial development.

Metalclad filed suit under Chapter 11, charging the Mexican government with violating the expropriation and fair and equitable treatment provisions. Absent reconciliation between the two parties, the company was entitled to plead its case before an arbitration tribunal. The latter sided with the plaintiff on both counts. The 2000 ruling said the Mexican government had failed to fulfill its obligation to provide "a transparent, clear and predictable framework for foreign investors." The panel criticized what it found to be misleading and inaccurate assurances by federal and state officials that their permission was sufficient to commence operation of the facility. It further ruled that the municipal government had exceeded its legal authority in demanding a local construction permit.[44] In declaring that the treatment of Metalclad constituted acts "tantamount to expropriation," the tribunal was the first to equate procedural actions by government with expropriation. The definition of indirect expropriation under Chapter 11 was effectively expanded to official regulations that reduced the value of corporate property.[45]

Defenders emphasize the absence of any significant new legal principles in Chapter 11, the contents of which merely replicate concepts contained in many bilateral investment treaties. Two Canadian scholars argued that the "uniqueness" of these investor–state dispute resolution provisions "derives from the decision by the three NAFTA parties to embed them within a broad trade and investment agreement, expanding the prospect that they would be interpreted on a broader basis than they would be as stand-alone provisions." Although they conceded that some litigants had made "creative and expansive claims suggesting a very broad scope for Chapter 11," they felt that the number of tribunal decisions (as of 2001) in favor of investors was relatively small and "narrowly conceived."[46] The authors noted that in all instances when governments lost an arbitration hearing involving environmental actions, the decision never questioned the legal validity of the underlying regulations. Arbitrators ruled only that they had been applied in a discriminatory and confiscatory manner in a specific situation.[47] Even more important is the fact that arbitration panels cannot strike down laws and regulations; they can only demand that a government compensate a winning plaintiff for financial damages incurred from official actions.

Some lawyers laud the chapter for giving investors an overdue boost in their historically tenuous legal standing vis-à-vis foreign governments.[48] "Governments remain free to regulate, but on a basis consistent with jointly developed rules set out in . . . trade and investment agreements." This argument holds that the power of the state to compel must be balanced by the right of the governed to hold the state accountable in law. Because governments abuse power, make mistakes, and sometimes intentionally implement measures that financially injure foreigners, allegedly it is misguided to think that holding governments accountable threatens democracy. "Foreign investors should be compensated for unfair and discriminatory treatment, and they should be confident that they can operate in a predictable business environment based on the rule of law. . . . The real risk is that rational debate about free trade and investment will be stifled under the weight of anti-free trade hysteria."[49]

A third perspective on NAFTA Chapter 11 incorporates elements of both praise and condemnation and then adds a dollop of uncertainty. It contends that on the one hand, its content and objectives are sound in principle. But on the other hand, it surmises that if the officials who drafted it had a crystal ball at the time, they would have inserted qualifying language. Most of the original advocates assumed that complaints and demands for arbitration would mostly target the Mexican government and would deal with expropriation and traditional regulatory encumbrances on foreign businesses. They assumed incorrectly on both accounts. Whereas the United States and Canadian governments were used to being the plaintiffs in investment disputes handled under bilateral treaties, both found themselves frequent defendants under Chapter 11. And much to the dismay of environmental groups, many of the complaints challenged antipollution policies. The synthesis approach holds that most of the unfortunate unanticipated consequences of this provision could be corrected by some relatively minor amendments.

To see what a revision might look like, one need look no further than the wording of the investment protection provision written into the U.S. free trade agreement with Central America and the Dominican Republic that came ten years after NAFTA. The revisions in the investment chapters came about "in direct response" to guidance provided by Congress.[50] The new agreement states that nondiscriminatory regulatory actions designed and applied to protect the public welfare (health and the environment, principally) do not constitute indirect expropriations "except in rare circumstances." Other original provisions are included to expedite dismissal of "frivolous" claims and calls for establishment of an appellate body to review financial awards ordered by arbitration tribunals.[51]

The eclectic view also espouses a wait-and-see attitude in lieu of final judgment. Chapter 11 is viewed as a work in progress with a number of important questions yet to be resolved. First, how important is the "intimidation factor?" Will national and local governments in fact ease up on enforcement of laws to protect public health and safety if confronted with the possibility of paying out many millions of dollars in compensatory damages? On the one hand, the roughly $35 million paid out for five lost cases by the three governments through 2005 is hardly financially crippling. On the other hand, the possibility exists of future payoffs amounting to several hundreds of millions of dollars in addition to large cumulative legal costs associated with what might be an increasing volume of arbitration cases. These contingencies might encourage the U.S., Canadian, and Mexican governments to back off strict enforcement of public health, environmental, and worker protection actions that are challenged as violations of NAFTA. Those who worry about a perverse descent into a "pay the polluter" system point to the settlement reached between the U.S.-based Ethyl Corporation and the

Canadian government. The latter rescinded a ban against a gasoline additive declared to be a public health risk, and in return the company accepted payment for damages that were a fraction of the $250 million it originally demanded.

Future complaints filed by aggrieved corporations could go in either of two opposite directions. Legal counsel may push the envelope with an array of clever arguments that expand the anti-expropriation clause well beyond what governments had intended. A different scenario is that the unexpected outcome of the complaint brought by the Methanex Corporation against the state of California may cause "plaintiff intimidation."[52] The arbitration panel surprised many people in unanimously ruling that the provisions of Chapter 11 did not apply because California's actions were not motivated by intent to harm foreign companies. The arbiters wrote that even if they had jurisdiction, they saw no evidence in this case of indirect expropriation. Potential corporate litigants might have second thoughts about seeking arbitration in view of another part of the panel's ruling: Methanex was told to pay the U.S. government $4 million to cover its legal expenses.[53] Legal activity under Chapter 11 in the future may increase, decrease, or be altered by amended language. The best forecast of its long-term effects is: "It depends."

Privatizing Regulation: The NGOs

NGOs have become a third actor in the dialogue conducted between MNCs and national governments. The term *NGO* has been defined in various ways owing to the great variance in these organizations' structures, size of membership, and budgets (some of which exceed $100 million annually). As agents of civil society, they are independent, nonprofit, value-centered organizations that operate in the broad political expanse between individual citizens and their government, excluding only profit-making business entities. The numerous policy fields in which they are active include scrutinizing corporate behavior, protecting the environment, promoting workers' rights, defending human rights, disbursing foreign aid and humanitarian relief, promoting the economic interests of developing countries, and monitoring the work of international organizations. Their strategies vary, as does the geographic scope of their activities—some are local, some national, others global. Estimates of "multinational NGOs," that is, those with international programs, range from 20,000 to 30,000. (Inclusion of every national and small local organization worldwide would put the total in the millions.)

Literally thousands of NGOs are interested in the "cross-cutting" theme that big companies responding to the invisible hand of the marketplace are not likely to act in harmony with the interests of society as a whole. NGOs display varying degrees of antipathy toward MNCs (most preach reform, a few have the more radical agenda of bringing big corporations to their knees) and to the globalization of production and capital movements. The transformation of these convictions into unofficial, but status quo–shaking actions constitutes a new form of quasi-regulation of multinationals.

The impact of NGOs in the FDI realm has induced hundreds (if not thousands) of MNCs to behave in ways inconsistent with pure pursuit of efficiency and profit maximization. These were voluntary actions not legally required by law or regulatory edict, and seldom if ever recommended by shareholders. The emergence of thousands of activist groups has forced large corporations "to make decisions in new ways, factoring in variables that once could be ignored: the costs and benefits of capitulation versus compliance, the competitive dynamics of concession, and the personal beliefs and preferences of top management."[54] Just as no responsible senior management team would ignore specific demands or complaints aimed at them by a determined host government, no responsible management today would refuse to give a fair hearing to specific demands or complaints aimed at its company by influential and determined multinational NGOs. The corporate social responsibility movement would not have become a significant part of the MNC experience without the intense pressures from NGOs that hit critical mass only in the 1990s. The behavior of high visibility multinationals today is more restrained and civic-minded than it would be had many of them not been on the receiving end of civil society's aggressively unrelenting lobbying tactics. Few CEOs would have acted purely on their own volition to commit their companies to comply with codes of conduct or to abandon profitable business strategies to do the "right thing" to protect workers' rights or the environment.

Literally hundreds of NGOs have become very savvy in public relations techniques in support of their efforts to shift MNC behavior into what they judge to be a more socially beneficial direction. They have the skills, resources, and depths of popular support that make it unwise for companies to confront them head-on in the battle for public opinion.[55] "In the contest between NGOs and companies, size is no advantage."[56] In fact, it can be a disadvantage: The bigger the brand name, especially for consumer goods, the bigger the potential financial hit from widely circulated and vitriolic criticism by a nonprofit organization ostensibly speaking on behalf of the public's welfare. NGO tactics to modify MNC behavior begins with quiet persuasion. If that does not produce acceptable results, the message shifts to publicly embarrassing corporations and fomenting dissatisfaction among their customers. The next step is usually use of Internet-enabled swarming by a phalanx of nonprofit activist groups from many countries. The result is a bright, globally visible spotlight illuminating what they have identified as the targeted company's injurious or unethical behavior. Should a corporation refuse to modify that behavior, it might face an escalation of tactics that can include physical attacks on corporate property, disruption of annual company meetings, and organized transnational consumer boycotts. NGOs have been very good at getting out in front of issues by sensing emerging shifts in public concerns and values. "They should be, since they are usually born during one of those shifts and depend for their survival on keeping up with them." NGOs do not simply respond to these shifts; they often help redirect and control them.[57]

Efforts by NGOs to intimidate/enlighten corporations have been greeted with both approbation and opposition. The deciding factor is perceptions, mainly the evaluator's acceptance or rejection of two ideas. The first is the relative validity of the message of NGOs on the need for greater protection of labor and environmental standards. The second is whether maximizing economic growth and increasing living standards are best achieved by leaving MNCs relatively free to deal with the rewards and risks of the marketplace.

A strong case can be made that advocacy groups, for better or worse, have achieved a high rate of success in convincing MNCs to be responsive to their various demands for behavior modification. Success is indirectly demonstrated by NGOs' continued disinterest in the traditional lobbying technique of petitioning governments for new laws and tighter regulation of global companies. It has proven quicker and more effective for them to make corporate executives squirm. Success is also demonstrable by published references to instances of corporate capitulation that are so voluminous that only a short list is practical here. Pharmaceutical giants have lowered their prices of drugs to LDCs and withdrawn lawsuits against governments in poor countries who were not enforcing patent enforcement of drugs to combat HIV/AIDS and other infectious diseases. Some coffee retailers have responded to the desire of some consumers to buy coffee that has been certified as "fair trade" goods, whereby growers are paid "fair" prices for their crops. Retailers and bankers have been convinced to cease doing business with foreign lumber companies recklessly denuding forests. Wal-Mart, the biggest retailer in the world, thought it appropriate to begin a program to hold its many non-U.S. suppliers accountable for upholding high levels of environmental and social standards.

Nike became a classic case study of successful civil society pressure when it responded in the 1990s to a spreading consumer backlash to revelations of relatively poor working conditions and low pay in the Asian factories making its popular line of athletic shoes. The unusual situation here is that these factories were not owned or operated by Nike; they were locally owned contractors who were for the most part conforming to local laws and pay scales. Clear and present threats of reduced sales through a tarnished brand name caused Nike and other companies, including Levi Strauss, Adidas, and the Gap, to refuse to do business with alleged sweatshops. They agreed to assume permanent responsibility for ensuring more Western-like treatment (excluding pay scales) for workers employed by foreign contractors.

Yet another manifestation of the impact of NGOs is the several international business organizations and coalitions that have been created to promote corporate social responsibility compatible with pursuit of financial success. Two examples are the World Business Council for Sustainable Development and Business for Social Responsibility. Some corporations open up their factories and those of their major contractors to outside inspection and certification of compliance with established labor standards; evaluations are provided by business-supported, nonprofit organizations like Social Accountability International and the Fair Labor Association. Unilever is one of many multinationals issuing annual corporate environmental and social reports.

A high winning percentage by NGOs may be fact, but the desirability on balance of their victories is a hotly contested issue. Public interest activists staunchly believe in the virtue of their mission because they consider efforts toward a more equitable society and a cleaner environment to be positive goals outweighing any other consideration. The opposing school of thought is critical of what they see as self-appointed carriers of the moral torch and ask, "who elected the NGOs to define and protect the public's interest?" Critics assert that these groups are no more inherently democratic or publicly accountable than the corporations they pillory. Some claim they are less so. Elected governments must account to their citizens, and corporations must account to their shareholders and to government agencies charged with enforcing corporate laws. NGOs need only account to their interested contributors.[58] Some avid supporters of the free market dismiss these organizations as special interest groups who may be unimpressed with the profit motive, but are very motivated to generate publicity that can maximize financial contributions. It has been suggested that inaccuracy seldom stops a message from being posted on the Internet, the communications medium of choice for most advocacy groups. Anecdotal evidence exists of questionable actions by individual organizations, running the gamut from conducting a misinformation campaign, presenting conjecture as fact, to issuing inaccurate or unwise policy guidance stemming from too narrow a frame of reference or overeagerness to impose Western values and economic standards on developing countries.[59]

"The best of them, the ablest and most passionate, often suffer most from tunnel vision, judging every public act by how it affects their particular interest."[60] Jagdish Bhagwati declared, "No NGO, or government, has the wisdom or the right to lay down what corporations must do. Social good is multidimensional, and different corporations may and must define social responsibility, quite legitimately, in different ways."[61] The incipient backlash to the NGO movement has grown to the point that at least one group disdainful of it has launched its own Web site offering a critical perspective on the activities and claims of corporate gadflies.[62]

The infrequently articulated third possibility is that the net impact of the rise of an activist civil society on international business cannot be generalized. Effects can be positive or negative on balance, depending on specific circumstances as well as on the company and NGO involved; in other words, "it depends." Just how extensive are the qualitative changes in MNC behavior directly attributed to the "privatization of regulation" cannot be measured with anything close to precision. There is no definitive compilation of cases where MNCs capitulated to NGO "name and shame" campaigns, nor is there a subcompilation determining whether the capitulations were advisable.

Back to the Future

No one can rule out the eventual emergence of a brilliantly conceived enunciation of policies and behavioral standards that would produce an optimal trade-off between governmentally imposed regulation and corporate pursuit of competitively priced goods and profits. The problem is that the formidable assets necessary to resolve the many problems standing in the way of a regime acceptable to all parties are not being allocated to this quest. The reason is perceived lack of urgency. National governments and MNCs can live comfortably with status quo–based, decentralized, and largely ad hoc guidelines affecting FDI policies and MNC performance. Most corporations and many governments perceive the greater danger to their goals is a groundswell of public support for an NGO-designed regime unfavorable to their perceived self-interests; better not to risk opening a Pandora's box by getting too ambitious.

Whatever one's position on the need for a comprehensive multilateral agreement on FDI, it is clear that doubts about the cost-effectiveness of expending the time, energy, and political capital necessary to produce a document acceptable to all factions are strong enough to deflate enthusiasm at least for the foreseeable future for going full steam ahead with negotiations. A strong, committed constituency for universal investment rules is yet to be created. As Raymond Vernon put it, "A long period of experimentation and travail will be needed before anything like a comprehensive international regime for transnational corporations takes shape."[63]

Notes

1. Their value has been most evident in times of economic stress when governments faced internal political pressures to adopt trade barriers or depreciating currencies as means to discourage imports and stimulate exports. Governments often deflect these pressures by pointing to the need to follow international rules against such actions.
2. Robert Gilpin, *Global Political Economy—Understanding the International Economic Order* (Princeton, NJ: Princeton University Press, 2001), pp. 300–301.

3. Stephen Young and Ana Teresa Tavares, "Multilateral Rules on FDI: Do We Need Them? Will We Get Them? A Developing Country Perspective," *Transnational Corporations*, April 2004, pp. 1, 18–19.

4. Data source: UNCTAD, "Recent Developments in International Investment Agreements," August 30, 2005, available online at http://www.unctad.org/sections/dite_dir/docs/webiteiit20051_en.pdf; accessed October 2005.

5. If one of two countries imposed zero or minimal corporate income taxes, no double taxation could result and no tax treaty would be necessary.

6. Data source: UNCTAD, "Recent Developments in International Investment Agreements."

7. This provision is often extended to include a most-favored-nation clause that says that any favorable special treatment extended by the host government to subsidiaries of third-country companies will be equally extended to subsidiaries of the treaty's other signatory government. In other words, if country A gives favorable tax treatment to the local subsidiaries of companies headquartered in country K, it would be obligated to extend the same special benefits to subsidiaries of companies from country B.

8. Two other Uruguay Round agreements partly touch on FDI policies: the General Agreement on Trade in Services and the Agreement on Trade-Related Aspects of Intellectual Property Rights.

9. To be listed on the New York Stock Exchange, companies now must adopt and disclose a code of business conduct and ethics for directors, officers, and employees.

10. Estimate of the International Chamber of Commerce, as quoted by Susan A. Aaronson, "Oh, Behave!," *International Economy*, March/April 2001, p. 41. The article also contains a chart summarizing the scope and administration of nineteen codes of corporate accountability.

11. Details of Social Accountability International's programs are available on their Web site, http://www.sa-intl.org.

12. OECD, "The OECD Guidelines for Multinational Enterprises," Policy Brief, June 2000, p. 1, available online at http://www.oecd.org/dataoecd/52/38/2958609.pdf; accessed October 2005.

13. Ibid., p. 4.

14. OECD Watch, press release dated September 22, 2005, available online at http://www.oecdwatch.org/content.htm; accessed November 2005.

15. OECD Watch, "Executive Summary," *Five Years On: A Review of the OECD Guidelines and National Contact Points*, available online at http://www.OECDWatch.org/docs/oecd_watch_5_years_on.pdf; accessed November 2005.

16. UN Global Compact, "Corporate Citizenship in the World Economy—The Global Compact," September 2004, available online at http://www.unglobalcompact.org; accessed November 2005.

17. Data source: http://www.unglobalcompact.org; accessed November 2005.

18. Amnesty International, Human Rights Watch, the Lawyers Committee for Human Rights, and Oxfam International, "Letter to Louise Fréchette Raising Concerns on UN Global Compact," April 7, 2003, available online at http://web.amnesty.org/pages/ec-gcletter070403-eng; accessed November 2005.

19. William H. Witherell, "An Agreement on Investment," *OECD Observer*, October/November 1996, pp. 6–7.

20. "The Sinking of the MAI," *The Economist*, March 14, 1998, p. 81. The article did go on to say that "Less obvious is how, and where, to write [such rules]."

21. Available online at http://www.citizen.org/print_article.cfm?ID=1676; accessed May 2005.

22. Martin Khor, "Globalization and the South: Some Critical Issues," UNCTAD Discussion Paper no. 147, April 2000, p. 44, available online at http://www.unctad.org/en/docs/dp_147.en.pdf; accessed November 2004.

23. "MAI—Democracy for Sale?," available online at http://econwg.igc.org/MAI; accessed March 2005.

24. Lori Wallach, "Everything You Wanted to Know about the Multilateral Agreement on Investment," Public Citizen, 1998, p. 1; a revised version of this report is available online at http://mondediplo.com/1998/02/07mai.

25. The Council of Canadians, "The MAI Will Put the $queeze on Canada," and "The Multilateral Agreement on Investment," undated reports available online at http://www.flora.org/flora/archive/mai-info/flyer.htm and http://www.canadians.org/sitemap.htm; accessed February 1999.

26. OECD, "The MAI Negotiating Text (as of 24 April 1998)," available online at http://www.nadir.org/nadir/initiativ/agp/free/mai/mai.pdf; accessed August 2005, emphasis added.

27. Stephen J. Kobrin, "The MAI and the Clash of Globalizations," *Foreign Policy*, fall 1998, p. 102.

28. Ibid., p. 99. Ironically, the worldwide coordination of the NGOs' offensive and their ability to get the word out to people who had never heard of the negotiations would not have been possible before the information technology revolution that also accelerated the globalization process so disliked by most of civil society.

29. Khor, "Globalization and the South," p. 42.

30. Ibid., p. 43.

31. David Robertson, "Multilateral Investment Rules," in Bijit Bora, ed., *Foreign Direct Investment—Research Issues* (London and New York: Routledge, 2002), p. 317.

32. Donald McRae, "Introduction," in Laura Ritchie Dawson, ed., *Whose Rights? The NAFTA Chapter 11 Debate* (Ottawa: Centre for Trade Policy and Law, 2002), p. 5.

33. This point was confirmed in two interviews with legal counsel at the Congressional Research Service and the U.S. Department of State, December 2005.

34. NAFTA members may not compel local subsidiaries of companies headquartered in another member country to agree to a minimum percentage of domestic content in their output, minimum percentages of output to be exported, import/export balancing, or mandatory technology transfer.

35. The case had not been resolved as of May, 2006.

36. Public Citizen, "Canadian Cattlemen for Fair Trade v. United States—Mad Cow Disease" (undated), available online at http://www.citizen.org/documents/CanadianCattlemen_for_FairTrade.pdf; accessed October 2005.

37. Naomi Al-Or, "NAFTA Chapter Eleven and the Implications for the FTAA: The Institutionalization of Investor Status in Public International Law," *Transnational Corporations,* August 2005, pp. 123–24, available online at http://www.unctad.org; accessed November 2005.

38. Public Citizen, "NAFTA Chapter 11 Investor-State Cases," September 2001, p. viii, available online at http://www.citizen.org/documents/ACF186.pdf; accessed August, 2004.

39. Ibid.

40. International Institute for Sustainable Development, "Private Rights, Public Problems," 2001, p. 46, available online at http://www.iisd.org/pdf/trade_citizensguide.pdf; accessed October 2005.

41. Fernando Bejarano Gonzalez, "Investment, Sovereignty, and the Environment: The Metalclad Case and NAFTA's Chapter 11," in Timothy Wise, Hilda Salazar, and Laura Carlsen, eds., *Confronting Globalization* (Bloomfield, CT: Kumarian Press, 2003), p. 17.

42. Anthony DePalma, "NAFTA's Powerful Little Secret," *New York Times,* March 11, 2001, p. III 1.

43. Katherine McGuire, "Commentary," in Dawson, *Whose Rights?,* p. 173.

44. The panel awarded the company $16.7 million in compensation, an amount considerably less than the $90 million originally sought by Metalclad.

45. Many analyses of this episode differ in their criticisms of the main players: some disparaging the ethics of Metalclad, others questioning the motives of the Mexican municipality. The main sources of this discussion of the Metalclad case are: Gonzalez, "Investment, Sovereignty, and the Environment"; Public Citizen, "NAFTA Chapter 11 Investor-to-State Cases," pp. 11–14; and Gary Clyde Hufbauer and Jeffrey J. Schott, *NAFTA Revisited, Achievements and Challenges* (Washington, DC: Institute for International Economics, 2005), pp. 231–33.

46. Michael M. Hart and William A. Dymond, "NAFTA Chapter 11: Precedents, Principles, and Prospects," in Dawson, *Whose Rights?,* p. 147.

47. Ibid., p. 153.

48. In the words of an American negotiator involved in drafting Chapter 11, private investors in the first generation of bilateral investment treaties were disadvantaged in having to ask their home government to seek arbitration with the host country on the grounds it had violated its treaty obligations. The problem was that a home country's response might be based on political considerations. If so, redress for economic harm inflicted on an investor by a foreign government was contingent on the political will and the political calculation of its own government. The latter might arbitrarily choose not to take up an investor's complaint with a host government, perhaps because the home country had a comparable practice or needed the host country's vote in the UN. Source: Daniel M. Price, "Chapter 11—Private Party vs. Government, Investor-State Dispute Settlement: Frankenstein or Safety Valve?" *Canada-U.S. Law Journal,* 26(1), 2001, p. 112.

49. Ian A. Laird, "Chapter 11 Meets Chicken Little," *Chicago Journal of International Law,* spring 2001, p. 229.

50. Summary of "The Dominican Republic-Central America-United States Free Trade Agreement," available online at http://www.ustr.gov; accessed November 2005.

51. Ibid.

52. Methanex is a Canadian producer of methanol, an ingredient used in the manufacture of a gasoline additive whose use was banned in California after growing evidence that it was contaminating groundwater. The company countered that absence of conclusive scientific proof meant the action amounted to unfair treatment and an indirect expropriation of its assets. It demanded $970 million in compensatory damages.

53. Bureau of National Affairs, "NAFTA Panel Rejects Methanex's Investment Claim over MTBE Ban," August 11, 2005, available online at http://www.bna.com/itr/arch309.htm; accessed October 2005.

54. Debora L. Spar and Lane T. La Mure, "The Power of Activism: Assessing the Impact of NGOs on Global Business," *California Management Review*, spring 2003, pp. 96–97.

55. Michael Yaziji, "Turning Gadflies into Allies," *Harvard Business Review*, February 2004, p. 110.

56. "Living with the Enemy," *The Economist*, August 9, 2003, p. 49.

57. Yaziji, "Turning Gadflies into Allies," p. 14.

58. Gary Johns, "The NGO Challenge: Whose Democracy Is It Anyway?," June 2003, pp. 6, 4, available online at http://www.ngowatch.org; accessed October 2005.

59. One of the most frequently cited errors in calculation involved Greenpeace's campaign to force Royal Dutch Shell to dispose of an abandoned oil platform from the North Sea on land instead of burying it at sea. After independent assessment agreed with Shell's assessment that deep-sea disposal would be less harmful and might even be beneficial, Greenpeace apologized for an error in calculation, and Shell's original plan was implemented. For additional details, see David Baron, "Going Head to Head," *Stanford Social Innovation Review*, spring 2003, available online at http://www.ssireview.com; accessed November 2005. Another much second-guessed NGO initiative was the successful campaign in which Nike was convinced to force its Pakistani contractor that made soccer balls to fire all child workers and commit itself to using only adult employees. The fate of those children is unknown, but local traditions and economic conditions suggest no reason to assume they returned to school or upgraded their standard of living.

60. Jessica T. Mathews, "Power Shift," *Foreign Affairs*, January/February 1997, p. 64.

61. Jagdish Bhagwati, "Coping with Antiglobalization—A Trilogy of Discontents," *Foreign Affairs*, January/February 2002, p. 7.

62. See, for example, the American Enterprise Institute–sponsored http://www.ngowatch.org, and Corporate Social Responsibility Watch at http://www.csrwatch.com, sponsored by the Free Enterprise Education Institute.

63. Raymond Vernon, *Exploring the Global Economy* (Lanham, MD: University Press of America and the Center for International Affairs of Harvard University, 1985), p. 96.

PART IV

Three Bottom Lines

12

THE CASE FOR FOREIGN
DIRECT INVESTMENT AND
MULTINATIONAL CORPORATIONS

A n objective and thorough evaluation of foreign direct investment (FDI) and multinational corporations (MNCs) must accept the qualification that neither phenomenon is in all ways and at all times economically and socially beneficial in its impact. An unequivocally positive, thumbs–up evaluation arrives at a different conclusion: The available evidence categorically demonstrates that the benefits of these international business phenomena dramatically outweigh their very manageable costs. Perceived net benefits to the global commons are so great that a clear-cut policy recommendation easily follows. Governments should stay in the background and foster a favorable, hands–off business climate for domestic firms and foreign-owned subsidiaries. What is best for society is to let the private sector do what it does best: allocate resources in the most efficient manner, produce good products at reasonable prices, create jobs, introduce new products, and generate wealth for shareholders and stakeholders. The case for FDI dismisses most of the arguments advanced against FDI and MNCs as being either exaggerated, oversimplified, or factually inaccurate.

The principal purpose of this chapter is to distill the main arguments into a thorough and convincing case in favor of MNCs and FDI. The objective is to showcase the many "reasonable" arguments supporting the view that society and governments should emphasize the discipline and incentives of the marketplace to further increase the world's material well-being and reduce its poverty. Winning converts to this viewpoint is not an objective. In fact, the chapter has a subtle agenda. It is to implicitly advance the idea that when the one-sided arguments that follow are weighed against the contradictory one-sided arguments of the next chapter, a relatively open-minded reader should encounter hesitation and equivocation. Such a reader should entertain the thought that because both make some sense, choosing one as representing the absolute, stand-on-its-own version of the truth is a flawed approach. Introduction of doubt is a preliminary step to suggesting the attractions of an eclectic middle-ground analysis that emphasizes the need to appreciate the heterogeneity of the subject, the need to shun generalizations, and acceptance of the scarcity of absolute truths in an ocean of subjectivity.

As in the next chapter, the contents of this chapter do not necessarily reflect the author's views, and individual assertions may or may not be backed up with what he regards as adequate evidence. The presentation should be considered the equivalent of a legal brief designed to interpret reality in a way that influences the opinions of those who read it. Although the most dubious, least substantiated praise has been excluded, this chapter as a whole is intended to be argumentative, not a demonstration of the scientific method at its most precise. The most important commonality of the individual arguments presented here is that each possesses sufficient credibility to preclude its being dismissed as patently untrue or irrelevant. The order in which the arguments are presented roughly follows a macro to micro sequence; order does not imply importance. Too much subjectivity and imprecision are involved to credibly argue that accurate weights can be assigned to each of the benefits cited.

The Compelling Economic Logic of FDI and MNCs

The case in favor of FDI and MNCs can be summarized succinctly and convincingly: it would make no sense to arbitrarily turn back the clock in an effort to reapportion economic power that may or may not be too heavily concentrated in a relatively few very large MNCs. Turning back the clock presupposes being able to do the apparently impossible, namely, providing good answers to several core questions. Globalization of production as opposed to what? What is a better alternative? How much less independence should MNCs possess, and what criteria should be used to make that determination?

Reverting to a relatively low-key, low-tech nineteenth-century-style economic order would roll back living standards to a degree that would be neither politically acceptable nor economically justifiable. Economic growth rates would surely decline. Small mom-and-pop operations may evoke nostalgia, but they cannot afford the colossally high fixed costs of developing and manufacturing increasingly sophisticated manufactured goods. Reverting to government-owned and operated economies would be equal parts economic and political tragedy. Taking such a disastrously self-defeating step backward would be tantamount to ignoring the not-so-distant lessons learned from the implosion of Soviet-style communism. Any system that rests on the absurd notion that a few planners are smart enough to fine-tune the millions of economic transactions that take place every day in a country's economy is doomed to failure. Bureaucratic meddling pales in comparison with the core premise of the free market: Pursuit of individual interest cumulatively adds up to the overall betterment of society. A system that protects property, contracts, and personal initiative also provides protection against the arbitrary power of the state.[1] The private sector makes mistakes, too. But in a free market environment, the inept and unresponsive disappear unless subsidized by taxpayers, whom governments seldom if ever ask if they want their tax payments used to bail out failing entrepreneurs and companies.

Private enterprise, regulated "within reason" by market-savvy politicians, is the first-best means of accomplishing the most important economic goals. They include allocating human and material resources in the most efficient manner, generating and sustaining economic growth, raising standards of living, and reducing poverty. The proliferation of MNCs has brought about the most efficient global allocation of capital in history. These companies are uniquely adept in determining where on the planet business costs are lowest and where among 190 countries they will get maximum returns on their money.

Reliance on free market forces and encouragement of MNCs is not a guaranteed formula for instant economic success free of missteps. Getting an intricate mix of essential policies just right on a country-by-country basis is no easy task for any government. Adoption of market-based reforms is a necessary but not sufficient act for a country to steadily increase the material well-being of its people. The suggestion that capitalism in general or MNCs in particular are a panacea for domestic or international economic problems is a straw man. The "quick fix did not work" argument has been used by clever opponents of free markets to point out that reliance on the private sector has failed to put all countries on a short road to prosperity that is devoid of potholes and detours. Turning entrepreneurs and companies loose—in the right way and to the right degree—to pursue their self-interests is only a part of the equation. The right kinds of economic regulations and institutions, together with a competent and honest government, need to be in place as well. Those who point to lingering inequities in the global economy make no believable case against market-oriented economics and offer no better alternative. Communism made equal distribution of income a top priority, but succeeded only in making everyone poor, except for a handful of Party leaders.

MNCs emerged as a logical and inevitable outgrowth of the generic corporate structure that has proven its worth over the course of three centuries:

> The company has been one of the West's great competitive advantages. . . .
> Civilizations that once outstripped the West yet failed to develop private-sector companies—notably China and the Islamic world—fell farther and farther behind. It cannot be just coincidence that Asia's most conspicuous

economic success is also the country that most obviously embraced companies—Japan.[2]

The virtue of MNCs is that they represent the most advanced and most efficient form of the corporation. "Relative to their domestic counterparts, multinationals are larger, pay their workers higher wages, have higher factor productivity, are more intensive in capital, skilled labour, and intellectual property, are more profitable, and are more likely to export." It is not surprising that MNCs possess these attributes "given that to become a viable multinational, a firm must have outperformed domestic and foreign rivals."[3] Corporations did not invent "multinationalism" as part of an orchestrated plot to facilitate making ever greater profits. Instead, going multinational was mostly a case of necessity born in the economics of the high-tech sector and perceived necessity of increased growth and profits. Going multinational was progressively facilitated by technological and scientific innovations and a more liberal international economic order, all of which freed business from the confines of its home market.

Large, financially successful global companies got that way and stay that way by being very good at giving the public what it wants and needs: quality goods and services at competitive prices and a steady procession of new products and cost-cutting methods for old ones. Well-managed companies do not rest their on their laurels after reaching a comfortable plateau. They correctly equate complacency and static sales with the first step in becoming an unsuccessful company flailing against better managed competitors. When these companies start or add to overseas production, it is not necessarily a zero-sum game for the home country; the presumption of offsetting declines in domestic jobs and production is seldom documented. New or enlarged overseas subsidiaries seldom cause corporations to lose their status as relatively fast-growing businesses in their home market. If anything, international expansion is likely to invigorate a firm and enlarge its product line, sales, and profits. The most probable outcome in such companies is more, not fewer jobs.

A good way of assessing the strengths and gifts of MNCs is to recognize their unrivaled array of propriety assets, namely the ownership advantages that convinced them they could succeed in foreign markets against local competitors expert in how business is done there. In addition to their proprietary technology, multinationals derive competitive strength from patented and trademarked brand names, the ability to organize and integrate production across countries, the ability to establish sophisticated marketing networks, and so on. Taken together, in the judgment of the UNCTAD Secretariat, these advantages mean MNCs "can contribute significantly to economic development in host countries" (as long as the company transfers at least some of its advantages and the host country has the capacity to make good use of them).[4] When manufacturing or service companies set up overseas subsidiaries to enhance their competitive positions in the international marketplace, it is in their self-interest to ensure that those factories or offices

> perform at their highest level possible in terms of quality, reliability, time-liness, and price. The plants are designed to capture all potential economies of scale, and to sustain a position at the cutting edge of industry best practices. "Parental supervision" of the subsidiary is intimate and ongoing, and both technologies and business practices are frequently upgraded.[5]

A thriving overseas business presence is increasingly a requirement and indicator of overall success; this connection applies to corporations headquartered in industrialized and developing countries alike. American companies with global operations account for the majority of domestic U.S. investment in physical capital (plants and equipment) in the manufacturing sector. "This helps raise U.S. productivity by providing more inputs for people to work with." American MNCs perform the majority, between 50 and 60 percent, of total U.S. research and development. "This helps raise U.S. productivity by leading to improved technologies for producing products more efficiently."[6] Relatively large increases in worker productivity explains why American companies with overseas operations are able to pay their workers higher wages on average than those who are not multinationals. Because global operations increase net income and competitiveness, the ability of American corporations to raise the U.S. standard of living "depends crucially on their ability to undertake foreign direct investment abroad."[7]

The economic benefits of MNCs are further demonstrated by the close statistical correlation between countries with relatively good domestic economic performances and relatively strong ability to attract inward FDI. A close correlation also exists between poorly performing national economies and a minimal presence of nonextractive foreign subsidiaries. Economic and political factors inimical to a prosperous domestic economy discourage FDI by creating poor investment climates. Domestic economic success appears to promote inward direct investment more than the other way around. The result is that the presence or nonpresence of MNCs in the manufacturing sector is usually a reliable litmus test for the quality of a country's domestic economic performance. Market-seeking direct investment is attracted first and foremost by the spending power of local consumers; poor domestic economic policies are inconsistent with increasing consumer spending power. Efficiency-seeking foreign subsidiaries are attracted by relatively low wages, but only in the context of a favorable economic and political environment.

Japan and South Korea are the most notable exceptions to the rule that FDI follows and reinforces domestic economic strength. The two countries shunned foreign-owned or -controlled subsidiaries in the early phases of their remarkable

BOX 12.1 Inward FDI as a Barometer of Economic Development

Economic data suggest that the relative amount of inward FDI in a (nonoil) developing country is a good indicator of how well or poorly that country has done in its efforts to develop. An interesting positive four-way statistical correlation is discernible between market-based economic policies, above-average GDP growth rates, a relatively strong export sector, and an above-average presence of MNCs. Conversely, an equally interesting negative statistical correlation exists between nonmarket economic policies, below-average growth rates, a relatively weak export sector, and a below-average presence of MNCs. Although it is vulnerable to an accusation of selectively choosing the statistics to make a preconceived point, a comparison of key economic indicators for Singapore and India suggests that the presence of FDI can be a mirror image of the degree to which a nation is employing successful development strategies.

Singapore's policy of actively courting incoming FDI has been backed up by specially designed business-friendly policies and an emphasis on providing an educated workforce and modern infrastructure. The country was very successful in attracting a long line of increasingly sophisticated foreign-owned manufacturing, service, and R&D subsidiaries (see chapters 7 and 9). India's postcolonial aversion to any form of foreign intervention in its internal affairs and a penchant for socialistic economic policies was, until recently, so resolute as to be a big factor in making it a laggard in economic progress in comparison to most Asian countries. Efforts to implement economic reforms and build better infrastructure in India continue but have not progressed sufficiently to allow development of a strong manufacturing sector or allow the country to dispel its reputation for being inhospitable to foreign subsidiaries (see chapter 7). If a strong, competitive, and largely home-grown services sector had not emerged at the turn of the century, the upturn in India's growth rates in recent years would have been much lower. (The success of services is directly attributable to the facts that India's telecommunications network is arguably the jewel in its infrastructure crown, and the sector tends not to be as closely regulated as manufacturing.)

Readers can draw their own conclusions about the FDI–economic growth-export relationship from the statistical comparisons that follow.

	Singapore	India
Population	4.2 million	1.1 billion
Per capita national income	$21,000.00	$540.00
Value of FDI inward stock	$147.3 billion	$30.8 billion
Per capita value of inward FDI	$35,000	$36.00
Total exports (excludes reexports)	$80 billion	$56 billion
Per capita value of exports	$19,000.00	$20.00

Data sources: World Bank for population and per capita national income; UNCTAD for FDI; and World Trade Organization for exports. The statistics are for 2003–2004.

economic recovery and development after World War II. However, some foreign economists attribute many of the economic problems Japan and Korea unexpectedly experienced in the 1990s to a delayed reaction to their prolonged market-distorting emphasis on industrial policy that discouraged the presence of foreign imports and investments. Government planning has a high propensity to channel too many resources to relatively inefficient sectors, a mistake associated with the tendency to target industries for government support on the basis of political fiat and friendships more than economic logic. The correlation between the degree of inward FDI and domestic economic performance is suggested in box 12.1, where key economic indicators for Singapore and India are compared.

Direct Economic Benefits to the Host Country

FDI is more than a transfer of money, just as MNCs are more than just oversized versions of domestic companies. A unique synergy of economic benefits and technical knowledge is inherent in relatively high-quality inward direct investment. The whole is larger than the sum of its parts. FDI was characterized by *The Economist* as being more than "mere 'capital': it is a uniquely potent bundle of capital, contacts, and managerial and technological knowledge."[8] The more dynamic MNCs bring to host countries *best practices*—techniques or methodologies that have proven to be the best ways of doing things—in development of new technology, management and marketing skills, information processing, human resources, and so on. FDI provides a net beneficial impact to the host country when it comes in the form of hard to replicate "integrated packages that place host-country plants on the frontier of industry best practices, and keep them there."[9] John Dunning wrote that one of the unique competitive advantages of a large MNC in our knowledge-based, globalizing economy "is its ability to identify, access, harness, and effectively coordinate and deploy resources and capabilities from throughout the world."[10]

The most direct benefit of FDI has been described as a foreign subsidiary using sophisticated means to produce goods in a host country that "embody the latest and best technologies, in a facility that uses state-of-the-art production methods. The result can be lower prices and higher quality goods and services for consumers in these countries" as well as relatively higher wages to its employees (see next section).[11] Many foreign subsidiaries not only bring with them advanced production methods, but also the employee training programs and managerial know-how needed to make maximum use of the technology.[12]

FDI has demonstrated that it provides a greater long-term contribution to GDP and income growth in host countries than the two other major private capital flows, bank loans and portfolio investments. Direct investment's uniquely long-term time perspective makes it relatively less volatile. As demonstrated during the Asian financial crisis in the late 1990s, it is far less likely to exit if a host country incurs short-term problems. Though foreign borrowing is often used to finance consumption, FDI is usually used for productive investments to expand or update production capacity or infrastructure.

A McKinsey Global Institute study of FDI in five sectors spread over four advanced developing countries described the single biggest impact of FDI on host economies as the improvement in the standards of living of the populace, "with consumers directly benefiting from lower prices, higher-quality goods and more choice. Improved productivity and output in the sector and its suppliers indirectly contributed to increasing national income."[13] The boost to the standard of living of consumers in host countries is the hidden success story of FDI because "consumers are a fragmented, less vocal political body than, say, incumbent domestic companies"—and antiglobalization demonstrators. The case studies suggested to the think tank's analysts that although a limited number of jobs are periodically lost "through elimination of inefficient local players or streamlining inefficient production operations," benefits to the consuming public and increased national wealth more than compensated.[14]

One of the most important economic benefits of incoming FDI is the cross-border transfer and diffusion of technology. MNCs are now the world's number one source of new technologies in the manufacturing, information processing, telecommunications, oil exploration and drilling, and mineral extraction sectors. Cutting-edge research and development in the high-tech sector has become incredibly complex and enormously to prohibitively expensive, but the need for and benefits of innovation are universal. Large MNCs are, with increasing frequency, the only organizations capable of financing and exploiting R&D on a grand scale. What allows them to do this is their ability to sell the resulting products in mass volume in markets worldwide (the concept of economies of scale is discussed in chapter 6), blue-chip credit rating, and opportunity to defray costs by entering into strategic alliances with other financially well-off MNCs.[15]

The simplest forms of technology transfer consist of (1) a new foreign subsidiary's utilizing proprietary technological capabilities superior to those of host country companies, and (2) expertly designed programs to train local workers in state-of-the-art manufacturing processes. Some leakage, that is, domestic spillover, of technology is likely to occur because thousands of local citizens may have an opportunity to observe a typical foreign company's operations on a first- or secondhand basis. Technology spillovers occur in several ways. One involves resignations from a foreign subsidiary by highly trained workers who take their advanced knowledge to an existing local company or set up their own businesses.

Competitive pressures are another source of spillovers. Local competitors may determine that their survival requires them to imitate as closely as possible the best practices of a foreign-owned subsidiary. This strategy would be implemented by indigenous companies adopting better management practices and investing in updated capital equipment (two good examples of where this has happened are telecommunications and retailing), both of which tend to increase efficiency and lower prices. These results in turn create additional benefits for a host country's economic well-being. In a word, FDI increases the level of *competition* in host countries. When greenfield investments add to the number of market participants, consumers can expect lower prices, more choice, and accelerated introduction of new products and services—not to mention more jobs.

Anecdotal evidence shows that diffusion of technology also takes place when MNCs provide special training and financial resources to their local suppliers of intermediate goods and of services. It is in the self-interest of foreign manufacturers to upgrade local suppliers' technological capabilities, improve their quality control and on-time delivery performance, and help them lower costs. In the 1980s, the Singapore-based subsidiary of a European electronics multinational helped its most important local suppliers automate their production facilities and occasionally bought needed machinery and leased it to them. When needed, the company also helped retrain the suppliers' workforces. To enable these same Singaporean suppliers to reach economies of scale, the European company and a nearby American-owned electronics subsidiary provided marketing expertise that enabled some of the local contractors to begin selling components in foreign markets. After first selling to overseas subsidiaries of the two MNCs and then exporting to independent buyers, three of the indigenous Singapore firms that started out as suppliers of printed circuit boards to local MNCs grew to the top rank of electronic manufacturing services companies.[16] A second example of MNC-local economy linkage via technology transfer is Dell's assistance to a Chinese electronics firm it contracted to build Dell-branded flat-screen TVs. The Dallas-based company helped the contractor reconfigure assembly lines to increase output and advised it on quality control, cost-cutting, and exporting.[17] Far more common is the basic form of so-called backward linkages between foreign subsidiaries and the host country economy: increasing purchases of goods and services from local companies resulting in expansion of existing domestic businesses and creation of new ones.

An additional benefit of inward FDI is its ability to fill two financial gaps that exist in most countries. The first is a shortfall of available private investment capital resulting from insufficient domestic saving and/or government budget deficits. Absent the foreign investor, expansion of indigenous production and jobs through construction of a new production facility would not have taken place. A financially sound MNC has greater internal financial resources and greater ability to borrow in capital markets than just about any firm operating only within one country. The second financial gap is the shortfall experienced in most countries of foreign exchange to pay for desired imports. Efficiency-seeking

FDI designed as an export platform will generate dollars, euros, and so on, much of which will likely remain in-country. MNCs have an edge on domestic companies in the ability to export because of advanced proprietary technology, lower average costs from economies of scale, greater knowledge of world markets, and the possibility of extensive intrafirm trade, that is, exports to a sister subsidiary of the company located in another country.

For transition countries, FDI can be particularly effective as a stimulant to economic development by "accelerating the transition from a planned to a market economy. This is because it helps speed up industrial restructuring and the development of markets and market-oriented behaviour of economic agents."[18] Even the U.S. economy enjoys measurable benefits from incoming FDI. A statistical analysis by two International Monetary Fund (IMF) economists suggested that FDI led to "significant" productivity gains for domestic firms. The size of FDI spillovers was categorized as "economically important" because they accounted for an estimated 11 percent of the productivity growth of American manufacturing firms between 1987 and 1996.[19]

Finally, foreign-owned or -controlled manufacturing subsidiaries are attractive because they mostly are more efficient than purely domestic companies. In short, they produce more product per input of capital or labor. "The evidence on productivity, whatever the measure, is close to unanimous on the higher productivity of foreign-owned plants in both developed and developing countries." In some cases, this higher productivity is a function of the higher capital intensity or larger scale production of most foreign subsidiaries relative to domestic manufacturers.[20] Foreign-owned or -controlled companies tend to be the "most dynamic and productive firms" in China. Output of foreign-invested industrial firms in that country expanded at four times the rate of local enterprises during the 1994–97 period, and their labor productivity was almost twice that of state- and locally owned enterprises. Research suggests that domestic enterprises benefited from the presence of foreign MNCs "both through increased sales and positive spillovers."[21]

More Jobs, Higher Incomes

One does not read about subsidiaries of MNCs being hampered by vacancies caused by their inability to hire enough new workers or by rapid turnover of existing staff. The reason is that these jobs are in high demand, and the reason they are in high demand is that wages, benefits, and working conditions on average are well above prevailing local standards. Establishment of a foreign-owned or -controlled manufacturing subsidiary in most cases has meant creation of new jobs requiring above-average skills and therefore paying above-average wages. The primary motive for national and regional governments giving incentives to attract incoming MNCs is expectation that high-quality, relatively high-paying jobs will be created, always and everywhere a high-priority political goal.

As an empirical matter, "there is virtually no careful and systematic evidence demonstrating that, as a generality, multinational firms adversely affect their workers, ... worsen working conditions, pay lower wages than in alternative employment, or repress worker rights." In fact, a large body of empirical evidence exists "indicating that the opposite is the case." Foreign-owned subsidiaries increase wage levels "both by raising labor productivity and by expanding the scale of production," and in doing so improve the conditions of work.[22] An Organization for Economic Cooperation and Development (OECD) survey in 2001 found "compensation per employee of firms under foreign control in all countries was substantially higher than the average for national firms."[23] To compensate for any possibility of pro-MNC bias in these sources, consider the conclusion by the economic development-oriented Overseas Development Institute located in Great Britain: "Almost all evidence shows that FDI and foreign ownership are associated with higher wages for all types of workers."[24]

In reviewing 1994 data, Edward Graham calculated that average compensation paid by foreign affiliates of U.S. manufacturing companies was 1.4 times as large as average domestic manufacturing wages in high-income countries (about $10,000 more in absolute terms), 1.8 times those of middle-income countries, and twice the average manufacturing wage in low-income countries.[25] Critics who decry low salaries paid by Western companies in lower-income less developed countries (LDCs) ignore basic laws of economics. Hourly wages are relatively low in LDCs in large part because prices of basic consumer staples like housing, food, and clothing are much lower. The local purchasing power of salaries is therefore higher than it appears when the local currency is converted into dollars at the nominal exchange rate. The other important reason wages are lower in LDCs is that workers on average have lower productivity levels than their counterparts in industrialized countries. Wage increases outpacing productivity increases is a classic cause of inflation.

As to why MNCs provide greater pay and benefits than domestic producers, the short answer is "it depends" on the supply of qualified workers, the company's human resources standards, its line of business, and the host country. The basic reason is that relatively large MNCs possess world-class technological, managerial, and marketing know-how that significantly increase their relative efficiency, a virtual prerequisite for competing successfully in what are for them literally foreign environments for conducting business. Manufacturing subsidiaries of MNCs typically use technologies that make their workers more productive than those of less sophisticated domestically owned rivals.[26] Pay differentials to some extent reflect the industry composition of FDI that is weighted toward relatively high-wage industry sectors: high value-added manufacturing and services.[27]

A frequent motivation for paying higher wages is the desire to minimize employee turnover. This not only reduces costs of training new workers, it also cuts down on the number of experienced personnel leaving and taking their knowledge of a foreign subsidiary's advanced operating procedures to competitors. In some countries, workers may be reluctant to work for foreign companies because of a cultural stigma attached to working for a Western company. In the case of Japan, higher wages by MNCs are needed to offset their not offering guarantee of lifetime employment as large Japanese companies do. No matter what the reason, large MNCs have the financial resources to pay relatively well, especially in LDCs where salaries are relatively low.

There is little evidence that FDI makes workers in host countries who are not employed by foreign-owned companies worse off. Nor is there sufficient evidence to prove the long-standing criticism that FDI hurts the labor force of home countries. "Outward U.S. FDI, if anything, in the aggregate tends to create rather than destroy U.S. job opportunities in high-wage, export-oriented industries." Viewed in full perspective, "outward direct investment helps rather than hurts U.S. workers" (see chapter 9).[28] There is merit in the arguments that the brunt of job losses in industrialized home countries mainly affects lower skilled workers and that the arrival of a subsidiary with sophisticated manufacturing processes does not mean a bounty for unskilled workers in the host country. Everything is relative, however. What matters most is that as a whole, FDI provides the greatest good to the greatest number. In the case of eBay, an online auction and buy/sell site, the relatively few jobs created at its overseas subsidiaries are geometrically outnumbered by the number of jobs and income flows created by small businesses and local artisans being able to show and sell their wares with no overhead by using the company's universally accessible Web sites. The company believes that it further defies the image of MNCs exacerbating the gap between the few rich and the many poor by making new and used goods available to the masses at relatively low prices.[29]

Foreign-owned factories get good grades for adhering to high safety and health standards. Image-conscious MNCs will think more than twice about violating workers' rights, such as overtly blocking unionization efforts, lest such actions be damned on the Internet sites of nongovernmental organizations (NGOs) around the world. Factories derided as being sweatshops are not subsidiaries of American, European, or Japanese multinationals. They are locally owned companies whose labor practices are not subject to the laws of their overseas clients' countries. Most MNCs also bring with them in-house training and incentives programs designed to expedite the promotions of exceptional employees. Although hard data are lacking, the relatively generous labor policies of multinationals suggest the likelihood that most provide vacation, sick days, and pension plans at levels comparable to or better than the average of local companies.

The Multiple Benefits of High-Quality Investment

To dramatize the potential for high-quality FDI to unleash a chain effect of positive economic effects, let us imagine a best-case scenario of a new foreign-owned manufacturing subsidiary whose multiple beneficial economic effects so clearly exceed any downsides that the host country clearly is better off having received it. This hypothetical investment from heaven is a newly built greenfield plant to manufacture most of the components for and assemble a computerized medical diagnostic device. No domestic companies are crowded out because none produce anything like this newly invented and patented product. The land acquisition, construction, installation of production lines, training of workers, and all other preproduction expenses are financed by capital transfers from the foreign company's headquarters to the new host country, where it is converted into local currency. Other than receiving the standard tax breaks and some minor improvements in transportation infrastructure, the company neither demands nor receives any special incentives.

A thousand new jobs are created, mostly requiring relatively skilled workers who will still need advanced training by the subsidiary in how the medical device works and in the parent company's assembly techniques. Sales increase both within the host country and in neighboring countries (some of whom have free trade agreements with the host) because the device is reasonably priced and proves to be the most successful means of early detection of the illnesses it was designed to search for. The plant's production capacity is soon enlarged, paid for mainly with reinvested profits. The labor force grows. Experienced local workers are promoted to management positions previously held by expatriates. Purchases of components from local vendors grow steadily as they become increasingly adept at meeting the foreign company's standards of quality, on-time delivery, and cost. Some of the suppliers are able to ingratiate themselves with the foreign subsidiary because they were started by former employees of the plant who became well-schooled in its needs and procedures.

Exports from the plant steadily increase, and most of the subsidiary's growing foreign exchange earnings is exchanged for local currency to pay for rising domestic expenses and to pay for imports of new, cutting-edge machinery. The nature of the assembly process for the medical device has no negative impact on the environment. The host country's corporate tax rate is average so there is no incentive for the parent company to manipulate transfer prices or to dodge taxes.

Over a slightly longer time span, the host government's focused strategy of attracting makers of scientific and medical instruments bears fruit. Thanks in part to official funding, expanded vocational training programs at technical and engineering colleges and management training programs significantly upgrade the quantity and quality of the local labor force. This factor, along with the success of the original foreign investment and an aggressive, well-designed government promotion effort, begins to attract companies in this and other targeted sectors. The result is an expanding cluster of foreign makers of sophisticated instruments whose factories are built by local contractors. A virtuous cycle produces sustained increases in output, employment, exports, and tax revenues. Poverty and unemployment in the country are not eradicated, but a significant number of workers come out ahead. They either directly benefit from the higher real wages allowed by increased productivity in the incoming MNCs or indirectly benefit by selling to their fellow countrymen the additional goods and services associated with higher living standards. Others are indirectly helped by the increased government spending on social services facilitated by the increased collection of corporate and individual income taxes. Measurable harm inflicted on the public at large is nil.

This idealized version of incoming FDI is rare, but not fiction. The reality of recurring benefits to recipients of FDI is demonstrated in the three case studies presented in the final section of this chapter. Detractors of free market economics will complain that most developing countries do not have the human and physical infrastructure and quality of governance to attract and reap maximum rewards from high-quality direct investment. This is an accurate assessment. The larger point is that responsibility for this condition lies with individual countries, not with MNCs.

The Critics Are, at a Minimum, Confused

Part of arguing the case in favor of FDI and MNCs consists of pointing out the flaws in the arguments made against them, either out of confusion or deliberate distortion. In its 2004 outlook for Asian economies, the Asian Development Bank caustically observed, "One cannot help but note in passing that some of the strongest criticisms of [MNCs] emanate from countries with the smallest FDI presence."[30] Another large source of loud criticism, one might note, is middle- and upper-class youth from rich countries who have not suffered directly at the hands of MNCs, and certainly never worked for one, but whose value systems simply abhor big business. Even the more moderate, better informed critics misconstrue cause and effect relationships and wrongly hold multinationals responsible for creating many of the world economy's very real shortcomings. The MNC is largely a product of its environment, often shaped by forces beyond its control (see chapter 3). People are not poor because some big global companies are profitable and their senior executives are well paid. Multinationals are not the cause of global poverty, illiteracy, or an uneven distribution of income. If the collective governments of the world have not cured these problems, MNCs cannot be expected to accomplish these feats. Instead, domestic and global companies should be given credit for at least alleviating many of these problems in countries where they have been given the chance to thrive.

Efforts to link exploitation of the masses and democracy deficits with MNCs are supported by little hard evidence beyond scattered anecdotes that do not demonstrate systemic failures. Clear-cut examples of social injustices and economic exploitation by the many small and medium-sized manufacturing companies with only one or two foreign subsidiaries and multinational service companies are nearly nonexistent. The major U.S.-based Internet search engine companies are going multinational, but they are far from being threats to abuse highly paid, skilled information technology workers, fix prices (certainly not as long as their services remain free), visibly add to distortions in income distribution, despoil the environment, or Americanize foreign cultures (especially if their Web site is in the local language). Furthermore, the idea that multinationals could be a serious threat to democracy and personal freedom "appears strange, if not ridiculous."[31] Outside of natural resource seekers, multinationals are seldom active and influential in dictatorships of the Right or Left.

The case against MNCs also suffers from the critics' fallacy of always pointing to the usual suspects to demonstrate international business behavior at its worst. It is a less than stellar methodology when the misdeeds of a relatively few miscreants—mining and oil companies, United Fruit, ITT, and so on—are repeatedly retold and are extrapolated to create a one-dimensional model of gigantic, evil global companies with far too much power for anybody's good. Extractive companies often operate in very rough neighborhoods and by necessity will behave accordingly to survive. To extract the oil or minerals they seek and the world needs, they must accommodate the government of the host country, no matter how benevolent or evil it is. This is not an apology for their actions, just a reminder that they represent only one narrow kind of multinational enterprise and are not typical of the species.

The aforementioned Asian Development Bank report, continuing its unusually blunt language, said it is "important" to emphasize that MNCs "generally adapt to the local commercial environment. Any assessment of their impact needs to make due allowance for this factor." Foreign-based MNCs "cannot reasonably be expected to behave any differently from local firms." For example, foreign subsidiaries will have little choice but to make payments to local leaders if corruption is deeply embedded in the host country's business and political cultures. Technology spillovers are likely to be limited when the local human capital base is weak. In sum, "it is important to diagnose the root cause of a particular problem, rather than engage in an exercise of 'guilt by association.' "[32]

The bank's report, though properly justifying some corporate behavior under extreme circumstances, underestimates the growth of good corporate citizenship whether for altruistic reasons or concerns about threats to sales, market share, and profits. MNCs in the manufacturing and services sectors have observed the downside of controversial business practices that at a minimum can generate torrents of bad publicity and calls for government interventions to be transmitted around the world via the Internet, and at worst result in customer boycotts. "When multinational corporations go abroad, they take more than their capital and technology with them. They also take their brand names, their reputations, and their international images." This reality has become especially important in recent years as major U.S., European, and Japanese multinationals have come under intense scrutiny by the international media and activist NGOs, much more so than local firms.[33]

When locally owned, nonexporting companies in countries like Vietnam, Bangladesh, or Honduras exploit workers, few in the West know or deeply care. These abuses are given a free pass as purely internal matters by activists in the North. The situation changes radically when those same producers become suppliers to multinationals like Reebok, Nike, Levi Strauss, or Disney. The perceived missteps of large MNCs have become targets of the wrath of a growing number of a relatively new kind of multinational institution: influential NGOs concerned with human rights and environmental protection. Responding to well-orchestrated, global public outcries has become a genuine bottom-line concern for companies finding themselves in the glare of a worldwide spotlight portraying them as callous robber barons. "Under these circumstances, the old Leninist link between multinational firms and foreign exploitation seems outmoded or even contradictory. Rather than having an interest in subverting human rights, corporations—particularly high-profile firms from open and democratic societies—may well see the commercial benefits of promoting human rights." In an international order increasingly sensitive to international media and transnational activism, "U.S. multinationals could be—indeed may already be—a powerful instrument in the pursuit of human rights."[34]

Unfair invective is also hurled at MNCs for "deserting" host countries for lower production costs elsewhere. If a foreign-owned company sees tax rates as well as power and telecommunications costs steadily rise, the local educational system falter, and political stability decline relative to other markets, what is the right course of action? Should it ignore free market emphasis on efficiency? Does the company have a moral obligation to stay put and protect its workers today but risk a potentially devastating long-term decline in sales? Don't host countries have some obligation for providing a competitive environment for foreign subsidiaries?

A major distortion to the critics' case is their unremitting comparison of the global sales of corporations to the size of countries' economies. These two measurements are compiled on a completely different basis, the result being that a direct comparison grossly exaggerates the dollar size of MNCs. Apparently the jeremiad that a majority of the 100 largest economies in the world are corporations and MNCs have grown as large as countries is too good a rallying cry to abandon merely because a few economists have pointed out that it is factually wrong (see box 3.1). The power of MNCs is also exaggerated by critics wrongly equating sales volume with ability to set prices and bombard consumers into submission with nonstop, globe-circling advertising. "The evidence bears out the proposition that companies do not dominate markets, but rather that markets dominate companies. Privatization and international economic integration have made markets more competitive and . . . companies less powerful within their markets."[35] Even in an era of shrinking numbers of major automobile makers, General Motors, the world's largest carmaker, has watched its market share steadily deteriorate in its own home market. The chief cause of this decline for the past several years has been the inability of GM—or Ford—to devise long-term antidotes to the steadily growing popularity of cars produced by the North American subsidiaries of Japanese companies and to steadily rising costs of medical benefits paid to its workers and pensioners.

The Race to the Bottom Is a Myth

The major flaw in the critics' assertion that MNCs are gravitating to countries with the lowest labor standards and least enforcement of environmental protection laws is the absence of evidence to support it. Empirical data is also lacking to support the ancillary argument that countries are in a competitive race to reduce their labor and environmental standards to attract high volumes of FDI. The data for many years have shown unequivocally that nonextractive foreign subsidiaries are concentrated in high-income, high-wage countries with vigorous enforcement of antipollution statutes, and at the same time are nearly absent in the poorest countries with the lowest wages (see chapter 7). If governments were in a genuine race to promise higher profit margins to foreign companies, the countries attracting the most FDI should have well below-average wage rates and workers' rights, and they should be choking on pollution.[36] They don't and they aren't.

The so-called race to the bottom is a chimera. Indeed, "a growing body of research suggests . . . that foreign direct investment is generally beneficial to developing countries, creating the socioeconomic conditions conducive to the improvement of human rights and environmental quality in host countries."[37] Because most MNCs place a premium on recruiting and retaining skilled, disciplined labor and usually bring with them the same advanced pollution abatement equipment used in their home countries, it is more credible to assert that a race to the top is under way. Workers lacking discipline, skills, commitment to come to work every day, initiative, and literacy are not attractive to corporations even at pennies per hour.[38] An MIT study quoted the head of a Hong Kong company with extensive production facilities in China as bluntly saying, "If you pay peanuts, you get monkeys." Guided by this calculation, the company's Chinese subsidiaries pay far above-average local wages to be able to "hire people with the right kind of education, motivation, and willingness to stay with the company."[39]

Wage rates are but a fraction of the costs of producing all but the simplest goods. More important is the sum of the costs of raw materials and components, labor productivity, utilities to power a factory, taxes, transportation, compliance with local business regulations and licenses, worker training and recruiting, security for plant and key personnel, and so on. The costs of constantly recruiting and training new workers in a high-turnover situation tend to be downplayed or ignored outright by those without managerial experience in the manufacturing sector. Furthermore, the really important measure is not absolute levels of wages and benefits but unit labor costs, which are the labor costs of producing a given value of production.[40]

The ample evidence that MNCs on average pay wages well above prevailing local rates was discussed previously and does not need to be repeated. What does need mentioning is that "there is no solid evidence that countries with poorly protected worker rights attract FDI. If anything, investors apparently prefer locations in which workers and the public more generally function in a stable political and social environment in which civil liberties are well established and enforced."[41] It is unrealistic to expect MNCs to force changes in local laws and attitudes in developing and in-transition countries that do not provide full freedoms to workers to form unions and bargain collectively. The important point is that despite claims of a sellout of labor to placate giant corporations, the data do not show any significant *deterioration* of freedom of association rights since the 1980s. "On the contrary, they show that the move to democracy in developing countries has been accompanied in several [of these countries]—notably in Latin America—by some improvement in the protection of workers' right to associate."[42]

Studies to determine if FDI is being drawn to countries with minimal environmental standards invariably conclude that they are not. Reality is just the opposite of what critics of MNCs claim. The arrival of foreign manufacturing subsidiaries is positively correlated with high levels of environmental protection. A World Bank working paper concluded, "Pollution control is not a critical cost factor for most private firms" and environmental protection expenses "are generally not a critical factor in location decisions."[43] The authors of another World Bank study reported that after conducting a variety of empirical tests, they "found almost no evidence of pollution havens. Instead, we find that foreign firms are less polluting than their peers in developing countries." Pollution abatement costs as a variable in determining the geographical distribution of FDI were found to be "very small, if not zero." This result was deemed "not surprising in light of the fact that pollution abatement expenditures are only a tiny fraction of overall costs."[44]

Existence of an environmental race to the bottom was "not substantiated by the data" according to a study by three scholars. The most common corporate environmental practice in their sample was adoption of a single stringent internal corporate standard on a universal basis. Although the authors of the study found that a few companies with less-than-stellar finances and management are from time to time tempted to choose locations with lower antipollution regulations, there "appear to be forces that encourage MNCs to integrate and standardize their environmental practices globally." In many cases it is cost-effective to adopt global corporate standards that exceed local requirements. This allows for the efficiencies that come with standardized company procedures. It also avoids the potential costs of retrofitting when environmental laws become more stringent.[45] This kind of upgrade inevitably happens after a country has enjoyed prolonged economic growth. A growing middle class typically demands cleaner air, water, and land, and the government has enough revenue to respond.

The relatively low cost of installing its most advanced antipollution technology in all its factories in all countries also appeals to the average MNC as a means of protecting the corporate reputation from accusations of being an insensitive polluter. Maintaining universally high environmental protection standards also avoids the occasional confrontation with local officials and multilateral NGOs unsatisfied with the fact that a particular foreign subsidiary is technically in compliance, but with relatively low national environmental protection standards. An important but often overlooked factor is that advanced pollution abatement technologies that concentrate on changes in the manufacturing or production process (rather than at the smokestack level) "can actually lower operating costs rather than raise them."[46]

Country Case Studies: Virtuous Cycles and High-Quality FDI

A good way to assess the benefits of a new foreign subsidiary to a host country is to take a long-term perspective, one that can incorporate the possibility that the initial investment will generate additional phases of economic activity. Agglomeration economies and the demonstration effect (see chapter 7) explain how successful FDI in itself can be a magnet for additional investments. Assessing a new foreign subsidiary in isolation by assuming that no favorable secondary and tertiary effects will be forthcoming is often a mistake.

The fallacy of short-sighted judgment in evaluating the net value of a direct investment project is demonstrated in the case of Alabama's quarter-billion-dollar incentive package in 1993. Much criticized at the time, it was the price of convincing Mercedes-Benz to build an automobile assembly plant there instead of another southern state. State officials in the moment did appear to be overly generous if the incentives are measured in terms of the prorated cost of each initial job created and contrasted with the alternative of increased state spending on schools and social welfare. When measured by the bigger, longer term picture, however, this is a classic case study of a risky but ultimately cost-effective investment. To paraphrase the title of an old song, "Cars Fell on Alabama."

In 1993, Alabama had no experience in manufacturing automobiles, but it is projected to be the one of the largest automobile-producing U.S. states in 2006, when output is scheduled to reach three quarters of a million vehicles annually. The early success of the pioneering Mercedes subsidiary prompted a major expansion, completed in 2005, that increased production and doubled its workforce to 4,000. Alabama's incentives and the smooth start of this subsidiary led to the second phase of the virtuous cycle: attracting other carmakers. Honda opened an assembly plant in 2001 and three years later added a second production line that significantly expanded the plant's output and workforce. Hyundai (from lower wage South Korea) began operations of its $1 billion-plus plant in 2005 and should equal Honda's annual output of 300,000 vehicles when it reaches full production. Toyota opened a plant to make engines for SUVs and pick-up trucks in 2003; it broke ground two years later for a major expansion designed to nearly double output and workforce.[47]

The clustering effect blossomed as third- and fourth-round effects from the initial Mercedes-Benz investment appeared, first in the form of a big inflow of prime contractors to the manufacturing, assembly, and engine plants and second when subcontractors began opening plants. The linkages between automakers and parts makers were still growing in volume and economic impact at the end of 2005. Capital investments in Alabama by dozens of new and expanding suppliers totaled an estimated $780 million during the first ten months of 2004, creating an estimated 3,437 new jobs in the process.[48] The automobile and auto parts industries in total invested some $6.4 billion and created 35,000 jobs between 1993 and mid-2004. A trade association promoting cooperation and sharing of technical information among parts and subcomponents producers in the state had nearly 400 member companies in 2004.[49] Viewed in a broader perspective, the automobile cluster is embellishing the state's image and helps fuel other economic development efforts, according to a senior official of the Economic Development Partnership of Alabama.[50] The virtuous cycle continues even further by contributing to what economists call the multiplier effect; the growing incomes of the workers at these plants generate spending, which in turn stimulates increases in retail businesses and new home sales. The increase in retailing entrepreneurs and employees adds a whole new round of income and spending. Rising payrolls are especially welcome in a state that had been suffering from a shrinking tax base brought on by the import-induced declines in production and jobs in textiles and apparel—at one time Alabama's core industries.

A similar virtuous cycle was experienced far away in Slovakia. Well thought-out and executed policy strategies led to considerable success in attracting MNCs. Inward FDI was the main reason the country, an economic backwater in the mid-1990s with a stagnant GDP and nearly 20 percent unemployment, was transformed into one of the fastest-growing countries in Central and Western Europe by 2005. The combination of the demonstration effect, a good geographic location with good transportation links, tax and labor law changes initiated by a probusiness government, relatively low labor costs (about one-eighth those of high-cost Western European economies), financial incentives, membership in the EU, and political stability collectively contributed to the upsurge in FDI. Like Alabama, the biggest investments have been by automobile makers: Volkswagen (the country's largest company and largest exporter), Peugeot Citroën, Kia-Hyundai, and Ford. If, as projected, Slovakia produces 850,000 cars annually in 2007, it will become the world's largest car producer on a per capita basis.[51] When the assembly plants are at full capacity and suppliers have finished setting up their plants, more than 30,000 new jobs will have been created in a country of just over 5 million people.

Costa Rica's CINDE (Coalition of Development Incentives), the nonprofit, nongovernmental agency responsible for coordinating promotion of incoming FDI, is properly credited with playing a crucial role in convincing Intel to build a massive assembly and testing plant for its state-of-the-art microprocessors (see chapter 7). A virtuous cycle quickly followed after it became fully operational in 1998. An estimated five percentage points of Costa Rica's 8 percent GDP growth (or 60 percent of the increment) in 1999 was attributable to the start-up of this one plant. Its $330 million of value-added accounted for approximately 7 percent of real GDP that year.[52] Hundreds of well-paying jobs were created, in most cases for workers whose existing knowledge and skills were enhanced through advanced technical training. A potentially inflationary upward spiral in salaries did not occur, the presumed reason being an anticipated increase in the supply of skilled labor stemming from creation of new programs in institutions of higher education and jumps in enrollment in existing engineering and vocational programs.[53] In addition to internal employee training programs, Intel provides financial support for degree and certificate programs in institutions of higher learning in technology and engineering, updated teachers' training, and advanced English language training. The subsidiary's strongest educational link is with the Costa Rican Technology Institute, whose Intel Associate status allows it to apply for company-funded grants for specific R&D projects as well as funding for faculty and students to engage in educational exchange activities.[54]

Linkage to the Costa Rican economy also came from Intel's training of an estimated one-third of its local suppliers to increase their performance quality and decrease prices.[55] Last but not least, the Intel plant dramatically demonstrated that Costa Rica was an attractive location for sophisticated high-tech assembly operations. This status enhances the potential for future development of a cluster of sophisticated electronics producers and their suppliers. The country's "greater clarity" in its strategic objectives for attracting FDI, "appropriate national policy instruments, and solid institutions" have combined to produce a major example of the potential benefits of incoming MNCs. Costa Rica "without a doubt... has become a shining example of how economies can progress towards better conditions in the framework of assembly operations, since it upgraded these activities in two major steps: from natural resources to apparel and from apparel to electronics," according to a UN report.[56]

Major success stories in attracting high-quality direct investments usually are related to a jurisdiction's operation of an effective investment promotion effort that impresses foreign companies that have many potential sites to choose from. "Recruiting" efforts concentrate on what country and state governments have targeted as high-quality manufacturing and service sectors that are a good match for the assets at their disposal. Alabama's industrial workforce training program was ranked number one in the United States in a 2004 survey of industrial site selection consultants by *Expansion Management* magazine. The program uses its own funds to recruit, evaluate, and put selected applicants through a preliminary training program in basic factory skills. Those who make the grade are referred to in-state automakers, thus providing them with a ready-made pool of prescreened workers.[57]

Postscript

The reader is reminded that this chapter, like the one that follows, is designed to present the most convincing, credible case possible for one side of an ambiguous and contentious issue. Although no factually untrue statements were knowingly made, the arguments presented herein do not necessarily represent the author's views. The data advanced in support of these arguments do not necessarily meet the author's standards of full academic rigor.

Notes

1. Daniel Yergin and Joseph Stanislaw, *The Commanding Heights* (New York: Simon and Schuster, 1998), pp. 389–90.
2. John Micklethwait and Adrian Wooldridge, *The Company* (New York: Modern Library, 2003), pp. xx–xxi.

3. Gordon H. Hanson, "Should Countries Promote Foreign Direct Investment?," February 2001, p. 13, available online at http://www.unctad.org/en/docs/pogdsmd pbg24dg.en.pdf. accessed February 2005.

4. UNCTAD, *World Investment Report 1999,* Overview, p. 31, available online at http://www.unctad.org; accessed December 2004.

5. Theodore H. Moran, *Beyond Sweatshops—Foreign Direct Investment and Globalization in Developing Countries* (Washington, DC: Brookings Institution Press, 2002), p. 117.

6. Matthew J. Slaughter, "Global Investments, American Returns," Report prepared for the Emergency Committee for American Trade, 1998, p. 51, available online at http://www.ecattrade.com, accessed November 2004.

7. Ibid., pp. 29, 51.

8. *The Economist,* February 24, 2001, p. 80.

9. Moran, *Beyond Sweatshops,* p. 162.

10. John H. Dunning, "Globalization and the Knowledge Economy," in John H. Dunning, ed., *Regions, Globalization, and the Knowledge-Based Economy* (New York: Oxford University Press, 2000), p. 28.

11. Edward M. Graham, *Fighting the Wrong Enemy—Antiglobal Activists and Multinational Enterprises* (Washington, DC: Institute for International Economics, 2000), p. 5.

12. JBIC Institute, Japan Bank for International Cooperation, "Foreign Direct Investment and Development: Where Do We Stand?," Research Paper no. 15, June 2002, p. 1, available online at http://www.jbic.go.jp/english/research/report/paper/pdf/rp15_e.pdf; accessed March 2005.

13. McKinsey Global Institute, "New Horizons: Multinational Company Investment in Developing Economies," October 2003, Executive Summary, p. 1; available online at http://www.mckinsey.com/mgi; accessed November 2004.

14. Ibid., chap. 1, p. 17, and Introduction.

15. Medard Gabel and Henry Bruner, *Global Inc.—An Atlas of the Multinational Corporation* (New York: New Press, 2003), p. 126.

16. Moran, *Beyond Sweatshops,* p. 125. The Singaporean companies are Flextronics, NatSteel Electronics, and Venture.

17. "Dell Finds Success in China's Maturing Market," *Wall Street Journal,* July 5, 2005, p. A8.

18. Magdolna Sass, "FDI in Hungary—The First Mover's Advantage and Disadvantage," *European Investment Bank Papers,* 9(2), 2002, p. 77.

19. Wolfgang Keller and Stephen R. Yeaple, "Multinational Enterprises, International Trade, and Productivity Growth: Firm-Level Evidence from the United States," IMF Working Paper 03/248, December 2003, p. 34, available online at http://www.imf.org; accessed September 2004.

20. Robert E. Lipsey, "Home- and Host-Country Effects of Foreign Direct Investment," in Robert E. Baldwin and L. Alan Winters, eds., *Challenges to Globalization—Analyzing the Economics* (Chicago: University of Chicago Press, 2004), p. 358.

21. Wanda Tseng and Harm Zebregs, "Foreign Direct Investment in China: Some Lessons for Other Countries," IMF Policy Discussion Paper, February 2002, pp. 19–20, available online at http://www.imf.org; accessed July 2005.

22. Drusilla Brown, Alan Deardorff, and Robert Stern, "The Effects of Multinational Production on Wages and Working Conditions," in Baldwin and Winters, *Challenges to Globalization,* p. 322.

23. OECD, "Measuring Globalisation 2001," main findings available online at http://www.oecd.org; accessed March 2005.

24. Overseas Development Institute, "Foreign Direct Investment: Who Gains?," ODI Briefing Paper, April 2002, p. 2, available online at http://www.odi.org.uk; accessed October 2004.

25. Graham, *Fighting the Wrong Enemy,* p. 94.

26. Ibid., p. 88.

27. Lipsey, "Home- and Host-Country Effects," p. 345.

28. Graham, *Fighting the Wrong Enemy,* pp. 95, 83.

29. Telephone interview with Matt Brannick, president of eBay International, September 2005.

30. Asian Development Bank, *Asian Development Outlook 2004,* p. 260, available online at http://www.adb.org/Documents/Books/Ado/2004/Ado2004_Part3.pdf; accessed April 2005.

31. David Henderson, "The MAI Affair: A Story and its Lessons," n.d., p. 59, available online at http://www.cairnsgroupfarmers.org/ni/reportspapers/maipaper.pdf; accessed September 2005.

32. Asian Development Bank, *Asian Development Outlook 2004,* p. 260.

33. Debora Spar, "Foreign Investment and Human Rights," *Challenge,* January/February 1999, pp. 70, 75.

34. Debora Spar, "The Spotlight and the Bottom Line," *Foreign Affairs,* March/April 1998, p. 12.

35. Martin Wolf, *Why Globalization Works* (New Haven, CT: Yale University Press, 2004), p. 225.

36. Again, China should be considered an exception.

37. Minxin Pei and Merritt Lyon, "Bullish on Democracy," *National Interest,* winter 2002/2003, pp. 79–80.

38. The real test of the cost of labor is productivity, or output per unit of work, not hourly wages.

39. Suzanne Berger and the MIT Industrial Performance Center, *How We Compete—What Companies around the World Are Doing to Make It in Today's Global Economy* (New York: Currency-Doubleday, 2006), p. 260.

40. Ibid.

41. Brown, Deardorff, and Stern, "The Effects of Multinational Production," p. 321.

42. JBIC Institute, "Foreign Direct Investment and Development," p. 86.

43. David Wheeler, "Racing to the Bottom? Foreign Investment and Air Pollution in Developing Countries," World Bank Policy Research Working Paper no. 2524, January 2001, pp. 5, 11, available online at http://www.worldbank.org; accessed May 2005.

44. Gunnar S. Eskeland and Ann E. Harrison, "Moving to Greener Pastures? Multinationals and the Pollution-Haven Hypothesis," World Bank Policy Research Working

Paper no. 1744, March 1997, pp. 27–29, available online at http://www.worldbank
.org; accessed December 2004.

45. Glen Dowell, Stuart Hart, and Bernard Yeung, "Do Corporate Environmental
Standards Create or Destroy Market Value?," *Management Science,* August 2000, pp.
1072, 1060.

46. Ibid., pp. 1062–63.

47. Barbara Sloan, "Alabama Takes Spotlight in Detroit," *Partners,* spring 2005, pp. 28–
32, available online at http://www.edpa.org/pdfs/spo5art6.pdf; accessed June 2005;
and "Automotive Brief—Toyota Motor Corp.: Auto Maker Will Nearly Double Size
of Alabama Engine Plant," *Wall Street Journal,* September 27, 2004, p. 1, available
online from the ABI/Inform Database; accessed June 2005.

48. "Automotive Suppliers Invest $779 Million in '04," *Birmingham Business Journal,*
December 24, 2004, p. 6, available online from the ABI/Inform Database; accessed
June 2005.

49. Data source on the Automotive Manufacturing Improvement Network of Alabama:
"Suppliers in Alabama Join Forces," *Automotive News,* November 15, 2004, available
online from the ABI/Inform Database; accessed June 2005.

50. Steve Sewell, as quoted in "Car Industry No Longer 'Fledgling' in Alabama," *Knight-
Ridder Tribune Business News,* May 9, 2004, p. 1, available online from the ABI/
Inform Database, accessed June 2005.

51. "Once a Backwater, Slovakia Surges," *New York Times,* December 28, 2004, p. W1.

52. Data sources: Felipe Larrain, Luis Lopez-Calva, and Andres Rodriguez-Clare, "Intel:
A Case Study of Foreign Direct Investment in Central America," Harvard Center for
International Development Working Paper no. 58, December 2000, p. 14, available
online at http://www.cid.harvard.edu; accessed October 2004; and U.N. Economic
Commission for Latin America and the Caribbean, *Economic Survey of Latin America
and the Caribbean, 1999–2000,* p. 181, available online at http://www.eclac.org;
accessed April 2005.

53. Larrain, Lopez-Calva, and Rodriguez-Clare, "Intel: A Case Study," p. 31.

54. Ibid., pp. 23, 5.

55. Ibid., p. 26.

56. U.N. Economic Commission for Latin America and the Caribbean, *Foreign Investment
in Latin America and the Caribbean,* 2003, pp. 17, 75–76, available online at http://
www.eclac.org; accessed April 2005.

57. "Work Force Training: Providing a Competitive Advantages for Expanding Companies," *Expansion Management,* August 15, 2004, available online at http://www.
expansionmanagement.com; accessed June 2005. The training program, part of
Alabama's two-year college system, had been ranked in the top ten of the magazine's
survey since 1997.

13

THE CASE AGAINST FOREIGN DIRECT INVESTMENT AND MULTINATIONAL CORPORATIONS

An objective and thorough evaluation of foreign direct investment (FDI) and multinational corporations (MNCs) must accept the qualification that neither phenomenon is in all ways and at all times economically and socially harmful in its impact. An unequivocally critical, thumbs-down evaluation arrives at a different conclusion: The available evidence categorically demonstrates that the negative effects of these international business phenomena dramatically outweigh their very meager benefits. Perceived net costs to the global commons are so great that a clear-cut policy recommendation easily follows. Governments should do what they are elected to do: run the country, promote the interests of the majority, and vigorously act to reduce if not eliminate the many harmful and inequitable effects of big multinational companies. What is best for society is to have the public sector ensure more equitable distributions of income and the benefits of globalization. The case against dismisses most of the arguments advanced in favor of FDI and MNCs as being either exaggerated, oversimplified, or factually inaccurate.

The principal purpose of this chapter is to distill the main arguments into a thorough and convincing case against MNCs and FDI as they currently operate. The objective is to showcase the many "reasonable" arguments supporting the view that society and governments are off-course in believing that markets, if left alone, will work wonders in broadly increasing the material well-being of the world's people and reduce poverty. As with chapter 12, this chapter has a subtle agenda. It is to implicitly advance the idea that when the one-sided arguments that follow are weighed against the contradictory one-sided arguments of the previous chapter, a relatively open-minded reader again should encounter hesitation and equivocation. Such a reader should entertain the thought that because both make some sense, choosing one as representing the absolute, stand-on-its-own version of the truth is a flawed approach. Introduction of doubt is a preliminary step to suggesting the attractions of an eclectic middle-ground analysis that emphasizes the need to appreciate the heterogeneity of the subject, the need to shun generalizations, and acceptance of the scarcity of absolute truths in an ocean of subjectivity.

As in the previous chapter, the contents of this chapter do not necessarily reflect the author's views, and individual assertions may or may not be backed up with what he regards as adequate evidence. The presentation should be considered the equivalent of a legal brief designed to interpret reality in a way that influences the opinions of those who read it. Although the most dubious, least substantiated condemnations have been excluded, this chapter as a whole is intended to be argumentative, not a demonstration of the scientific method at its most precise. The most important commonality of the individual arguments presented here is that each possesses sufficient credibility to preclude its being dismissed as patently untrue or irrelevant. The order in which the arguments are presented roughly follows a macro to micro sequence; order does not imply importance. Too much subjectivity and imprecision are involved to credibly argue that accurate weights can be assigned to each of the downsides cited.

The Inevitability of FDI-Induced Harm

An UNCTAD report makes the case succinctly and convincingly: "Not all FDI is . . . always and automatically in the best interest of host countries."[1] The accuracy of this statement begins with the larger truth that irreconcilable differences between nation-states and MNCs guarantee that their interests are not fully compatible. Profit maximization is inherently linked with maximization of efficiency but not necessarily maximization of national economic and social goals. Multinationals have no incentive to place the needs of host countries before their own. The inevitable result is that most FDI activity is either detrimental or of minimal value to the economic and social orders of the host. Furthermore, nothing in the relentless pursuit of growth and profits suggests that the majority of FDI activity is beneficial to home countries.

Companies, whether domestic or multinational, are not committed to treating any country as an equal partner in a common pursuit of financial gain. The people who run corporations are not hired and paid to be big picture–seeing altruists who put the public good of host and home countries ahead of the good of the company. Privately owned manufacturing corporations are neither charities, social services providers, nor regulated public utilities. They are established to reward the financial commitment made by their owner/investors by selling goods and services that the public needs and wants, not to champion social causes. An international consumer boycott and accusations of being baby killers were necessary to get Nestlé and other multinational producers of infant formula in the 1980s to address the health problems their products were causing in less developed countries (LDCs). Contaminated water and the absence of facilities to sterilize and refrigerate turned what was a safe product in the North into a dangerous substitute for breast milk in the South—although it remained legal to sell.[2] Press articles regularly report reluctance by automobile companies to issue voluntary recalls for defects not yet proven to be a *dire* safety risk. In the executive suite, the burden of proof is always on the employee who proposes doing something socially magnanimous but harmful to the bottom line.

Conscious commitment to putting the public good first is least likely to be found in corporations operating on a global basis. MNCs are not merely large versions of domestic corporations. They are huge organizations with unprecedented control over economic resources. They are not just business firms, but the most complex and most highly developed agents of world capitalism, operating in the most important branches and the most highly concentrated sectors of advanced economies.[3] In the opinion of the late Raymond Vernon, a distinguished early scholar in the field, "The multinational enterprise has come to be seen as the embodiment of almost anything disconcerting about modern industrial society." MNCs did not become magnets for criticism by chance or bad luck. As a rule, he felt they are "conspicuously well-endowed with money and knowledge; they are entrenched in industries difficult to enter; and they are viewed as foreigners in the eyes of most governments with which they deal." In Vernon's view, MNCs' presence in LDCs "has drawn the hostility of those eager to develop a strong national identity free of outside influence, those repelled by the costs of industrialization, those at war with capitalism as a system, and those distrustful of the politics of the rich industrialized states."[4] These feelings can be fully justified.

As corporations go global, their growing competitiveness and financial power weaken the institutional base of national economies. "This inhibits equity and legitimacy."[5] The mistaken belief that domestic investment cannot be equally effective as a means to promote development and increase jobs has caused the majority of the world's governments to opt for the short-sighted, quick-fix strategy of urging foreign companies to open subsidiaries. In bending over backward to ingratiate themselves with MNCs, government leaders regularly place foreign corporations' demands ahead of the needs of the citizens who elected them.

Because multinationals by definition move resources and do business on a global scale, they are "less concerned with advancing national goals than with pursuing objectives internal to the firm—principally growth, profits, proprietary technology, strategic alliances, return on investment, and market power."[6] "Stateless corporations have given rise to corporate states."[7] An inherent contradiction results from the desire of MNCs to integrate activities on a global basis with little regard for national borders while the people and government of a host country seek to integrate foreign subsidiaries in the best way possible into their national economy.[8] "If not adequately regulated, FDI can compound economic, financial, and social problems."[9] The problem is that adequate regulation is not always forthcoming. Many governments lack the ability to stand up to big foreign corporations and impose regulations compatible with national needs rather than the demands of these companies. If a government is too weak, out of touch, or corrupt to promote suitable policies, sovereignty will be no match for MNC power.[10] Ultimately, an assessment of the probable impact of MNCs on host countries turns on how effectively the government of the host country performs its role as maker of policy and defender of what it is judged to be the national interest.[11] Too often, that performance is ineffective.

Manipulation of transfer prices is a prime example of how corporate self-interest can surreptitiously siphon off benefits due to countries in which they are doing business. Internal accounting legerdemain allows MNCs to engage in a kind of high-tech tax evasion. Transfer prices refer to the prices that different units of the same business organization (for our purposes, a parent company and one of its overseas subsidiaries) charge one another for finished products, components, factory machinery, or services. Transactions between related parties do not typically follow the market-directed rules of arm's-length transactions between unrelated entities. Multinationals can establish internal costs that arbitrarily raise or lower transfer prices to minimize the amount of taxes or tariff duties owed to national governments.

Profits of a parent company can be enhanced simply by charging higher prices for goods and services sent to subsidiaries located in relatively high tax countries, thereby minimizing or eliminating the subsidiary's profits and thus reducing tax liabilities. If a subsidiary is operating in a low tax country, transfer price legerdemain would consist of charging it artificially low prices, thereby maximizing profits where they will be taxed least. National tax agencies are exercising increased vigilance to discourage manipulation of transfer prices, but outsiders probably will never be able to completely penetrate the caliginous haze that shrouds real costs within massive corporations conducting tens or hundreds of thousands of transactions annually among their subsidiaries in dozens of far-flung countries. This problem might explain why a private study found that subsidiaries of U.S. corporations operating in four major tax havens (the Netherlands, Ireland, Bermuda, and Luxembourg) had 46 percent of their profits in these four jurisdictions in 2001, but only 9 percent of their employees and just under 13 percent of their plant and equipment.[12]

Artificially low transfer prices can also be applied to shipments to subsidiaries in high tariff countries, thereby depriving importing countries of another form of revenue. Artificially high transfer prices invoiced by headquarters can also serve as a clandestine means of evading host government restrictions on the amount of profits that foreign subsidiaries can remit to their parents.

Corporate actions showing disdain for the interests of the host country are not always the subtle handiwork of the accounting department. The combination of anger, fear, and aggressiveness has led companies to intervene directly in the domestic political sphere. Information on the frequency of such behavior is hard to come by because shady activities involving political leaders and executives of foreign corporations are not conducted in public and not always exposed. One of the classic examples of this phenomenon, ITT's intervention in Chilean politics in the 1970s, is discussed shortly.

All things considered, questions are constantly and understandably raised about who controls MNCs and by what means. Their demonstrated capacity to harm the public's well-being makes them too dangerous to be left to their own devices. The idea that MNCs can police themselves is illusory, and the relatively new concept of corporate social responsibility is disingenuous. As a study by Christian Aid concluded, "While there are some companies that act responsibly much of the time, and many companies that act responsibly some of the time, the [corporate social responsibility] landscape is uneven." The organization has seen too many cases where the "rhetoric and the reality are simply contradictory." Because corporate social responsibility "can become mere a branch of PR," Christian Aid opined that self-policing of corporate promises of responsible and ethical behavior is a "completely inadequate response to the sometime devastating impact that multinational companies can have."[13] Harvard Business School Professor Michael Porter characterized corporate social responsibility as "a religion filled with priests, in which there is no need for evidence or theory. . . . It is all a defensive effort, a PR game in which companies primarily react to deal with the critics and the pressure from activists."[14] Many people believe that enlightened corporate statements notwithstanding, the dominant philosophy of business executives was perfectly summed up by Milton Friedman in 1970: "There is one and only one social responsibility of business—to use its resources and engage in activities designed to increase profits so long as it stays within the rules of the game."[15]

At the same time that harmful consequences of FDI and some of the duplicity by MNCs are part of the public record, the presumed economic benefits of concentrating production in the lowest-cost locations are another cruel deception. These benefits exist only in economics textbooks and corporate press releases. The consuming public at large should take with the proverbial grain of salt the claim that the increase in our material well-being over the past half-century is mostly attributable to the spread of MNCs. The growing domination of world markets by fewer and bigger companies with increasing power to set or influence market prices is at best a mixed blessing. Unless one has sold an MNC's stock at a profit, there is no way to unequivocally demonstrate that MNCs have been indispensable in raising living standards. Despite the efficiency hype from supporters of MNCs, no one has demonstrated that establishment of new foreign subsidiaries always or even mostly results in lower prices rather than bigger profit margins. Neither has it been proven that domestic companies on average could not have reached the same level of efficiency, or at least come close, as did incoming FDI.

MNCs Are Too Powerful and Inherently Anticompetitive

A common criticism of MNCs has always been that their very function is to make competition imperfect. By limiting the number of competitors in the market, they distort the economic process and obtain monopoly rents (excess profits) through dominant market shares. Their actions have made them "agents of a new mercantilism, which has historically tended toward some form of imperialism."[16] Big global companies may not have a conscious malign intent, but they cannot escape having a malign impact on the quest for greater economic good for the greater number. The outlook is for more of the same: increasing concentrations of market power in quasi-monopolistic MNCs that grow progressively larger in size, in part through a continuous series of cross-national mergers and acquisitions. Fewer MNCs "are gaining a large and rapidly increasing proportion of world economic resources, production, and market shares."[17] The most disquieting aspect of the bigness trend is the degree to which large and powerful MNCs increasingly dominate world markets in the strategic industrial sectors: telecommunications, information and software, electronics, machinery, automobiles, pharmaceuticals, mass media, and so on.

The downside of an international economic order dominated by large MNCs was first recognized in the 1960s by Stephen Hymer, a pioneer scholar in the field (see chapter 6). He foresaw what indeed has materialized: increasing worldwide asymmetries in the distribution of economic power and benefits. A system based on powerful global companies enjoying monopoly rents centralizes high-level corporate decision-making positions "in a few key cities in the advanced countries, surrounded by a number of regional sub-capitals, and confine the rest of the world to lower levels of activity and income.... Income, status, authority, and consumption patterns would radiate out from these centers along a declining curve, and the existing pattern of inequality would be perpetuated."[18] More recently, a labor union official suggested that the "benefits of the global economy are reaped disproportionately by the handful of countries and companies that set rules and shape markets."[19]

A large-scale MNC entering an average-sized host country market usually is able to parlay its financial and technological power and its management and marketing skills into an oligopolistic if not a monopolistic position in the local market. A highly competitive and ambitious MNC expands, structures, and confines the development of the host economy. It introduces new production, but may by this very act permit no other introduction of competing production. "Thus the normal constraints . . . of competition in products and prices may not be present."[20] Crowding out of domestic producers is a risk whenever incoming direct investment is in head-on competition with locals (i.e., when a foreign-controlled subsidiary is market-seeking rather than an efficiency-seeking export platform). Local firms have been driven out of business and new firms discouraged as the results of MNCs' being more efficient, having better access to financial resources, engaging in anticompetitive practices, or all three.[21] Crowding out can also occur when cash-rich MNCs offer higher salaries to lure the most productive workers away from locally owned businesses.

Another aspect of the anticompetitive bent of MNCs is their propensity to cartelize. The apex of international cartel behavior existed during the Depression years of the 1930s when sales and profits shrank and most governments looked the other way. Corporate efforts to control output and prices on a worldwide basis were concentrated in those raw materials and manufacturing sectors, for example, steel, chemicals, and aluminum, where the products were similar and the number of competing producers was limited. Collusion extended to mutual agreements on market share allocations and exporters charging the same prices in foreign markets as those agreed on by domestic producers.[22] In today's world, formal understandings are not an absolute prerequisite limiting competition across national borders. If three MNCs dominate the world market for a given product, three unilateral, uncoordinated decisions not to aggressively compete for market share through low prices become the economic equivalent of a cartel.

Low-Quality FDI Can Be Worse Than None at All

Advocates of multinationals like to talk about high quality incoming direct investment (see chapters 8, 12, and 14) that create good jobs and produce high-tech goods. By ignoring the (allegedly) greater preponderance of low quality direct investments that are more harmful than beneficial to host countries, advocates are telling only partial truths. First of all, a significant proportion of new FDI since the 1990s has been in the form of mergers and acquisitions, in which the initial effect is simply a transfer of ownership from a domestic to a foreign company. A capricious absentee landlord and a drain on the host country's foreign exchange holdings can easily negate the few to nonexistent positive effects of a foreign takeover. Second, foreign-owned subsidiaries often function as islands cut off from the mainland of the domestic business sector and devoid of linkages and knowledge spillovers.

Third, many jobs in foreign subsidiaries, especially in LDCs, are relatively dead-end, involving unskilled, low-paid, and monotonous work with no hope for advancement.

If incoming direct investment was guaranteed to produce positive externalities (for example, spillovers of technology and enhanced worker skills, and extensive linkages with local businesses), the prospect of anticompetitive tendencies and other negative effects would, in most cases, be a risk worth taking. That these externalities may never materialize can be seen in the case of the Irish economy, one of the great success stories from inward FDI. The links between foreign subsidiaries and local businesses were virtually nonexistent until the government came to the realization in the 1980s that indigenous high-tech export-oriented firms were not emerging and there was no indication that the presence of growing FDI would inspire creation of any in the foreseeable future. All signs pointed to the government giving too much preference and assistance to foreign MNCs and ignoring indigenous businesses.[23] Today, spillover and linkage effects are better, but still limited mainly to low-end support industries. By way of example, locally owned printing plants have increased in great number in response to the demand by U.S. software firms for instruction manuals. "On the whole, the belief that competition would whip native industries into shape has not been sustained. Instead, it has snuffed them out."[24] Ireland is at risk for becoming overly dependent on the kindness of foreigners.

The lack of a spillover effect by foreign-owned automobile assembly plants in Mexico further demonstrates how MNCs and local business can live in two separate worlds. Despite being in Mexico for forty years, foreign automobile plants reportedly have generated relatively little business for local suppliers and have not transmitted much technological know-how. The Volkswagen plant there stresses the point that it buys 60 percent of its parts domestically, but the "local" suppliers are virtually all foreign-owned and import most of the materials they use. "In spite of the fact that Mexico has been host to many car plants, we don't know how to build a car," said a local academic.[25]

To dramatize the potential for low quality FDI to unleash massive harm, let us imagine a bad news scenario of a new foreign-owned manufacturing subsidiary whose multiple deleterious economic effects so clearly exceed its benefits that the host country clearly would have been better off without it. This hypothetical investment from hell is born as an acquisition of a local producer of toiletries and cosmetics, so no net increase in production results. The takeover is financed by borrowing from a local bank, the parent company having been able to get favorable loan terms on the basis of its excellent global credit rating. No foreign exchange flows in. Less capital is available for lending by the banking system to indigenous businesses and entrepreneurs.

No new jobs are created. In fact, many existing ones are lost. In connection with implementation of the parent's lean production techniques, up to one-third of the acquired company's labor force is summarily dismissed. Most if not all senior executives and top managers are replaced with expatriates from corporate headquarters. Workers who remain are told that if they do not meet higher assigned production quotas, they will also be heading out the door—and that they should not even think about trying to unionize. Those that stay may be taught to use more sophisticated machinery, but their job skills are not significantly enhanced. They remain assembly line workers knowing only how to turn out endless batches of bath soap and lipstick.

Pricing strategy finds the "sweet spot" that allows output to be sold below the prices of domestic competitors but still earn a modest profit. This is only a temporary business strategy. The foreign company's long-term plan is to become a quasi-monopolist, raising prices after a sufficient number of local competitors are driven out of the market by the combination of clever advertising of a world-class brand name and low prices. Marketing will be aggressive enough to discourage local entrepreneurs from entering the market and providing new competition.

Profits notwithstanding, the new foreign subsidiary differs from the domestically owned company that was acquired in that it pays no corporate income taxes. This is the result of its being granted a tax holiday by the host government as an inducement to make the investment. Once this exemption ends, the MNC plans to use transfer prices (see previous discussion) to produce paper losses for its subsidiary in the host country. Profits earned by the subsidiary in question will be booked to a subsidiary in a country with lower taxes. At least one of the newly retooled plants will increase water pollution levels. Contingency plans call for any efforts by the host government to tighten regulation of the subsidiary to be rebuffed by a carrot-and-stick strategy. Campaign contributions to influential politicians will be made simultaneously with threats to close the local plant(s).

Further economic harm comes in the form of adverse effects on the host country's balance of payments. Although no capital flowed in to pay for the initial investment, the foreign company regularly remits profits to headquarters in lieu of reinvesting to expand or upgrade the subsidiary. It regularly imports raw materials, intermediate goods, assembly line machinery, and business services, having determined that local suppliers cannot meet its demanding requirements. The subsidiary does not export. The aggregate result is a drain on the host country's limited foreign exchange earnings that might otherwise have been spent on imports needed to meet basic human needs and promote economic development. A low-income country should not be forced to freeze or cut back on imports and internal investment to export capital to cash-rich parent companies in affluent industrialized countries.

As harmful and unappealing as a manufacturing subsidiary with this profile would be to a host country's economy, it is not an absolute worst-case scenario. A more definitive version of the ultimate undesirable incoming direct investment would be an amoral foreign mining company truly adroit at bribing government officials (a profile that a cynic would say excludes only a very few multinational mining and petroleum companies). On day one, it begins secretly depositing vast sums in the offshore bank accounts of the host country's top leaders. In return, the foreign company's subsidiary is allowed to pay well below-market value royalties for the ores or oil it recovers. It also receives quiet assurance that environmental protection laws will not be vigorously applied to its local mining or oil drilling operations. After denuding the countryside of its mineral riches, the MNC quickly removes its equipment and personnel, leaving the locals to deal with the negative spillovers of land ravaged from open pit mining, water pollution, depleted natural resources, and so on. Spillovers of knowledge and technology to the host country are nil, as are lasting benefits.

Neither Fairness nor More Efficiency

Workers have waged an uphill, largely unsuccessful battle since the Industrial Revolution for an equitable share of the income generated from their physical efforts. As noted in chapter 5, the estimated gap has grown to the point where the average U.S. corporate president earns in just one business day what the average rank-and-file worker earns in an entire year. The globalization of production has dealt a serious setback to this struggle by further shifting the balance of power in favor of the corporation. For many years, the average manufacturing company has enjoyed greater mobility in moving across national borders than labor. More recently, progress in technology, reduced communications and transportation costs, and the knowledge-intensive nature of the information technology sector have made it even easier and less expensive for medium and large corporations to relocate factories and service facilities to lower cost countries. Another recent trend is the increasing ease with which MNCs that become dissatisfied with wage rates or governmental regulation in one country can find qualified labor in another country willing to do the same work for less money, another government willing to impose fewer restrictions, or both.

The MNC has corrupted the core dilemma of economic policy: finding the optimal trade-off between pursuit of fairness (equity) and efficiency. The growing trend to transferring production to subsidiaries in lower cost/lower wage countries reduces labor's share, already too small in the eyes of most people, of the economic pie. However, the new workforce will be less, or at best equally, productive compared to the workers they replaced. Efficiency in the narrow sense of the term has not been increased; instead, the reduction in salary outlays exceeded the decline in productivity in the newly opened foreign subsidiary. A huge question is how the MNC responds to the bonanza it gets from reduced production costs. It has two options: lower prices or generate higher profit margins and greater rewards to shareholders (through higher stock prices and increased dividends). The consensus answer is that in most cases, prices remain unchanged and profits rise.

The growing propensity of production lines being shifted to lower cost countries, sometimes in connection with financial incentives being provided by the new host country, is best described as a "ratcheting down to the bottom."[26] As a result of their denouncing a race to the bottom that does not literally exist, some of the more strident critics of globalization are often summarily dismissed; this does a disservice to the genuine plight of relatively well-paid production line workers. Attention is diverted from the fact that the negotiating position of factory workers at MNCs is deteriorating badly. They face unprecedented threats to job security, salaries, and retirement benefits as companies use their mobility advantage to find ever cheaper labor in the far corners of the world.

Sometimes a company does not physically transfer an assembly line to another country, but workers still suffer economic setbacks. De facto ratcheting down occurs when a company demands that its production workers "voluntarily" agree to givebacks in the form of lower wages, increased hours worked, stricter work rules, or all of the above. This demand is backed up by management explaining how increasing competitive pressures leave it no alternative to move production to another country unless it can reduce labor costs.

The increasing frequency with which manufacturing companies move their subsidiaries to another country is eroding a classic argument about the relative attractiveness of FDI inflows as long-term commitments. Permanence is no longer a sure thing, and their longevity premium over shorter term, more volatile capital flows like bank borrowing and foreign portfolio investment has started to erode. Prosperity based on the presence of MNCs has become hostage to a self-absorbed movable beast. A global jobs auction is now under way. MNCs "are, in effect, conducting a peripatetic global jobs competition, awarding shares of production to those who make the highest bids."[27]

The full human toll from MNCs' increasing mobility is unknown because a complete count cannot be made of instances where production continued uninterrupted after workers quietly capitulated to management ultimatums and accepted reduced incomes and benefits. Even if the percentage of workers hurt by this trend is a relatively small percentage of the total workforce, the absolute numbers appear to be growing, and little or nothing is being done to give comfort to or diminish the injury of the many workers whose jobs and earning power have been and will be adversely affected.[28] The intensifying need to placate the demands of MNCs is curtailing government's ability to respond to the plight of the unemployed with increased spending. "Just when working people most need the nation-state as a buffer from the world economy, it is abandoning them."[29]

Workers in the more industrialized countries of Western Europe have achieved the highest average levels of salaries, job security, vacation time, and social benefits ever measured. The quality of life attained by skilled workers in the industrial sectors of those countries has come to symbolize the magnificent possibilities of capitalism with a heart. The bounty of the economic system tipped in favor of the working majority. However, believers in the Marxist view on exploitation of the masses may yet have the last laugh. The writing on the wall becomes clearer every day: Labor's share of national income and its leisure time appear to have peaked and regressed well into the early stages of decline. The main cause: the ratcheting down syndrome. Europeans feel no guilt for enjoying the good life and believe they deserve to retain it. The fact is that they "have gained politically and socially what many Americans say they want ... but have been unable to achieve politically. Americans, too, would like to have employment security, more flexibility, more leisure, fewer worries about health care and pensions."[30]

Germany is the best example of globalization's tightening squeeze on European labor. Absorbing what are widely regarded as the world's most expensive labor costs has not prevented the country's major manufacturers from continuing to be world-class competitors and the backbone of the country's long-running trade surplus. Despite its much smaller economy, Germany passed the United States in 2003 to become the world's largest exporter of goods. The workers' skills and relatively high productivity notwithstanding, time seems to be running out on the quality of life achievements of the German labor movement. Large employers are avidly exploiting new opportunities for reduced costs and increased profit margins in Central Europe. The average cost of wages and benefits paid to relatively skilled labor in Hungary, Poland, the Czech Republic, and Slovakia is estimated to be as low as one-sixth of the equivalent German rate when longer work weeks are included in the comparison. Now that these countries are members of the European Union, they have become ideal locations for efficiency-seeking FDI, more specifically export platforms for industrial shipments to Western Europe.

Central Europe is to German workers as Mexico is to American workers: They are the lower wage neighbors whose workers are highly productive when placed in a foreign subsidiary with state of the art technology and managerial supervision from the parent company. Factory workers in Germany and the United States have been hard hit, more than in any other country, by domestic corporations building a growing percentage of their new plants in other countries and switching existing production to a subsidiary in a lower cost country. "All new [automobile] plants built in Europe will be built in Central or Eastern Europe," the chairman of French auto giant Renault was quoted as saying.[31] The setbacks suffered by German workers are easily demonstrated by the series of concessions made by their unions in 2004 in return for job security. Across-the-board givebacks to the electronics giant Siemens by the powerful union IG Metall were the most dramatic. In return for the company's agreement not to shift mobile phone production for at least two years from two German plants to Hungary, the workers in these plants will work an additional five hours a week (from thirty-five to forty hours) at no increase in pay, which equates to a cut in the hourly wage rate. In addition, downward adjustments were made in Christmas bonuses and vacation pay.

Less dramatic concessions (effectively wage freezes) were granted later in the year to DaimlerChrysler and Volkswagen, in both cases to defuse their threats of shifting production eastward. Workers at a GM Opel plant in Germany agreed in early 2005 to reductions in scheduled future wage increases and more flexible working hours; this was the price of convincing GM to build new models of Opel and Saab in the German plant rather than at its subsidiary in Sweden. An educated guess about future labor-management trends in Germany and elsewhere in Western Europe is that the givebacks of 2004 are the wave of the future.

Second-tier wage countries in Europe enjoy no immunity from the FDI ratcheting down process. When Volkswagen announced in late 2002 that it intended to lay off 500 of the 5,000 workers at its assembly plant in Pamplona, Spain, the five unions representing workers at the plant initially took a hard-line position in opposition. They soon became more conciliatory in response to the advice of a senior union official at the carmaker's main plant in Germany. Wages for workers at the Spanish plant were well below their German counterparts but more than double those in Slovakia, where the company had been expanding manufacturing capacity. An overly rigid position, the union official warned, would likely result in management shifting significant production from Spain to the east. Several weeks later, the Pamplona workers accepted a 5 percent pay cut, and VW canceled the layoffs. In the age of globalization, the union official later lamented, "one has to be willing to go in a different direction."[32] Only a few years earlier, winning this sort of concession would have been unthinkable for most Western European companies. European unions had long waged a bitter fight against even modest givebacks to employers while demanding and winning pay raises and shorter work weeks.[33]

The ratcheting down process started in the high-wage countries but is now in full swing in moderate-income countries. Foreign subsidiaries have already begun abandoning Mexico and Central Europe in the continuing move down-market to still lower wage countries. In the process, Hungary and the Czech Republic have become giant intake and outtake conduits for FDI. At the same time that MNCs are being attracted to Central Europe, others are closing subsidiaries they established just a few years earlier and heading east, mainly to China, in search of even lower wage/lower cost locations.[34] Flextronics, a multinational electronic manufacturing services company under contract to assemble the Microsoft Xbox game player, originally opted to assemble it in Hungary. Not quite a year into production, it shut down the production line and moved it to southern China, where the wages were considerably lower. In yet another example of the need to avoid overgeneralization and look at facts on a case-by-case basis, employment in Flextronics' Hungarian plant remained steady in the early 2000s. Ironically, it was partly due to a new contract for final assembly of TV sets made by a Chinese company, presumably for sale in Europe.[35]

A prime example of ratcheting down is the automobile wire harness industry, which binds wires that deliver electrical current to accessories like headlights and power windows. The first stage of production migration went from the United States to Mexico. Then, as automobile assemblers intensified demands on their suppliers for periodic price reductions, the labor-intensive assembly of wire harness in Mexico began looking expensive to some of the companies that had relocated there. The second wave of migration commenced when they began moving subsidiaries to lower wage Honduras and still lower wage China; the result has been a decline in Mexico's share of exports of the product to the U.S. market.

Declining wire harness production is only one small part of the larger trend of foreign companies abandoning Mexico for a lower rung on the international income hierarchy. In 2002 alone, an estimated 200,000-plus manufacturing jobs were lost in that country. The principal cause was the departure of more than 300 plants, mostly U.S.-owned export platforms known as maquiladoras that had been engaged in labor-intensive work. Once again, the most frequent destination was China, where total production costs were low enough to offset its greater distance from the American market.[36] "Mexican workers are in the untenable position of not earning enough for a good life, but too much for job security. It's a treadmill that's trapping developing countries as they struggle to keep what had been Americans' jobs."[37] Another strain on the already inadequate social safety net in Mexico will result from the multiyear staged reductions in corporate income tax rates that began in 2005, part of an effort to make the country more business-friendly.

Ultimately, the effect of ratcheting down is to further reduce labor's share of total income and further increase the already unequal distribution of income. "A world in which the assets of the 200 richest people are greater than the combined income of the more than 2 billion people at the other end of the economic ladder should give everyone pause," wrote a U.S. union official.[38]

An Open Door to FDI Can and Does Threaten Self-Determination

MNCs are the main reason that a globalized economy distributes most of its benefits to a small, already wealthy minority, leaving the majority helplessly to cope with the harm and disadvantages inherent in MNCs. At some point in every country, incoming FDI becomes excessive—it crosses a line at which point it begins inflicting an unhealthy loss of economic autonomy on the host and begins handing foreign investors an unhealthy degree of influence over the country's economic future. The excessive power accruing to the big multinationals inevitably comes at the expense of the public good and democratic principles. Critics have warned that gigantic corporations, answerable only to themselves, are pushing societies into an amorphous, disenfranchised mass in which individuals and groups lose control over their own lives and are subjugated to these firms' exploitive activities.[39]

Western Europe and Canada became sensitive in the 1960s to the possibility of suffering an intolerable and irreversible loss of control over their economic destinies after watching waves of American MNCs enter and become critical components of their domestic economies. Both went through long periods of angst in an unsuccessful effort to find cost-effective ways of capping this growing dependence. Although they never imposed formal barriers, their disquiet persists today, especially in sectors like mass media that are perceived to threaten a nation's cultural heritage.

Japan and Korea took a far more restrictive stance against incoming FDI in the post–World War II period. In a word, they effectively banned it in the belief that it came with too many harmful strings attached. Neither suffered significant economic harm by doing so, relying instead on domestic saving and borrowed foreign capital to finance very high rates of domestic investment. Industrialization was successfully carried out by national champions, members of keiretsu groups in Japan and chaebols in Korea.

Japan expressly excluded majority-owned foreign investment, with only a few exceptions until the 1970s, when intense pressure from the United States led to a reluctant, gradual easing of barriers to FDI. Japanese economic planners worried that the presence of foreign companies would interfere too much with their grand design for economic recovery. The consensus view was that foreigners could never understand and accept the unique rules of the Japanese version of capitalism, especially the unwritten but rigid mutual obligations of the government–business relationship. If foreign companies wanted to profit from Japan's economic recovery, they were required to do so in a passive manner that did nothing to interfere with economic self-determination. They had to team with a local partner owning at least 50 percent of a joint venture or license their technology to a Japanese company.

Prior to an about-face in attitude in 1998 forced by the Asian financial crisis and its aftermath,

> The general fear of Korean industries being dominated by foreign entities—a fear deeply rooted in memories of Japan's colonization from 1910 to 1945—was too widespread inside Korea for the government to accommodate foreign management. Even today, there is a lingering suspicion that FDI is really just a means for foreigners to control Korean industries.[40]

Americans long viewed this foreign trepidation and resentment as overly emotional, unsophisticated xenophobia. By the late 1980s, however, many Americans familiar with FDI issues had adopted the same stance, never mind the large size of the U.S. GDP relative to the inflow and the continuing U.S. status as the largest outward direct investor by a wide margin. The catalyst triggering the sudden outbreak of not unfounded American fears of excessive loss of economic autonomy was the surge in FDI by Japan, much of which consisted of acquisitions. The country was widely viewed as unfairly having tens of billions of dollars to invest in the United States by virtue of being an adversarial trading partner that restricted imports, aggressively pushed exports, and did not allow foreign takeovers of Japanese companies. The Japanese encouraged further resentment by developing an infatuation with trophy acquisitions (Rockefeller Center, two Hollywood movie studios, Pebble Beach Golf Club, and so on).

All things considered, some thoughtful Americans felt the volume of FDI inflows in the 1980s was excessive even for the world's largest national economy. For example, there was the warning, "The heaviest price paid by Americans is the loss of a measure of political independence. The political activity generated by foreign investors becomes more visible daily."[41] The presumably internationalist associate editor of the journal *Foreign Policy* worried that

> Foreigners with fistfuls of devalued dollars now comb America for banks, businesses, factories, land, and securities. . . . The most pervasive concern about foreign investment is that it will reduce America's economic and political autonomy. . . . Particularly worrisome is the growing reliance of American high-tech start-up companies on foreign partners for cash and manufacturing expertise. The quid pro quo is usually a transfer of new technologies to the foreign investors, creating future competitors.[42]

Those who believe history repeats itself were in their element in June 2005, when two closely timed announcements from China triggered a visceral American reaction poignantly encapsulated by the *Wall Street Journal* headline "China Inc. Looks Set to Outdo Old Japan Inc."[43] A Chinese appliance maker announced a cash bid for Maytag, and a Chinese oil company (partly owned by the Chinese government) announced its intention to take control of Unocal Corporation, an American oil company. The latter takeover proposal created the image in many Americans' minds of the new owners diverting petroleum from American SUVs to Chinese military vehicles. Public opinion was further agitated by the (correct) belief that increased FDI inflows from and acquisitions by China were facilitated by its enormous bilateral trade surplus with the United States. Furthermore, many Americans believed the bilateral surplus to largely be the result of China's unfair trading practices and maintenance of an undervalued exchange rate to enhance its already formidable competitiveness. Even more serious, some Americans worried that Chinese outward FDI would help finance its long-term foreign policy agenda of diminishing the U.S. role as an Asian power.

MNCs are the cat's paw of globalization's threat to cultural autonomy. Mass media, food, clothing, and restaurant companies, mainly from the United States, have bulldozed a lot of people from other countries into adopting tastes and lifestyle preferences of an alien, highly materialistic society. National cultures and values are being diluted on a worldwide basis to an unprecedented extent. Simmering resentment to the perceived Americanization of the planet was demonstrated by José Bové, a French farmer-activist whose anger (and flair for publicity) impelled him to wreck a local McDonald's restaurant. His actions were wrong, but he spoke for a rising frustration abroad when he denounced the company as a symbol of the "standardization of food" and a general indicator of what was wrong with the world. To him, the Golden Arches "represents globalization, multinationals, and the power of the market. Then it stands for industrially produced food bad for traditional farmers and bad for your health."[44]

Case Studies: Extractive MNCs Are Still Masters of Bad Corporate Citizenship

Not even the most ardent supporter of FDI and MNCs can excuse the malodorous record of harm these companies have inflicted on host countries by natural resource–extractive companies. These kinds of subsidiaries have been caught in unethical, illegal, and harmful acts in numbers far greater than their share of total global direct investment. With geology dictating where they invest overseas, they do not have the option of shopping for a pleasant investment climate as do their relatively refined counterparts in the manufacturing and services sectors. To protect their mining and cultivation rights, they have frequently intimidated and bribed relatively weak, inexperienced third world governments. If bribes are used to secure sweetheart deals consisting of below-market royalty payments and re-duced corporate taxes, the inhabitants of poor countries are denied the full benefits of what usually are nonrenewable sources of national wealth. The public good is also harmed if MNC payments to officials' offshore bank accounts buy exemptions from compliance with local environmental protection laws.

The long historical record of misdeeds by primary sector subsidiaries inspired and sustains the criticism that MNCs make no effort to promote democracy or protect human rights. They rebuff this criticism with the hollow claim that they need to respect national sovereignty and follow the rules of operation laid down by governments, whether democratically elected or authoritarian regimes of the right and left. Though literally true, this defense omits reference to their efforts to topple governments when respect for the sanctity of national sovereignty is inconvenient.

In an admirably dispassionate historical study of MNC operations in devel-oping countries, Daniel Litvin is less critical than resigned to what he views as something akin to congenital misconduct by foreign-owned extractive companies operating in LDCs. He writes that the complexity of the relationships suggests a systemic problem, an apparent outgrowth of the "inherent limits to the capacity of large multinationals to manage social and political issues in developing countries effectively." Repeatedly and in a pattern "too pronounced to be coincidental . . . multinationals have exercised their power in unplanned, unsophisticated, or self-defeating ways."[45]

Historically, extractive MNCs have been the ones most frequently caught contravening local laws and interfering in the domestic political affairs of the host country. The United Fruit Company was an indirect participant in the 1954 overthrow of the democratically elected president of Guatemala, Jacobo Arbenz. Fearful that some of the company's vast property would be expropriated as part of a land reform program, senior executives of United Fruit fanned the flames of fear in the U.S. government that the overtly left-leaning Arbenz administration would lead to the spread of communism in Central America. The company then quietly aided and abetted a CIA operation that culminated in a successful military coup restoring right-wing leadership. United Fruit won the battle but lost the war. Over the long term, its power over the Guatemalan government waned. Disclosure of its role in the toppling of the government permanently tarnished the company's reputation, and it is still linked to the decades of low-intensity civil war in Gua-temala that were unleashed by the coup.[46]

Another example of MNC interference with national sovereignty unfolded in 1960 shortly after the country then known as the Congo received its indepen-dence from Belgium. Union Minerè literally financed the brief secession of Katanga, the province where its massive mining operations in copper, uranium, and cobalt were located. Fearful of an upsurge in nationalism and the spread of political chaos in a country ill-prepared for a smooth transition to statehood, the company diverted its considerable tax payments from the national government to the much friendlier and protective provincial government.[47]

A more recent case study of an MNC plotting the overthrow of a government it found inconvenient involved ITT Corporation, a U.S.-based services conglomerate. The drama began in 1970, when the company decided it needed to protect its Chilean telephone business from the perceived threat of nationalization. It first actively sought to thwart the election of Salvador Allende, a Marxist, as president, and then after he was elected, to engineer his ouster. In the process, ITT not only engaged in a variety of illegal and unethical in-country activities on its own against Allende the candidate, but also urged the Nixon administration to impose economic sanctions against Allende's administration and the CIA to engage in disruptive clandestine activities against the regime.[48] Later, an internally inspired military coup resulted in Allende's death. ITT may have won the battle but it lost the war. The company never fully dispelled suspicions in the United States, Chile, and elsewhere that it was involved in Allende's demise.[49] Once again, it was a case of corporate malevolence creating a situation in which all concerned parties were hurt.

A corporate public relations offensive continues to trumpet the theme that big business has accepted the need to act in a more socially responsible manner—because it is the right thing to do, and a negative public image is bad for business. The image of kinder, gentler CEOs has created a widespread impression that the insensitive, swashbuckling mindset epitomized by extractive MNCs is over. This image is inconsistent with the facts. Despite learning from history that efforts to topple host governments tend to be bad for business and despite sincere efforts by some companies to be guided by the corporate social responsibility ethic, reports of injurious and/or callous behavior continue unabated. The prolonged pollution in Indonesia traced to Newmont Mining Corporation was described in chapter 8. Shell oil company in 2005 was still dealing with a public relations disaster created by the widespread perception that it has been a co-conspirator, along with the government of Nigeria, in the persecution of people living in the oil-rich regions of that country. Indigenous peoples have been brutally suppressed by the Nigerian army when complaining about the water and land pollution caused by oil drilling and about their not receiving an equitable share of the royalties paid by the oil companies. After investigating the situation, a nongovernmental organization (NGO) concluded, "Acknowledging the difficult context of oil operations in Nigeria does not . . . absolve the oil companies from responsibility for the human rights abuses taking place in the Niger Delta: whether by action or omission they play a role."[50]

Turning to Latin America, a question can be raised: Are multinational mining companies helping reduce poverty in Peru? Not according to a study by Christian

Aid. The economic benefits currently being provided to Peruvians by FDI in mining often accrue to the already well-off and "are easily outweighed by the high costs borne by the poor. Rather than reducing poverty, the evidence suggest that mining many be entrenching it" through greater pollution, land seizures, and reduced education and health care services in the remote villages where mining is concentrated. Policy changes, including reduced corporate taxes, over the past decade have been successful in attracting multinational mining companies to Peru, but they "have not led to improvements in the lives of the rural poor who have to live near the mines."[51]

Oil and other natural resource–producing MNCs can indirectly contribute to economic malaise in a host country even if they are paying a fair price for extracted natural resources. The ultimate benefits of resource-seeking FDI are only partially determined by the monetary value of the hard currency royalties generated by exports. The principal variable is how effectively the government spends the revenues generated. The record here is not good. Some observers have suggested, with only slight exaggeration, that oil and other valuable raw materials have been a curse to those countries receiving large amounts of royalty payments for them. The inflow of financial riches seems to encourage national laxity and overconfidence, insufficient financial controls, corruption, and wasteful spending in these countries far more than economic development and poverty reduction (see chapter 8).

Offshoring: The Newest Phase of the Disenfranchisement of the Majority

The latest socially disruptive by-product of the twin trends of constant change in technology and the constant ratcheting down of working-class leverage in dealing with management is *offshoring*.[52] This term does not yet have a single, universally accepted definition. It is used here to describe the business strategy of transferring the work done by relatively high-skilled, high-paid *service* employees in industrialized countries to workers with comparable skills and education in LDCs whose salaries are significantly less. The new workers can be employed at an overseas subsidiary of the MNC doing the layoffs or at a locally owned business services firm, most likely located in India or the Philippines.

Technological progress in computing power and telecommunications has transformed an increasing number of service jobs from nontradable sectors to tradable ones; in short, a steady array of service jobs are joining manufactured goods in becoming vulnerable to foreign competition. With an ever-increasing amount of business activity being digitalized and with the growing availability of well-educated, English-speaking, relatively low-wage workers overseas, hundreds of millions of new workers have been added to the global labor pool. In some respects, the growing offshoring of jobs is merely another phase of companies concentrating economic activity in the lowest cost location as they seek an ever-increasing level of efficiency in using the world's limited resources. Offshoring might have remained just a footnote in the larger trade policy debate if the movement of jobs from the United States and Western Europe had stopped at what might be described as its first phase. No big political backlash resulted from the initial overseas transfer of lower skilled services jobs, mainly rote data entry of credit card and mortgage applications, the writing of long, elementary software code, and call centers answering customer questions. The political firestorm began as the quantity and quality of services jobs being exported increased.

The real meaning of offshoring is that the relatively few owners of capital and corporate executives have reached another milestone in their efforts to give themselves more money by giving less to the working majority. In the services sector as in manufacturing, if a company switches production to a lower cost locale overseas, it has the choice of increasing its profit margin or passing the savings on to consumers via lower prices. When it comes to allocating the financial gains from offshoring, look for corporate greed, especially among U.S. MNCs, to select the profit-enhancement option. Offshoring is just another way for international business to communicate the message to workers that they are losing the right to rising incomes and job security. Only executives and shareholders are guaranteed benefits from the globalization of production. When the high-skill jobs of software engineers, radiologists, architects, legal and financial researchers, accountants, and tax professionals can be done more cheaply overseas and with no precipitous drop in quality, incomes and standards of living in relatively affluent countries are at greater risk than ever before. New York Senator Charles Schumer coauthored an op-ed article in the *New York Times* in which he expressed concern that the United States might be "entering a new economic era in which American workers will face direct global competition at almost every job level. . . . American jobs are being lost not to competition from foreign companies, but to multinational corporations, often with American roots, that are cutting costs by shifting operations to low-wage countries."[53]

One of the reasons that long-term predictions about the number of service jobs moving offshore are especially tricky is that a small self-correcting element may come into play. If and when offshoring begins to destroy the jobs of economists, corporate public relations flacks, and general purpose intellectuals, the ranks of supporters for a hands-off approach to MNCs and liberal trade will be decimated, and the ranks of opponents will swell in number. Sooner or later, a broad-based political backlash against job insecurity will rebalance the corporate-dominated economic order.

Postscript

The reader is reminded that this chapter, like the previous one, is designed to present the most convincing, credible case possible for one side of an ambiguous and contentious issue. Although no factually untrue statements were knowingly made, the arguments presented herein do not necessarily represent the author's views. The data advanced in support of these arguments do not necessarily meet the author's standards of full academic rigor.

Notes

1. UNCTAD, *World Investment Report 1999*, p. 155, available online at http://www.unctad.org; accessed November 2004.
2. Kathryn Sikkink, "Codes of Conduct for Transnational Corporations: The Case of the WHO/UNICEF Code," *International Organization*, autumn 1986, pp. 820–21.
3. Volker Bornschier, "Multinational Corporations in World System Perspective," in Wolfgang Mommsen and Jurgen Osterhammel, eds., *Imperialism and After—Continuities and Discontinuities* (Boston: Allen and Unwin, 1986), p. 243.
4. Raymond Vernon, *Storm over the Multinationals—The Real Issues* (Cambridge, MA: Harvard University Press, 1977), pp. 19, 27, 145–46.
5. Dani Rodrik, "Governance of Economic Globalization," in Joseph Nye Jr. and John Donohue, eds., *Governance in a Globalizing World* (Washington, DC: Brookings Institution Press, 2000), p. 348.
6. U.S. Congress, Office of Technology Assessment, *Multinationals and the National Interest: Playing by Different Rules* (Washington, DC: U.S. Government Printing Office, 1993), pp. 1–2.
7. Maude Barlow, as quoted in Robin Broad, ed., *Global Backlash* (Lanham, MD: Rowman and Littlefield, 2002), p. 43.
8. Stephen D. Krasner, *Structural Conflict: The Third World against Global Liberalism* (Berkeley: University of California Press, 1985), p. 179.
9. Oxfam International, "The Emperor's New Clothes," Briefing Paper no. 46, 2003, p. 8, available online at http://www.oxfam.org; accessed January 2005.
10. David Fieldhouse, "A New Imperial System? The Role of the Multinational Corporations Reconsidered," in Wolfgang Mommsen and Jurgen Osterhammel, eds., *Imperialism and After—Continuities and Discontinuities* (London: Allen and Unwin, 1986), p. 234.
11. Ibid.
12. Steven Rattner, "Why Companies Pay Less," *Washington Post*, May 18, 2004, p. A19, quoting a study conducted by Tax Notes.
13. Christian Aid, "Behind the Mask—The Real Face of CSR," 2004, available online at http://www.christian-aid.co.uk; accessed May 2005.

14. European Business Forum, "CSR—A Religion with Too Many Priests? Michael Porter," EBF Debates, 15, 2003, available online at http://www.ebfonline.com/at_forum/at_forum.asp?id=421&linked=418; accessed June 2005.

15. As quoted in Michael Hoffman and Jennifer Moore, eds., *Business Ethics: Readings and Cases in Corporate Morality* (New York: McGraw-Hill, 1984), p. 157.

16. Fieldhouse, "A New Imperial System?," p. 236.

17. Martin Khor, "Globalization and the South: Some Critical Issues," UNCTAD Discussion Paper no. 147, April 2000, p. 4, available online at http://www.unctad.org/en/docs/dp_147.en.pdf; accessed September 2004.

18. As quoted in Fieldhouse, "A New Imperial System?," p. 228.

19. Jay Mazur, "Labor's New Internationalism," *Foreign Affairs*, January/February 2000, p. 80.

20. Henry J. Steiner and Detlev F. Vagts, *Transnational Legal Problems*, 2nd ed. (Mineola, NY: Foundation Press, 1976), p. 1185.

21. UNCTAD, *World Investment Report 2003*, p. 105.

22. Geoffrey Jones, *The Evolution of International Business* (London: Routledge, 1996), p. 124.

23. Eileen Doherty, "Evaluating FDI-Led Development: The Celtic (Paper?) Tiger," 1998, p. 6, available online at http://www.ciaonet.org; accessed November 2004.

24. Ibid., pp. 9, 12.

25. Tina Rosenberg, "So Far, Globalization Has Failed the World's Poor," *New York Times Magazine*, August 18, 2002, p. 32.

26. I learned this term from Steven Beckman, director of the Governmental and International Affairs Department, United Automobile Workers.

27. William Greider, *One World, Ready or Not—The Manic Logic of Global Capitalism* (New York: Simon and Schuster, 1997), p. 82.

28. Lori G. Kletzer, "Globalization and Job Loss, from Manufacturing to Services," *Economic Perspectives*, Federal Reserve Bank of Chicago, Second Quarter, 2005, p. 45.

29. Ethan B. Kapstein, "Workers and the World Economy," *Foreign Affairs*, May/June 1996, p. 16.

30. Peter Meiksins and Peter Whalley, "Should Europe Work More, or America Less?," *International Herald Tribune*, August 11, 2004, available online at http://www.iht.com; accessed August 2004.

31. "Detroit East," *Business Week*, July 25, 2005, p. 49.

32. Neal Boudette, "As Jobs Head East in Europe, Power Shifts away from Unions," *Wall Street Journal*, March 11, 2004, p. 1.

33. Ibid.

34. See, for example, "A Chill Wind Blows from the East," *Business Week*, September 1, 2003, p. 44.

35. "Hungary Eager and Uneasy over New Status," *New York Times*, March 5, 2004, p. W1.

36. See, for example, Asian Development Bank Institute Discussion Paper no. 17, November, 2004, p. 3, available online at http://www.adb.org; accessed February 2005; and *Business Week*, July 26, 2003, p. 35.

37. "Jobs Don't Pay Enough to Loosen Poverty's Grip," *Detroit News*, November 21, 2004, available online at http://www.detnews.com, accessed December 2004. Another business executive was quoted elsewhere as saying that unrelenting pressures to move production out of high-cost countries is a rat race. He might have added that in a rat race, the winner is always a rat.

38. Mazur, "Labor's New Internationalism," p. 80.

39. Robert Gilpin, *Global Political Economy—Understanding the International Economic Order* (Princeton, NJ: Princeton University Press, 2001), p. 291.

40. Kim Wan-Soon and Michael Jae Choo, "Principal Barriers to Foreign Direct Investment in Korea," in *Korea's Economy* (Korean Economic Institute, May 2003), p. 28.

41. Martin and Susan Tolchin, *Buying into America—How Foreign Money Is Changing the Face of Our Nation* (New York: Times Books, 1988), p. 17.

42. Thomas Omestad, "Selling off America," *Foreign Policy*, fall 1989, pp. 119, 125, 135.

43. June 24, 2005, p. C1.

44. As quoted in Joe L. Kincheloe, *The Sign of the Burger—McDonald's and the Culture of Power* (Philadelphia: Temple University Press, 2002), p. 3.

45. Daniel Litvin, *Empires of Profit—Commerce, Conquest and Corporate Responsibility* (New York: Texere, 2003), pp. xii–xiii.

46. Ibid., pp. 113–40. Another good source of information on this incident is Stephen Schlesinger and Stephen Kinzer, *Bitter Fruit—The Untold Story of the American Coup in Guatemala* (Garden City, NY: Doubleday and Company, 1982).

47. Litvin, *Empires of Profit*, pp. 155–67.

48. Joan E. Spero and Jeffrey A. Hart, *The Politics of International Economic Relations*, 5th ed. (New York: St. Martin's, 1997), pp. 259–60.

49. ITT subsequently ran into a series of management mishaps, some related to excessive diversification and acquisitions; it effectively disappeared in 1994 after being split into three separate companies.

50. Human Rights Watch, "The Price of Oil," January 1999, available online at http://www.hrw.org; accessed January 2005. For additional information on Shell and Nigeria, see Litvin, *Empires of Profit*, pp. 249–63.

51. Christian Aid, "Unearthing the Truth—Mining in Peru," February 2005, p. 15, available online at http://www.christian-aid.org.uk; accessed April 2005.

52. *Outsourcing* is a more frequently seen term, but it is not used here because it is too broad; it can apply to purchases of goods or services from either another domestic company or a foreign one. Vertical supply networks, whereby companies buy intermediate goods from other companies, has existed for many years.

53. Charles Schumer and Paul Craig Roberts, "Second Thoughts on Free Trade," *New York Times*, January 6, 2004, p. A23.

14

AN AGNOSTIC CONCLUSION
"It Depends"

Few people who have read the previous thirteen chapters will find it surprising that the conclusions reiterate and reinforce the main themes that have pervaded the analysis and argumentation in those chapters:

- Foreign direct investment (FDI) as process and multinational corporations (MNCs) as corporate entities are heterogeneous phenomena, and as such their nature and impact should be assessed on a disaggregated basis. Any individual foreign subsidiary can have a good, bad, neutral or uncertain impact, or some combination of the four. Effects likely will differ between host and home country. It all depends on specific circumstances.
- Perceptions vastly outnumber demonstrable facts; in many cases, observers mistake their perceptions for absolute truths.
- Generalizations almost always are oversimplified and misleading.
- A number of methodological problems block a fuller, more accurate understanding of the FDI/MNC phenomena, including inadequate statistical data, the difficulty of distinguishing between cause and effect, and their dynamic nature as seen in their continuing evolution into new forms and kinds.

What is surprising is that these almost self-evident hypotheses should constitute an analysis of the subject that is somewhere between highly unusual and unique. This is not to suggest that these ideas are completely original or a radical departure from the mainstream literature. Other authors have made at least oblique references to heterogeneity and the need for disaggregation. As noted in chapter 1, however, these allusions are no more than brief, incidental remarks inconspicuously buried in the middle of a paragraph that then quickly moves on to other matters. The nearly total absence of the themes of this study as core arguments in the long-standing public and academic discussions of FDI and MNCs is a major error of omission.

For better or worse, the conclusions do not unlock all the secrets of FDI and MNCs. It would be ideal to be able to distill the data and argumentation of previous chapters into one all-encompassing theory that explains why the process of FDI exists, unravels the collective nature and impact of the entities known as MNCs, and devises an all-inclusive matrix tracing the cost-benefit ratio of hosting foreign subsidiaries. This would be a genuine breakout intellectual accomplishment; but alas, it is beyond our reach. Instead, this chapter deals mainly with what we cannot know about the subject and the question of why the concepts of finality and closure are incompatible with a dispassionate, objective study of the FDI/MNC phenomena. It has the relatively modest assignment of expanding on the theme of "it depends." It seeks to enhance the credibility of this approach through references to brief statements in the literature that support the underlying premises of this thesis.

Restating the Argument, Getting More Relevant Answers

The long-standing public disagreement on the attributes/harm of FDI and MNCs rolls along with no end in sight. This is partly due to the complex and abstract nature of the subject matter. The dual image is also due to the circuitous route by which individuals make a judgment on the desirability of these phenomena. Personal assessments begin, often unconsciously, in one's larger value system concerning economic ideology and political philosophy. Values cannot be branded as right or wrong; feelings aren't verifiable hypotheses. Although the basic metrics (sales, profits, employees, debt, etc.) of corporate performance can be readily gleaned by reading annual reports to shareholders and to the U.S. Securities and Exchange Commission, the overall essence and total impact of an MNC cannot be quantified or scientifically measured.

People approve or disapprove their *perceptions* of MNCs, not the literal thing. Invariably, positive perceptions emanate from a favorable attitude toward free markets and economic efficiency. Negative perceptions about MNCs flow from giving priority to promoting a fair and just society and from a dislike and distrust of any organization whose top priority is seeking profits. To narrow the perceptions gap on MNCs, it would be necessary to narrow perceptions gap on the biggest disagreement in political economy, namely, markets versus government and the importance of a symmetrical income distribution. That is not going to happen; a full resolution of conflicting economic ideologies is not in the offing. A desirable, more achievable, and less ambitious alternative is to follow the path implicitly recommended in this study: a different approach to the assessment of the FDI and MNC phenomena.

The majority of people and institutions who have written in this area have sought to answer the wrong question: Are FDI and MNCs good or bad for society and the world economy? Too often the literature and public policy discussions want to make a sweeping and unequivocal case one way or the other—as if the object being studied had universal, unchanging characteristics. Touching a few parts of a metaphorical elephant is not adequate to conduct an objective, in-depth inquiry. The best short answer to the mega-question of whether FDI and MNCs are mostly good or bad is that sometimes they are a good thing, sometimes a bad thing, sometimes neutral, and sometimes the data are too inconclusive to make an informed judgment. Case-by-case circumstances determine the respective degrees of presumed benefits and harm by individual foreign subsidiaries on host and home countries.

Most discussions of these phenomena also suffer from inadequate analytic emphasis on the exogenous variables that can be more important factors than the MNCs themselves in determining certain aspects of their nature and impact. A proper analysis requires full appreciation of the large extent to which the nature of MNCs and FDI are the effects of business-related technological change as well as the extent to which their impact is the effect of preexisting conditions in host countries. Treating MNCs as stand-alone independent variables causing good or evil is a mistake.

A few steps toward consensus are likely if a different model of the FDI/MNC phenomena is employed, one that reduces reliance by both sides of the debate on what arguably are oversimplified polemics. More promising is an effort to broaden acceptance of the idea that stereotyping MNCs is a fallacy. More studies of FDI and MNCs need to dwell on the large gray area between the two extremes of all-inclusive admiration and fear and loathing. An analysis is long overdue that explains why the question of whether multinationals are good or bad is *not* an either/or proposition as conventional wisdom suggests. It *is* an "it depends" proposition requiring extensive disaggregation. Better to accept diversity, inconsistency, ambiguity, and uncertainty as unavoidable complicating factors. Better to realize that with disaggregation, one realizes that only *some* multinationals are fully worthy of admiration or loathing, whereas others reside in the gray area of ambiguity. Pronouncements of unqualified verdicts as to good or bad are part of the problem, not the solution. They help perpetuate an intellectual and policy stalemate.

This study has tried to present the merits of an agnostic, centrist model based mainly on the argument that FDI and MNCs are both hopelessly heterogeneous. Different inputs produce different outputs. Because the behavior of tens of thousands of MNCs from dozens of different countries over several decades has run the gamut from utterly disgraceful to ultra-beneficial, it is a simple matter to illustrate *any* kind of behavior by selectively choosing a few anecdotes from the vast corporate history archive. For anyone with a bias, the temptation is strong to start with a predetermined conclusion and choose examples of corporate behavior that ostensibly support it.

The research methodology used here is premised on the belief that a few anecdotes and case studies cannot prove that one particular point of view is irrefutably correct when another carefully selected set of examples will give equal support to an entirely different assessment. Logic suggests that the very act of observing dissimilar behavior by MNCs and different effects of FDI on host countries of incoming direct investment undermines the concept that a single universal truth exists about whether the virtues of international business outweigh the evils—or vice versa. Data manipulation is not difficult if the intent is to find support for a preconceived conclusion. If making the argument that all-powerful MNCs can force host governments to do their bidding, one should point to small, poor countries with indecisive or corrupt leaders; it is here that corporate leverage is most likely to be maximized. For support of the opposite argument, that national sovereignty trumps private enterprise, cite China as the antithesis of the need to kowtow to foreign business executives. Beijing has shown itself to be singularly adept in exploiting the eagerness of foreign MNCs to invest there by exacting substantial concessions, such as transfers of state-of-the-art technology, as the price of admission.

To assign the labels of "mixed record" and "inconclusive" to the FDI/MNC experience is not as cerebral an effort as developing a unified theory explaining the causes, behavior, and impact of FDI or a partial theory predicting that the combination of certain stipulated variables produces a predetermined result. However, these vague labels are consistent with the process of FDI and the entities known as MNCs being end-products of an infinite number of variables. In mathematical terms, it does not make sense to assume uniformity when the forces shaping the management, output, and finances of each subsidiary come from a gene pool of colossal size. The statistical universe being studied consists of tens of thousands of parent companies pursuing dozens of different kinds of operating procedures and business objectives in the primary, secondary, and tertiary sectors; hundreds of thousands of subsidiaries, some small and some enormous, some greenfield and other takeovers of local businesses; and some 200 host countries and territories creating economic and political environments that range from incubators of economic progress to executioners of the human spirit. The literally uncountable number of possible outcomes is the essence of heterogeneity and explains why FDI and MNCs are so diverse that in the aggregate they can legitimately be praised and condemned in the same breath.

The answer to the conundrum of whether MNCs in the aggregate should be given a free pass from government interference because of their alleged ability to use economic resources with maximum efficiency or should be subjected to more vigorous regulation to curb their tendencies to act as price-gauging monopolists *is obviously somewhere between these two extremes.* The exact spot of truth, wrote John Dunning, will be determined by (1) the efficiency of the resource allocation mechanism prior to the entrance of MNCs, and (2) market conditions under which multinationals compete that vary, among other things, according to industry and country.[1]

Experiences with incoming direct investment vary on a country-by-country basis. Ireland and Singapore harnessed it to elevate themselves from also-rans to superbly performing national economies. Countries in Sub-Saharan Africa and Central America at various times have been badly exploited by foreign-owned extractive companies. In none of these cases is the impact of foreign subsidiaries typical of the world at large. The vast majority of countries have had more mixed, muted, or unremarkable experiences with FDI. Another set of countries has no experience at all, having been unable to attract foreign companies because of relatively unstable economic and political environments, along with the absence of marketable natural resources.

Hungary exemplifies ambiguity inasmuch as its relatively brief experience with FDI demonstrates the taking-the-good-with-the-bad syndrome. It was the first mover among Central and Eastern European countries to open its doors, a policy that brought it a lot of FDI, along with many costs and benefits.

> But what is the balance? Expert opinions cover the full range, from those who believe that opening up was the best that Hungary could have done to those who think that the country could not have done worse. Critics of the FDI strategy claim that the massive inflow of transnational corporations turned the country into a colony of foreign capital. Experts at the other end of the spectrum posit that FDI (and the free-market economy in general) solves all . . . economic and social problems. *Of course, the truth lies somewhere in between.*[2]

At best, an eclectic-skeptical approach to multinationals will gain adherents only slowly. Adherents of market-based policies will not easily let go of the idea that in being able to efficiently produce goods and services, create jobs, and rationally allocate capital and real resources, MNCs should be left free to be the ultimate expression of a globally interconnected capitalist marketplace that will promote positive competition, innovation, and progress for everyone.[3] Advocates of a more equitable society will resist just as hard before letting go of the perceived need to rein in large, powerful, self-serving companies able to easily shift production to more attractive countries and acting as if they had been awarded a license to put their profits above everyone else's welfare.

Regrettably, one of the few things the antagonists have had in common is rejection of more nuanced, balanced position as their intellectual center of gravity. The two polarized positions equally obscure the real story of the nature and effects of the FDI/MNC phenomena. This is a serious flaw that helps sustain the inconclusive debate. Mutual inflexibility also has the unfortunate effect of continuing to block consensus on binding multilateral agreements to establish mandatory guidelines and standards of behavior for governments and companies alike. The result is perpetuation of the current system of haphazard, overlapping voluntary guidelines in lieu of a system that enforces limits on extreme behavior by both corporations and governments.

Unqualified, blanket praise and blanket condemnation of FDI and MNCs are not supported by a solid body of empirical evidence that holds up under close scrutiny. Although most of the more strident arguments on both sides fall somewhere between exaggerated and patently untrue, many of the tempered criticisms and tempered laudatory comments are credible. The efforts at even-handed analysis that (hopefully) pervade previous chapters are based on the proposition that any single foreign subsidiary has the *potential* to bring over-whelming benefits—and the potential to wreak havoc. "The ambiguous—and sometimes contradictory—empirical findings indicate that FDI must no longer be considered to be a homogenous phenomenon."[4]

On one hand, no inherent affinity exists between the national interest of a country and the self-interest of an MNC. Their priorities are dissimilar. Governments seek to spur economic development and social stability within a national context. MNCs take a global perspective to strengthen their competitiveness and bottom lines; they are not created to function as nonprofit public service institutions. They typically have far greater loyalty to their home countries than to their host countries. Corporate neutrality is manifested only in efforts to minimize taxes owed to both. Few MNCs would have the economic power to promote a more even distribution of wealth in the countries where they operate subsidiaries even in the unlikely event they made that their highest priority.

On the other hand, animus is not inevitable between sovereign states and the multinationals, as is clearly demonstrated in Singapore and Ireland. Governments are in the best position to *redistribute* wealth in a manner deemed equitable, but private enterprise has consistently proved itself superior in *creating* wealth. Private enterprise provides the main impetus—through increased productivity, job creation, and product innovation—for rising standards of living, a cherished goal in governmental efforts to keep the electorate happy. The official and private sectors need one another. Governments need tax revenue to pay for the social safety net, and corporations and their employees are a good source of that revenue. Corporations need favorable laws and regulatory policies. Mutual gain can result when government officials and MNC executives work harmoniously with each other.

Qualify and Disaggregate, Don't Generalize

The infinite variables associated with multinational production of goods and services impede a unified explanatory and predictive theory. The search for common denominators is foiled by the limitless combinations of variations and disparities among subsidiaries and home country economic conditions. No single, inherent logic is responsible for the growth of MNCs. Their expansion was not linear. Although the growth of FDI was not a random process, "it is evident that systematic factors behind its growth must not be oversimplified. There are no easy generalisations about the consequences of multinational investment."[5] Acceptance of a single, integrating theory of FDI/MNCs is further complicated by the reality that "we can probably dream up a theory model to produce any result that we want [and] justify any policy we desire."[6]

If country differences and the many different kinds of direct investments are assumed to be the critical determinants of the impact of inward FDI on individual host countries, "the main lesson might be that the search for universal relationships is futile."[7] The line of inquiry should shift away from how FDI as a whole affects all countries to more disaggregated questions. At best, by examining the empirical evidence, "we can greatly narrow the range of sensible theories as candidates for use in policy analysis."[8] Generalizations are of little use. We need more systematic data on two specific variables. First, can specific kinds of subsidiaries be closely linked with positive or negative results? Second, can specific kinds of host country conditions be closely linked to favorable, unfavorable, or neutral effects of FDI on the local economy?

It is "safe to conclude that there is no universal relationship between the ratio of inward FDI flows to GDP and the rate of growth of a country."[9] "The nexus between FDI and overall investment as well as economic growth in host countries is neither self-evident nor straightforward, but remains insufficiently explored territory."[10] "Whether or not foreign direct investment is beneficial or exploitative will continue to depend on the type and volume of investment, its terms, and the policies of the host government."[11] The authors of another study did not find any definitive link between inward FDI and the enhancement of economic development in host countries. In effect saying "it depends," the authors said the reason for their equivocation was that "the exact nature of the relation between foreign MNCs and their host economies seems to vary between industries and countries. It is reasonable to assume that the characteristics of the host country's industry and policy environment are important determinants of the net benefits of FDI."[12] It then follows that the many imponderables of kinds of subsidiaries and host country environment means that "ensuring a large quantity of FDI alone is not sufficient for the objective of generating growth and poverty reduction."[13]

The questions of why and where companies establish overseas subsidiaries also are best answered with the all-purpose imprecision of "it depends." Some academics do acknowledge the difficulties of a precise, finite answer. The determinants of FDI decisions are too diffuse to be "straightforward," said one, adding that "we are still in the process of uncovering what we don't know."[14] Bruce Blonigen also admitted that "in the final analysis, the empirical literature is still young enough that most hypotheses are still up for grabs" and that most determinants of FDI are "fairly fragile statistically." However, he did not indicate agreement with the implied assumption in this study that this is the natural, probably permanent state of our understanding of these phenomena. Like most academics, he optimistically looked forward to the day when a greater availability of micro-level data would clear up some of the current unknowns.[15] That practitioners inhabit a different culture from that of academics is suggested in a Wall Street economist's relatively simple explanation of why companies decide to produce overseas. Joseph Quinlan also fails to find any single explanatory paradigm, but he does not suggest that further research will or needs to produce an all-purpose model of MNC behavior. "The global motivations of firms are as diverse and complex as both their business lines and the global markets themselves. They are in constant flux, changing and adjusting to prevailing market circumstances."[16] The behavior of overseas direct investments is individually shaped by the distinctive history, strengths and weaknesses, business models, product mix, technical know-how, and so on of headquarters. The geographical breakdown of the Whirlpool Corporation's international production operations (see box 14.1) is indicative of how corporate decisions on where goods are produced reflect specific circumstances more than textbook formulae.

The Need to Distinguish between Things That Change and Those That Do Not

Another demonstration of the complexity and diversity of our subject matter is the applicability to it of two contrasting aphorisms: "The only constant is change" and "the more things change, the more they remain the same." The inherent difficulty of disentangling the temporary from the permanent has contributed to embarrassingly poor forecasting of new FDI and MNCs trends. "Each phase in the growth of multinational business brings out the extrapolators."[17] The problem is that their projections have been largely inaccurate. In the three decades after World

War II ended, conventional wisdom was sure that the edge in American industry's technology, innovation, and marketing prowess was going to make it a permanent world-beater, subjecting other countries to also-ran status. The superstar designation was later yanked from the United States and transferred to Japan in the late 1980s, just a few years before the Japanese economic miracle imploded.

A select few ideas remain accurate and relevant over many decades. One of them was introduced by Charles Kindleberger back in 1969 and still rings true: FDI is "a subject in which it is necessary to judge case by case, on the basis of the relevant circumstances, before coming to conclusions about the effect of one or another action."[18] This succinct truism unfortunately has been swept aside by the embrace of generalizations by the public, companies, governments, non-governmental organizations (NGOs), and academics. Similarly, no updating is needed to the U.S. Department of Commerce's pointed summary of the MNC policy debate published early in 1973:

> The apparent conflict between the multinational corporation, with its supranational point of view, and the nation-state, with its national eco-nomic concerns and special interest groups, has given rise to a host of economic and political problems. What is at issue . . . is the degree of freedom that should be allowed the multinational corporation or the nature and extent of regulation that should be imposed on its present operations and future growth in order to make it better serve divergent national interests.[19]

Quantifying the degree of freedom that should be accorded MNCs is, after four decades, still a quintessential subjective value judgment and an unresolved, contentious policy issue.

Respect for timelessness is good up to a point. The problem is that viewing the process of FDI and the operations of MNCs in static terms is a greater mistake than ever. The information technology revolution has accelerated the pace of change in the business world to an unprecedented degree (see more detailed discussion to follow). Evaluations of FDI and MNCs past and present cannot be more than a snapshot in time, useful for looking back but of little or no value in divining the outlines of future trends. Chapter 3 discussed how advances in science, technology, communications, and transportation have altered the structure and facilitated the geographic reach of the corporation. The persistence of change in business economics long ago made it illogical to assume that the optimal market for companies would forever be the unscientifically drawn na-tional borders of the large, medium, and small nation-states in which they origi-nated. The snapshot metaphor is also relevant for pointing out the right and wrong ways to properly assess the effects and desirability of a foreign subsidiary. An initial investment may deteriorate or flourish in ways totally unanticipated at its inception. Critics who berate all extensions of financial incentives to MNCs by national and regional governments ignore the possibility that the factory in question may substantially expand its output, labor force, linkage with domestic firms, taxes paid, and exports; furthermore, it may lead to other foreign companies establishing subsidiaries. Making snap judgments is flawed methodology. Patience and a long-term perspective are what is called for.

Chapter 3 also noted the endless series of new kinds of MNCs arriving on the scene. Imagine your bewilderment if in 1990 someone had told you that by summer 2005, Apple Computer would have a multinational operation called iTunes that sold more than 500 million units of something called downloadable songs in nineteen countries.[20] Furthermore, the music would be played on something called a hard drive marketed as something called an iPod, and digitalized songs would be sold on a fully automated basis over something called the Internet. Also try to imagine what entirely new kinds of MNCs will appear over the next two decades.

As the world economy continues to be more tightly integrated and the revolution in information technology continues to alter the business environment, competition more likely than not will become increasingly severe. Industry consultants McKinsey & Company see the coming of "extreme competition" that will "make the pressures of the 1980s and 1990s look tame by comparison."[21] The ever-increasing pace of technological of change "will have an impact on you, no matter what you do for a living. It will bring new competition from new ways of doing things, from corners that you don't expect" was Andy Grove's (the retired head of Intel) version of a wake-up call to industry.[22] Corporate executives seem far more sensitized to the consequences of the constant of change than do corporate critics. Changing market conditions have led to the strongly felt belief in nearly all corporate boardrooms that size matters and that only superlarge companies will survive in an increasingly competitive world marketplace. Since perceptions define reality, the result has been increased reliance on overseas expansion through new subsidiaries as well as mergers with and acquisitions of foreign companies to achieve steady growth and increased economies of scale. Again, this is a case of international business being subjected to the same market pressures and adopting the same strategic responses as domestic-based businesses. In the United States, at least, it takes the form of large national chains all but wiping out individually owned clothing and hardware stores, pharmacies, fast food outlets, and so on. Domestically and externally, the dominant trend is toward bigger companies.

One of the ironies in the FDI/MNC saga is that what drives senior executives to create ever-larger MNCs is at least as much fear of their companies' being bypassed or outflanked by competitors as it is self-assured drives for profit maximization and market power. An argument could be made (unprovable in a court of law) that for many years, the main catalyst for fewer and larger companies in various industrial sectors is more feelings of insecurity and vulnerability among senior executives than the imperialistic aggression allegedly embedded in capitalism. Gillette Corporation explained its decision to merge with Procter & Gamble as coming from the need for greater resources to drive growth. As a company with a mere $10 billion in annual sales, senior management perceived it as suffering increasingly severe constraints from having to compete against companies with "exponentially greater sales, reach and resources."[23]

To avoid a false generalization, it must be pointed out that while the increased popularity of mergers and acquisitions has indeed created "bigger bigness" and diminished competition, it also has produced costly mistakes as well. Major operating problems and declines in shareholder value (falling share prices) are fairly common events following the honeymoon of recently married idiosyncratic corporate cultures. Repercussions such as money-losing sales or write-offs of product lines that did not mesh in the new company are not uncommon. The lack of certainty that a mutual quest for bigness produces a comfortable integration of companies is demonstrated by the complex and expensive problems encountered in the mergers between Time Warner and America Online, Daimler-Benz and Chrysler, and Hewlett-Packard and Compaq Computer.[24]

Size has never inoculated even the largest MNC against infection from endless changes in market conditions. The rapid attrition in companies included in the Dow Jones Industrial Average and Standard & Poor's 500 Index over the past five decades speaks to the imperative for companies to perpetually reinvent themselves or face stagnation or extinction. Corporate restructuring to offset failure to keep pace with rapidly changing market conditions and consumer tastes is common even in such world-class companies as IBM, Sony, and Unilever. A new breed of executive has evolved: the turnaround specialist who moves from company to company, attempting to reverse the downward spiral initiated by the previous CEO's mistakes and inaction. General Electric, the lone surviving company from the original Dow Jones Industrial index, today sells an array of goods and services completely different from its early years, the result of its current offerings not being invented 100 years ago.

Changes in what is considered acceptable behavior in the marketplace represent another shift in the business environment that does not necessarily favor corporations and the people who manage them. Thousands of NGOs, linked worldwide by the same telecommunications networks that contributed to the rise of globalization, now regularly threaten a barrage of embarrassing publicity and consumer boycotts if a targeted company, invariably an MNC, refuses to terminate activities deemed harmful to human rights, workers' rights, or the environment. Firms increasingly blink first in such confrontations, a response largely unknown just a few years ago. Reluctant decisions to modify profitable but publicly criticized corporate operations are no longer uncommon. Corporate executives increasingly feel it necessary for their firms to exude the aura of social responsibility and on occasion sacrifice some short-term profits in return for long-term customer and public goodwill.

The Enron Corporation debacle and the parade of ensuing U.S. corporate scandals triggered major changes in corporate regulation and governance, while also shattering senior executives' longtime ability to hide behind the cloak of nonaccountability. The U.S. government's success in securing guilty verdicts in its crackdown on crime in the suites has altered the thinking of all executives, and the actions of most. When Bernard Ebbers was sentenced to twenty-five years in prison for massive accounting fraud while CEO at the WorldCom Corporation, it sent a loud message to big business that a major shift had occurred in the risk/reward ratio for illegal activity. Yet another tilt away from corporate omnipotence is Wal-Mart's reversal of the traditional business model in which manufacturers set the prices of the goods they sold to wholesalers and retail chains. The company's unprecedented market power and commitment to low prices are strong enough to force vendors around the world to accept the rock-bottom prices demanded by Wal-Mart or suffer painful declines in sales from not being on the shelves of this multinational retailing juggernaut.[25]

The constant of change in the corporate world does not make big companies or their well-compensated senior executives recipients of widespread sympathy, but it does affect the manner and pace of doing business. Well-known economist Jagdish Bhagwati suggested the adjective kaleidoscopic to connote the emergence of a constant shifting in international competitive advantage among companies. Today, you have it, tomorrow you lose it, and eventually you might regain it, as witnessed by the shifting ups and downs in the Boeing-Airbus rivalry. His metaphor is also applicable to FDI, where accelerating change in the kinds and activities of MNCs means that the patterns visible today are likely to quickly rearrange themselves into new shapes, like a revolving kaleidoscope.[26]

Although Stephen Hymer retains guru status among MNC theoreticians, his intellectual contribution has been diminished by the significant evolution of international companies since the 1960s, when his thoughts coalesced. He presumably was thinking of traditional FDI—producers of chemicals and machinery and seekers of natural resources—in 1970 when he cast doubt on the proposition that MNCs are endowed with superior efficiency. Multinationals, he argued, are large companies operating in imperfect markets, and economic theory raises questions about the "efficiency of oligopolistic decision making, an area where much of welfare economics breaks down, especially the proposition that competition allocates resources efficiently and that there is a harmony between private profit maximization and the general interest." Allocative efficiency "does not apply to direct foreign investment because of the anticompetitive effect inherently associated with it."[27] His skepticism does not appear applicable to today's multinational information technology and communications companies. They, too, have changed a basic business model through constant price reductions while steadily introducing more technologically sophisticated goods and services.

Data Limitations and Other Caveats

We know that there is a lot we still do not know about FDI and MNCs, but not exactly what or how much. "Any analysis of foreign investment has to be heavily qualified by data constraints," the Asian Development Bank cautioned.[28] UNCTAD's *World Investment Report* for 1999 noted that "the economic effects of FDI are almost impossible to measure with precision." Each MNC represents a "complex package" of company-specific strengths and drawbacks that are "dispersed in varying quantities and quality from one host country to another" and are difficult to isolate and quantify.[29] Despite intensified research efforts, "economists know surprisingly little about the driving forces and the economic effects of FDI." Few undisputed insights exist on which policy makers can definitely rely. "The economic effects of FDI do not allow for easy generalizations. Empirical studies on the growth impact of FDI have come up with conflicting results."[30] The complexities of the subject have caused academic assessments to resort to either an econometric analysis of the relationships between inward direct investment and "various measures of economic performance, the results of which are often inconclusive, or to a qualitative analysis of particular aspects of the contribution of [MNCs] to development," which usually lack precision because they do not attempt to measure costs and benefits quantitatively.[31] The implication here is that the door is wide open for perceptions to produce multiple versions of truth.

Sizing up the impact, good and bad, of FDI is further constrained by our inability to divine what would have happened if past realities had not played out as they did. The nature of counterfactual situations makes it impossible to know for sure if host and home countries would have been better off *without* certain direct investments that were made and better off *with* certain investments that did not take place.

A precise figure for how much direct investment is out there still does not exist. Nor is it certain that it should be calculated at the original cost, current market value, replacement cost of the subsidiary, or all three. The result is that policy analysis is formulated with barely adequate statistics. Statistical limitations are hard to eliminate when there can be no guarantee that every company engaged in this activity fully, accurately, and promptly reports all outflows and all reinvestments and profit remittances to their host and home countries' statistics gathering agencies. The totals reported for new investments financed by local borrowing and reinvested earnings are notoriously incomplete. Some LDCs reputedly have wholly inadequate data collection capabilities. Not all countries define FDI in the same way. Some countries compile FDI flows from applications for new FDI that may or may not actually take place. The cumulative impact of these statistical shortcomings is an annual discrepancy between recorded global inflows and outflows of FDI that averaged nearly $100 billion annually in 2001 and 2002.[32] A final problem is that data for the current value of cumulative FDI, that is, stock numbers, suffers from reliance on original purchase prices, a procedure explained by the difficulty of accurately calculating current values for hundreds of thousands of subsidiaries.

All things considered, it is no surprise—and not inappropriate—that many academic studies have concluded that more research is needed on this subject.

Country Case Study: The Complex Relationship between Canada and Inward FDI

Canada's attitudes toward and its experiences with FDI and MNCs are illustrative of why there are so few simple situations and simple answers associated with these phenomena. Massive amounts of capital inflows from the economic giant to its south give Canada the image of having to sleep next to an elephant, all the while hoping it doesn't get rolled over on and crushed. Canadians have two conflicting visions of the considerable U.S. ownership of their manufacturing and mining sectors. The first part of the love/hate feeling is appreciation for the jobs, capital, advanced technologies, efficiencies, and linkage with domestically owned businesses that foreign subsidiaries can bring with them. The second part is fear of serious, irreversible dilution of Canadian political and economic autonomy and its culture—"the Americanization of Canada" for short.

The major twists and turns in Canada's FDI policy suggest a fluctuating ambivalence. By the 1960s, the period of enthusiastic welcoming of new inward direct investments was over, and Canadians had begun worrying aloud about the implications of having the highest ratio of foreign ownership of industry to GDP of any industrialized country. Various government reports and the message of the nonpartisan yet dramatically named Committee for an Independent Canada eventually caused a shift in public opinion too strong to ignore. The Foreign Investment Review Act of 1974 was born of the clear consensus that FDI policy needed to be redefined to realize more benefits and fewer externally generated constraints on Canadian self-determination. The legislation created the Foreign

Investment Review Agency (FIRA) with the mandate to screen applications for takeovers and greenfield FDI to ensure that each offered "significant benefit" to Canadians. The determinations were to be made on the basis of standard economic criteria, such as employment effects and extent of technology transfer. Complicating the process was the fact that the FIRA did not have power to approve or reject applications to invest; instead, it made recommendations to a Cabinet committee, which had the final say. Some important facts about the procedures are indisputable: Some 90 percent of new business applications as well as a large majority of takeovers were approved, and an important loophole deliberately allowed existing foreign investors to expand or diversify without having to seek approval. It was also a fact that Canada's share of international FDI flows began to decline. It was assumed (but never proved) that the review process was the chief cause of this downturn; public opinion again began to shift.

The reality created by perceptions, was that the new policy was excessively costly and politicized. The sentiment grew that it was making Canada a less desirable destination to foreign companies. Rather than going through the hassle of convincing the FIRA of their investment's merits, a growing number of foreign investors were presumed to be looking to more hospitable host countries that did not feel the need to apply a formal benefits test before allowing FDI inflows. As one Canadian writer put it, the high ratio of FIRA's approvals "neither reflect applications that were withdrawn before a decision could be rendered nor investors who were deterred from applying either because they feared delays [which did occur] or that they could not meet the significant benefit test."[33] The FIRA review policy was abolished shortly after Brian Mulroney's Conservatives gained control of the government in late 1984. Investment Canada, the agency created to replace it, was given the mandate to promote and facilitate investment by both Canadians and foreigners. The review process was effectively eliminated except for FDI in the highly sensitive cultural sector that includes media. The face of Canadian FDI policy to the outside world eventually became International Trade Canada, an agency whose mandate is promoting inward FDI, not discouraging it or passing judgment on its merits.

A counterintuitive fact has encouraged the Canadian business community to support a more open policy toward inward FDI. The image of a small, scrappy underdog trying to avoid being swallowed up by a flood of incoming MNCs from the rich, powerful neighbor to the south overlooks sizable *outward* FDI by Canadian multinationals. Strange as it sounds, the recorded value of Canada's cumulative outward FDI stock exceeded the value of inward foreign investment, US$370 billion versus $304 billion in 2004. The country's outward FDI stock as a percentage of GDP was 37 percent in 2004, more than double the comparable figure for the United States (17 percent).[34] Canada's FDI in the United States is not inconsequential. At $134 billion, the value of its U.S. FDI in 2004 was 62 percent of the value of U.S. direct investment in Canada.[35] If this figure is adjusted for the fact that Canada's economy and population are only about 10 percent of comparable U.S. figures, the common perception that FDI between the two countries follows a one-way route from South to North is debunked. Canada has also lost its status as the industrial country with the highest ratio of inward FDI to GDP; at 30.5 percent, it is slightly below the same figure for Western European countries as a group.[36]

Four Final Thoughts on Reshaping the Public Dialogue on FDI and MNCs

A more productive international dialogue would result if it ceased to be dominated by uncompromising advocates and critics. Partial reconciliation of conflicting perceptions/viewpoints begins with greater acceptance of the notion that FDI and MNCs are composites incorporating tens of thousands of individual foreign subsidiaries whose nature and effects do not conform to any single formula. Instead of the antagonists putting their energies into securing bragging rights for having proved that MNCs are good or bad, the public, government officials, businesspeople, NGOs, and academics should seek a better understanding of the major variables. The following are four suggested guidelines for making the dialogue/debate more productive and conciliatory.

First, the kinds of FDI and MNCs are so diverse that a multitude of possible results is inevitable. The quality of the vast majority of foreign subsidiaries falls between the extremes of ultra-high quality and ultra-low quality. "The literature has, however, tended to treat FDI as a homogeneous resource benefiting the recipients in the same manner and has neglected any potential differences in the quality of FDI received."[37] The more insightful governments demonstrate their awareness of these differences through targeting, that is, offering generous incentives to the kinds of FDI that their research has found will provide maximum stimulus to their economy and standard of living. To make such a determination, several critical variables must be examined. The most important are how extensive will the foreign subsidiary's linkage be with the indigenous business sector; how extensive will be technology transfers and opportunities for positive knowledge spillovers; will it require skilled, relatively high-paid workers (and is there an adequate local supply of such workers); what is the potential for the subsidiary's expanding its labor force and output; to what extent will it contribute to hard currency-earning exports; and is it a greenfield project or merely a takeover of an existing local company? Despite the views of hard-core advocates, nonextractive investment projects do not automatically stimulate sustained growth. Incoming MNCs "may preserve the technological backwardness of the host country by transferring low value-added activities. They may lead the host country to overspecialize in a few products, thus exposing it to the business cycles of the world economy."[38]

The economic and regulatory policies along with the political environment of the host country is the second super-variable that needs greater understanding. It can be divided into two phases. First, individual country characteristics are the most important determinant of how much (if any) and what kinds of direct investments will be made. MNCs don't like to gamble with the time, money, and prestige associated with starting and operating overseas production facilities. To some extent, they don't have to gamble; corporations have a choice of more than 200 countries and territories when seeking a good fit for an overseas investment site. Second, economic policies, the skill level of the workforce, and the extent of regulation imposed on the operations of foreign-owned factories influence their structure and the level of efficiency at which they operate. Instead of arguing in black-and-white generalities, discussions of FDI and MNCs should try to confirm whether subsidiaries are in fact more likely to have beneficial effects on host countries when they "are able to take advantage of all economies of scale, and are driven by competitive pressure to upgrade their technologies, quality control procedures, and management practices continuously."

A local subsidiary seems most likely to be at the forefront of best practices when it has been designated as a key link in the parent company's distribution network and a direct contributor to its competitiveness in world markets.[39] Subsidiaries having this status are located in countries with market-oriented policies, skilled labor, good infrastructure, rule of law, and so on. More information is needed on the extent to which overseas investment projects are in fact doomed to low-quality status if they are forced by nonmarket host country policies to be "oriented toward small, protected, domestic markets and/or prevented from being incorporated into the parent's supply chain by joint venture or domestic content requirements imposed by the host country." Overseas factories in such cases "do not achieve full economies of scale, nor utilize the most advanced production techniques."[40]

Second, another reason that definitive evaluations of our subject are elusive is the difficulty of distinguishing cause and effect and the lack of attention given to this problem. Chapter 8 discussed the equally plausible arguments that FDI can be a cause of growth in a host country's economy and that a proven record of economic growth can cause companies to invest there. The world is globalized in part because of the proliferation of MNCs. However, causal factors "also work in the opposite direction: there are many multinationals because the world is globalized."[41] Multinationals should not be identified as the causes of the benefits and dislocations caused by major technological advances and structural transformations of the international economic order. They are mainly effects.

Being multinational is a compelling strategy for responding to a world economy increasingly integrated by efficient communications and transportation and low or no trade barriers, and to a business environment characterized by intense competition and high fixed costs.

Third, when reading about or listening to discussions of FDI and MNCs, everyone should keep in mind that the writers and speakers (the author of this book included) are communicating educated guesses at best and propaganda at worst, not hard, indisputable scientific fact. Consider the institutional affiliation of all sources of information. Do they have a personal stake in how public policy affects MNCs? Examine their methodology for signs of bias and preconceived notions. Never underestimate the primacy of perceptions and value judgments in assessments of any issue in the social sciences, especially one as multifaceted, dynamic, abstract, ambiguous, and heated as this one.

Fourth, it is time to ignore what is probably the most unnecessary contretemps of the public debate: The alleged race to the bottom by rapacious MNCs. This metaphor is grossly exaggerated to the point of irrelevance (see chapters 7 and 12). For MNCs outside the natural resources sector, the vast majority of decisions on where to invest are made on the basis of two criteria. For purposes of market expansion or protection, overseas production goes to countries where there is an already large and a projected growing demand for their goods. Efficiency-seeking direct investments go to where net profitability will be highest by calculating what is left after all expenses (wages, transportation, power, bribes, high labor turnover, shipping delays, and so on) are deducted from the selling price. Focusing on gross costs, namely, low wages, is financially misguided. Undoubtedly, a few companies with less than stellar ethics and financial positions have been attracted to countries where labor and environmental standards are poorly enforced. This is another case of at least a few examples of all kinds of corporate behavior being out there for the finding. The real issue is the frequency and reasons that companies shift production from one country to another in what is a limited ratcheting down process.

The thoughts presented here not only tie together the main points of previous chapters, they also serve as the point of departure for the recommendations presented in the final chapter.

Notes

1. John H. Dunning, *International Production and the Multinational Enterprise* (London: George Allen and Unwin, 1981), pp. 36–37; emphasis added.
2. Magdolna Sass, "FDI in Hungary—The First Mover's Advantage and Disadvantage," *European Investment Bank Papers*, 9(2), 2004, p. 86; emphasis added.

3. Medard Gabel and Henry Bruner, *Global Inc.—An Atlas of the Multinational Corporation* (New York: New Press, 2003), p. 120.

4. Peter Nunnenkamp, "Foreign Direct Investment in Developing Countries: What Economists (Don't) Know and What Policymakers Should (Not) Do!," 2002, p. 30, available online at http://www.cuts-international.org; accessed January 2005. Nunnenkamp's advice is an example of the aforementioned dead-on accurate idea in the academic literature that is stated all too briefly, without follow-up, and without attracting the attention it deserves.

5. Geoffrey Jones, *The Evolution of International Business* (New York: Routledge, 1996), pp. 310, 314.

6. James R. Markusen, "Multilateral Rules on Foreign Direct Investment: The Developing Countries' Stake," prepared for the World Bank, October 1998, p. 57, available online at http://www2.cid.harvard.edu/cidtrade/Issues/markusen.pdf; accessed March 2005.

7. Robert E. Lipsey and Fredrik Sjöholm, "The Impact of Inward FDI on Host Countries: Why Such Different Answers?," in Theodore H. Moran, Edward M. Graham, and Magnus Blomström, eds., *Does Foreign Direct Investment Promote Development?* (Washington, DC: Institute for International Economics and the Center for Global Development, 2005), p. 40.

8. Markusen, "Multilateral Rules on Foreign Direct Investment," p. 63.

9. Robert E. Lipsey, quoted in *Does Foreign Direct Investment Promote Development?*, pp. 24–25.

10. Nunnenkamp, "Foreign Direct Investment in Developing Countries," p. 32.

11. Neil Hood and Stephen Young, *The Economics of Multinational Enterprise* (London and New York: Longman, 1979), p. 359.

12. Magnus Blomström and Ari Kokko, "How Foreign Investment Affects Host Countries," World Bank Policy Research Working Paper no. 1745, March 1997, p. 33.

13. Dirk Willem te Velde, "Policies towards Foreign Direct Investment in Developing Countries: Emerging Best-Practices and Outstanding Issues," March 2001, p. 50, available online at http://www.odi.org.uk; accessed March 2005.

14. Bruce A. Blonigen, "Foreign Direct Investment Behavior of Multinational Corporations," *National Bureau of Economic Research Reporter*, winter 2006, available online at http://www.nber.org/reporter/winter06/blonigen.html; accessed February 2006.

15. Bruce A. Blonigen, "A Review of the Empirical Literature on FDI Determinants," NBER Working Paper no. 11299, April 2005, p. 29, available online at http://www.nber.org; accessed December 2005.

16. Joseph Quinlan, *Global Engagement* (Chicago: Contemporary Books, 2001), p. 23.

17. "Survey of Multinationals," *The Economist*, March 27, 1993, survey p. 18.

18. Charles P. Kindleberger, *American Business Abroad* (New Haven, CT: Yale University Press, 1969), p. 36.

19. U.S. Department of Commerce, "The Multinational Corporation—An Overview," in *Multinational Corporations*, a compendium of papers published by the U.S. Senate Committee on Finance, February, 21, 1973, p. 42.

20. Data source: CNN Money, "iTunes Japan Sells 1M Songs in 4 Days," August 8, 2005, available online at http://money.cnn.com; accessed August 2005.

21. "Extreme Competition," *McKinsey Quarterly*, February 2005, available online at http://www.mckinseyquarterly.com; accessed March 2005.

22. Andrew Grove, "Only the Paranoid Survive: Book Preface," available online at http://www.intel.com/pressroom/kits/bios/grove/paranoid.htm; accessed January 2005.

23. Gillette Corporation, *2004 Annual Report*, p. 4, available online at http://www.gillette.com; accessed May 2005.

24. Nevertheless, the sequel to Andy Grove's well-known business primer, *Only the Paranoid Survive*, might well be *Only Large Paranoid Enterprises Will Survive*.

25. The pressure to meet the low Wal-Mart price possibly has forced some suppliers to shift production to lower wage countries.

26. Jagdish Bhagwati, "A New Vocabulary for Trade," *Wall Street Journal*, August 4, 2005, p. A12.

27. Stephen Hymer, "The Efficiency (Contradictions) of Multinational Corporations," *American Economic Review*, Papers and Proceedings of the Eighty-Second Annual Meeting of the American Economic Association, May 1970, pp. 441, 443.

28. Asian Development Bank, *Asian Development Outlook 2004*, endnote 2, p. 264, available online at http://www.adb.org; accessed January 2005.

29. UNCTAD, *World Investment Report 1999*, overview, p. xxvi, available online at http://www.unctad.org; accessed April 2005.

30. Nunnenkamp, "Foreign Direct Investment in Developing Countries," p. 7.

31. UNCTAD, *World Investment Report 1999*, p. xxvi.

32. Calculated from Annex table B.2, UNCTAD, *World Investment Report 2003*, p. 372.

33. Russell Deigan, *Investing in Canada* (Scarborough, Canada: Thomson Professional Canada, 1991), p. 7.

34. Data sources: Annex tables B.2 and B.3 of UNCTAD, *World Investment Report 2005*, pp. 308 and 314.

35. Data sources: Tables 1.2 and 2.2, U.S. Commerce Department of Commerce, Bureau of Economic Analysis, *Survey of Current Business*, July 2005, pp. 51, 53, available online at http://www.bea.gov; accessed August 2005.

36. Data source: Annex table B.3, of UNCTAD, *World Investment Report 2005*, pp. 313–14.

37. Nagesh Kumar, *Globalization and the Quality of Foreign Direct Investment* (New Delhi: Oxford University Press, 2002), p. 4.

38. Sass, "FDI in Hungary," p. 77.

39. Theodore H. Moran, "Strategy and Tactics for the Doha Round: Capturing the Benefits of Foreign Direct Investment," December 2002, p. 7, available online at http://www.adb.org/economics; accessed November 2004.

40. Ibid., p. 8.

41. Giorgio Barba Navaretti and Anthony J. Venables, *Multinational Firms in the World Economy* (Princeton, NJ: Princeton University Press, 2004), pp. 278–79.

PART V

Recommendations

15

AN AGENDA FOR
FUTURE ACTION

The dual objectives of this book are to offer a more accurate understanding of the diverse nature and effects of foreign direct investment (FDI) and multinational corporations (MNCs) and to stimulate a more relevant public policy discussion. These objectives are based on the author's belief that past portrayals of these phenomena do not do justice to their nature, effects, or importance domestically and internationally. This situation is not the result of indifference or deliberate design. The sheer breadth and complexity of these mostly abstract subjects is partly responsible. But so, too, is the mutual failure of the two contesting schools of thought to appreciate that both are partially correct, partially wrong, and partially beside the point. The unacknowledged subliminal roles of perceptions and ideology in shaping what passes for reality perpetuate an endless cycle of irreconcilable, often oversimplified claims and counterclaims that perpetuates a divisive, stagnant, unshakeable, and ultimately unnecessary stalemate. It is as if the advocates and critics of FDI and MNCs each donned blindfolds, touched a few parts of the metaphorical elephant, came to contradictory conclusions as to its total nature and impact, and stubbornly rejected any need to accommodate the other's assessment.

The proposals that follow are designed to serve the aforementioned objectives of this study. They were formulated in the hope that, if well received, they would contribute to a better understanding of the subject and better public policies, both of which would serve the common good.

1. *The two ends of the political spectrum and all in between should accept the overwhelming likelihood that on virtually every significant issue involving these international business phenomena, different perceptions of reality will create four legitimate sets of conclusions: positive, negative, neutral, and indeterminate.* Their relative validity and relevance will differ according to circumstances. This "quadruple bottom line" approach likely will be increasingly appropriate in the

future as forms of FDI and MNCs become ever more diverse and transitory in composition. Multinationals will continue to change and evolve as long as external stimuli keep changing. Analysis of FDI and MNCs needs to be aware of and keep pace with these changes. This is unlikely given the current propensity of most interested citizens, government officials, business executives, and researchers to employ faulty methodology. Like the blind men in the parable, they feel rather than see. They focus on narrow aspects of the process of FDI or on particular MNCs and then extrapolate well beyond their data base. At the end of the day, they still want to judge the merits of FDI and MNCs on an either/or basis. This is a flawed and oversimplified approach.

If objectivity and accuracy are what is being sought, the first-best approach is to emphasize diversity, not seek an all-inclusive prototype. This stands a better chance of narrowing the chasm between supporters and critics than continuation of the status quo. The real-world policy dialogue would then be in a better position to devise win-win rules and procedures that will increase the benefits of FDI as well as reduce its costs—to home and host countries, and to workers and owners of capital.

2. *Pay less attention to one-size-fits-all positive or negative evaluations of the nature and impact of the entire universe of FDI and MNCs. Accept the compelling evidence of inherent heterogeneity and the fallacy of sweeping generalizations.* Resist the idea that there is a homogenous composite enabling a simple yes or no vote as to the overall desirability of MNCs. Discount all assessments and value judgments (including the ones in this book) regarding FDI and MNCs because of the near inevitability that statements about their nature and impact reflect to some extent the larger political values of beholders—values that differ and legitimately so.

Hard, incontrovertible truths on these subjects are in very short supply, but opinions based on limited data are not. As argued in chapter 4, there is no such thing as a standard or prototypical form of FDI or MNC. Measuring clear-cut cause and effect relationships and isolating foreign investment activity from domestic economic activity is getting progressively more difficult. A report by the secretariat of the Asian Development Bank offered a superb summary explanation of why there is no such thing as a "typical" foreign-owned subsidiary:

> It is increasingly difficult to characterize and typify foreign [direct] investment. In most economies, it enters practically all sectors. It originates from industrial and developing economies . . . It ranges from the global investments of the world's largest corporations to smaller cross-border investments. The distinction between foreign and domestic investment is increasingly blurred, especially when a country's diaspora [e.g., China] is actively involved. A world of increasingly seamless national boundaries also connotes highly fluid capital whose characteristics are often difficult to

discern. . . . In assessing the impact of FDI, a key issue is one of attribution, in the sense of discerning causality. . . . In most cases . . . causality appears to be either weak or nonexistent.[1]

3. Emphasize inclusiveness and transparency as the transcendent principles in all future efforts to reach multilateral consensus on new or more specific rights and obligations for both governments and MNCs. Government, business, and civil society should improve the means by which they communicate both quantitatively and qualitatively. A better understanding of the nuances of MNCs and FDI as well as mutual acceptance by these three "constituencies" of the proposition that none of them has anything close to a monopoly on wisdom about these phenomena can improve the communications process.

Maximum inclusiveness and transparency will not guarantee excellent policies and honorable behavior, but they will maximize checks and balances and provide maximum oversight of the major actors. Human beings are imperfect. Because institutions are composed of humans, they, too, are imperfect. Even the most respected organizations cannot guarantee that their leaders will not occasionally succumb to corrupt, greedy, narrow-minded/self-serving, or just plain stupid behavior. Leaders of any and all organizations—governmental, corporate, and nonprofit—have shown themselves capable of becoming intoxicated with power, overly righteous about their vision of the public good, or indifferent to the interests of the public at large. Some will continue to do so, even with tightened rules affecting the conduct of international business. "Rules exist to govern behavior, but rules cannot substitute for character."[2]

4. Create an ongoing "quadralogue" among governments, business and nongovernmental organization (NGO) representatives, and academic and institute researchers. It would be charged with slowly but surely working through the trade-offs necessary to achieve more specific, mutually advantageous multilateral FDI agreements affecting the behavior of both the private and official sectors. No critical need exists at present for immediate establishment of an FDI regime, and no master formula exists for resolving the deep philosophical differences toward the relative merits of MNCs. Nevertheless, a simple procedural change in the way that four key actors communicate with each other might at least partially loosen the Gordian knot choking off consensus on a proper allocation of rights and obligations for governmental policy making and MNC activities. Governments have talked mostly to other governments; MNCs have talked mostly to other companies (and occasionally to UN officials); NGOs, including labor unions, have mostly talked to other NGOs and periodically to MNCs; academicians and researchers have mostly talked to other academicians and researchers. The four constituent groups need to talk more extensively to one another and spend less time communicating only with counterparts.

A kind of four cultures syndrome has materialized; it is characterized by an ineffective communications process that is sustained by turf-protection concerns and distrust of the other three actors. Incredibly, no public record exists of any extended talks among representatives of all principal constituencies in the FDI/MNC debate being held to identify and broaden overlapping areas of agreement. A more formal and comprehensive multilateral consultative framework holds great promise for a more effective system than today's scatter-shot collection of bilateral investment treaties and voluntary codes of conduct. Opinions about FDI and MNCs are entrenched and antagonistic, but they would not necessarily be impervious to a patient, friendlier four-way dialogue. Because these opinions do not represent state-of-the-art incisiveness, even a small reconciliation of their differences would be a step in the direction of mutual benefit.

A group comprised of respected, well-informed representatives from business, government, NGOs, and academicians-researchers agreeing to serve for an extended period of time should be convened on a permanent basis on neutral ground, perhaps a forum cohosted in Geneva by UNCTAD and the World Trade Organization. Participants in the quadralogue would be selected by the respective constituencies. Their mandate, with no fixed deadline, would be to compile a growing list of broadly defined but enforceable commitments that would be acceptable in principle to governments, MNCs, and relevant NGOs. The ultimate objective would be to reach enough agreements that a de facto multilateral FDI regime gradually emerges, one that would not necessarily be a cure-all, just an improvement over the current patchwork quilt. No set of behavioral rules for MNCs will forever prevent determined executives from violating them and behaving in a manner detrimental to society. Nor can a multilateral agreement prevent determined political leaders from implementing "outlawed" FDI policies. A means of punishing violators does, however, create disincentives for taking actions outside of consensus-based norms.

5. *Give more attention to the thesis that not all incoming FDI is created equal: Any given foreign subsidiary can make invaluable contributions to domestic economic growth and rising incomes, and any given subsidiary can be more harmful than beneficial. Differences in the quality of individual foreign-owned or -controlled subsidiaries should be the guiding principle in the formulation and administration of economic policies toward incoming FDI.* These policies should recognize and respond appropriately to the wide range of differences in the nature and effects of the many forms of FDI and individual MNCs. Governments, especially those of relatively vulnerable (to the power of big MNCs) developing countries, should formulate policies that (1) distinguish between the types of FDI that are appropriate for their individual circumstances; (2) encourage the entry of FDI considered desirable, while discouraging or disallowing FDI considered less appropriate to the country; and (3) make FDI policies serve wider national objectives and development needs.[3]

6. *Developing countries on a case-by-case basis should consider adopting a nonpolitical system of screening inward FDI to discourage the least desirable investment projects and encourage potential foreign investors to design a mutually beneficial investment project to improve its chances of gaining government approval.* An efficient form of screening run by technocrats can allay at least some of the concerns about MNC exploitation of less developed countries (LDCs) while not significantly antagonizing potential foreign investors. International organizations, such as the World Bank or UNCTAD, should consider providing free technical training programs for the people who will judge applications in nonindustrialized countries. The target audience would be government and private sector technocrats; the subject matter would focus on creation and operation of a government-sanctioned facility, perhaps with private sector input, to screen applications for incoming FDI on a quick, professional, and nonpolitical basis. The more advanced developing countries that can afford to be selective should look to the techniques used by the investment promotion agencies of Ireland, Singapore, and Costa Rica as the gold standard for attracting relatively high-quality FDI. The least developed countries presumably need to be less selective in allowing incoming manufacturing FDI, but they still could impose a screening process and more stringent regulatory conditions on extractive MNCs.

Developing countries would disproportionately benefit if the proposed quadralogue could devise meaningful multilateral restraints on the ability of governments to extend overly generous financial incentives to foreign-owned companies looking for investment sites. If the "no one wants to disarm first" syndrome can be overcome through concerted action, more taxpayers' money can be channeled from large corporations' bottom lines to serve domestic goals with potentially higher long-term pay-offs, for example, improved human capital and physical infrastructure.

7. *Appreciate the critical need to preserve and maximize competition among the larger MNCs.* There is probably no stopping them from growing ever bigger in size and increasing global market shares for their goods and services as they respond to competitive pressures and follow economies of scale strategies to minimize production costs and maximize profitability. This absolutely does not mean that passive government acquiescence to corporate gigantism is acceptable. Because further cross-border mergers of already large MNC manufacturers suggest further concentration (few major competitors) in key industries,[4] all countries have an interest in ensuring vigorous enforcement of reasonably comparable national antitrust laws. *Governments should increase their ability to identify collusion among corporate giants.* Discouraging collusion and promoting transparency and inclusiveness will improve the world's chances to maximize the benefits and minimize the costs of FDI and MNCs. Big corporations per se are not a problem, argues Swedish economist Johan Norberg, as long as they are exposed to competition that

threatens to harm them financially should they "turn out products inferior to or more expensive than those of other firms. What we have to fear is not size but monopoly."[5]

8. *Encourage the poorest LDCs to embrace the economic priorities practiced by the more advanced emerging market economies: Before seeking incoming FDI, they should get the domestic and economic fundamentals right, that is, enhance human capital and create the good governance and private sector-accommodating environment that has had a high statistical correlation with increased economic growth and rising growth rates.* LDCs "should provide a stable, noninflationary, micro and macroeconomic environment, with appropriate legal and regulatory infrastructure, that rewards both domestic and foreign investment."[6] These countries should accept the abundant evidence that a domestic order that repels inward FDI or a policy stance that systematically excludes or limits it, is unlikely to be an order that can successfully generate sustained economic development and poverty reduction. Developing countries should also be guided by the proposition that the more vibrant the domestic business sector, the more likely incoming foreign subsidiaries will forge links with the domestic economy by procuring locally produced goods and services. Courting MNCs, however, should not require these governments to capitulate to costly and egregiously self-serving corporate demands for economic concessions.

9. *Address the legitimate criticisms of the antiglobalization movement.* Judgments on the relative merits of MNCs are properly made in the larger context of attitudes toward globalization. This is a mega-trend that promises continued economic prosperity for many people, but not all and perhaps not even for most people. It is a trend that probably cannot be reversed short of causing grievous economic harm on a worldwide basis. Internationalization of production arguably is preferable to the alternatives, but increased efforts are necessary to ameliorate its more egregiously undesirable features—beginning with efforts to stabilize the widening gap between beneficiaries and victims of globalization.

It is disingenuous and counterproductive to ignore the fact that some people and some communities have been and will be economically disadvantaged by forces unleashed by globalization. Although it is inevitable that a relatively small number of entrepreneurs, investors, and executives will gain disproportionately from globalization, more ought to be done to strengthen the social safety nets that soften the financial distress of those that have been harmed. In political terms, market-oriented international economic policies are put at risk if increasing numbers of people perceive that the system worships profits and views workers as expendable inputs. Market-oriented policies will be attacked by people who believe that at the same time their standard of living is stagnant and their job security is declining, the wealthy minority is getting steadily richer—absolutely and relatively. "Employment insurance" could be provided to significantly offset lost wages and benefits (e.g., health care and pensions) suffered by the relatively few workers displaced by

MNC production shifts or increased imports and unable to find suitable new jobs. It would be a win-win situation if these benefits included enhanced technical training designed to make less skilled workers more employable and elevate them to the ranks of those having a positive stake in the trend toward greater internationalization of production. The response to those that say such a program would be too expensive is that it would be cheaper than imposition of what effectively is a sales tax on *all* consumers when imports are restricted or cost-reducing MNC production shifts are blocked by governmental fiat.

10. *Intensify the research agenda on the FDI/MNC phenomena in both qualitative and quantitative terms.* Although it is unlikely we will ever definitively know all that would be useful to know, a moderate increase in understanding these phenomena more likely than not will demonstrate the heterogeneity and variability of FDI and MNCs rather than perpetuate the false and distracting notion that their nature and impact is overwhelmingly good or bad on an all-inclusive basis. A number of priority research topics present themselves. The variables determining whether a direct investment project will be high quality and beneficial, marginal, or low quality and costly to the host country need to be more clearly identified. A related question is whether any statistical relationship can be found between the arrival of certain kinds of investment by certain kinds of companies and above-average increases in growth and per capita income in host countries. Another worthy effort would be increasing our understanding of how the domestic variables of human capital and the economic and political environment affect the success or failure of incoming foreign subsidiaries. Other important factors that need to be better understood are the numbers and relative pay scales of jobs created by incoming foreign-owned subsidiaries, the relative importance of factors that MNC executives find appealing and repelling for specific kinds of direct investments, and what have been the effects, good and bad, of incoming FDI on domestic competitors in host countries.

Governments should spend a modest amount of additional money to improve the data on FDI flows and the monetary value of cumulative inward and outward direct investments. Governments should also expend the nominal amount of effort that would be necessary to bring greater worldwide uniformity to definitions and measurement criteria. Governments should collect data (on a confidential basis) from foreign-owned subsidiaries located within their jurisdiction to more fully and accurately measure the flows of hard currency these subsidiaries both bring into host countries and remit overseas. At a nominal cost, this procedure would provide valuable insights into the domestic and balance of payments impacts of inward FDI. Similarly, a better understanding of FDI's effects on foreign trade could be gained if countries required confidential reporting on the imports and exports of inward direct investments and published the aggregate results.

A detailed, case-by-case examination of thousands of overseas subsidiaries in lower income countries to determine the extent (if any) that each increased the number of relatively high-paying jobs, transferred state-of-the-art technology, established linkage to domestically owned businesses, increased exports, and encouraged subsequent FDI inflows would be illuminating. Although no quick, easy, or inexpensive task, such a study could geometrically increase our relatively limited understanding of how well or how poorly—and under what circumstances—the various kinds of multinationals have boosted economic performance in those LDCs where they have a significant presence. Another addition to the research agenda of the larger industrial countries should be a comprehensive examination of the push and pull factors responsible for companies closing entire plants and moving production to overseas subsidiaries. It also would be useful to have greater insights into how frequently this has occurred and to give more thought to remedial policies in the home country that might ease the plight of at-risk workers.

Hopefully, foundations, corporations, and governments will support an expanded research effort in the belief that the advancement to knowledge about a very important but inadequately understood set of public policy issues would be worth far more than the costs.

11. *Encourage the use of innovative ideas to assist the least developed countries to attract and reap the benefits of incoming FDI (assuming willingness to simultaneously address internal shortcomings).* Relatively wealthy countries should consider reducing the corporate tax rates on profits remitted from designated LDCs, including export-processing zones, as an incentive to invest in them. The World Bank and other regional development banks should establish additional programs in the poorest countries similar to the Bank's initiative to counter corruption in Chad. It was designed to ensure a minimum percentage of the country's revenues from foreign oil companies is transferred directly into escrow-like accounts to benefit the current and future population rather than being diverted into the pockets of the elites or used to buy military equipment and weapons. A stipulated percentage of Chad's oil bonanza is to be earmarked for externally administered accounts divided between those designated for current development projects and poverty alleviation programs and one reserved for future use after oil reserves are depleted. The peoples of other poor countries hosting big money extractive FDI would surely benefit from a similar version of externally controlled bank accounts.[7]

A Closing Thought

To describe the nature and impact of FDI/MNCs in all-encompassing or immutable terms is to repeat the mistakes of the blind men separately touching individual parts of the elephant. A full and proper appreciation of these animals requires observers to scrutinize and compare all major physical and behavioral characteristics of all species of elephants. Moving from metaphor to specifics, the best way to assess FDI and MNCs is to accept the thesis that the appropriate answer to most of the important questions about them is "it depends." Disaggregation and appreciation of the heterogeneity of these complex and dynamic phenomena can lead to more accurate insights into their nature and effects as well as to the most appropriate policy responses. An analysis of FDI and MNCs that mislabels perceptions as fact and proffers wobbly generalizations to prove its arguments is "irrelephant."

Notes

1. Asian Development Bank, *Asian Development Outlook 2004*, pp. 259–60, available online at http://www.adb.org/Documents/Books/ADO/2004/part030000.asp; accessed July 2005.
2. Alan Greenspan, "Commencement Address," May 15, 2005, Board of Governors press release, p. 5.
3. Martin Khor, "Globalization and the South: Some Critical Issues," UNCTAD Discussion Paper no. 147, April 2000, p. 44, available online at http://www.unctad.org/en/docs/dp_147.en.pdf; accessed September 2004.
4. In the early weeks of 2006 alone, press reports indicated that Mittal Steel had made an offer to buy Arcelor, the world's second largest steelmaker; if consummated this could lead to further consolidation in the world's steel industry. In addition, General Electric and Hitachi, both large producers of nuclear reactors, made a joint bid to take control of Westinghouse Electric, a major British nuclear technology company.
5. Johan Norberg, *In Defense of Globalization* (Washington, DC: Cato Institute, 2003), p. 210.
6. Theodore H. Moran, *Foreign Direct Investment and Development* (Washington, DC: Institute for International Economics, 1998), p. 29.
7. The program early on ran into major complications. Chad's government demanded that the amount of cash earmarked for the escrow accounts be reduced and transferred to current expenditures.

Index

Agglomeration economies, 158–159, 166, 301–303

Alabama
  inward FDI, 301–303, 304

American University, 110

Anti-globalization. *See* Globalization: opposition to

Asian Development Bank (ADB), 296, 297, 345, 356

Automobile industry, 138–144, 302–303
  U.S. import barriers, 141

Baken, Joel, 105, 112

Balance of payments, 188, 215

Barnet, Richard J., 22–23

Best practices, 191, 289, 349

Bhagwati, Jagdish, 275, 344

Bilateral investment treaties, 260, 264, 266, 267

Blonigen, Bruce, 339

BMW Group, 140, 143

British East India Company, 43

Brookings Institution, 192

Buchanan, James M., 101, 103

Business Roundtable, 208

Canada, 47, 247, 265, 322
  policy toward inward FDI, 346–348

Capitalism, 103–104, 285. *See also* Markets, benefits of

Catholic Relief Services, 188

Caves, Richard E., 186, 199, 200

Cemex Corp., 88

Central American Free Trade Agreement, 271

Central Europe, 319–320, 321

Chad, 189, 362

Child labor, 190

Chile, 80
  and ITT Corp., 187, 326

China, 68, 103, 129, 183, 207, 220, 335
  effects of FDI on trade, 207
  inward FDI, 51, 58, 109, 135, 142, 151, 156, 161–164, 170, 227, 249, 292, 321
  outward FDI, 89, 134, 136, 194–195

Christian Aid, 312, 326–327

Citigroup Corp., 84, 128

Civil society. *See* Nongovernmental organizations

Coca-Cola Company, 85

Codes of conduct, 261–263

Comparative advantage, 222–227, 229. *See also* Foreign direct investment: and international trade

Corporate culture, 64–65

Corporate executives
  salaries of, 104

Corporate social responsibility, 31, 275, 312

Corporation
  benefits of, 99
  downsides of, 105–106
  evolution of, 30
  governance, 32–34
  nature and purposes of, 27–32
  regulation of, 29

Corruption, 100, 172, 248, 297, 325, 344

Costa Rica. *See also* Intel Corporation: and Costa Rica
  inward FDI, 214–215, 227, 303–304

Council of Economic Advisors, 221

Crowding-out, 74

DaimlerChrysler Group, 139, 140, 143, 167, 320, 343
Dell, Michael, 153
Dell Corp., 209, 291
Deloitte & Touche, 156
Democracy deficit, 108
Depression, Great, 46, 243, 253–254, 314
Developing countries. *See* Less developed countries
Disaggregation, need for, 13, 14, 15, 120, 338, 363
Double taxation treaties, 260
Dow Chemical Corporation, 167
Dow Jones Industrial Average, 23, 343
Drucker, Peter, 24, 32
Dunning, John H., 42, 44, 45, 126, 127, 224, 289, 336
  eclectic paradigm, 125–126
Dutch East India Company, 43

eBay Corporation, 82, 133, 134, 294
Eclectic paradigm. *See* Dunning, John
Economies of scale, 122, 224–225, 291, 349. *See also* High technology
Economist, The, 172, 235, 264, 289
Efficiency-seeking FDI, 69–70, 130, 140, 186, 198, 287, 350
Electronics manufacturing services, 84
Emergency Committee for American Trade, 208
Emerging markets, 181–182
Encarnation, Dennis, 221
Equity versus efficiency, 18, 93, 336
Ericsson Corp., 157
European Union (EU), 49, 129, 136, 160, 221, 241, 253
  and national sovereignty, 244
Exchange rates, 134
Export processing zones (EPZs), 72
Expropriation. *See* Nationalization
Extractive industries, 47, 156 198, 297, 325. *See also* Resource-seeking FDI

Fair trade goods, 274
FDI Performance Index, 184
Fieldhouse, David, 18, 241
First-to-market, 132
Flextronics Corp., 84, 321
Ford Motor Company, 23, 46, 139, 142, 299
Foreign direct investment (FDI). *See also* Multinational corporations
  assessments of. *See* Multinational corporations: assessment of
  benefits of. *See* Multinational corporations: benefits of
  cause and effect issues, 16, 42–44, 185, 286, 287
  definition, 36–39
  disadvantages of. *See* Multinational corporations: disadvantages of
  and economic growth, 57–58, 170–171, 206, 338, 349–350
  efficiency-seeking. *See* Efficiency-seeking FDI
  and exports, 217–222
  extractive companies (resource-seeking). *See* Extractive industries
  factors attracting inward FDI, 155–159
  factors discouraging inward FDI, 154–155, 168–172
  flows, annual, 48
  greenfield subsidiaries, 73
  and gross domestic product (GDP). *See* Multinational corporations: and gross domestic product
  heterogeneity of, 62–65, 127, 157, 332, 335, 356, 363
  horizontal, 71
  impact of. *See* Multinational corporations: impact of
  importance of, 53–59, 121
  incentives. *See* Multinational corporations: incentives from governments
  and international trade, 58–59, 129–130, 206–212

and labor, 70, 80, 108, 150, 292–295, 300, 317–321, 328, 360–361
manufacturing companies. *See* Manufacturing FDI
market-seeking. *See* Market-seeking FDI
mergers. *See* Mergers and acquisitions
and nation-states. *See* Sovereignty, national
protection of export markets, 129
quality of, 15, 64, 188, 196, 198, 295–296, 314–317, 349, 358, 361
reasons for, 68
regime, lack of, 253–259, 266, 276
regulation of, 253–263, 336
relative to world economic output, 54, 56, 107
services companies. *See* Services FDI
stock of (book value), 48
strategic asset-seeking. *See* Strategic asset-seeking FDI
subsidiaries' sales. *See* Multinational corporations: subsidiaries
theories, 25, 118–126
in the United States. *See* United States: inward FDI
vertical, 71–72
Fortune 500, 23
France, 45, 257, 265
Free trade agreements. *See* Regional free trade agreements
Friedman, Milton, 312

General Electric Corp., 130, 157, 241, 343
General Motors Corp., 23, 46, 76, 139, 142, 207, 299, 320
Germany, 45, 319–320
inward FDI, 167, 340
outward FDI, 70
Gillette Corp., 343
Gilpin, Robert, 53, 97, 242, 255
Global Compact, UN, 262–263
Globalization, 239–240, 317
opposition to, 106–109, 360

Global production networks, 72
Global Reach, 22–23
Goodman, Louis W., 88
Google, Inc., 82, 134
Governance, quality of, 153, 158, 164
Government
benefits of, 103–106
Governments versus markets, 94–98, 109–111, 255
Graham, Edward M., 206, 293
Great Britain. *See* United Kingdom
Great Depression. *See* Depression, Great
Grove, Andrew, 23, 342
Guatemala, 187, 325

Haier Group, 89, 194
Hecksher-Ohlin theorem, 119, 122, 223–228. *See also* Comparative advantage
Heritage Foundation, 171
Hertz, Noreena, 108
Heterogeneity. *See* Multinational corporations: heterogeneity of
High technology (high-tech), 81, 327–328. *See also* Economies of scale
economics of, 52, 122–123
Home countries, 256
Honda Motor Company, 139, 142
Honduras, 321
Hong Kong, 200
Host countries, 14, 256–257
Human capital, 197, 297
Hungary, 319
inward FDI, 57, 153, 215–216, 321, 336
Hymer, Stephen, 121, 124, 126, 344
Hyundai-Kia Corporation, 139, 140–141, 167

IBM Corp., 23, 130, 194
Ideology, economic, 20, 29, 93–98, 186, 319
Income distribution, 107, 337

India, 289, 327
  inward FDI, 163–164
  outward FDI, 89, 129
Indonesia
  inward FDI, 199
Information technology revolution. *See*
  High technology
Infrastructure, 158, 164, 166
Intel Corporation, 129
  and Costa Rica, 86, 168, 214–215, 249,
    303
  foreign subsidiaries, 130–131, 137–138,
    157
Interdependence, economic, 107, 247
International Monetary Fund (IMF), 246,
  253, 254
International trade. *See* Foreign direct
  investment: international trade;
  Comparative advantage
Internet companies, 52, 82, 132, 134, 297
Intrafirm trade, 207
Ireland, 173
  effects of inward FDI, 70, 212–213
  inward FDI, 57, 153, 159–161, 207, 229
Israel, 137–138
ITT Corporation, 187, 297, 312
  and Chile. *See* Chile: and ITT Corp.

Japan, 103, 257
  inward FDI, 154, 200, 216–217,
    221–222, 287–289, 294, 322–323
  outward FDI, 50–51, 70, 77, 134,
    141–142, 208
Joint ventures, 75, 76

Khor, Martin, 266
Kindleberger, Charles, 25, 122, 240, 341
Kobrin, Stephen J., 239
Kodak Corp., 46
Kokko, Ari, 195
Korea (South), 199, 322
  inward FDI, 217, 287–289, 323
Krasner, Stephen D., 235, 241
Krugman, Paul, 227, 228

Labor. *See* Foreign direct investment:
  and labor
Lee, Kuan Yew, 213
Lennon, Vladimir, 106, 298
Lenovo Corp., 194
Less developed countries (LDCs), 78, 104,
  180–186, 257–258, 359, 360
  attitudes toward FDI, 50
  benefits of FDI in, 190–193, 293
  effects of inward FDI in, 79–80,
    184–199
  harm of FDI, 187–189, 309–310
  heterogeneity of, 181–183, 193
  inward FDI, 50–51, 58, 151–152
  least developed countries, 362
  outward FDI, 87–90, 192–193
  variables, economic, 193, 195–200
Lever Brothers Corporation, 46
Licensing, 119–120
Linkage. *See* Multinational corporations:
  linkages with host countries
Lipsey, Robert, 221
Litvin, Daniel, 325

Manufacturing FDI, 80–81
Market concentration, 359. *See also*
  Multinational corporations: as
  oligopolists
Market imperfections, 96, 122
Market-seeking FDI, 67–69, 156, 186,
  287, 350
Markets, benefits of, 98–103
Markets versus government. *See*
  Governments versus markets
Mathews, Jessica, 246
Mauritius, 88
McDonald's Corp., 83, 128, 324
McKinsey and Company, 137, 342
McKinsey Global Institute, 290
Mercedes Benz, 302
Mergers and acquisitions (M&As), 51,
  64, 73, 74, 135, 139
Metalclad Corp., 269–270
Methanex Corp., 272

Mexico, 109, 267
  inward FDI, 199, 220, 269, 315, 321
Microprocessors, 215, 226
Microsoft Corp., 84
Mitsubishi Motors, 143
Monterrey Consensus, 190
Moran, Theodore, 192, 198
Morgan Stanley, Inc., 135
Müller, Ronald, 22–23
Multilateral Agreement on Investment
  (MAI), 263–266
Multinational corporations (MNCs). *See
  also* Foreign direct investment
  allegiance to home country, 35–36
  and anti-globalization arguments. *See*
    Globalization: opposition to
  assessments of, 20, 22–24, 337, 341–343,
    345–346, 363
  benefits of, 284–296, 334–335
  cause and effect issues. *See* Foreign
    direct investment: cause and effect
    issues
  competition among, 52
  debate over impact of, 19, 22
  definition, 34–36, 39
  disadvantages of, 309–319, 334–335,
    349
  as dynamic phenomena, 21
  and economic growth. *See* Foreign
    direct investment: and economic
    growth
  efficiency-seeking. *See* Efficiency-seeking
    FDI
  and environmental issues, 300–301, 350
  evolution of, 41–47, 356
  exports by, 207. *See also* Foreign direct
    investment: and exports
  extractive companies (resource-seeking).
    See Extractive industries
  geographic concentration of, 149–152,
    183, 300–301
  and gross domestic product (GDP),
    54–58, 298–299, 338
  growth, need for, 128

  heterogeneity of, 5, 13, 14, 18, 62–65,
    127, 157, 356, 363
  impact of, 13, 96
  importance of. *See* Foreign direct
    investment: importance of
  incentives from governments, 165–168,
    247
  and international trade. *See* Foreign
    direct investment: and international
    trade
  and labor. *See* Foreign direct
    investment: and labor
  linkages with host countries, 290–291,
    295, 315, 348
  manufacturers. *See* Manufacturing
    FDI
  market-seeking. *See* Market-seeking
    FDI
  mergers. *See* Mergers and acquisitions
  monopolies. *See* Multinational
    corporations: as oligopolists
  and nation-states. *See* Sovereignty,
    national
  number of, 12, 14, 47, 63
  as oligopolists, 22, 106, 123, 313–314
  quality of. *See* Foreign direct
    investment: quality of
  reasons for. *See* Foreign direct
    investment: reasons for
  regulation of. *See* Foreign direct
    investment: regulation of
  sales by overseas subsidiaries, 48, 57–59,
    206, 298–299
  services companies. *See* Services FDI
  size, 85–86
  strategic asset-seeking. *See* Strategic
    asset-seeking FDI
  subsidiaries, 14, 38, 63, 71–75
  technology's impact on, 44, 52. *See also*
    High technology
  theories. *See* Foreign direct investment:
    theories
Multinational enterprise. *See*
  Multinational corporations

Nader, Ralph, 239–240
National treatment, 260
Nationalization, 249, 260, 267, 265
Netherlands, 45, 87
New United Motor Manufacturing, Inc., 76
Newmont Mining Corp., 199, 326
Nigeria, 100
    inward FDI, 171–172, 326
Nike Corp., 85, 274
Nissan Motor Company, 139, 140, 142, 144
Nokia Corp., 226
Nongovernmental organizations (NGOs), 100, 110, 111, 189, 258, 261, 263, 272, 357, 358
    activities of, 245–246, 272–276, 294, 298, 343–344
    opposition to MAI, 264–265
Norberg, Johan, 101, 359
North American Free Trade Agreement (NAFTA)
    Chapter 11, 266–272
Nunnenkamp, Peter, 193

Offshoring, 83, 89, 129, 327–328
Ohmae, Kenichi, 35, 237
Oil companies, 78–79, 362
Oligopolies, 344. See also Multinational corporations: as oligopolists
Organization for Economic Cooperation and Development (OECD), 254, 264, 293
    Guidelines for Multinational Enterprises, 262–263
Organization of Petroleum Exporting Countries (OPEC), 78, 249
Overseas Development Institute (UK), 199, 293
Ownership advantage, 121–122, 125–126
Oxford University Press, 81

Perceptions of FDI, 19, 332, 333, 350, 355
Performance requirements, 170

Peru, 326–327
Pharmaceutical industry, 123
Philippines, 207, 327
Porter, Michael, 225, 312
Portfolio investment, 37, 289
Primary sector. See Resource-seeking FDI
Privatization, 73, 136
Product life-cycle theory, 124–125
Public choice theory, 101–102
Public Citizen, 264, 268–269

Quinlan, Joseph, 339

Race to the bottom, 108, 150, 299–301
Regional free trade agreements, 136
Regulatory environment, 153, 158, 169
Research and development (R&D), 122, 123, 139, 140, 287
Resource-seeking FDI, 66–67, 78–80, 198, 325, 327. See also Extractive industries
Ricardo, David, 222–223
Risk diversification, 130
Rodrik, Dani, 185
Rosenau, James, 246
Ruggie, John, 238
Russia, 45, 46, 249

Sarbanes-Oxley Act, 34
Saudi Arabia, 80
Schumer, Senator Charles, 328
Secondary sector. See Manufacturing FDI
Servan-Schreiber, Jean-Jacques, 49
Services FDI, 53, 81–84, 256, 327–328
Shareholders, 29, 31, 96
Shell Oil Company, 326
Siemens Corp., 45
Silicon Valley, 135, 158
Singapore, 173, 208, 291
    effects of inward FDI, 212–213, 289
    inward FDI, 85, 161
Singer Sewing Machine Company, 45
Slovakia, 320
    inward FDI, 226, 303

Smith, Adam, 99
Sovereignty at Bay, 240
Sovereignty, national, 234–241, 243–244, 247, 248, 322–324, 325, 335
Spatz, Julius, 193
Stakeholders, 31, 32, 96, 256
Standard Oil Corp., 45
Starbucks Corp., 83, 128
Stiglitz, Joseph E., 109
Strange, Susan, 237
Strategic alliances, 75–76, 139
Strategic asset-seeking FDI, 70–71, 140, 156
Subsidiaries. *See* Multinational corporations: subsidiaries
Sweatshops, 189, 294

Taiwan, 199, 207
Tariff jumping, 129, 156
Technology. *See* High technology; Multinational corporations: technology's impact on
Technology transfer, 54, 191, 290, 291, 298, 362
Tertiary sector. *See* Services FDI
Toyota Motor Corporation, 76, 139, 142
  direct investment in United States, 131
Trade, international. *See* Foreign direct investment: and international trade
Trade-Related Investment Measures, 170, 260–261, 267
Transfer prices, 311
Transnational actors, 244–245
Transnational corporation. *See* Multi-national corporations
Transnationality index, 86–87
Transparency International, 100, 172
Transparency, 357
Triad countries, 123, 150, 156

Union Minerè, 325
United Fruit Company, 45, 297, 325

United Kingdom, 45, 139
United Nations Code of Conduct on Transnational Corporations, 266
United Nations Conference on Trade and Development (UNCTAD), 48, 64, 87, 88, 151, 153, 154, 167, 184, 192, 196, 207, 216, 217, 221, 254, 286
  World Investment Report, 86, 183, 190, 200, 206, 345
United States
  effects of FDI on trade, 208–212
  as hegemon, 53
  inward FDI, 51, 89, 135, 138, 154, 167, 169, 212, 323–324, 347–348
U.S. Congress, 100, 102, 110
U.S. Department of Commerce, 210, 212, 341
U.S. International Trade Commission, 210, 220–221

Venezuela, 100
  inward FDI, 171–173
Vernon, Raymond, 124, 126, 240, 276, 310
Vertical integration, 52, 71–72, 220
Volkswagen Group, 143, 315, 320

Wages, 149, 286, 292–294, 317–321. *See also* Foreign direct investment: and labor
Whirlpool Corporation, 340
Whistle-blowers, 111
Wire harness industry, 321
Wolf, Martin, 100, 242
World Bank, 100, 155, 169, 171, 189, 191
World Economic Forum, 172
World Trade Organization (WTO), 56, 207, 246, 253, 254

Yahoo! Inc., 82, 134
Yergin, Daniel, 78
Yum! Brands, Inc. 135